# WILD GENESIS

*A True Story Of Adventure, Friends Lost,
And Maturity Found*

## WAYNE WASECHKA

Copyright © 2018 by Wayne Wasechka

All rights reserved. No part of this book may be reproduced or transmitted in any form or by any means, electronic or mechanical, including photocopying, recording, or any information storage and retrieval system, without permission in writing from the author.

ISBN: 978-1-948638-91-3

PUBLISHED BY

Fideli Publishing, Inc.
119 W. Morgan St.
Martinsville, IN 46151

www.FideliPublishing.com

# The Neighborhood

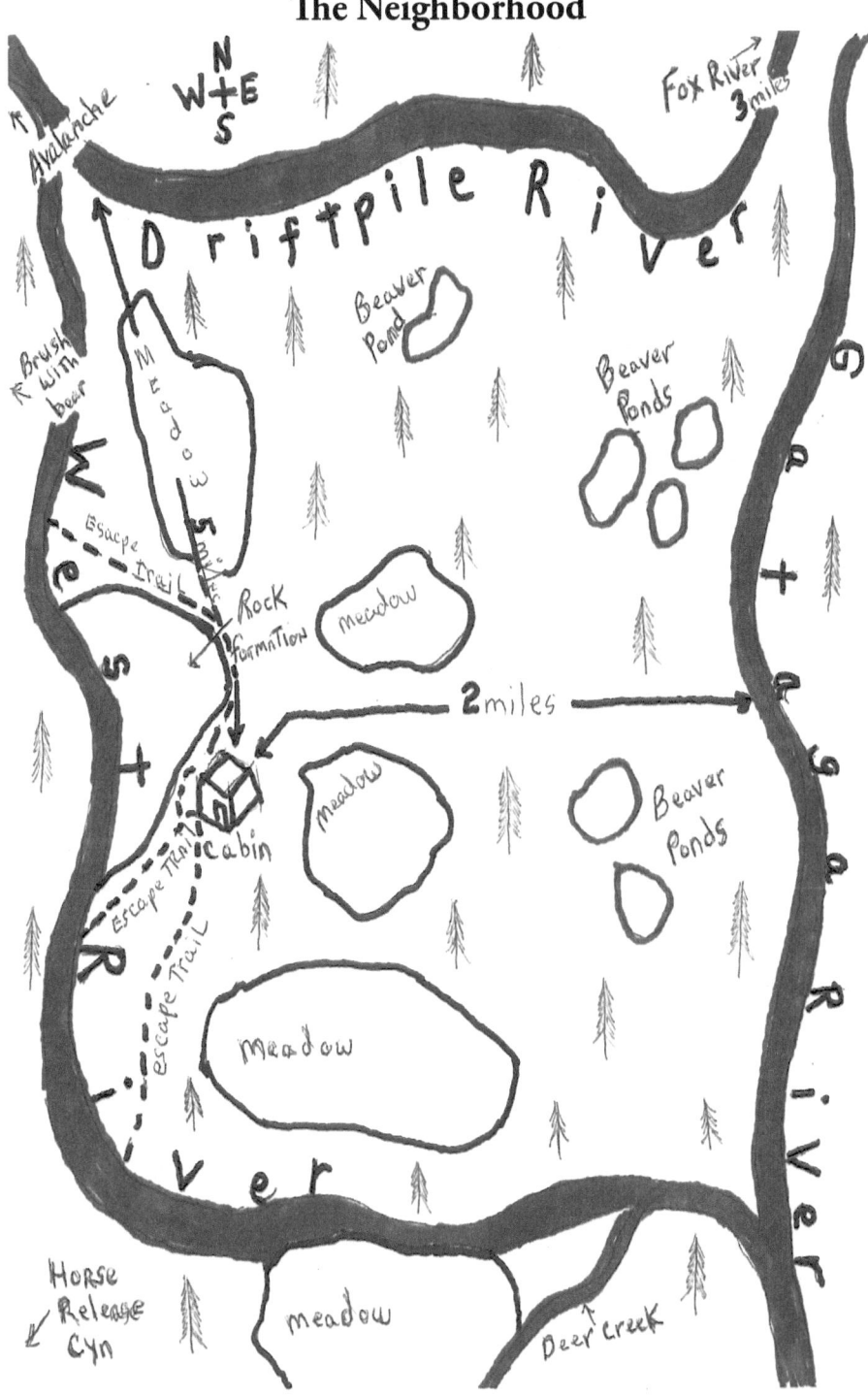

The cabin sits between the Rocky Mountains
and the Omineca Range of mountains.

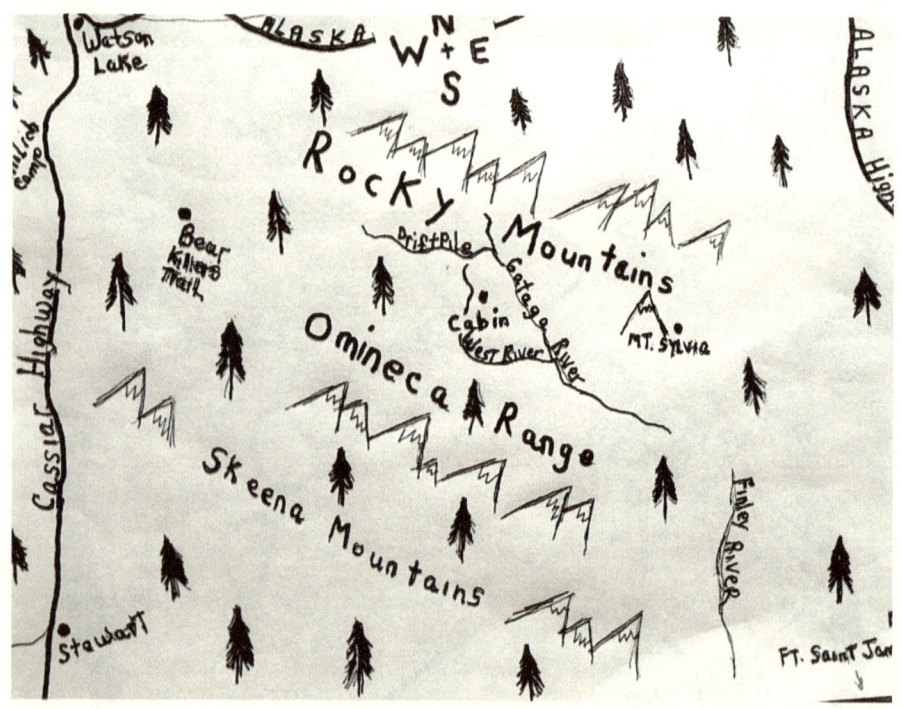

# INTRODUCTION

I love this Earth as I love myself.

Given the nature of our society today, I doubt that many men have examined themselves and taken stock of all that has been provided to them by birth (wealthy parents) and wondered what it would have been like to have earned it himself. I am among those who question what the term self-reliance means. As a young man, I pondered if I could survive a life independent of others.

What follows is the actual account of my journey with my friend George into the wilderness of British Columbia, Canada. It is beneficial for the reader to keep in mind that I wrote the journal that is the basis of this book starting in 1976.

For the most part, this book is a boring narrative, mundane routines sometimes interspersed with moments of terror. Unless otherwise indicated a single day has passed since the prior entry was made.

I commenced this expedition to seek a re-birth and learn about self-reliance. The cost, in terms of money and personal sacrifice, is chronicled, as are some of the details of which one must be aware when making a trek such as the one we made.

Some people may find the descriptions of events unbelievable, but I promise that I speak with a straight tongue. All of the names used in this book are fictitious. The miles traveled are based upon the best educated guesses of my pal George and me.

I read somewhere that a horse may stride at four miles per hour. So by traveling five hours at four miles per hour one would travel 20 miles. Of course, George and I had to compensate for detours, so we deducted a mile or two if we did not travel in a constant straight line during a ride. We also relied on topography maps to locate landmarks that lined up with what we saw.

Not many others knew of, or understood, my love of nature or comprehend my attitude toward personal property. I do not find this surprising, since each person is consumed with his or her own life. To me, personal ownership of the land has seemed a travesty, the thought that a person can claim ownership to what is not theirs alone to claim. This pretense is then passed from generation to generation, without concern for the land itself.

Food, weapons, clothing, cars, horses, and the like may be owned, given away, sold, or destroyed. This Earth, however, is the mother force in the power from which I believe all things come. Although man in his conquest to control all things may try, nothing may be done to moderate this Earth; nothing may make it less precious for all who tread upon it. Even in the most rundown slums of the inner cities the Earth is not in disarray, just the buildings and the hopes of the tenants are depleted.

What person may hike through a meadow without marveling at a single blade of grass, which is food for some or perhaps a soft bed for others? Is Mother Earth any less stunning than the prettiest woman or less important than the air we breathe?

As you might imagine, George and I expected to encounter foul weather, and so, often times the entries may be somewhat short due to the wet or otherwise inclement weather. I will do my best to describe accurately both the surroundings and what I was feeling at that time.

Finally, George and I developed an appreciation for what would be the ever-present, overshadowing fact that we would be alone, far from society.

As humans, we would have no control over events, as we would no longer be at the top of the food chain.

In days past, a person could find much open space close to the city, but no more.

We will soon have to leave our own country to visit pristine lands once so accessible to all. If you choose to believe that you are accountable for the state of nature on this planet, then you have no grander concern.

# Contents

Introduction ..................................................................................... v

| | | |
|---|---|---|
| Chapter 1 | Why Do This Crazy Thing? | 1 |
| Chapter 2 | Preparation | 6 |
| Chapter 3 | The Genesis Begins | 11 |
| Chapter 4 | Summer 1976 | 51 |
| Chapter 5 | The Valleys Beyond The Cassiar Mountains | 60 |
| Chapter 6 | Autumn 1976 | 66 |
| Chapter 7 | Winter 1976 | 80 |
| Chapter 8 | Spring 1977 | 146 |
| Chapter 9 | Summer 1977 | 180 |
| Chapter 10 | Autumn 1977 | 208 |
| Chapter 11 | Winter 1977 | 233 |
| Chapter 12 | Ride To Civilization | 325 |
| | Epilogue | 341 |

# 1

# WHY DO THIS CRAZY THING?

Anyone who has stopped and scrutinized themselves hoping to discover what they are as a human being may attest to the laws of nature. Take as an example the guy who drinks an alcoholic beverage and then drives his car. It is possible that he may get home this time without issue, or perchance the next time, but nature is unforgiving and eventually the guy will wreck his car. One does not fool nature.

I have subscribed to the Lakota Indian Tribe simplistic attitude toward life, and for this reason I think that my life has been more diverse than it otherwise might have been. I believe that the Earth is mother. She provides food, water, and the abundant wildlife that most take for granted.

The overseer of this universe in my eyes is the Great Spirit, Wakan Tanka. This spirit is not a single being but rather more like the collective energy of many present and past relatives. Everything in the world is alive and is a part of the whole.

With these basics in mind, I am left to answer your question: why do this crazy thing?

To trust my answer, you must accept that I believe that I have lived a previous existence, though I've caught only short glimpses of it over time, and that the spirit from that life exists in me now. Long before this journey had been considered, or undertaken, that spirit existed deep within me. This spirit is not a demon, or a holy being, or an object. It is instead knowledge that I have flourished in the past in an environment such as the one we will experience, the raw loneliness of the wilderness.

This belief is common among certain societies and is accepted as a possibility by others. My belief is based upon a number of things, the most compelling of which is the feeling of being totally free when I am in the forests and the mountains.

I have long sensed that I can anticipate any situation and deal with it, if prepared. Never have I felt alone or afraid in the mountains. When I close my eyes, I hear the melody of the songbird. I smell the scent of the most fragrant flower. The wind, no matter how light, touches my face and carries those fragrances to me. With eyes open I see the immense spaces beckoning me to come explore. Through each fish or other meal harvested, I taste the life giving fare so richly offered by Mother Nature. Each of my senses absorbs the clues and signals to survival.

I have seen a place in the mountains for the first time and felt that I knew the place from before, like a long lost friend returning. At any given moment, I feel captivated by this lifestyle. It was my desire to re-trace the footsteps of a previous lifetime, a time when I roamed this Earth as a mountain man. It was my desire to know that I could survive the wilderness.

It was my wish to see the images that danced daily in my mind becomes a reality. I wanted to build a cabin, cut the trees, strip the bark, and feel a tinge of fear at the sight of a wolf. I wanted to know what self-reliance is. Over the years as I grew up, it became clear to me that at some point I would attempt a long-term trek into the back-country wilderness.

During my high school years and beyond, friends whose company I considered desirable arranged weekend camping trips in the mountains of Southern California. This entailed a two- or three-hour drive and the evening rush hour to grab a campsite near a splashing stream before they were all taken. In the event of an emergency, one could drive to the local hospital 30 minutes away and be taken care of.

These outings amounted to, in fact, nothing more than a reasonable excuse to abuse alcohol! Though I always went along willingly, and drank my share of the fire water, I found myself often resenting the manner in which we drunken woodsmen fancied ourselves a Davey Crocket or a Jim Bridger.

Even I, with my lack of field knowledge, knew the laws of nature. It takes time in the wild to learn to read the signs around you, and none of us fall-downs had a clue about what was going on around us. I made up my mind over time to embark upon this wilderness escapade.

Growing up I attended catholic grade school through eighth grade. I mention this because of a connection made there. I played on the football team in eighth grade, and we had made it to the championship game. I played tight end, most often positioned on the end of the offensive line, for reasons that I could not understand, considering that I weighed all of 130 pounds. Across the line from me during that game stood a kid who rose five foot eight inches tall and outweighed me by 50 pounds and appeared to be salivating at the chance to drive me into the ground. This kid stood out, being a loud-mouthed white boy on an otherwise all African-American team.

My assignment as the tight end called for me to block him on running plays and to try to get open on passing plays. He roughed me up on the running plays, and I made him appear slow and unable to cover me on passing plays. We won the game on a last second touchdown that I had nothing to do with.

Fast forward some 12 years, and while then living in Los Angeles, I tried out for my company softball team. As fate would have it, that same kid, who weighed in now at 200 pounds while maintaining his five–eight frame, also tried out. It took but a second for us to recollect where we had met before. We both made the team and for the next couple of years were roommates off and on. We fished and hiked together in the mountains, and on occasion, in the Sequoia National Forest.

George was a brazen white boy who grew up in the poorer inner city of south central Los Angeles. He tried his best to fit into the community by acting as brash as possible. By being loud and obnoxious, he found that he could intimidate people.

The blacktops of the city park basketball courts and the grass of the baseball field were his domain. George was a fine athlete overall.

He had traveled on a limited basis outside of California but had never spent a lot of time out of Los Angeles.

Among his talents, he was an excellent cook. George had a knack when it came to barbecue. He was also fearless. George would not back down to anyone regardless of size. I once witnessed him challenge a whole softball team to a fight.

He lacked no skill when fishing and knew how to handle guns well. George was a ladies' man, or so he tried to portray himself. He talked to any girl, white, black, or brown, or as he boasted, 16 to 60, blind, crippled, or cuckoo. George was ever ready to take any one of them home for the evening.

Being for the most part unattached, my life became a series of on and off girlfriends, a lot of partying, and a succession of meaningless jobs. At one point I sold vacuum cleaners and at another worked at a screw manufacturing company.

I entertained serious thoughts of making my long anticipated trip to the wilderness more often at this time.

George bought in to the idea right away, and we took more remote camping excursions. We went to the Eastern Sierras, Yellowstone, and to Yosemite National Park. We found back-country places to fish and learn the habits of wildlife.

After being depressed from yet another breakup with a girl, I made the decision that I would indeed begin preparation for an extended expedition into the mountains. George and I wondered who we might recruit to join us, as three would be better than two so that we could form a majority-rules governing system.

After soliciting a select group of people, Nick, who was going through a bitter divorce, agreed to join us to get as far away from California as possible. Nick was an acquaintance of George's, a person I had met on a softball team.

As the days passed, we spent time talking about purchasing the supplies necessary for the trip.

With the help of an insider, George and I landed jobs at a construction site in downtown Los Angeles, each making five hundred dollars a week. This proved to be the vehicle that would allow it all to happen.

We each agreed that whatever equipment the individual deemed essential, he would purchase, while community-needed supplies would be split three ways. This would help keep us each focused on the benefit of the whole.

We each held secret reasons for wanting to make this journey and another of mine was for what I called religious purposes.

Without preaching, I will declare that having any belief forced on one is not natural. We all find reasons to believe in something more powerful than ourselves, as it gives us a reason for being, a sense of comfort knowing that we are protected.

One thing rings true, however. Upon this Earth the laws of nature are real. Nature may be a religious experience to some. It is easy to understand why. For me, it is easier to feel in harmony with nature than with any of the religions with which I am familiar.

In order to become proficient in the ways of nature, it is necessary to participate in them bit by bit, from the view of an objective onlooker. The lessons taught by nature must be learned and remembered as soon as possible. Once the participant has learned his lessons, it naturally follows that he will want to put the lessons to use. Armed with the knowledge that open space was shrinking as the population grew, I felt that if ever I was to test my knowledge of the lessons I had learned, it must be soon.

I was keenly aware that as the years went by, I would become less fit to undertake such a journey.

In conclusion, I languished at a point in my life where nothing pulled me in a direction as much as the desire to re-live the past in the present. I went into this adventure knowing that death was a possibility, if not an eventuality, though no more so than life in the city. I loved the feeling of expectation that such a journey into the unknown aroused.

These are the reasons why I planned to do this crazy thing.

# 2

# PREPARATION

It is one thing to say that you are going to live in the wilderness and quite another thing to actually do it. By December of 1975 George, Nick, and I had made definite our plan to leave for British Columbia, Canada, in April of 1976. The reason for departing in April was to try and arrive in advance of the snowmelt, which would be at its peak in May, thus reducing the number of swollen rivers that we would have to cross to reach our destination. We knew that this might require us to travel through wet and snow for a longer period of time, however, the alternative possibility in our minds was not worth the risk.

During the summer of 1975, after long consideration and much discussion, the majority decided that our destination would be an area north of Ft. Saint James, Canada, which we consider to be the doorstep to the vast interior expanse of the Canadian province of British Columbia.

Shortly after acquiring the required maps from a Canadian topographical map distributor and reviewing them, we found an area of dense forest where the Rocky Mountains and the Omineca Range of Mountains run parallel south of the Alaska Highway and east of the Cassiar Highway. The remote location, and the abundance of water in the form of lakes and rivers, made this a desirable place to go. It would be easy to conceal ourselves in such a dense tree-covered wilderness, and without doubt, the hunting would be excellent.

Working the construction job for three months brought in the needed cash, and once I had enough, I quit my job. For the next two months I spent several hours daily in the library, reading at length about the region, the wildlife that lived there, and the habits of each critter. This was a labor of love, time-consuming though it may have been.

Over time we compiled a list of equipment that we deemed indispensable, the most significant piece of which was the rifle that each of us would carry. Knowing that the grizzly bear was the primary threat to us, we compared the 30.30 to the 40.440 Marlin lever action rifle. The 40.440 was the obvious choice. The shell is three inches long and half an inch in diameter. The bullet is flat on top so that it is not re-directed by hitting a limb on a tree.

The rifle cost $265.00. A box of 25 rounds cost $10.00. I purchased $400.00 worth of shells. I also purchased a used Colt 45 side arm for $100.00 and 300 rounds of ammo.

George purchased the Marlin rifle, a Smith & Wesson 45, and a shotgun with an over/under 410/22. This was a slick gun. It had two barrels, the top barrel a .22 caliber and the bottom barrel a .410.

Nick also purchased the Marlin rifle, and he had a side arm at home.

In addition to the weapons our list included, but was not limited to:

| | | |
|---|---|---|
| Knives | U clamps, 4-inch diameter | Pots and pans |
| Hammers | Outdoor thermometer | Flat griddle |
| Two-, four-, and six-inch nails | Hunting bow/arrows | Rice |
| Axes | Logging saw | Flour |
| Ropes | Canvas bags | Grain |
| Draw shave | Maps | Oats |
| Pulley | Binoculars | Vitamins |
| Cement trowel | Rain gear | Suntan lotion |
| Painters canvas drop cloth | Clothing and boots | Salt and pepper other spices |
| Sharpening stone | Snowshoes | Plastic wrap to store food |
| Plastic drop cloth | Sleeping bags | 16 ounces of marijuana |
| Chisels | Canteens | Three pounds of Bugler brand |
| Cross bow | Five-gallon water container | rolling tobacco |
| Gun oil | Books | |
| Door hinges | Stratego / cards | |

As we gathered the necessary equipment, each of us faced a gut-check as we shelled out the money for a one-way train ticket to the unknown. It was then that Nick had a change of heart. He decided to stay and contest his divorce. I could think of nothing to say that might change his mind, so George and I revised our plan and will now go together. Having two parties involved, governing would no longer be majority-rule. Now George and I would have to discuss and debate major decisions. I hoped that George would most often defer to my suggestions as far as showing the way, since I was more familiar with maps and compasses.

We leaked clues of our intention to friends, some of whom ridiculed us, saying, among other things, that we were full of shit. Be that as it may, we had convinced ourselves that we would at the very least make an effort to succeed.

In this world, every person's future may be measured in minutes because that may be as long as one has left of life.

So I asked myself, "Why walk a path that may lead to doubt? Why miss such an opportunity to explore and perhaps invite regret? Why not instead live my dream and one day tell the children who follow what this Earth was once like? Why not meet the future doing what I am here to do? Why not put my lessons to the test and accept any failure as my own?"

Like others in my age group, I was seeking to discover who I was. What I was put on this Earth to do. It is probably safe to assume that most young people come to a point in their life where the figures of authority seem to be more intent upon forcing their will upon their children than focusing on what the young person wants and needs at that particular point in time.

I am not suggesting that parenting is an easy task, nor am I saying that parents generally are not in touch with their child's emotional state, but it takes all kinds of people to make this world go round.

In my mind, without doubt, the Fifties era in which I was born fueled the current situation faced by my parents. They seemed unable to relate to both their peers on one level and their children on another level. Instead, they became frustrated and threw their weight around, sometimes literally. There was little discussion, the adults dug in their heels and declared what would be since they said so.

From fourth grade through eighth grade I went to catholic school and then entered into the public school system, which were overwhelmingly attended by African-American students, some of whom had little or no guidance at home. As a result, a lot of petty crime occurred in the schools and on the public transportation system.

My parents, it seemed, were in tune with other things. The Watts riot traumatized both my parents, but I believe it scared my father more. I recall as an 8-year-old that during the 1964 riot, my father and uncle sitting on the porch as Army jeeps patrolled the streets, the crews manning .50 caliber machine guns, seeking curfew violators and keeping an eye on burned out and looted stores, all within blocks of our home.

I could never understand how my some of my relatives could be so bigoted considering their heritage. All migrated from the tough streets of Brooklyn where they lived in true middle class fashion. I could see no distinction between a white man and a black man trying to support his family, as long as both did it lawfully. The behavior I witnessed was no more than ignorance and a lack of the most basic consideration for something different, and it fed racism on all sides.

During this decade, specifically 1966, I became aware of music with the emerging hippie scene. The Beatles had a lifelong effect on me, and I have been a rocker since I can remember. For the duration of the 1960s, I was exposed to protests on TV, drugs at social gatherings, music, school, and the party scene.

Throughout high school in the 1970s I worked hard enough to get by, to have cigarette money and beer money. I grew my hair longer and spent more and more time learning firsthand about life. Late in my senior year I got a car.

Still later I got a car that ran! A gorgeous used 1964 Cadillac Coup De Ville. She was my liberator! No longer was I bound by how far I could hitchhike or by which friend could give me a lift somewhere.

I altered my way of thinking more to what it is today. I found myself now more in control of my destiny and able to pursue almost anything I wished. What teenager has not screamed with glee in their moment of liberation? The Caddy lasted for three years before I blew up the engine.

In the days that I owned the Caddy, I spent a lot of time in the mountains with friends. Somewhere between buying the Caddy and the death of the Caddy, I formed the belief that it was safer to be in the wild than it was in the city. I took weekend trips to the Sierras and camped often enough to appreciate that environment more than I did the city life.

For most young people I knew in high school during the 1970s, all 17-year-olds lives beat to the same drum. There was always a party to go to on Friday night after the football game. Saturday nights, another party, and school during the rest of the week.

Upon graduating from high school, I found a job and felt unhappy, without a goal. I felt lost. I had no purpose. I had no understanding of what I was put on the planet to achieve or even in which direction I was heading.

As a result, I began to study more in depth the ways of Native Americans. I read every book that I could find, and over time, with the help of those wise Grandfathers, learned what was considered sacred. I found those things to be more meaningful to me than any religion I had ever heard of.

Foremost among these sacred things is respect. Respect for those who share the Earth with me. Respect for my animal brothers. The manner in which a man conducts himself is sacred. The pipe and the buffalo are both sacred. I choose to live in such a sacred manner that I would respect all, until shown that my respect is not deserved. It still makes sense to me that if I fail to respect nature, I will pay a price. The wilderness easily supports anyone who knows how to attain the rewards that it offers.

I left home for reasons that never existed. My parents were not the reason I left, but rather a convenient excuse that I gave myself. In truth I felt lost, unable to approach my parents, and like others of my generation; I kept searching for an identity. I spent the following couple of years off and on roving across the country in nomadic fashion, taking odd jobs to earn money for food and cigarettes. Otherwise I roamed without aim, with no real intention.

In the beginning, my top-most priority had to be avoiding contact with law enforcement, as being under-age, still 16 at this time, I realized that any potential encounter could spell my return home, or to juvie. I traveled during the spring of 1973 through the Southwest, staying along the highways and on the outskirts of towns. For me, the open desert represented an escape route if necessary. There were times in the desert when the temperature went from more than 100 degrees during the day to near freezing at night. I spent one night under a highway bridge with my teeth chattering, the structure rumbling each time a truck passed over it.

As the summer progressed, I hitchhiked my way to Colorado, where I made friends and spent the winter of 1973. I found a sense of brotherhood among the people living there, a sense of teamwork. The people living in these communities came from other places and built large canvas shelters to assist runaways comparable to myself. We all did equal work and shared in the rewards.

Moving on in the fall of 1974 I traveled through Colorado with a sleeping bag, a backpack full of clothes, and my knife. Later in the year I left Colorado with the intention of going back to California for a brief visit with friends and family, but I never quite made it all the way.

# 3

# THE GENESIS BEGINS

Last night, April 14, 1976, George's brothers threw us a farewell party. The general consensus is that we will return in a couple of months, tops. The party seemed somewhat strange in that no one seemed to think that the morning would come and that we would be gone. The conversations were the kinds that take place at weekend parties, not what one would expect when someone is going on such a major expedition.

I had mixed emotions at the time. I knew that I would miss my friends and family and yes, even Los Angeles, with all of the routines that had clocked our lives until now. George spent the night with his girlfriend. I stayed at George's brother's house.

I took time to thank the Great Spirit for giving us the power to learn and asked that he watch over us in the wilderness.

The newspapers report that this has been the worst winter on record in parts of Canada, and experts said that the worst was likely not over. I feared that we would be facing the end of winter rather than the beginning of spring.

**Spring 1976, Vancouver, British Columbia**

We arrived in Canada yesterday, April 15th, amid a driving rain, which made things less than perfect. In my mind's eye, I had pictured a sunny day greeting us, but this was the reality. We rented a hotel room nearby, nothing fancy, but dry and a place to sleep.

We had arranged to meet Galen Gen in town the next day, and he would fly us to a town named Prince George. We now stood some 200 miles from there.

As the day wore on, the rain changed to snow, and things settled down. I began to feel more comfortable. Touring around the city, we found Vancouver to be clean, populated with smiling people. We had dinner and bought a six-pack of beer and ambled to our room. We were both too thrilled to sleep, so we drank beer and smoked, and then quite relaxed, we watched TV.

\* \* \*

Late this morning we met Galen, to whom we were introduced through a mutual friend, at a local bar. Galen was ex-military, having served in Vietnam as a navy pilot. He seemed to always be looking over his shoulder, so to speak, and was armed with a handgun in his waistband. I can't be sure that I would want to spend a great deal of time around this man, as he seems rather skittish.

After two drinks, Galen had us load our things into his truck, and we drove to the municipal airport and pulled up alongside a single-engine float plane. Galen had agreed to fly us, and our gear, to Prince George for the sum of $100.00 each. We had already made arrangements to buy our horses. We stored our gear on the plane and planned to fly out at 6 a.m. the following morning.

Returning to the bar, we played pool and consumed several more rounds.

George and I wandered to our hotel at 10 o'clock.

\* \* \*

I am writing from the Krable Ranch, where we purchased our horses and tack.

This morning we touched down after a flight over rugged wilderness, with spectacular lakes and streams dotting the landscape. Snow-capped mountains and valleys passed below us. In the back of my mind I questioned my sanity. We made a stop in Quesnel for something that Galen needed to take care of. We then flew on to Prince George.

We exchanged good-byes with Galen and waited on the side of the highway for our ride.

It arrived 40 minutes later, and we loaded our gear into a 1966 Ford truck. We drove toward Vanderhoof, British Columbia. Chet, a ranch hand on the Krable spread, was our guide. After 10 miles, we arrived at the Krable Ranch.

Via phone and U.S. mail, we had arranged to buy five horses and two saddles, as well as pack frames for the pack horses for $1,600.

In the corral to which we were led stood 10 horses of different sizes and breeds from which we could choose. I selected a brown and white paint, a horse with large black eyes and white socks on three legs, the other sporting a brown sock. She stood smaller in stature than the other horses, but she was well defined. I shall call her Canoni (Ca-no-nee), which is a Lakota word meaning wanders in the woods.

George's choice, a gray Appaloosa, was broad and tall. The three packhorses that we selected were run-of-the-mill brown horses.

Reality came to the fore as we now had our means to traverse the highlands and forests. Tomorrow morning, we will go forward into the past, and I will get my chance to partake in my genesis in the wild.

Chet drove us to town, where we purchased our supplies at the general store and the hardware store. One hour and $470 later, Chet brought the load to the ranch. George and I stacked the supplies neatly near the corral. Once finished, George and I hiked a short ways and smoked a pipe load of weed. We spent half an hour chatting about the horses and then meandered to the main house. Mr. Krable invited us for dinner. After a spectacular dinner of fried chicken with biscuits and gravy, we traipsed to the cabin, where we slept.

* * *

It is evening as I write. We rode 10 miles before finding a camping spot, where we pitched our tents and now sit, having coffee.

We awoke animated this morning, as the sun lit the eastern sky. We loaded each packhorse with 100 pounds of supplies and additional gear. We anticipated that these supplies would be enough to get us to where we would live and we hoped, through the first few months.

Ready to begin this once-in-a-lifetime journey, to test our potential, capture our capacity for fear and adventure, we would determine if we had the ability to survive whatever this land threw at us.

Packed and eager to ride, Mr. Krable wished us luck, and we ventured away from civilization, riding into the mountains. The long-awaited dream has finally manifested, and now we face our destiny.

As we traveled northwest, the terrain consisted of smooth rolling hills in the valleys. Deep snow blanketed the surrounding mountains, but the ground was more muddy than snow-packed. Rain accompanied us almost from the start this morning, and the day has been wet and somewhat chilly. The riding trails that we followed were muddy, and the soil in general was wet, making for a gloomy ride. Nevertheless, the thrill of being here, and the majesty that we see all around us, makes the misery well worth it.

In the early afternoon, after roving 10 miles, we found our campsite at the base of a towering rock formation, which has an overhanging ledge to keep the rain off of us. With the fire burning, and shielded from the wind, it does not seem so bad. Of course, I reminded George not to allow the fire to get too hot, since it could heat the ledge above us, and it could then fracture and fall on us. George made soup for dinner.

Beyond the glow of the fire, it is quiet and dark. As I peered into the darkness that surrounds us, I thought about something that I read not too long ago. It spoke about the Seventh Arrow. According to the Grandfathers, who passed the belief from generation to generation, The Great Spirit showed the people a medicine wheel, which contained four gifts. Every male child arrived on earth with one gift bestowed by the Great Spirit.

From birth, expectations demanded that each man would attain the other three gifts in his lifetime. Once all four gifts had been acquired, (Wisdom, Illumination, Innocence, and Perception) the tribe considered him whole, and he would know the Seventh Arrow. When a man had gained all four gifts, the tribe presented him with a war shield depicting two half-moons facing each other. Since wisdom is thought to come with age, those who attained the Seventh Arrow generally did so as elder men.

I do not know what number of men achieved this goal, but it would seem that it would be a low number, due to war and other dangers associated with the Indian ways.

In order to be more easily understood, these gifts were assigned a different bearing on the horizon. In addition, they were each assigned a color and an animal to represent them. Four gifts reside on the medicine wheel, one gift for each direction. The gift of the North is Wisdom and Knowledge. As one might guess, this gift was most often realized in old age, never often in youth. This proved by far the hardest gift to acquire because of the constant conflict between the white people and the tribes. It is far easier to kill with weapons than to progress with Wisdom.

The color chosen to represent the North is white. This color represents purity. So the Grandfathers decided that the most beloved of all animals, the buffalo, would be assigned to represent the North. Tatanka, the buffalo, chosen for its legendary durability graces the wheel.

The gift of the East is Illumination. This is the ability to show the world how much you love yourself and everything around you. In combat, Illumination was used to impress the enemy with courage and daring. Parents are required to teach their children that which brings peace and prosperity to the tribe. In general, Illumination gave the seeker love and self-respect.

Because of its great mastery and dominance over the sky, the eagle was selected to represent the East. As it relates to the sun and its illumination, yellow or gold is used to represent the East.

Next on the medicine wheel is the South. Perhaps the least mastered of all mankind's abilities is the ability to truly trust himself, to find his Innocence. He must learn to rely on his inner voice that speaks truth, regardless of whether he chooses to hear it.

The color chosen to represent the South is green because of the relationship between green and the spring, the time of re-birth, the time for genesis. The creature chosen to represent the South is the mouse, due to its size and innocence.

The gift of the West is Perception. This is the ability to look within oneself and accept what is found. You may make the world perceive you as one thing, and that does not really matter in the long run because you can't hide from yourself.

Because perception requires a lot of strength, the bear is chosen as the animal to represent the West. Often the seeker felt lost, without purpose before finding this gift, and for that reason, black was selected as the color to represent the West.

It is my belief that I was born with Perception, the gift of the West. I have also worked to attain Illumination, the gift of the East.

George believes he came into the world with the gift of the East as well. He is loud and even brash. He cusses a lot and is fearless. He does not easily buy into these beliefs and is here to be away from the city. Each passing day here in the wilderness, I will strive to attain the gifts that I now lack.

\* \* \*

## THE THIRD WEEK OF APRIL BEGINS

We rode at a comfortable pace and reached Lake Tezzeron. We have traveled 26 miles. The terrain has been manageable, though muddy, and this has allowed us to keep our steady pace. In most places the mountains are tall and surround us. We have seen signs of animals but have not spotted anything significant as of yet. Both George and I ride with our heads turning, constantly surveying the landscape around us.

We have made camp for the night, and George is cooking pancakes for our dinner. For the moment we are content, anxiously awaiting tomorrow.

\* \* \*

I write these notes as the sun fades through the dark grey cloudy sky. Sometime after midnight it started to rain, and drizzles stayed with us all day. I like the fact that the rain deadens the sounds in the mountains, wetting the brush and dirt. With the slightest breeze it feels chilly on our hands and faces.

We ate our first kill today — a rabbit George hit using the bow we brought with us. The meal was more ceremonial than filling.

We made camp after riding 20 miles. We tried our luck fishing in Lake Tezzeron. We did not catch any fish. We tried several different lures of varying sizes, running at various depths, but fate had other ideas.

\* \* \*

Today we fished Lake Tezzeron but realized marginal success at best. Using salmon eggs, I managed to land two adolescent trout. George also caught one, his being the largest, a 14-inch fish. We enjoyed these for lunch.

The rain has continued off and on, and it has been cloudy all day. Earlier in the day we heard the call of the true dog for the first time, one wolf howling to another somewhere in the distance. It was a sound that made us pay attention.

So far our 47-mile excursion has been horseback riding and camping. I am excited for the days to come, when we have found our cabin location.

\* \* \*

Early in the day we crossed the Nation River. It is quite impressive. It runs swift at this location, affording no shallow crossings.

Having at last found a place to cross, and succeeding, we built a fire and dried our cloths. The features of the land have changed, now thick green forest envelops us in all of its majestic glory. The rain was unrelenting for most of the day, a sprinkle, but wet, nonetheless.

The horses have been well behaved thus far. They do not seem to mind the muddy conditions or the rain. They follow our lead. Canoni makes me proud as I imagine how I look from another's perspective, sitting tall and straight as I traverse the land.

Our ultimate destination is a valley that lies at the foot of the Cassiar Mountains, right where they meet the Rocky Mountains. Judging by the progress that we have made so far, it will take another three weeks to get there.

I can't adequately describe how enormous this land seems. The mountains tower over us and the dense fog makes a man seem insignificant. The overwhelming feeling that we are strangers in this land looms ever-present as we weave our way deeper into the unknown.

\* \* \*

We traveled 10 miles this day. Early in the ride, we approached the base of the first range of mountains that we must cross, known as the Omineca Mountains. The weather has continued damp and chilly, making the ascent somewhat more dangerous. The highest peak is near 8,000 feet, according to the topography map. We will be exposed to the coldest temperatures as we summit the highest valley, then once on the other side it shouldn't take more than a few hours to reach the flat valleys.

We traced the valley trail as it wound its way higher and higher into the pass, the snow becoming deeper as we went. Late in the day, the sun broke through the clouds; the warming rays were what we needed. We summited the pass in late afternoon and found relief from the breeze that had picked up on the front side of the mountain.

We have set up camp for the night on a flat piece of ground. George is gathering firewood as I write, and I will go and prepare the tinder that we will use to start the fire.

We now have the fire burning. George will make chili beans and coffee for dinner.

Being camped on the side of a mountain is rather strange, there never seems to be true level ground upon which to set our tents. So while in my tent, the uneven ground makes for a pain in the lower back. I guess that that could also be from riding horses all day.

George has mentioned that he has blisters on his butt, which caused me to laugh, until I realized that I have them as well.

Soon dinner will be ready, so I will put away my journal now.

\* \* \*

We have been seven days on the trail. Our best estimate is that we have covered 87 miles, including today.

We made our descent from the pass in much the same way as yesterday, following the natural flow of the valley. As we descended, the snow became shallow, and by afternoon we had reached flat land. It rained again, and so we decided to set up camp and give the horses a rest.

Before we left California, weeks before, in fact, we wrote down some thoughts that we had at the time, thoughts that we would take with us.

Here are a few of them:

When we arrive at the right place, and the land offers timber to protect us, we will know that it is our spirit speaking to us, telling us to build there.

I am man, made of thought and will, and nothing sits above my will. We seek pride and happiness, and nothing compares to the joy that I feel in nature. I have one life, my own, and so I will appreciate that life. I own the strength of choice, and nothing can detour my choice. I will take the risk that comes from adventure.

## ON THE SUBJECT OF DYING IN THE MOUNTAINS:

Living in the inner city jungle, competing for everything one possesses drains the life out of one. Every night I am thankful for having survived the gangs, the police, and the smog. At least if I die in the mountains I will have died in peace. (George)

## ON LIVING IN THE WILD:

To live, it is essential for the person to become one with his surroundings and intermingle with everything upon the land.

The teachers tell us that all things know of their harmony with every other thing and know how to give away to each other, except man.

We begin with the spirit of man and work down through the laws of nature. If the unthinkable happens, I am to bury George in a deep grave, with heavy rocks piled on top. George has agreed to erect a scaffold and lay my remains upon it, for a period of three days, after which time he will set fire to the scaffold.

\* \* \*

Two days have passed, and we have covered an additional 55 miles and are camped a short distance south of the Ingenika River. We have decided to camp here and start fresh in the morning. I shot a rabbit after making camp using the .22 caliber rifle. George is cooking it on a roasting stick.

Clouds obscure the moon as it climbs in the east, foretelling a dark night ahead. We let the horses graze while hobbled, the front feet tied slackly with three feet of rope, preventing the horses from galloping away. I feel especially tired tonight and think I will sleep well.

\* \* \*

Today we came to the second major river that we must cross, and this crossing has come at a price. Upon seeing the Ingenika River, we realized that this was not a river that we could wade across, as it ran swift and was perhaps a hundred feet wide. It ran flat and without rapids where we were, although the current swirled in earnest.

Our first task was to construct a raft to float the supplies across the river. Using Lodgepole pine we completed the raft in two hours.

We flipped a coin to see who would swim across to set up the pendulum system with a rope and pulley that we would use to guide the raft across the river. George lost the toss and prepared to swim across.

George took a rope that we had brought for this purpose and slipped it over his shoulder through his arm. He jogged upstream several hundred yards and dove into the water. He was forced downstream by the current as he swam across. It appeared he would not get to the other side, but being a strong swimmer, he made it.

First thing out of the water he let out a yell that may have been heard in sunny California! He built a fire and dried off while I organized the supplies. George tied one end of the rope to a tree and ran it through the pulley. He tied the other end to an arrow before shooting it back across the river. I secured my end of the rope to the raft and loaded it with gear. In this manner we moved all of our gear in three trips.

Before I crossed the river, I chased the horses into the water and watched as they swam across. They swam well, but as they neared the far bank, one of the packhorses was swept into deep, faster-moving waters, sending it downstream, around the bend and out of sight. George collected the others as they clambered out of the water.

In order for me to cross and bring the rope with me, we decided to use a device that we had brought for that type of thing. George shot the rope across to me, and I tied my end high in a tree. George secured his rope so that my side was at a higher angle. The device that we refer to as a pulley is built to allow the rope to fit on a wheel that is outfitted with handles. With the rope strung across the river, the rider places the wheel on the rope and holds onto the handles as they glide above the water. We thought that this would allow me to ride the pulley across, hanging from it by my safety belt if necessary to rest. I got ready and took the leap out over the river.

The system worked fine until I neared George's side, when the rope on my side of the Ingenika River slipped and slid down the tree. This caused the rope to slacken and my progress to be stopped 10 feet short of George. He tried to figure out a way to get me across. He decided on holding a branch that I could grab onto and be pulled in.

As he searched for the branch, I relaxed my grip on the wheel to rest my arm muscles, as we had done many times before. This time, however, the belt on my harness slipped and tightened, closing around my stomach. I was being suffocated by my own body weight! Being unable to draw a breath, I became lightheaded. I tried to yell out to George, but the river drowned out my call.

I tried to climb up the harness safety rope to the wheel, but I didn't have enough strength. I then thought about cutting the harness safety rope and taking my chances in the Ingenika River. Visions of the packhorse rushed into my mind as I drew my knife from its shield. I realized, as I saw the veins on my arms swelling to three times their normal size that I was not going to make it off of that rope. I feared that this was where I would die.

I burned inside with anger at my misfortune, while at the same time flailing away in vain in my attempt to gain the wheel all the time stunned by the thought of dying, having come so far but achieving nothing. I heard George bellowing, but I could not locate him.

At this point my strength failed me, and I watched my knife drop into the water below me. Everything seemed as if a dream. In my subconscious mind I wondered how long it would be until I passed out. I slipped into a semi-sleeping state, able to hear the water below but not caring about it. I felt a tug on my arm, but I gave no thought to that.

Then I was at ease, no longer in a panicked state, now asleep. In the next instant, I opened my eyes, and hearing the river, knew that I was alive. George stood over me with an expression of relief on his face. I could not get up for a full 10 minutes. I had that feeling that one gets when one's foot goes to sleep, but throughout my entire body.

The two or three minutes that the incident lasted seemed like 15 full minutes while it was occurring. People say that one see one's life flash before their eyes when one is close to death. I did not experience this.

I was driven to fight for survival until I became too weak. By then, not much oxygen remained in my brain.

George crowed, "Tonweya, you were not conscious when I pulled you closer so I could reach you. You were out for another two minutes once I unhooked your safety belt. The veins in your neck stood out half an inch, but I knew that I would reach you before you died!"

Over the next hour we talked about the whole event and smoked several bowls of weed in the process. We decided to stay there for a few days to recover.

George made an admission. "When you called out to me I thought you were kidding, and I did nothing. Then I saw the fear in your eyes, and the pain that you seemed to be in and knew that the distress was real. It took me a minute or two to find a branch strong enough to pull you out".

Once my ass settled into the sand, George rode his horse downstream to see if he could locate the packhorse, without success. There was a lack of sentimental emotions on this occasion since we had to care for the remaining livestock. We would now have to divide the 150 that that horse had been carrying between the two surviving packhorses. They would now be carrying near 250 pounds each, far more weight than we ever anticipated.

This would affect the distance that we could travel without endangering the animals. During the crossing, we lost two pieces of gear, our folding lawn chairs and a canvas tarp that we had intended to use as a shield for our campfire, to break the wind. It was useful in reflecting heat in one direction. It also kept most of the smoke from blowing into our faces as it cut the wind. George will miss this most as he does most of the cooking.

Although this day is over now, it was painful on numerous levels.

\* \* \*

It's been a day since my brush with death, and I'm making this entry to remind myself of how precious life is and how thin the thread is between life and death. I never thought that by letting go of that wheel I would find myself struggling for life, having done it many times before. The reality of death is never seriously considered, until one find themselves facing it. One second you are doing whatever, and in the next instant you are fighting for your life. One becomes aware of how short that last breath of life is. Even in that instant that I thought of death, nothing changed or was disrupted, nothing altered except my world, which was almost gone.

Yet the beauty of British Columbia is such that I gladly and willingly accepted the risks associated with it. No man would rather die than live. Looking around me perhaps I appreciate the trees and sky more. Even the cold seems not as bad. I am alive thanks to George, and I owe him a debt that I may never be able to repay.

Then again, if all things truly come full circle, I may yet have a chance to repay the debt, especially living out here.

\* \* \*

The last day of April has past, and May is upon us. We rode 15 miles today and have set up the tents and dug the fire pit.

While we have been out here for less than two weeks, it seems that time has slowed down, or perhaps time has disappeared. There is day and night, so much to observe and respond to, that time has become irrelevant. We don't have dinner at six o'clock, we have dinner before dark.

Riding for six to eight hours a day wears on us. We both toddle around like old men and have blisters on our ass. The reality of how hard things can be has set in.

Late this afternoon a shower passed overhead, so we sat inside George's tent telling stories from our past.

George told me of a time that he won a substantial amount of money playing cards. This happened late at night in a bad neighborhood in southwest Los Angeles. He had won the big pot and was motivated to get home. He didn't notice two men follow him out of the club. As he reached his car and unlocked the door, the men demanded the money that they knew he had. George swung at one of them, knocking him down. As he bolted for the club, the other man pulled a gun and fired in George's direction, missing him, the bullet smashing into the wall of the club. He fired several more times, missing each time.

George made it through the door as a bullet smashed the glass in the door! Within minutes the police swarmed the area but did not find the two men.

This type of incident is common in Los Angeles at any time. This is only one example of how cheap a life is considered there.

\* \* \*

We have been on the trail for two weeks. We rode all day today with a stiff, cold wind in our faces. Travel has been sadistically miserable, each minute a literal pain. I estimate the wind to have been gusting at 25 miles per hour. I'm sure that the wind-chill temperature was below freezing.

We have traveled to a point 100 miles north of Fort St. James, and we have another hundred miles to go before reaching our target area.

Thus far the journey has been as spectacular as we could have imagined, other than the weather. We have suffered no lasting injuries to ourselves or the remaining four horses.

Having set up camp, George is cooking rabbit stew over the fire in a black cast iron kettle.

Today for the first time, I thought about those people in the civilized world, those who have no idea where or how we are. They are better off not knowing. Some of them would worry. The rest will soon forget us. Out of sight, out of mind.

Sitting in our tents is like sitting in nothing at all. Sometimes we hear a gust of wind far down the canyon, and it rolls toward us, getting closer by the second. The wind violently shakes the tents, to the point that we think that it might pick us up and blow us away. Then in a heartbeat, it is gone, and things are quiet. The silence gives way to the distant sound of another gust. This goes on for hours sometimes, and tonight is one of those nights.

\* \* \*

The tents survived the night, as did we, although with little sleep. This morning that wind has not stopped and will make for another cold ride.

We rode 12 miles today, and the wind-chill made it feel icy cold. We shot a rabbit and roasted it for dinner. We found a nice spot to set up camp, at the base of a gigantic rock formation, which will block the wind. For this reason, we have a fire and a belly full of hot meat. George crept into his tent half an hour ago; I can hear him snoring. Another day closes.

\* \* \*

Two days later, the dawn broke to a bright, cloudless sky, auburn rays reaching down from the heavens. For the first time in three weeks we saw the sky, without fog or rain clouds. Without the wind that has accompanied us for the past two days, the rays of the sun felt amazing. We appreciated the sun so much that we rode 10 miles in five hours. We stopped early in the afternoon and made camp. The rest of the day we spent lying in the sun, heads resting on our saddles.

I remember as a kid, lying in the grass or on the sand at the beach with my eyes closed, on a nice summer day, as somewhere in the distance a song played, and the music drifting on the air. The one thought in my mind today was how good the sun felt on my body. I pray that many more days like this are in our future.

George managed to catch two trout in a nearby stream and will soon cook them for dinner. In weather such as we see here, coffee is a tasty treat while it lasts.

* * *

Early in the day we crested a range of mountains, passing through one pass and then descending into a long sheltered valley on the other side. On the floor of this valley, the snow was less than a foot deep; however, we could see that it appeared much deeper on the mountains that stood to the west.

We spent time clearing a 20-foot circle in the shallow snow that remains on the ground, in which we set up the tents and dug a fire pit. Then it took us an hour to find dry firewood, which proved frustrating, as everything at lower altitudes seems to be damp.

Once we had the fire going, George pulled out the map and placed his finger on where he thought we were. He pointed to a spot northwest of Fleet Peak.

I disagreed. "George, I think we are farther north by 20 miles."

After a lengthy discussion, I gave an inch. "Okay, tell me your calculations."

"I am going on a gut feeling." George got defensive.

I grew annoyed. "George, your gut feeling could get us lost or worse. The compass and the maps indicate that we are within five miles of Fishing Lake. I'll tell you what, if we don't see the lake by noon tomorrow, we can travel in any direction you wish."

George acceded, and I could see him having doubts. What better chance to get him to put faith and trust in my skills? That is, unless I was wrong too.

* * *

We have been on the trail for three weeks and have traveled 122 miles.

We saddled up and rode the dusty trail as the sun crested the horizon. As the day brightened, we spied a herd of elk in the distance, perhaps 25 strong. Among the herd were a few new calves.

We rode north, keeping the mountains on our left. Three hours after starting out, we passed Fishing Lake. I caught sight of George looking toward the sky while rubbing his hand over his lips when it sank in that he missed his guess by so many miles

I hoped that this would be a lesson learned. Of course, I was feeling a bit cocky as I loudly cleared my throat, my grinning face a dagger to his pride.

Another couple hours of riding brought us to an area where the ground was grassier and less rocky. In the distance, we heard the faint sound of rapids.

I knew what lay ahead. I dropped the lead from my packhorse and spurred Canoni into a gallop. George did the same, and we rode for a minute, stopping along the tree-lined bank of a feeder stream that ran into the McCook River. This stream was wide but shallow, four feet at the deepest point.

We waited for our packhorses to catch up, and we crossed without any issues. On the other side, we unpacked the horses and let them drink from the McCook River and eat the sparse grass along the bank. We continued riding for another mile or so and stopped.

Eyeing the surroundings, we found the trees to be plentiful, tall, and the proper diameter needed for building a cabin. Green grass grew under our feet. Fishing would not be a problem with the many streams running down from the mountains.

This valley is a natural migration path, which should make hunting easier. Why spend more time and energy heading for a far distant place that might not be any better than this place. We took our decision to stay in this area. For the next few days we planned to search for the perfect ground upon which to build our cabin. As a general point of reference, we are located between the Omineca Range and the Rocky Mountains.

\* \* \*

After riding through the valley for three miles scouting a location to build on, we came upon a soft, sloping rise in the terrain. We liked this slope, as it would allow water to run off and not pool around the structure.

A spectacular granite rock formation jutted into the sky, with a river some 200 feet below the top on the back side of the formation. This river was not marked on the map, so we were surprised to see it. We knew that the formation would shield us well from any bad weather coming from the west.

So, for the next three months or so, this was where we would live, in our little tents as we construct our home.

We saw signs of various animals while riding. The one that most impressed me was a lone set of grizzly tracks, which ran from east to west through the valley. By the depth of the impression, we could tell that this was an adult bear. We also saw deer, elk, and fox tracks.

Our spot was replete with thick stands of ponderosa pine and Lodgepole pine trees. The two would make a fine blend of wood in sizes with which we could work. We would use the ponderosa for the walls and floor of the cabin and the Lodgepole for the roof.

We ate a dinner of trout and pork and beans.

\* \* \*

Rain returned today as if on cue. We rode into the forest and marked the trees that we would cut. We spent hours selecting them, all while a steady rain fell.

We did not fish today, so we are eating chili beans. George mixed in some greens, and the flavor was decent enough.

We relax by the fire as I pen this entry. The clouds have disappeared. The night will soon be black and cold. A million stars shine down on us tonight, now and then one falling from the heavens, burning up with a dazzling display of fire in its wake.

The warmth of the fire feels good on my face. We wonder aloud what tomorrow will bring.

\* \* \*

Two physically exhausting days later, we have spent most of our time in the last couple of days away from camp, felling trees, using a logging saw for this purpose. Once on the ground, we cut, or to be more accurate, chopped the limbs off of the tree, leaving the log ready to be cut to length. We dragged them into the sunlight. They will be stripped of bark and left to dry.

Over the past two days, the rain has stuck around, with periods of intermittent sun. We have had fair luck fishing in the unforeseen river, which I will name the West River, since it is west of where our cabin will stand, catching several trout and a white fish. This was a nice change from eating red meat for dinner.

We have begun taking the vitamin supplements that we brought with us, each of us at 500 mg of vitamin C and 500 mg of iron every other day.

The rain has systematically soaked everything. Our tents form a buildup of condensation during the night from our breathing. By morning, everything in the tent is damp. Since the sun has remained elusive, our things never fully dry.

Traveling back and forth to work on the logs is dreary, with everything so wet and quiet. The birds don't sing. We hear the distant racket of a lone woodpecker.

To keep our minds off of the weather, we either fish, cut trees, go for short hikes, or ride our horses. Any way you slice it, we stay wet.

* * *

As if fulfilling an eventuality, it seems that spring has fully arrived, and it appears as though it is time for everything to grow. Many species have dropped their young, and it is evident that the lessons of life have begun.

Today I rode out of camp to a favorite spot that I have come to enjoy in the week that we have been in this area. I found a slope north of our building site that overlooks a set of rapids on the West River, some 30 feet below. A series of trails lead from the water up to the level ground upon which I stood. Dense brush and grass concealed my presence. The West River flowed from my left to my right. A line of trees propagates the bank, as the river winds around a bend and out of sight.

Below me a mother grizzly bear stood with her two young cubs in a pool just above the falls. The mother hunted for fish, as her curious cubs bounced along the shore.

Mother was cinnamon-colored, her head a somewhat lighter shade, almost blonde. I would estimate that she weighed between 350 and 400 pounds.

Once when the cubs jumped into the water, they were washed over the falls into the current below. Mother, oblivious to the current with her immense weight, was caught off guard when her young were swept downstream. She watched intently.

I patiently analyzed the scene as this event unfolded. Each time the young bears regained their footing they swam to the far bank, climbed onto shore, and padded back to Mama along the sandy shore.

While my attention was upstream checking out Mother's reaction when her cubs went over the falls a second time, one of the cubs hauled himself out of the water on my side of the river. I was oblivious of this and so paid little attention downstream. Then I heard the cub cry out with a long high-pitched shriek, inciting terror within me as I was sandwiched between Mama and her cub. Downstream, I could see it hastening along the shore towards the inclining trail that led to me!

In an instant, I felt the ground vibrate and heard the vulgar huffing, grunting exhale of Mama as she charged up the incline on my left. In a flash she had bolted past me, within a foot or two! I could have reached out and touched her head. As she rushed past me, I fumbled with my rifle.

My mind was clouded by confusion. I tried to process what was happening. I leaped backwards away from the opening in the tall grass that hid me, and fell onto the dirt trail, attempting to cock my rifle. Raising to my feet my eyes tracked Mama, and she was now very near the river. My rifle now cocked, rested firm against my cheek and I took my finger off of the trigger. I was shaking and my knees were unstable.

I subconsciously wondered why Mama had not attacked me. I imagine that she had to be as startled as I. In an instant it all became clear. The cub's cry had come as a result of a male grizzly, which had been wandering along the river, hidden from view among the trees. It rushed to the edge of the river to investigate the cub, and perhaps kill it, as males are known to do.

By now, Mama had reached the river and with a great splash hurdled in, prepared to do battle. I heard the collision and the loud growling as the two fought. Mama tore clumps of fur from the male bear, while attempting to bite his neck and mouth, causing him to run into the forest. The cub in the meantime, had just about stumbled upon my position, and soon it passed 10 feet in front of me.

I thought it best to leave because Mama would be agitated and sure to press the issue. I backed away from the ledge and skedaddled to Canoni, mounted, and rode toward camp, and to a higher vantage point that overlooked the scene of the clash.

I could see that Mama had reunited with her cubs, while the male was nowhere to be seen. It would be difficult to describe the ferocity in Mama bear's growl, short of saying the sound seemed to vibrate through the air, the horse raspy sound demanding submission. It is something that I will not soon forget. I will forever remember how close Mother came to me before I even knew she was charging. She covered 20 yards in the blink of an eye.

I perched on Canoni for a short while, recounting the incident in my mind, trying to regain my composure. I understood that even if I had had the rifle cocked and ready, I would not have gotten a shot off before Mama reached me.

The last time I saw the male bear he jogged across the West River, far up on the bank, heading toward the valley, off to another place. I learned a lesson that common sense dictates one should not have to learn: never take your eyes off of an adult bear, especially if she has cubs.

Mother learned that the river harbors dangers, and the male bear learned that a mama grizzly protecting her cubs can be four-legged death!

In all of my dreams and waking fantasies concerning being in the wild, I have never felt the power of an animal like I did today. My whole body turned to Jell-O in the moment. It was on shaking legs that I made it to Canoni. These were the most adrenalin-packed seconds of my life so far!

It was unusual for bears to be in the rivers fishing at this time. I would have expected them to be eating grass, bulbs, and roots.

And so ends another extraordinary day in the wilderness!

* * *

This morning, the sun greeted us with its warm rays, which felt terrific on our exposed skin. We set about cutting trees for the cabin. Today we went to the trees farthest from the tents, if for no other reason than to soak in the sun a little longer. We worked into the afternoon before heading to camp.

Along the way we pointed out and identified animal tracks that we came across. We noted a combination of wolf, rabbit, deer, moose, and elk, plus other unidentifiable tracks.

For dinner we ate the fresh fish caught by George a couple of minutes ago. From river to frying pan in five minutes, it does not get any fresher than that.

* * *

Today remained sunny and warm for the most part. We have felled what we think will be enough timber to erect the cabin, our home. I felt a desire to explore the wilderness around us, but George wishes to stay around camp and relax, so I will investigate tomorrow alone.

I am filled with anticipation and eagerness. The thought of seeing something that no other man has ever seen has always thrilled me. That is exactly what I came here to do. I will take Canoni, one packhorse, and enough supplies for one week. My plan is to go north along the Gataga River, which is situated two miles east of our building site.

George has indicated that if he decides to go riding, it will be east, on this side of the Muskwa Mountain range. He seems more aware of the vastness of this place than even a week ago. I am pleased that he wants to see what's out there. Tonight we smoke a pipe full of weed and will ride when the sun rises.

* * *

We have arrived at mid-May. I awoke before the sun had fully risen in the sky. Loading the packhorse, I was quiet as I rode out. As I navigated the soft ground, I could not restrain myself from urging Canoni into a run as my anticipation grew. The wind blew my hair straight out, its briskness stinging my face.

For the first time I was absolutely alone. I had never felt such a feeling of isolation, at least on this grand scale, before. I yelled a war cry at the top of my lungs and reveled in the thought of not being heard.

The mountains and valleys hold all varieties of life, and one always hears sounds. What is different here is that often I hear one sound at a time rather than a number of them at once. Everything is not happening at the same time.

I am not sure that I am more than five miles from our base camp, but I will set up for the night, regardless.

With my tent up and being warmed by the midday sun, I rest on a rock, listening to the sound of the gentle wind as it blows through the evergreens, making a slight whistling sound.

I hobbled Canoni, and she eats grass near the tent. I will eat some beef jerky and wash it down with water. No, this is not a great meal, but it will put something in my empty stomach.

* * *

I have ridden 20 miles from camp since departing yesterday. I have seen signs of animals in the area. This will be an excellent chance for me to test my skills assembling snare traps.

Having accomplished this task, I will see if I am successful in the morning. A snare trap is fairly easy to create. I simply found a trail that showed signs of travel and set up the sticks that hold the trap in place. The design was such that a rabbit running along the trail would wander into the trap, and the loop would then tighten around its neck. More often than not, one finds the traps empty. These empty traps are dismantled and carried along for the next attempt farther down the trail.

It is curious how much more alert one gets the farther into the wilderness they go. I am in tune to every noise, every smell I encounter. I try to identify each in my mind to determine any risk.

I caught and will cook a rainbow trout that I caught in a nearby stream.

\* \* \*

This day's entry was supposed to be one of great accomplishment, as I did succeed in snaring a rabbit in one of the traps. Another event, however, overshadowed my triumph. After cleaning and cooking the rabbit for breakfast, I continued my journey through the thick forest of pine and cedar.

Something unseen by me spooked Canoni. She reared up and threw me to the ground. I rolled down an embankment, landing on my shoulder and neck. I immediately felt paralyzed. My leg ended up in an awkward position, and I could not feel it. I felt no pain at all. In fact, I felt nothing at all below my waist. I willed my body to roll off of my shoulder.

I could not determine what had spooked Canoni. In my mind, I pictured some archeologist in years to come finding my skeleton and wondering what the hell happened to this poor son of a bitch. After lying on the ground for some minutes, I felt an excruciating pain, a hot and searing pain, spreading to my shoulder, neck, back, and legs. I sat up and waited for the head-rush to pass before getting to my feet.

Shit! Where are my horses? Searching around the immediate area, I could see no horses. Many thoughts jumbled up my mind, the vast majority of them negative.

Limping through the trees, I ignored the pain, concerned only with finding Canoni. I found her and the packhorse a quarter mile from where I had fallen, grazing on the fine grass. Once I reunited with them, I smoked two bowls of weed in an effort to dull the pain. I didn't know which was greater, my relief that I was not paralyzed or dead or the pain in my body.

Though it was difficult and painful, I cooked the rabbit for dinner and am now in my tent trying to find a comfortable position in which to situate myself.

\* \* \*

I awoke this morning to, no surprise, stiff and sore neck and shoulder muscles. My lower back on the right side hurt every time I moved. Despite the discomfort of riding, I steered Canoni east, then swung south. The fishing in the lakes that dot the landscape is incredible, though the fish are small. I cooked two fish for lunch and then sustained my ride.

The valleys here are long and narrow. I will return to investigate them some more at some point. The next time I go exploring, it will be for more than one week.

This afternoon a thunderstorm came up, and heavy rain fell, accompanied by lots of lightning and thunder. Fog shrouded the peaks, making the landscape seem all the more ominous. I would guess the temperature to be in the low sixties, with no wind to speak of.

As I sit and recount the events of the day, I fight the urge to forge ahead and not return to George. There is so much to see here, but George would go crazy if I didn't return when I said I would. Tomorrow I will head to base camp.

\* \* \*

I have ridden 10 miles so far today. I judge the time to be early in the afternoon. I am resting the horses for a while and then will journey on toward camp, which is 15 miles from here.

As I gaze around, the mountains do not seem familiar, but I am sure that the Gataga River is to my left, so I will remain on the current path.

It is true that some people get lost in the forest because they fail to look behind them to see how the terrain appears from the other direction. For example, a huge rock formation will appear different depending on the direction from which you view it.

A thin line of gray clouds appeared on the horizon. The temperature fell as the sun set. I hoped that the rain would hold off until I rode the final 15 miles.

The rain did not hold off. I arrived in camp long after dark, accompanied by a light rain. As I surveyed the camp it was clear that George, his tent, and his riding and packhorse were gone. I figured that George went exploring, was camped somewhere, and would return tomorrow.

As I make this entry, rain falls hard against my tent. Being dry and warm, I relaxed to the sound of the rain.

\* \* \*

I have finished eating a breakfast of pancakes, coffee, and vitamin C tablets. The day is mild and sunny.

Deep green grass sprouts appear on the hillsides of this valley, more so on the southern-exposed landscape. Glancing higher up the mountain, I see a small herd of mountain goats moving along the cliffs, including several new born kids.

I plan to stay in camp until late afternoon and wait for George.

George rode into camp just after noon. "You have no idea how happy I am to be home!"

As strange as this sounded, I guess that even a plot of empty land is like a long lost friend when you call it home.

George described his ride to the east. "The hills were more rolling, and streams run everywhere. I saw a number of grizzly bears and two black bears with cubs. The small lakes dotting the terrain will surely be a mosquito breeding problem in the early summer, which will be upon us before we know it."

Summer is still weeks away from today, as we come to the third week of May. One could call it late spring presently.

"The grass there will be plentiful in summer, as there are far fewer trees than we see here." George gestured with his hands.

George also told of crossing many game trails and of hearing wolves howling in the distance several times.

In contrast to my good fortunes fishing, George did not have any luck at all. "To make matters worse, I crossed a range to our east and forded a wide stream that did not appear on the map. I sat on the bank of the stream with my feet in the water when a skunk strolled up beside me to take a drink!"

"I started to get up so that the skunk would have more room, but the skunk took the movement as a threat and sprayed me, catching me squarely from the waist down." George chuckled.

Despite spending that day and all of the next in the stream washing away the stink, George carried a trace of it with him. We both laughed about that one, George sitting outside his tent.

For our meal tonight George is cooking trout in canned tomato sauce, spiced with flavors too numerous to identify.

Clever as we are, we have used the empty cans to fashion an alarm system that we ring around our campsite. The cans have a string running through them and a small stone dangling from a string inside the can. If an intruder hits the barrier of string the stones hit the side of the can and we know where to face the danger.

\* \* \*

As we enter the third week of May, we have agreed to hold off building the cabin until later in the summer, to allow the logs to dry longer. We had planned to start sooner, just to be out of the tents. But as this will be our home, we wish to build it properly.

We sometimes feel vulnerable at night, with a nylon tent between us and the wild. For now we will settle into the routine of gathering firewood, fishing, and taking short exploration rides. We practice stalking game to keep our skills honed, killing only for meat. We also spend a lot of time talking about nothing at all, whatever comes to mind.

Sometimes we play practical jokes on each other, all in fun. At night George leaves his Levi's hanging on the tent roof, he says to air them out. One time I hid George's Levi's during the night. In the morning he felt sure that a predator had come into camp and stolen them. I gave his pants to him a while later, earning a punch in the arm as compensation.

Gathering firewood is an easy chore, as dead cedar trees and Lodgepole pine trees lean broken on the hillsides. We climb up to them, push the tree over, and make it tumble down, breaking up as it goes. We then pick up the wood and stack it in various locations near the camp. We have a lot of firewood already, several cords.

It has become necessary to dig a pit for the cooking fire, and we made a game of bringing a few river rocks to line the bottom of the pit. Any time we go near the West River for water, to fish or whatever, we stuff baseball sized rocks in our pockets. We see who can bring the most rocks. We think that this will make the heat reflect more and that food will cook at a higher temperature.

* * *

**FINAL WEEK OF MAY**

This morning, as is so often the case, nothing happened worth writing about. The usual routines recur. The sun has been bright during these few days.

We measured and cut trees, which were three to five inches in diameter, which we will use to construct a corral for the horses. This will be attached to the cabin, on the side opposite the rock formation that towers behind us. It will be 15 feet by 10 feet.

What made my day today materialized this morning when George decided that he would wash his long johns. As he washed one pair, he set another pair on a rock. A breeze blew the dry long johns into the water, and I glanced up in time to see George hop into the knee-deep water, trying to catch his under garments.

I couldn't stop laughing at the sight of him leaping from rock to rock, missing the long johns until at last they disappeared under the water and downstream. The pair he had been washing now lay in the sand on the bank, needing to be washed again. It's funny how I am sure that I will never forget this simple event.

We have been comfortable during the past week seeing mild sunny days and equally mild nights. Fish and rabbit have been our fare for the most part during that time. Canoni and the other horses are content spending their days lazily grazing on the abundant grass.

\* \* \*

Two days later, we were greeted this morning with light rain and a stiff wind. A typical mountain rainstorm had arrived. By midday, the rain cleared, leaving us with a sun-soaked afternoon.

While we relaxed in camp a mother fox and four kits visited. They seemed to not be afraid of us, coming within a few short feet of where we sat. Mother was beautiful, her tan and red coat and white-tipped tail contrasting perfectly with her black face.

One of the kits found a face cloth hanging from the tent rope and stole it, playing tug of war with his siblings. We welcomed the entertainment and were amused by the kits for half an hour, before they dropped the cloth and moved on into the forest.

More and more, birds of varying species fill the sky, their songs ringing from the trees. Deer can be seen on the hillsides and among the trees. Rodents, especially field mice, are becoming abundant. In fact, they have become a pain, running everywhere!

We have become vigilant about zipping up the flaps when we enter or exit the tent because we share an anxiety that the little buggers will make our tents their home. They provide a food source for many residents of the forest. Coyotes, wolves, and other predators feed on them regularly.

Of course, as the days pass, grizzly bears will become more of a factor in our everyday life. Ducks and other water fowl have become abundant. Spring is the season that I have waited to experience, and I would not trade this day in this place for anything!

\* \* \*

Today, destiny made an unannounced appearance. In doing so it turned an otherwise boring day into a remarkable celebration of life.

We awoke to a mild, sunny day, with birds singing their songs, seemingly just because they were happy.

I was reading a book in my tent when George picked up his fishing pole and tackle box. "I think I'll go fishing. Do you want to come along?"

"No, thanks. I'm going to stay here and read".

We spent a few minutes smoking a pipe full of weed, and then George departed toward the West River.

George yelled to me as an afterthought, "I'll be upstream on the far bank, the spot near the fallen tree."

After a few short minutes, I put down the book and decided to join him, at least to keep him company. I ventured north around the huge rock formation and straight down to the river. The trail that we had made from the many trips down showed the way.

A hundred yards north was a fallen tree that jutted out over the bank, making it a very nice place from which to fish.

I searched in both directions and saw no sign of George.

While crossing the water, I thought out loud. "How could he have gotten out of sight so fast?"

I quickened my pace. A sick feeling suddenly rushed into my gut. As I approached the fallen tree, I realized that the end had broken off. What my eyes took in next seemed like it happened in slow motion.

I saw George's tackle box spilled open next to the tree. From above, I could see a dark shadow in the water, which I recognized was George. He was under the water and not coming up. Only his arms stuck out of the frigid water. Without another thought I jumped into the water from the upstream side of the tree, so the current would push me into the rocks and I could stabilize myself. The water was four feet deep, with a strong current that could easily move a body.

I grabbed George by his jacket collar and forced his face out of the water. His body was stuck, and he couldn't lift his face higher out of the water on his own. His lips were purple; his eyes wide open, not blinking. Once his face was out of the water, he dramatically gasped for air.

I plunged my face into the icy water and saw that his leg was wedged between the broken end of the tree and a rock. The current was strong enough to bend him backwards, under water. My attempt to move the log was thwarted by the current, which kept it firmly in place. George's head was again forced under the water, and I knew that he would panic if I didn't do something quick. I knew that he was not going to be able to help me help him.

I realized that I would need to use leverage, and I clambered out of the water to find a strong tree branch. George grabbed my jacket and yanked me into the water. I pulled his face up and screamed at him that I would help him get out.

By now he was in a full-blown panic, choking and trying to breathe and spit water at the same time. White bubbles formed at the corner of his mouth. The current made it difficult to hold George out of the water. Finally he calmed a little and took several deep breaths.

I released my hold on him go and scaled the bank. I found a branch five feet long post haste. It was not straight, but I thought that I could manipulate it in the water.

I jumped into the shockingly cold water to resume the rescue and lifted George up out of the water. "George, when you feel the slightest movement, pull your foot free."

I knew that he couldn't feel his legs because I could not feel mine in the freezing water.

I managed to wedge the branch between the fallen tree and the rock against which it was pinned. I leverage my full weight on the branch, and George slipped out of his bind, groaning. I dragged him up the bank, and we untied his boot. His foot was swelling despite the water temperature. To be safe, I made a splint and tied it tight.

George is a large man, only five feet, eight inches in height, but he weighs 250 pounds. As a result, we took some 20 minutes making it back to camp.

As I sit here recounting the events of the day, George has agreed to leave the splint on for three days before we determine if the foot is broken. George is in his tent resting after we smoked a bowl of weed.

I have reviewed the incident in my mind, and I am proud of how I responded, being up to the challenge. Had I not gone down to the river, or had George hit his head on the rocks, this day could have ended a lot differently.

It would not have taken too much longer for that current to wear George out to the point where he couldn't lift his head up.

George offered profuse thanks. "Oh, man. I was fucked until I felt you pull on my jacket. You saved my life."

It is quiet once again. Soon I will attempt to catch a fish for dinner. I have re-paid my debt to George. I praise the powers that be for giving me the chance to do so.

I did not actually think that I would ever be able to re-pay George for saving my life, but the gods have allowed me to even the score.

\* \* \*

This morning marks three days since George's accident. That puts us at the start of June. We removed the splint from George's leg, and he does not believe that it is broken. Our relief is tempered by the stress of knowing that George won't be fit for heavy work or travel any time soon.

The 40 logs needed to build the cabin lay drying in the forest. In planning the structure, we settled on a 10 by 15-foot single-room cabin. It will stand six feet tall at the highest point. We will have a fireplace on one wall that measures four feet by four feet. The chimney will extend five feet above the roof. This will be our source of heat, as well as be our cooking fire when weather forces us inside.

From our many trips to the West River we have amassed a collection of a few hundred rocks, mostly hand-sized, but none larger than a softball. For now we concentrate on preparing the logs, examining them, and setting aside the thickest and straightest timber to be used for the roof. We picked the straightest remaining logs to use for the walls.

Our goal for today was to strip the bark from the trees using a draw shave. This is done by drawing back the scraping tool with its blade less than an eighth of an inch below the bark. Working for 10 hours we peeled 10 logs. George worked at a slow pace as he sat on the log that he was shaving.

My back and arms are sore from the intense energy required today. George cooked a rabbit for dinner, along with some rice. Not bad for one and a half men in the wilderness.

With each passing day, I gain a deeper sense of belonging here. The more we make this place look like home, the more it feels like home. As I write, we pass a pipe between us, the smoke relieving the aches and releasing our minds to wander.

* * *

Two days later, we continued the task of stripping bark from logs. The weather has turned overcast and a bit cooler than it has been of recent. After stripping 10 logs yesterday, we made a goal of matching that total today. The work is not unpleasant but strenuous. By noon we had stripped nine logs.

We took an hour break then stripped six more logs, for a total of 15 for the day. Tomorrow, we will try and finish the last 15 logs. George caught and cooked a nice trout for dinner, 17 inches in length. It tastes every bit as good as one can imagine a trout could taste.

Each night as I prepare to sleep, I tell myself that we are one day closer to sleeping indoors. George feels that he is healing well and uses a homemade cane that he fashioned out of a tree branch, more to be cool I think than anything else.

George and I have chatted about not leaving signs of our presence on the land and so we have scattered the shavings from the logs on the forest floor. Although this is another energy depleting chore, it is vital to us that we do it.

* * *

We got an early start today, and by midday, we had finished stripping the bark from the remaining logs. Not too bad, 40 logs peeled in two and a half days.

Now with the initial preparation done, we could make some essential cuts. The first step we took was to mark the end of the logs with a pencil with a half circle of eight to 10 inches. This task was fairly boring and repetitious. Once it was complete, we used the logging saw to make horizontal cuts at one-inch intervals until the half circle was defined.

Using an ax, we chipped away each of the cuts we had made, leaving a close outline of the shape we were trying to achieve. Using a chisel we cleaned up the cut, leaving a seamless cradle for the log that would fit into it. We managed to finish eight logs before it got dark, forcing us to return to camp.

George cooked trout in a cornmeal coating, and it was excellent.

While eating George caught a case of the funnies. "So where the hell is the beer guy"?

We both had a good laugh over that comment, George's laughter uncontrollable.

I will finish up for now so that we may share some conversation before we sleep.

* * *

It is evening now, we have finished our dinner, tonight we ate pancakes.

We woke up later than usual this morning but by midday were working on notching logs. We have become more efficient at using the ax to chip and the chisel to clean up. Now, George handles the ax, and I use the chisel. We finished up for the day late this afternoon, notching another 10 logs.

Our horses are all doing fine, for they lack nothing. We allow them to graze on the plentiful grass. We no longer have to use hobbles, as they understand that we are their protectors, and as such, they stay within sight of us. My Canoni never strays beyond eyesight.

My body is sore from the hard work.

George is sore as well. "My leg still hurts, and my back makes me feel a hundred years old."

It is nice to admire the workmanship of the cuts we have made, but much more hard work lies ahead.

\* \* \*

Today we worked on notching the remaining 22 logs, finishing 18 of them, leaving four for tomorrow. We were so dog tired tonight that we did not eat anything.

We are both in our tents, George already sleeping, as I determine by the snoring coming from his direction. As I make this entry every part of my body is sore. Just think, tomorrow is another day to notch logs.

I find no greater joy these days than to lie down at night and let this sore body refresh, although the soreness greets me each morning as sure as does the diversity in the weather.

\* \* \*

I write as we lounge in front of our campfire, having accomplished a lot today.

First thing this morning, we ate a good breakfast of pancakes, boiled rice, and coffee.

When we finished, we set about notching the last four logs. Once that was done, we stacked them, each one fitting precisely into the log above it. In a few cases we had to increase the radius of the notch, but most fit well. With each log we hoisted into place, we smiled with a sense of progress and pride. We framed the cabin, stacking the four walls six logs high, using 24 logs in total.

It rained early in the afternoon, so we stopped work and sat in our tents. Once the rain stopped, we took our horses out for a ride, going two miles into a canyon located south of our camp where the West River veers east to join the Gataga River. We rode side by side, imagining where any deposits of gold might be found in the streams.

Returning to camp, George cleaned a rabbit he snared, his first success using a snare trap, and also cooked some red beans. We made hot tea for a change from the usual coffee and water.

Looking at the cabin, I am filled with pride, for even as it sits half finished; it is now something noticeable on the landscape. I stare at the structure and am barely able to comprehend the fact that George and I have erected what will be our home with our own hands. This marks the first time that either of us has ever attempted such a feat, and so far I am quite pleased with the results.

\* \* \*

We worked on the cabin this morning, making more adjustments to the cuts than we did yesterday, but nothing dramatic. We now have four walls erected, and it is beginning to resemble a building.

With the walls secured, it is time to pack the spaces between the logs with the adobe we must make. This will require most of the day to complete, as we want to pack it thick to increase insulation.

George was able, with much effort, to draw out the shape of the door on the stacked logs using charcoal. We completed the packing of two walls, placing the mixture of grass, mud, and river sand tightly into the cracks and crevices in the logs.

George cooked fish and rice for dinner. We rolled a couple of cigarettes from the supply we brought with us, both enjoying one.

George struck a pose to show his physique. When we started out, he carried a beer belly, now he is trim and strong.

He spoke in his loud voice. "We should take some time out from work on the cabin and ride into the mountains, as a reward for our hard work so far."

I agreed, so we will ride tomorrow.

\* \* \*

This morning, as planned, George and I took off for the hills to ride. The air was cool and the water cold as we crossed the West River. Though it runs four and a half feet deep, it is sufficiently deep enough that our legs got wet. We rode in a westerly direction, up and over the first range of mountains.

We observed a mother grizzly and her two cubs, seeking food on the hillside opposite our location. We watched them for a while, our rifles at the ready, and were entertained by the cubs as they wrestled and frolicked behind their mama. Farther on, we saw a beautiful red fox, and later, a herd of deer.

We came upon a lake and decided to name it Luke Lake, after George's brother. George caught three fish in a matter of five minutes. We will fish here again, I believe, as it is not more than two miles from the cabin.

George presented a surprise today. He pulled six beers out of his saddlebag, which he had carried since we left the Krable Ranch. The last alcohol I had was at the bar the first night we arrived in Canada. We both got pretty buzzed on three beers apiece. I, in fact, literally stumbled around after the third beer and the third pipe full of weed.

We lingered there in that field of grass, enjoying the change in our mental attitude. A party in the wild! At one point we were treated to a flock of Canada geese flying overhead and skidding to a landing on the lake. Something to keep in mind when autumn comes later.

After riding to camp we ate a rabbit along with canned peas.

Then I located a piece of scrap wood that had been cut from the end of one of the logs. It was 24 inches long and approximately eight inches wide. With care I cut the piece in half, lengthwise, and instructed George to follow my lead. We cut two inches off of the rounded side of the piece to make that side flat. We both had a three-inch thick, 24 inch straight piece of wood.

"What the hell are we doing?" Bewildered, George threw his hands up in the air.

I smacked my lips. "We have just created support frames for the window that you will cut into the cabin, George."

We had plenty of four-inch-long nails to nail these supports in place.

As it got dark, we heard a wolf howling from somewhere not too far away. This served as a brief reminder that the sooner we finished the cabin the safer we would be, especially at night.

When thinking about this in retrospect, I knew things that had gone our way could have turned out differently. Specifically, I thought about how we convinced ourselves that we were not in danger when we heard the wolf pack or saw a grizzly bear across the meadow. We, of course, did recognize the danger, but we were convinced that we had the smarts and the weaponry to be safe from all eventualities.

I felt that in this way our brains kept us from being in a constant state of fear. For example, we couldn't be afraid to put down our rifles to use a saw.

Our rifles never left us, unless they were within quick reach. I personally felt most afraid at night, sitting in my tent, while the night creatures roamed about the land.

However, our two-tent city was now expanding to include our cabin.

\* \* \*

This morning we got to work on the cabin. Our immediate task was to complete the process of caulking the logs with adobe. We mixed quite a few batches and used it unsparingly.

Once we completed that job, we worked hard at getting three support logs into place on the roof. To accomplish this we propped three logs against the side of the structure, then using a packhorse, from the opposite side of the cabin, we dragged the logs up over the leaning logs and up the top where we positioned them strategically.

While I thought about how we would complete the roof, George cut into the front wall and took out a two-by-two foot square. We wedged the pieces that we had made the previous night into place and drove home the four-inch nails. The frame for the window was now in place.

Once we had finished, we stood back and admired our window work. Since we had no glass, we decided to make a tight-fitting shutter for the window that would open outward.

As we did not want to work on the roof today, we spent the remainder of the day cutting five-foot-long pieces of wood in half, using the hand saw. We would build the door from these materials. We brought brass hinges with us to use on our door. The door would be five feet high, so we would both have to duck when entering or exiting the cabin.

The fox we saw a week or so ago returned with her kits this afternoon. They seemed to feel at home as they ran all around the campsite. At one point, one of the kits swiped George's cowboy hat and played with it. George tried to get the kit to drop the hat, but the kit enjoyed the hat too much to let it go. After a few minutes, George threw a rock at the kit, and he dropped the hat long enough for George to pick it up. Other than being a bit dirtier, it was none the worse for wear.

The young foxes explored the interior of the half-built cabin, appearing and then disappearing back inside.

As we sat in front of the fire, mama fox and the kits settled in under a bush on the edge of camp, presumably for the night.

It has gotten too dark to write, so I will turn in for the night.

\* \* \*

Today the weather was excellent! According to the thermometer, the temperature rose to 64 degrees in the afternoon.

Right from the start this morning, we vowed to get the roof put on the cabin today. We used logs ten feet long for the three horizontal supports and a 15-footer for the center beam. Working non-stop, we got the supports in place in before mid-afternoon.

I couldn't imagine how difficult it would be to build the cabin alone. The logs were quite heavy, especially when we had to lift them above our heads. But the structure is really looking like a cabin now.

Tomorrow we plan to ride in search of more Lodgepole pine trees to use to finish the roof. We will take the saws, the axes, and three days' worth of dry food, along with a couple of ropes. We hope to find trees four-inches in diameter, which we will lay across the frame on the roof and cover with a canvas paint drop cloth and a heavy layer of moss and other natural material.

Our hope is that any moisture will roll off the sides of the cabin and not filter through the roof.

\* \* \*

We slept in this morning, waiting for the sun to rise before cleaning up the campsite and mounting our horses to find more Lodgepole pine trees. With our cabin situated on high ground of a sloping valley between two tall mountain ranges, I'm not sure that we could have selected a better spot to build.

We rode south along the West River on the search for the trees. We took our time, riding slow and quiet, watching as the landscape unfolded with each step. It is always fun riding with George because each of us misses less thanks to the eyes of the other. We enjoy more of the scenery riding together.

We pointed out critters to each other as we saw them. We saw a few deer, this particular herd having at least three fawns. At one point, we almost rode right into a mama grizzly bear as she rested on the trail on which we rode. As we crested a rise, she sat there, a hundred feet away, sniffing the air for a scent that we could not detect. It was obvious we had caught her off guard. She grunted as she bolted for the cover of the thick ferns that grew beneath the taller pines on the hillsides. It did not take long for her to run out of sight. As always we rode past the spot she disappeared from exercising caution, ever alert for any possibility.

In the early afternoon, we turned off the trail on which we had ridden all morning and followed a stream that fed into the West River. Along the stream, trees grew tall on either bank, pines of different species, and among the forest we discovered a stand of Lodgepole pine. The wood of the Lodgepole is soft and the bark not too hard on the hands.

We figured that we needed to cut 70 trees of four inch diameter, at least 10 feet long. We cut down 15 and then moved to another area and cut 15 more.

We stopped to eat our dinner, which consisted of a rabbit and pancakes. We used the last of the syrup that we brought with us. In the fall we hope to gather berries and make ourselves some berry syrup.

As I write this entry, the sun drops behind the mountains to the west. Darkness will not be long in coming. We heard an owl in the gathering twilight, asking who dared to intrude on its territory.

Once again, the feeling of being an insignificant fish in an immense ocean emerges as the stars grow brighter and the vastness of this universe becomes evident. It does take a brave man to look out over the fire into the blackness.

\* \* \*

Two days later, we got up early and cut more trees. We felled a total of 30 yesterday, just 40 more needed. During the morning a black bear approached our work area but was easily deterred by our loud voices and waving arms. George threw stones in the direction of the bear as well.

We finished eating a late lunch of trout and beef jerky. We then enjoyed smoking a bowl of weed and tied the trees into the bundles that the horses will drag to the cabin. Each bundle consisted of 15 trees, which would require three trips from here to the cabin. Grueling work for our horses but they must carry their share of the burden of building the cabin as well.

The sun is falling behind the mountains to the west leaving a brilliant array of yellow shades streaking the sky. Minute by minute the color deepens to red, then pink, and finally gray before all light is lost. With the darkness comes time to refresh this body and soul.

Tomorrow will be another working day among the open spaces of our valley.

* * *

June has reached beyond the halfway point.

This day broke to a layer of thick fog covering some areas nearby. After deciding to take the day off from labor yesterday, we got to it today. We cut the final trees, bundled them up, and prepared to start the first return ride to the cabin. With our two packhorses dragging 15 trees, we walked out in front of them, and only once did we have to re-tie any of the loads.

We arrived at the cabin with the second load half an hour after the sun had set, easing the burden from the horses and feeding and watering them. With the animals secured, we ate beans for dinner. A bright fire blazed, and it felt awesome to lean back against my saddle.

* * *

This morning the sun rose into an overcast sky, painting the clouds in wondrous shades of rose and pineapple. We rode to the cutting site with the intention of taking the remaining logs to camp before dark.

Again today, all manner of wildlife reacted to our passing. We saw a bull moose in the shallow water of West Lake. He seemed to be enjoying the day too. Butterflies in all sizes and colors fluttered from place to place. Wildflowers stood out as they bloomed in sharp contrast to the various shades of green. We arrived at the work area at noon, and taking just enough time to water the horses and let them graze on the grass, we split the bundle of trees among the horses and returned to camp. We arrived mid-afternoon, and after unloading the horses, relaxed.

George found some wolf scat near the cabin. We could tell that it was wolf because it was larger than other animal feces and had fur in it. Apparently the wolves came to visit or investigate but found us not home. I am sure they will return sometime. Hopefully we will have finished the cabin by then.

As we have seen previously, today, the mama fox and her kits came to play at the campsite. The smaller male likes taking sticks that litter the ground and chewing on them. George has given them names. Mama is Gloria, the female is Jackie, and the male is Beatle. George gave no reason for these particular names.

Having all of the materials necessary to build the roof, we began the process of nailing the Lodgepole pines to the frame of the roof. We laid the Lodgepole over the support beams so they face east which is the natural slope of the land.

Although it will be a much slower process laying the trees in this direction, this will allow the water to flow off of the roof easier and faster.

Our four-inch nails were not long enough to go all the way through the pines, so we hammered four nails into each tree, two on each quarter of exposed tree. In other words, we hammered the nails in at an angle rather than straight through the logs.

The weather was fair, so we were not concerned about working quickly. It was more important to go slow and make sure the pines were tight against each other when nailed in.

We quit working late in the afternoon and took a ride across the West River. We saw the usual deer and coyote, and many birds were evident as well. We found a single set of wolf tracks in the dirt, determining that this wolf was most likely the one who visited our cabin.

We have returned from fishing. We each caught a decent fish, mine was 17 inches. We fried my fish in a pan over the fire.

I can't think of another place in the world I would rather be. We have, over time, become familiar with the territory in which we live, thus, we feel more at ease and find it easier to see things out of the norm.

\* \* \*

Two days later, we have sustained our efforts putting the pines on the roof, taking our time, doing it right the first time. Our horses are all fine, each having plenty of food.

Aside from working on the roof, we must perform a series of daily chores, specifically, replace our water supply and firewood stocks. We must also exercise the horses and feed ourselves.

These kinds of days, when working so intently on the cabin, make the time go fast. At the end of the day, we sit near the campfire examining our handiwork and realize that we will finish the cabin before the first snow flies. I can't tell you how relieved we are at this knowledge.

George is in the process of making corn bread and trout for dinner. I must say that the corn bread looks more like pancakes but taste wonderful, nonetheless.

\* \* \*

June has reached the third week, bringing with it warm and sunny days. George and I have finished placing the roof supports and have secured them to the frame using four-inch nails. The fit between the poles is tight. We will place a canvas cover on the roof and use the thick, matted moss and boughs from the many Lodgepole branches as packing materials. We will use rocks to weigh the materials down even though the U-clamps that we brought work well. We are going through all of the extra labor adding the branches, hoping that this adds insulation and warmth to the cabin. Once we finish the roof, we will construct the fireplace.

Earlier this afternoon we cooked fish for lunch and now sit in the last of the sunshine, as it sets to our west.

We have seen Gloria, Jackie, and Beatle on a semi-regular basis. It seems that they have adopted our temporary spot on the Earth as their own. We try not to interact with them, but it is not easy to ignore a fox nipping at your heels. They are as daring as they are shy, dashing here and there through the area, yipping and barking at us and each other. Having the company is more fun than not.

*  *  *

Two days later, we finished the roof, and it is quite sturdy. We feel confident that it will also be waterproof. The moss, branches, and mud caulking appear natural.

This morning George went to work making the door for the cabin. He started by using his saw to cut the logs to the shape he marked prior. Once he had cut the logs to a height of five feet, we framed the cut in the same manner as we did the window. Once the frame was secured and the hinges screwed into the frame, we built a two-inch thick door, braced and sealed in two hours. George is hanging the door as I write this.

We have spent our last night by necessity outdoors! What a huge accomplishment! Yes, there it is our wilderness cabin, security from all that might threaten us.

*  *  *

It has been three days since I last wrote.

We have enjoyed sleeping in the cabin after working on it for so long. I can admit now that I am beyond relieved that we can sleep easier knowing that we won't be attacked in our sleep.

We have spent the past two days building what will serve as a refrigerator for us. In one of the taller trees near the cabin George fashioned a box in which we will store our meat. The box is made of Lodgepole sticks three feet long and four inches in diameter. He secured the sticks together with rope. It seems sturdy enough to deter animals from successfully stealing our meat.

After finishing that project, we fished. We wish to keep our body charged at all times, so we try not to overwork. We will begin to build the fireplace tomorrow.

\* \* \*

For breakfast this morning we ate trout and pancakes.

We began construction of the fireplace. First we will need to make a mud hearth, a wall of clay plastered over the stones of the fireplace. This will prevent the fire from cracking and chipping the stones. When we build the walls of the fireplace with logs, and our chimney of sticks and rocks, the clay will shield the wood so the fire will not ignite the wood and consume it.

We toiled on the fireplace all day long and managed to get the frame made and the logs formed on the outside. We also dug the hole for the broken river stones. I say broken, but really they were worn river rocks.

I caught a white fish and filleted it. The meat roasts over a fire now as I write. George complains of a sore back, while my neck and shoulders ache.

It seems that this condition is the new normal, waking up each morning, moaning and groaning when getting out of the sleeping bag.

\* \* \*

We have reached the final day of June. We spent much of the day adding more chinking to the walls of the fireplace. The walls are four to five inches thick. We added some golf ball sized stones to the walls as we went. We also added more chinking to the hearth.

George ate some jerky for dinner, but I was not hungry.

\* \* \*

July arrived today. We spent the day placing the clay in the chimney, adding one to two-inch river rocks once the walls were covered with several inches of clay. I felt pretty good about the fireplace being able to withstand the flames and heat while not catching fire.

George spent some time this afternoon fashioning a lock for the door. It is the same setup used in the old days to lock gates on army forts, a strong thick plank held in place by two L-shaped brackets. Of course, we both realize that a bear would have no trouble knocking the door down.

Anyway, tomorrow is another day, and it is nice to be secure inside.

* * *

Today we finished the chimney. The fireplace is ready for testing. George has gathered some firewood, and we're ready to light it.

The test was fruitful. The chimney works well, once heated up. We grew more confident with each new log that we put on the fire that the fireplace is insulated enough. Nonetheless, I will lay awake until flames die down this evening.

The chore ahead is to make furniture for the cabin, chairs and tables the most necessary items. George wants to make a couple of backrests and shelves for his food storage area.

When the fire is going and the window is shuttered, the cabin feels quite comfortable. It is obvious to us that the window will only ventilate when the door is open, since otherwise there is no cross breeze. So perhaps in summer we will open both.

George snared a rabbit today and is preparing it for our meal, along with some rice. In place of coffee we drank pine needle tea, which is somewhat bitter, but it does have a citrus-like taste.

During the afternoon, we saw Gloria the fox, but the two kits were not with her, which I found somewhat odd. She scavenged around the outside of the cabin, perhaps looking for food. After a while she went on her way, leaving George and me alone. These visits by the native residents always bring happiness to George and me, as we get the chance to observe our neighbors going about their lives.

Canoni and the other horses are fat and content, as usual spending the day eating the plentiful grass that surrounds us.

The food is ready now, so I will lay my pen down.

# 4

# SUMMER 1976

It's July 4th, and our country celebrates its 200th birthday today. I am patriotic and would have enjoyed being in the United States today to join the celebration.

This morning, as if on schedule, a rainstorm passed through the area, giving our cabin a chance to be evaluated for its moisture resistance. Much to our joy and even amazement, the cabin kept the water out totally. I couldn't find words to describe how satisfying and relieving it was to know that our cabin would keep us dry, protecting us from both the elements and beasts.

George and I talked today about the fact that we have been here for more than three months. We have stayed longer than people said we would. To be honest, the time has passed quickly, as we are always busy doing something. I imagine that our friends have forgotten us, as other things become pressing for them, but here we are, healthy and happy.

\* \* \*

Two days later, as the water level in the Gataga River is manageable, I talked George into going rafting with me. This had always been one of my fantasies.

Being July mattered not, the water was cold, but the weather is mild in comparison to earlier in the year. The Gataga River is located east of the cabin, a two-mile walk. The West River, which runs along the trees south of the cabin, empties into the Gataga further south of the cabin some seven miles.

Together we built a strong raft, eight feet long by five feet wide, the thing being quite heavy. We used nylon rope to lash the logs together, wrapping each log to make a tight fit. We fashioned a tiller on the back between a triangle-shaped frame. We hoped that this would be sufficient to keep it in a stable position.

We had no idea how long or how far this trip would go, but we decided to leave the horses at the cabin and walk back, whatever the distance turned out to be. I had whitewater rafting experience from rides on the Kern River and the Keweah River, both in California, while George has never been rafting.

Here, however, things would be a lot different, especially considering that we did not have life vests. I reasoned, however, that Lewis and Clark had not had life vests, either.

Anyway, all is ready for tomorrow. The feeling today is one of anticipation and maybe slight fear. It's funny how the macho traits come to the forefront when a group of men is out in the field. It is easier to absorb the adventure than to skirt it. You can never live down the story of how you chickened out of one.

Our dinner tonight consists of trout fished from the West River.

\* \* \*

Morning has come, and we are ready to slip the raft into the Gataga River. I hope that this is not the last entry in this journal, but if it is, let it be known that I live for this kind of adventure and excitement.

\* \* \*

Eight days later, we are at the cabin after our rafting trip, and I will recount the events of the past eight days.

We loaded our food, rifles, fishing poles and sleeping bags onto the raft and pushed it into the Gataga River, allowing the slow current to carry us downstream. We used the tiller and paddles to navigate. We had been through this first, rather deep part of the river several times, though we encountered no rapids.

Two hours after starting out we hit the first rapids, a minor set of rapids and eddies, which tended to spin the raft around, making it more difficult to maneuver between the boulders. At times we were pushed into boulders midstream, which often caused us to stop rapidly, often bouncing the contents on the raft around. We ran a few sets of rapids and felt more at ease about how well the raft would hold together.

Once past the rapids, we floated on calm water, winding through a gorge with steep walls on either side of us.

After floating for 20 minutes on calm water, we heard the faint sound of rapids in the distance. Not wanting to be surprised, we rowed to shore and beached the raft, hiking to a spot where we could see downstream. We saw rapids that dropped perhaps 15 feet over a 100 yard distance, impressing us even from where we stood.

This was more than we wanted to try, so we ported the raft around this section of the river. It took us a couple of hours to carry the raft and contents around the falls to a less volatile spot. Once past these rapids, we floated on calm water for the next hour, occasionally diving into the water and fishing along the way.

We wished that this kind of activity could go on indefinitely.

Later, we came to a sandy shore at a bend in the river. We decided to spend the night there. After beaching the raft, we built a fire, unrolled the sleeping bags, and cooked the fish that we had caught during the morning.

After dinner we enjoyed the night sky, the stars, the sounds of nature, and to top off the day, a smoke from our pipe. Our first day of rafting was splendid in every way.

The morning of day two also dawned bright with sunshine and a chill in the air. We cooked pancakes for breakfast and then packed up and slipped the raft in the water. It was easy going, and the world floated past us as if we were stationary.

Curious deer peeked out at us from the behind trees that lined both sides of the Gataga River as we passed. Birds with beautiful white and black feathers flew past us, eating insects on the surface of the water, never running out of energy.

A moose stood belly deep in a pond located off the Gataga River, lifting her head to watch us as we drifted by.

The Gataga River widened and flattened out as we entered a smooth, deep pool. We paddled to shore so we could hike downstream and look at what lay ahead. The water moved faster as we paddled, pulling us away from shore and into the center of the river. We rowed harder, trying to get close to shore. Catching us off guard, the raft hit a submerged boulder, throwing George off and spinning the raft around.

My first thought was to get the rifles and equipment off of the raft, since I knew that we would have to abandon it. I picked them up and slung them over my shoulder. With great force I threw the rifles to shore, making mental note of where they landed. Next I grabbed the sleeping bags and threw them to shore. The burlap sack with the frying pan and tin plates and cups followed, landing in the sand on the shore. I kept an eye on George, who was trying to swim to shore. I then dove into the water and swam toward the shore 10 feet away.

I flailed over a three foot waterfall and into an eddy below, and from there I was able to climb onto a rock and jump to shore. I searched downstream for George and saw him bobbing up and down in the water as he was being swept downstream. I was cold and shaking, so I feared that George might soon be suffering from hypothermia.

It was important for me to gather up at least the rifles before I went to search for George. I sat down on the sandy bank of the Gataga River and sucked in a long breath, let it out, and then told myself to be calm and think rationally.

I located the rifles 30 yards upstream and the sleeping bags another hundred feet farther upstream. I was unable to find the fishing pole that we had brought. I then made my way downstream, searching for George. Past the rocks and the rapids, I saw the raft bobbing unattended in a whirlpool, but George was nowhere to be seen.

I made my way downstream, straining my eyes, searching for George every step of the way. I was becoming convinced that he might be lost. The accident had occurred 10 minutes before, and I had found no sign of him. I had searched a good stretch of river on this side, but could he have been on the other side somewhere? Could I have missed seeing him in the water?

I found a place to cross, taking the rifles, cooking utensils, and sleeping bags with me. Once on the other side, I decided to resume my search upstream for a ways before I went farther downstream. I hiked upstream until I came to the raft, where I had seen no sign of George. I then went downstream without any idea of how far to search.

From atop a boulder in the Gataga River I saw George's body lying half in the water, his upper body on shore. He was on the opposite side of the river, and so I put the rifles and sleeping bags down and swam across to his location. I called his name but got no response. As I got closer to him I was relieved to see that his face was out of the water, as was his body up to his waist.

I could see that he had a bump on his forehead and scratches on his shoulder, from scraping upon the rocks, I assumed. I checked his pulse, and it was strong. I dragged him fully out of the water and placed him on his back on the sand. He opened his eyes much to my relief. His knee was swollen and discolored, he had blood on one shin, and his hand was also bleeding.

I gathered wood for a fire and was able to get it going in a few minutes. I collected enough firewood to last through the night. George lay awake with a dazed, disinterested look on his face. I placed a sleeping bag under George's head and set about cutting branches to make a lean-to. Once I had erected the structure, I dragged George to it and covered him with my sleeping bag.

I considered what to do next. I tore the sleeves off of my shirt and used two branches to make a splint for his knee and then concentrated on finding food. This was the same knee that George had twisted before. Having lost the fishing pole, we would have to find something else to eat other than fish.

I made three snare traps and placed them on rabbit trails in the forest.

I went back to George. "How you feeling, man?"

"I feel like I want to throw up. Everything hurts, Tonweya."

We smoked two pipe full of weed intending to help ease his pain.

I went and checked the traps. Nothing. As the sun was setting 15 minutes later, I checked them again, and one had done its job. A rabbit jerked as I neared it. I dispatched it with my knife and skinned it, taking the meat back to where George lay. I was proud of myself for being able to make meat when meat was necessary.

As I cooked the meat George spoke. "When the raft hit the rock, I was looking at the shore and was off balance when we hit. Once in the water, I realized that I would have to go with the current as I swam to shore. I hit a lot of submerged rocks, and even a submerged tree, but I do not recall hitting the first object."

That object was a huge boulder that he was swept into as he spilled over the rapids.

"I saw a boulder coming, and I put my feet out in front of me to deflect away from it. I remember that I glanced off of the rock, but my face hit it, making me woozy. Farther downstream I hit a submerged tree stump, and my damn knee bashed into it...hard. Finally, when I reached the shore I only had enough strength to climb partially out of the water."

"Go to sleep, my friend. I will keep the fire going and stand guard."

I arose with the sun the next morning. "I will hike back to the cabin and get the horses." I proclaimed to George.

I left him with the weed, the pipe, and what was left of the rabbit.

As I started upstream, I called out to George, "Keep an eye out for me in the next day or two."

Truth was I did not know exactly how far from the cabin we had floated.

The morning was cold, but with the sun coming up it would soon be tolerable for George. I planned to stride fast for two hours, then at a normal pace for one hour, and then fast for two, and so on.

The terrain at this part of the Gataga River was steep and rocky, so there wasn't a lot of room along the path, and I opted to follow an animal trail over the mountain rather than around it. As I reached the top, I yelled a final good-bye to George, who was a hundred feet below me and an eighth of a mile downstream, and started down the other side.

Even though I could not see the Gataga River at all times, I could hear it and knew it was always on my right side, so I stood no chance of getting lost.

I slept fitfully, or didn't sleep, as the case may be, the first night on the trail, with no sleeping bag. Staring up at the night sky I thought about George. I hoped that he was feeling less pain, able to smoke the weed.

I spent the second night on the trail after cross-country hiking non-stop the whole day. I guessed that I had covered 12 miles during the day. This night I found sleep easier and woke refreshed and eager to reach the cabin.

The third day, I traveled on, taking short breaks every few hours. I hiked past a four-foot tall, three hundred pound male black bear, who feasted on grass across an open meadow. I was careful to pass without disturbing this bear. By the end of the day, I was surprised that I had not yet reached the cabin.

I spent another night exposed to the elements, having my campfire to keep me warm.

With the dawn of the fourth day I hiked, my feet and back hurting from the long journey, but I soldiered on. Ultimately, late in the morning, I saw familiar landmarks. I reached the cabin midday. I fed Canoni and the other horses. It was too late to start back to George that day, and I wanted to get a good night's rest, so I got supplies ready for the morning.

On that fifth morning, even before the sun was wholly above the horizon, I packed some clean clothes for George and food for the trip. I took Canoni, George's Appaloosa, and one of the packhorses. I headed out along the same trail on which I came in.

As soon as it was light enough to see, I galloped the horses, and from then on, did the same whenever possible. I made a lot of progress, remembering the landmarks along the way. I knew that I was no more than a three-day ride away from George.

I made camp that night, anxious for the sunrise so I could ride on.

Feeding and watering the horses was a chore I wished that I didn't have this day, but it was required and so was done.

Night fell as I cooked a piece of venison and drank water for dinner.

At daybreak, I rode as hard as the terrain would allow. One more day on the trail and I should be able to locate George.

After another fitful night, the long-awaited dawn arrived, lifting my spirits. I packed the horses and set out. Later in the morning, at the top of the high ridge I had to cross, I yelled out to George and fired off three rounds. Seconds later I heard three shots reverberate around the canyon.

I appeared within view of George at midday. He was in less pain, and he was alert and glad to see me. I gave him a piece of dried venison and water to wash it down with.

"How are you feeling? Do you want to stay here another day?" I couldn't resist the urge to tease George.

He guffawed. "The hell you say. I want to get the hell out of here!"

George provided me with a bit of background. "During the twilight two nights ago, a mountain lion came to drink on the opposite bank of the Gataga River, and it stood there observing me for longer than I felt comfortable with. Eventually, it moved on, but I did not sleep at all that night. I was scared shitless, helpless as I am."

I helped him mount his horse, conscious of his pain. We rode slowly, but with each step his appaloosa took, George absorbed another shot of jarring pain. What had taken me an hour to travel alone now took two hours with George. Despite his agony, we rode all day, stopping late in the afternoon.

I made George as comfortable as possible, and we slept on the trail. George's spirits were lifted by the knowledge that we were on our way home.

\* \* \*

Three days have elapsed, and this morning we started out early, reaching the cabin late in the afternoon.

We were shocked, left staring open-mouthed, at the sight of blood and guts from our half-eaten packhorse in the corral! Our second packhorse had obviously been attacked and killed by a mountain lion.

And for all we knew, the mountain lion was still in the vicinity surveilling us. I placed a rope around the dead horse's leg and dragged it away from the cabin and into the forest across the meadow. I cleaned up the corral area the best I could and tramped inside to check on George. I was exhausted from the past few days, and the killing of our horse added more stress to my already substantial burden.

George has been resting for the last hour, and I have been writing this entry. The fact that we have lost another packhorse saddens and concerns me deeply. Not only will we be forced to leave some things behind when we leave, but we will be forced to work the one surviving packhorse harder than we would like.

I can find no silver lining in this situation. It is emotionally difficult seeing a part of our extended family killed and torn apart, through what we feel is no fault of our own. Nonetheless, the fact remains that we have seen two of our horses die.

I will cook something for dinner and see what tomorrow brings.

\* \* \*

As we begin the third week of July, we remain amazed by all that we see on a daily basis. This day dawned to a clear sky and warm sun. George feels better this morning, though his forehead is quite bruised, and his knee is inflated. His left eye is black, with blood coloring the white of his eye. He does look the part of a castaway.

The horses are getting fatter with the grass being more plentiful. They spend most of the day grazing. When they are thirsty, they walk to the West River, drink, and then return to the cabin area.

I caught two trout on a fishing excursion, which I cooked for dinner. George is resting as I sit on the rock formation behind the cabin, watching the sun sink into the horizon in a blaze of golden glory.

Despite the events of the last few days we look forward to what the next day, the next minute may hold. I, for one, am not sorry in any way for the decisions that we have made so far on this great adventure.

\* \* \*

Two days later, George is making progress in his recovery. His knee is less swollen, and his forehead is almost back to its normal size and color. He still sports a black eye, though it is appearing better by the day.

I took a ride south of the cabin today, identifying many animals. A herd of deer stood still and watched me from a distance through the dense forest. I observed a grizzly bear ambling in a meadow with a single cub following behind her. The cub was several hundred pounds, so I assume that it is in its second year of life. Farther on I spied a bull moose striding across an open meadow.

The weather stayed fair the whole time, making it an enjoyable ride.

Writing now from inside the cabin, I smell that George has created a stew of venison, trout, and some edible greens. The whole cabin smells like meat.

"We might as well be wearing a ham vest and pork pants, as much as it smells like meat in here." I joshed with George.

* * *

As the days have passed, George is mended, now able to get around with minimal pain. He limps, but he will have no lasting effects from the injury. He suffers pain when mounting his horse, so sometimes he waits at the cabin while I take my daily ride. He is able to fish and does it well.

Again today, we will eat fresh trout for dinner.

George gave himself a haircut today and looks more like a madman now than he did before. I found it difficult to hold in my laughter.

I will allow my hair to grow as long as it will.

* * *

We have reached the third week of July already. George and I have decided that we will take a long ride into the valley that lies beyond the ranges to the west. We will head for the Deadwood River in two days. We have both wanted to see this place, so see it we will. George is sure that his knee is fine, and he has been cabin-bound for long enough.

# 5

# THE VALLEYS BEYOND THE CASSIAR MOUNTAINS

We are ready to set out for the Deadwood River. In order to make travel easier, and to avoid another incident with mountain lions, we will bring our remaining packhorse on this excursion, as well as our tents and sleeping bags. I will also bring my bow on this tour. We have stacked firewood inside the cabin so that we will have dry wood upon our return. It is mid-morning as we ride out.

It is now late afternoon as I make this entry.

We rode at a methodical pace until mid-afternoon, when we stopped to eat and make camp for the evening. We estimate that we rode 10 miles today, and we are camped at the fork of the Rainbow and Kechika Rivers. The Kechika River is much grander, wider, and deeper than the Rainbow. We will follow the Rainbow River west until we find a spot suitable for crossing without peril.

George caught two nice trout, so we will eat well in a few minutes. Aside from the spectacular scenery, little else has occurred that deserves reporting.

\* \* \*

We rose at dawn, anxious to ride on. Filled with a sense of impending adventure, as in the old pioneer days of mountain men and trappers, we rode north at an aggressive pace. By early afternoon, we had covered 20 miles. We are five miles south of the Jack Stone River.

Game is plentiful here and easy to see.

Today, we twice encountered a strange smell. Again now, I faintly smell what I would describe as bad underarm odor combined with the smell of death, like a dead animal. I know that bears have a strong, pungent odor, but that is not what we smelled today. We had earlier noticed several trees broken at a height of 10 feet above the ground. We have also seen, from time to time, trees broken at a higher height, but they were burned and cracked by lightning.

We talked about it and have reasoned that the smell must be an animal that died in the area.

In reverence, we will keep the fire burning bright tonight.

While on the trail today, George shot a hare with his bow. We will eat it soon, as it is roasting over the coals now. This rabbit is the first live target that George has hit with his bow. Today was excellent practice for the winter hunt.

We have become accustomed to eating one meal per day, in part because of the hassle involved in cooking meals over an open fire and also in preparation for winter. Frozen meat will be difficult to cut, so we will eat a single meal daily as a rule.

I see the moon rising in the eastern sky, half full. It will provide a nice effect tonight.

\* \* \*

It's evening, and today we covered 10 miles. After rising with the sun and packing the horses, we crossed the Jack Stone River, clad in boxer shorts. On the other side, we dressed and rode into what had become dense forest, dictating that we weave our way in and out of trees. Of course, many trees had fallen, causing us further delay, thus making for a slow ride. We saw tall trees on all sides of us, and even though it was mid-afternoon, it appeared quite dark.

This forest was alive with movements and noises made by elk, deer, and maybe a bear or two.

For this reason we have decided to rotate the guard tonight. This is the first time that I can ever remember sleeping in such dense forest. The environment plays mind games on a person. Shadows move across fallen trees, making demons out of things that are not there. In the filtered light of a half moon, things seem much more alien.

When darkness set in a few minutes ago, we piled wood on the fire, and George has set up for first watch. I will sleep now and relieve George in four hours.

\* \* \*

Early this morning, I delighted in seeing the sun as it arose in the eastern sky. I took second watch from midnight. I won't admit to how the sounds of the dark night worked on me. Suffice it to say that my rifle was warm from my grip, and my eyes were in perpetual motion. The rhythm of George's snoring and an owl in a nearby tree kept me awake and ready.

Once George woke up, we packed and rode north, passing a lake called Denetiah Lake. Though we have covered a scant five miles, we have elected to stay here for the rest of the day, swimming and fishing in that lake.

The fishing is excellent here, both of us catching more fish using lures than we could recall catching before. We had trout and pine needle tea for dinner.

The grass is plentiful around the lakeshore, so we let the horses eat their fill. I slept in the afternoon and will no doubt sleep well tonight. George and I smoked a bowl, and as always, enjoyed the effects.

\* \* \*

Today, the riding was much easier as we emerged from the dense forest into a wide valley of knee-high green grass. As the breeze rippled through it, the grass swayed like a wave far into the distance. Butterflies darted about, as did colorful grass birds. As a result, we covered 20 miles today. Riding almost due north, we have arrived in a valley between the Kachika River to our east and the Dell River to the west.

During times when we hiked along with the horses, they ate their fill of grass.

Game is plentiful, as we have seen both deer and moose. As we strode through the grass, rabbits ran in different directions. We also spooked some blue grouse from time to time. We had no trouble harvesting two of them for dinner.

As I write this entry, I hear a wolf howl, and from another direction, the return call of the pack. Tonight the moon is closer to three-quarters full, a light band of clouds seemingly dividing it in half. The night air is cooler now than when we started, and for the first time we wear our heavy coats and gloves.

\* \* \*

This morning we received a shock upon waking. Last night was a clear cloudless evening, the untold millions of stars viewable, but this morning I stuck my head out of the tent, and I saw snow as far as my eyes could see. Though just a trace, the sight of the snow was a shock.

As I peered up through the trees, with the sun rising behind them, I noted water dripping as the snow melted. The sun's light refracted through the drops, creating a thousand rainbows. Within a couple of minutes, the angle of the sun made the rainbows disappear.

I was amazed that I had gone to sleep under a clear, cloudless sky and woken up to this.

I stoked the fire and coaxed it back to life, and after a minute or two, felt the warmth on my hands and face. As George exited his tent, I watched his face change from sleepiness to wide-eyed surprise.

We made a pot of coffee, and while each sipping a cup we talked about the eventuality of more snow falling in the coming weeks. We tried to calculate at what depth it would become difficult for the horses to travel.

From movies I had seen, I recalled that horses seemed to have no problem traversing through snow up to four feet deep. We decided that it would take a few more serious storms to accumulate that total.

As we rode, the sun warmed enough to melt all of the snow on south-facing terrain.

George shot a duck as it ate roots in a marshy area, using his shotgun early in the day. We rode a total of 20 miles today. As I write, the smell of roasting duck whiffs through the air.

\* \* \*

July slips away as we enter the final three days. It has been a week since we began our ride. We have traveled 85 to 90 miles. Today we rode 15. We are now 15 miles from the Deadwood River and a somewhat less than that to Deadwood Lake. Both are to the west of our current position.

Last night the temperature dropped into the low forties. A light frost covered the inside of the tents, causing us to have to turn them inside out to dry. Frost also draped the trees this morning.

Tomorrow, we should arrive at our destination. Perhaps we will spend a day or two at the lake, allowing the horses to rest.

We snared a rabbit while setting up camp and will enjoy it along with rice for our meal.

Tonight the moon is full, and the land is lit up enough to see deer moving as they forage for food. Of course, predators use the moon to their advantage in different ways as well.

Now alone in my tent with my thoughts, I try to picture what the trail ahead might hold, yet not ready to release the memories of what today brought, all the while drifting nearer to sleep.

\* \* \*

We woke up this morning, packed the horses, and rode northwest toward the Deadwood River. Even before we saw it, we could hear it, the faint sound of rapids in the distance.

With each new destination reached in the time that we had estimated, we became more and more cocky, more sure of our abilities. It was as though we knew we were right on track, but until we saw our destination, we weren't sure if we should feel sick in the pit of our stomachs or secure in our smugness.

We had thought about getting lost, even though I was tracking our progress on a map. Then, at the moment when we arrived at our target, we felt superior, like nothing could stop us from finding our way. As we emerged from the trees, we sat 20 feet above the Deadwood River. Looking in both directions, it was clear that we would not be crossing where we were. We decided to make camp and ride southwest the five miles to the lake tomorrow.

We were able to catch two fish and so will sleep on a full stomach.

\* \* \*

A single day has vanished since the last entry.

Today, as usual, we were up with the sun and ready to move out before it warmed up enough to feel our fingers. We made a turn toward the Cassiar Mountain Range and then a slight adjustment south. Although Deadwood Lake was five miles from last night's camp, it took us almost three hours to reach it, due to the heavy tree growth along the banks of the Deadwood River. We arrived as the sun blazed overhead, determined to stay a day or two.

We let the horses graze, and as they ate, we set up the tents, made the campfire circle, and gathered firewood.

As the afternoon wore on, we fished Deadwood Lake and smoked some weed.

By mid-afternoon we were full, relaxed, enjoying life.

We caught sight of a four hundred pound male grizzly bear, easily identified by its enormous size, across the Deadwood River, downstream a hundred yards. We watched as it walked upstream eyeing the bank for food. The breeze, such as it was, blew toward us, so the bear would not detect our scent. We allowed it to get 50 yards from us, and then we fired a few rounds into the air to scare it away. The bear disappeared into the trees not to be seen thereafter.

As the sun set, we talked about staying here for a few more day and then roving south toward the cabin. We have found the ride along the Deadwood River and the scenery here at Deadwood Lake to be spectacular. If I was an artist, I would wish to paint a landscape of what I see here today. A flat calm lake with not a ripple to disturb its surface. Crystal clear water reflects the reverse image of pines lining the shore, the sun sinking lower, lighting the land in different hues that I am not sure have names. The thick pine trees around the lake are 40 to 50 feet tall. Squirrels and birds make them home, and if we listen, the environment is noisy as the squirrels bark at us and the birds chirp from every direction. We have seen flocks of Canada geese flying overhead in a southerly direction.

# 6

# Autumn 1976

The summer season is already beginning to give way to autumn. So short is the alpine season of plenty. August has seen two days show her intention to stir things up. The air is cooler now, even during the day.

We have been on this trip for close to four months already. Today was a comparatively relaxing day, spent fishing and enjoying the weather with which we have been blessed. In late afternoon the breeze picked up, and we sat in camp waiting for it to die down so we might cook our meal. Within an hour the breeze calmed enough to allow us to safely tend to cooking. After dinner it became calm.

We built the fire high and bright, enjoying the heat it provided. George has decided to stay up and tend the fire. I am tired and will soon sleep.

As I gaze into the indigo sky, I see the lights of a passing jet, too high to hear, as it flies to its destination in another time, another world.

\* \* \*

Today we spent the whole day fishing and relaxing in the grass along the shoreline of Deadwood Lake. We threw in a line and caught our lunch, leaving more time to do nothing. After gathering more firewood, we discussed the ride back to the cabin, some 80 miles from our current location.

Examining the map, we intend to stay west of the Dell River, so we will only have to cross three rivers. On the way here we crossed five rivers. None of them were terribly difficult, but with the season changing, bringing afternoon showers and thunderstorms, we would rather not take the chance of a sudden flash flood striking while we make a crossing.

It is early autumn, and life is good. The animals we see all take advantage of the abundance of food. We saw a female grizzly with a single cub, eating sage grass while seeking the more rewarding wild berry patches sure to blossom this month.

While George was cooking some fish, a family of raccoons wandered into camp, determined to eat our dinner. They were noisy and a bit aggressive. When one of them pushed their luck, George chased them through camp with his walking stick. They clambered up the nearest tree and peered down at us.

After darkness had engulfed the camp, the raccoons slid down from the tree and ransacked our camp as best they could, scattering the fish bones from the fire to the ground around the tents. They knocked over the coffee pot as well. One of them even had the nerve to scale my tent, forcing me to push it off from inside.

I kept telling myself that we are visitors in their land, that this land is their home. They stood right outside the tents chattering at us. We let them throw their tantrum, and then they left, and we were able to sleep.

\* \* \*

For the first time on this ride, it rained hard during the early morning. We did bring our heavy coats with us but were lax in not bringing our rain dusters. The rain was heavy for half an hour and then lightened up to a steady drizzle. We remained sealed in our respective tents during the rainfall.

We traveled 20 spectacular landscaped miles during the ride today.

We spied countless deer as we sojourned on south, but we have not killed any because we are still too far from the cabin to haul it there before it spoils. We were visited by a peregrine falcon, which flew not more than 20 feet above us as we rode. In the next moment it was gone, and we were once more riding alone. We failed to score any meat today, so we will eat rice for dinner.

As I sit as an observer to all that occurs in this land, my appreciation is exceeded only by my amazement in how perfect everything interacts with everything else. For example, I noticed an elk strolling through the grass browsing. Scrambling step for step with the elk, a four inch tall black bird ate the insects that were disturbed by the elk, thus teaming up to provide a wonderful meal for both.

We see daily examples of this interaction and are endlessly fascinated.

\* \* \*

Travel today was anything but swift, but we managed to ride 12 miles. As I make this entry, it is raining, as it has been since noon.

Except for seeing an enormous bull elk trying to herd a female, the morning was uneventful. The male ran alongside the female and steered it into the herd. Once the new member was herded, it must have felt secure, as the elk seemed to be at ease in a short period of time.

Throughout the forest, we heard the occasional squeal of other bull elk as they tried to attract females and challenge rivals to fight. There will be much more of this in the coming month. They could be calling for other reasons I suppose, since it is too early for rutting season.

In the last 30 minutes of our ride today George caught sight of a moose lying in a shallow pond taking advantage of the water and vegetation.

We are now less than 50 miles from the cabin, so we will hunt tomorrow.

\* \* \*

The sun rose this morning bright and early, bringing with it the comfort that every creature seeks, the warmth that had been playing hide and seek for the last two days. As the sun rose higher, so did our spirits. We smoked a bowl of weed and set out for the cabin.

The wilderness appeared so much more surreal with a brilliant sun shining as opposed to when the sky was overcast. So much color is disguised under the clouds. The sun glistening on the back of a mallard duck comes to my mind.

We let the horses trot for a portion of the day, as it seemed to be their desire. Although we rode 25 miles, we made it 20 miles closer to the cabin, as we chose to deter around the Pitman and Frog Rivers rather than cross them. The runoff from the rain made them unsafe to cross, muddy and swift as they were.

Having chosen the detour, we did not hunt today, as it was too late, so instead we rode in different directions scouting for deer. George rode southwest, and I rode due south. We met later in the afternoon at our campsite. George said that he seen many deer at the base of Mt. McNamara, which is 10 miles from where we are now. We will ride there in the morning and hunt.

We will eat a duck that I disposed close to the Frog River earlier. This bird will be a taste different from our normal grub, and we will savor it, I'm sure.

The sky appears clear, and light fades as the earth is caught between day and night. Soon enough, we will sneak into our tents and wait for the morning to light the earth.

\* \* \*

This sixth August day delivered a beautiful sunrise. We started out early, as the sun rose, and we found ourselves at the base of Mt. McNamara by mid-morning. This mountain is more than seven thousand feet high.

We decided to stick close to the base and hunt in a counter-clockwise direction. We rode for a short while, hobbled the horses, and then stepped into the brush and trees.

George and I split up, George going a few hundred yards closer to the steeper incline of the foothills. I traversed along the more flat, sandy, dry streambed that rims the mountains. I found a rise in the terrain that held a well-worn game trail. I spied a spot above the trail 20 feet, hidden by brush and an outcropping of boulders.

I waited there to ambush any deer that might pass. As I waited, it occurred to me that George and I had not agreed on a time to meet up at where we left the horses. I figured that I would stay where I was until late afternoon and then meet him. I hoped George would do the same.

As the time passed, my legs cramped up from crouching in the same position for so long. I searched the landscape to see if any prey was coming and then stood and stretched. As I scanned farther down the trail, I saw the antlers of a buck, moving up the trail, perhaps 50 yards away.

I dropped back down into a shooting position, setting the arrow in the guide of the bow. It seemed like it took 10 minutes, though it was far less, for the buck to reach my position. I drew the string, centered the sight on the flank of the animal, and watched as the deer inched closer. What wind there was came from the south, into my face. Perfect!

What did seem strange to me was that the deer acted out of character by roaming this trail so late in the morning. The norm would be that it would rest or lay in a day bed on a ridge where it could smell the thermal air. The buck now stopped every couple of steps in order to glance over its shoulder, attentive to its surroundings, and then it grazed on soft leaves and twigs. After three or four more steps, he repeated the pattern.

The buck was now 30 feet away from me, and 20 feet below. I stood, taking aim with the bow fully drawn. I took two deep breaths to steady my aim and then released the arrow. It reached the target in a split second, smashing into the flank behind his front leg, striking his lungs.

The animal leaped high into the air and dashed into the dense brush. My first thought was that the arrow had somehow missed its mark, yet I saw it fly into the animal, so I could not have missed. I made my way down to where the deer stood when I shot it. On the ground I noticed a few drops of blood.

I shouldered my bow, took my rifle, and followed the drops of blood. As I walked into an open spot, I caught a glimpse of the deer going over the ridge. I tried to envision in my mind's eye how close to the heart of the deer the arrow had struck. I did not want to be chasing a wounded animal all over the mountains.

I climbed to the ridge without haste and could clearly see the blood trail getting more intense, easier to follow. I knew that the buck could not be too far away. The problem was that sometimes a wounded deer would retreat into dense brush, lay down to rest, and never get up. I did not want to lose this beautiful buck that way. But I found him on the downslope of the ridgeline.

I would have to get George to help me with this beast, as I could not move it alone. I did cut its stomach open and prop it up with a few tree branches. This allowed the meat to cool slowly and some said would make the meat taste better. The buck weighed close to 100 pounds, appeared reddish in color, and had a nice 12-point rack. I hiked to Canoni and rode to where I thought George would be but saw no sign of him or his horse.

The packhorse was tied to a tree. I decided to take the packhorse back and try to salvage my kill. Once at the spot of the kill, I field dressed the animal and slung the meat over the packhorse and returned to where George and I had split up. Still, no sign of him.

I unloaded the venison form the horse and sat in the grass waiting for George. He appeared half an hour later with a 50-pound load of meat over his shoulders.

As the afternoon wore on, George dressed out the meat. We found a tree a hundred yards from the campsite and hung the meat. We cooked two large steaks for our dinner, savoring the smell of the venison.

We cautioned each other about the fact that the hanging meat could attract bears and that we could do nothing about it other than to keep the meat a good distance from our tents.

The steaks were cooked to perfection, juicy and tender, making this perhaps the best meal I have had since the trip began. We could not have bought a better steak in any five-star restaurants, I would wager.

* * *

It is morning, a single day since the last entry.

After we turned in last night, I heard raindrops hitting my tent. It was a welcome sound, as the rain would help dampen the smell of meat in the air. Apparently this worked, as no bears trespassed on our chosen spot as far as we could tell.

As planned, we hunted, and by early afternoon we had bagged three decent deer. After cleaning and hanging the deer from the trees, we relaxed around camp the remainder of the day.

We will leave for the cabin tomorrow, since we cannot carry any more meat. We estimate that we have 120 of venison, enough to burden our packhorse.

For some reason, the thought occurred to me that I have not seen George keeping any kind of records. "Why aren't you writing anything down to remember this adventure?"

"No one will believe this story. What can we show them of it? We can't take the cabin or the horse's home with us. We have done nothing more than prove that we could survive the elements." George retorted.

It seemed sad to me that he would not by now be full of the life that surrounds us. It seemed unnatural that he would not want to let his brothers or his daughter read about what he had done, what he thought about while out in the wild.

I know that someday I will turn these notes into a book, which I will share with anyone with a dream that may be out of the ordinary. I hope to help others believe that they can live their dream if they are devoted and see the challenges through. It takes only preparation, courage, and commitment to succeed.

\* \* \*

We greeted the morning with a renewed energy, for by day's end we could be back at the cabin. We loaded the venison onto the packhorse and started out. We rode east for 10 miles, reaching Ridgeway Lake at midday.

The land here was dotted with a stand of new pine trees, as a result of a burn that occurred perhaps five years ago. A swath of land, four miles or more, had burned, and the boundaries of the burn were quite obvious. From where we were, the cabin lay less than 15 miles away.

We stopped at Ridgeway Lake and fished for an hour, catching a nice fish and cooking it for lunch.

We rode on, and three hours later we crested the ridge lying west of the cabin. What a beautiful sight, to see our brown tinted cabin standing alone against the green forested background, near the blue water of the West River, all set against the vastness of this wilderness.

We have completed a 16-day ride, covering 250 miles, through wilderness we had never seen before. I would say that that was pretty damn brave of us. With us we brought 120 of meat, which will see us through part of the coming winter.

A pronounced chill saturates the air tonight, and the days are not as long as they once were.

Our hunt and exploration sojourn was most gratifying for us both, and we have recounted the trip while relaxing in the cabin. Especially rewarding was the discovery of a pond northeast of the cabin that houses beavers. We saw both adults and two younger beavers in the pond. In point of fact, the one pool was indeed three ponds linked by a shallow waterway that led from one pond to the next. I would estimate each pond to be 50 feet across and six feet deep.

Once at the cabin, we got the fire going and the horses settled for the night. We talked of hunting different species to change up the variety of the meat that we would eat during the winter. We would, of course, smoke the better cuts of meat and save them for winter.

\* \* \*

As if on cue, we woke to the deep, chilled air of autumn. An overnight storm dropped snow on the higher peaks, and even though it is the second week of August, we feel the change in the air. We now face the fact that the short Indian summer is dwindling.

One good thing about the colder temperatures is that the meat will freeze solid in the box that we built in the tree.

We carry out our necessary mundane tasks, such as building a strong ladder so that we may reach the meat stored in the tree, collecting firewood, and digging channels in the ground to drain the water away from the cabin in case of heavy rain.

As the season has progressed, we have initiated a vitamin-enhancement regimen in an effort to build our resistance to illness. Outside at night the temperature now gets below freezing at times.

We did some work on the corral, adding six-inch diameter posts and stronger logs, making it much more secure. We made a windbreak for the exposed side of the corral by burying poles against the rails of the corral; so one side resembles a fort. The other side is built close to the cabin wall, so it is a wind block.

We thought about building an outhouse but have decided not to, as it would become a breeding ground for bacteria. We will use a hole in the ground for a week and then bury the waste. We then dig a different hole a few yards away. Of course these holes are a good distance from the cabin.

Going outside at night to pee is not fun at all! The colder nights speeds up the process, as we could freeze in a matter of minutes. Imagine entering a freezer, dropping your pants, and trying to take care of business. Yeah, that's what it's like.

Then we face the matter of hygiene. Every other morning I jump into the West River and wash the vital areas. I also wash my hair, which has now grown to the middle of my back. I hate dirty hair, so the instant headache from the cold water is worth it.

Every day we must bury or burn the bones from anything we've eaten, for obvious reasons.

During lulls in our day, I tend to wonder to myself what I am waiting for. I feel like a fireman, whose days consist of 23 hours of boredom and one hour of high danger and excitement. I await those unknown events that have not yet occurred.

\* \* \*

The wind picked up overnight, and by this morning, it blew hard, gusting at 60 to 70 miles per hour. It blew snow sideways as well during the moments of moisture.

Later in the day, early afternoon, the storms passed, and the wind died down, creating a wonderful postcard-like scene. The mountains surrounding us now sport a thick coat of snow. Against the azure blue sky, the vista was amazing. The temperature stayed cold for the whole day, not getting above 40 degrees according to the thermometer that we placed outside on the cabin.

In the forest somewhere we heard the rattling of antlers, a sign that the rut will soon begin. While I was relieving myself, I heard the wolf pack howling. We have become accustomed to hearing the wolves and so no longer become nervous when we hear them. As long as they keep their distance, we will have no problems.

During the past few days we have been observed by a hawk sitting high up in a tree on a dead branch near the top. Perhaps it will remain long enough to know that we are not a threat. We saw flocks of Canada geese flying south for the winter throughout the day. It is not too hard to shoot down a bird as they pass, as they are flying low.

We welcome the change from red meat. George considers shooting and cleaning the birds his task alone. Until the freeze set in, it had been impossible to stockpile meat, but now that it is colder, that is no longer an issue.

I have collected a number of feathers, and I am contemplating trying to make a headdress. Currently our rifles and binoculars adorn the walls of the cabin. I will also use a few of the feathers to decorate the mane of Canoni. My rifle will also now be adorned with feathers.

\* \* \*

This day we greeted bright sunshine and an unblemished sky. The stiff breeze, however, made it feel colder than the 50 degrees shown on the thermometer. I remembered reading that the average temperature in this region was 69 degrees during this time of year. At night the temperature drops close to or below freezing. It is nearing the end of autumn, and it will get colder.

I fished the Gataga River today, and for the first time in a long time, I was shut out, catching nothing at all.

Our daily routine has relaxed a bit, as we realize more of our goals. It seems that nowadays we are finished with our chores by mid-morning and then seek out things to keep us occupied.

George used a pine branch to form a basketball hoop, fixing it to a tree. A ten-inch diameter pine cone is our ball. You get the picture. You can take the boy out of the hood, but you can't take the hood out of the boy.

In the time here, we have accomplished much. We are both much better at our survival skills; our hunting skills have improved as well. George has also mastered the art of cooking the meat, which without his spices would be boring and repetitious. As always, George remains a master fisherman.

During our downtime we tend to think and talk about the family and friends that we left behind in favor of this land. In the long run we are able to move on to other things, and the depressive nature of those thoughts is forgotten, if only for a while.

\* \* \*

The second week of August is in the books. I am writing this dramatic episode after a night that we will never forget. We have finished cleaning up the remains of an aggressive wolf from in front of the cabin.

This whole incident began last night after dinner, as George buried the bones of the rabbit that we had eaten for supper. He spotted a single wolf watching him from a knoll across the West River.

George opened the door of the cabin. "There is a wolf on the other side of the river, sitting there watching us."

I grabbed my rifle, and we hotfooted it to the place where George had spied the wolf. We scanned the area with an abundance of caution for 10 minutes, and then, unable to locate the wolf, returned to the cabin. As could be imagined, a rising full moon added to the drama.

Later, we heard first the bark of a single wolf, then the howling pack, the wolves in communication with one another, I assumed. The noise stopped, and for a while it was a quiet, cold night. Inside, we were warmed by the fire, clad only in our long johns. We each smoked a cigarette and shared a pipe full of weed while we talked about how cool it was to be a part of this untamed world

"For all we know, the wolves could be right outside." George speculated.

Of course, we both knew that he was right, but we went on talking until it grew late.

George, as always, had his shotgun leaning against the wall next to him, and my rifle was within reach. As we lay there listening to the sounds of the night, we heard the faint sound of an animal becoming clearer, something nearer to the door than before.

"Most likely a deer." I threw out a guess, but that was not the first thing that popped into my head.

Yes, the wolves were our first thought. Without warning a scuffle broke out, and the silence turned to chaos. The pack of wolves attacked whatever it was outside of the cabin.

As quick as it had started, it was over.

The fire was glowing embers, but I could see George's face, more specifically, his eyes. He sat up in his sleeping bag and reached for his shotgun. I turned to grab a log to toss into the fire, and at that exact second, a loud and fierce snarl came from the other side of the door, followed by the door itself being rattled.

I was alarmed and snagged my rifle, aiming it at the door. George had his shotgun pointed at the door as well. We could not see what was going on, but we knew that the wolves could get inside one way, and we were facing it.

In my mind I imagined that the door would fling open and the wolf would be silhouetted against the moonlight, making for an easy shot. George had by now taken up a position at the cabin window, opening the shutter with his gun barrel. Without warning, the shotgun went off with a deafening blast, instantaneously filling the cabin with smoke. All I could hear was a loud ringing in my ears, but I could see George mouthing something, and then aiming his gun and firing a second round.

I yelled, "Goddammit, George, stop shooting!"

After the second blast, though I could not see the dead body of a wolf lying on the ground, I knew that if something had been there it would be dead now.

For two hours, we were afraid to open the door. I was perfectly happy to wait for the sun to rise, thank you very much. Besides, I was still too unsettled to hit a target.

Needless to say, we were not going to sleep any time soon. The remainder of the pack left the area, as indicated by the silence that followed the shooting.

It took an hour to settle down enough to write these details. This ordeal remained quite frightening.

With much apprehension and false daring, we opened the door and saw the wolf lying dead. Blood flooded and pooled on the ground behind the carcass. This female wolf was bigger than a domestic German Shepard, grey and white in color, and rigid in her death pose.

While I stood guard, George dragged the carcass away from the cabin and into the trees, where he buried it. We covered the blood on the ground with snow and cleaned up the blood and brain matter on the cabin wall with water.

My heart felt bad for my sister, Šung'manitu-tanka, the Lakota word for wolf. I knew also that George had no motivation to kill her, either. Things happened fast, as they often do. We had scant time to react.

I had heard about the fog of war, and in that brief second of confusion wondered if this was what that was like. I was glad that it was not the alpha male that had been killed.

George explained himself. "The first shot went off by accident. I hit the frame of the window, and the gun went off."

We deduced as much from the damage to the ground outside the cabin.

"I intended to scare the animal away when I fired the second round." George hung his head.

The gory results of this encounter were proof that there is little separating life and death here. There seems to be no middle ground, life is eligible to be extinguished at any moment. Any miscalculation may bring lethal consequences. We both agreed that we did not desire a repeat of this particular event.

\* \* \*

Three days later, we have neither seen nor heard the remaining members of the pack. The intervening days have been cool and windy at times. No rain or snow has fallen during this time. We have repaired the wall outside and have built a stronger door, using thicker logs.

Some things in nature are so unique that man can't even envision reproducing them. This morning I crept through the forest into a meadow and found a place to sit and observe. Hundreds of some breed or other of forest bird hopped to and fro across the meadow. These birds remained active, hopping, clinging, or dangling from tree branches. As with every species, a certain pecking order was in place for these winged creatures. They were competitive with each other in hunting the insects that populated the meadow. They were quick to defend against uninvited intruders.

We have remarked that every animal, regardless of size, has a comfort zone that can't be broached. Take a squirrel, for example. We could inch up to within a few feet of one and take a picture, but if we got any closer, the animal would run away or fight.

We have faced a couple of exceptions. If we breach the imaginary zone of a grizzly bear, it will, more often than not, become aggressive. Mountain lions are the same.

Sometimes, however, when a fox encounters us day after day, it has built up a tolerance to us and allowed that gap to close. It is fascinating to witness the laws of nature at work.

We spent the better part of today in the cabin, while outside a cold, steady rain fell. The wind has blown at times, making the cabin the best option for contented survival. The horses stand close to the cabin wall and do not seem to be adversely affected by the weather.

\* \* \*

Five days later, George and I have taken our horses to a canyon south of the cabin where we aim to let them graze unattended. Our thinking is that we will preserve the food source around the cabin for later consumption.

We have spent a total of five hours gathering firewood, replacing what we have burned over the last few weeks.

I casually strolled to the edge of the West River today, and as I scanned the river, I saw a contrast of greens and white. The pine trees held snow in their branches, and the snow covering the ground made for a scenic picture.

Beyond the trees I caught sight of a herd of eight deer browsing on grass that grows beneath the snow.

We have some time to kill now, so we will take a short hike.

Our jaunt on this day was enjoyable, though uneventful. Other than spying on elk and checking in on the beavers in the pond as they went about their day, we had nothing to hold our attention.

Our dinner today consisted of trout and pancakes and was fantastic.

\* \* \*

We enter the final week of August as we turn the page on our journey of a lifetime.

George and I have decided we cannot risk the possibility of our horses being attacked in the canyon so we hiked to the location, rounded them up and brought them back to the cabin. Our angst was unbearable.

George and I left the horses out of the corral while we cleaned it up. Our three horses create a lot of crap. A chipmunk played hide and seek with us as we cleaned up the pen, thinking that he could somehow scavenge a meal. Things never worked out for him, though.

During the afternoon, the days have become more fall-like, both in terms of the cooler air and in the distant sound of antlers locked in battle.

Unless we know of something important to do outside, we go indoors earlier than we did a month ago. We pass the time playing cards or a board game called Stratego.

\* \* \*

Things have remained the same for the last three days — nothing of note has happened. The weather has been nice and clear during the day but colder after sunset. The cobalt blue sky makes it feel welcoming here.

We have tried to take several short rides each day to alleviate the boredom of having nothing to do. We have ridden along game trails, scouting them out. Occasionally George or I set a snare trap with the expectation of harvesting a rabbit.

We have noted that the higher elevations brandish a thick blanket of snow. It seems that all of nature is getting ready for the inevitable winter.

Before we ate an early dinner, we saw a family of four river otters passing downstream as we strolled along the West River. It was clear they were having fun in the water, though early in the mornings it now sports a thin layer of ice around the edges. They noticed everything and were curious. We watched until they swam out of sight around the bend in the West River.

Back in the cabin, with a warming fire burning, we felt that it was nice to be home.

\* \* \*

## AUGUST SEES ITS FINAL DAY

Yesterday afternoon, dark clouds swept in from the north, bringing with them a cold front complete with arctic wind and steady snowfall. The snow fell through the night but has eased in the past hour. The snow has accumulated to a depth just under knee high. Needless to say, we will not be going anywhere far for a while.

George and I had a spur-of-the-moment snowball fight during the few minutes that it took to feed the horses. Two grown mountain men having a snowball fight in the middle of the wilderness made for good times. Since then we have stayed inside, reading or doing whatever.

George has begun reading a book that I brought along that tells the story of the journeys and family structure of the Lakota Indians in the late 1700s. It traces three generations through storytelling and the detailing of historic records. Each generation speaks of new discoveries, wars, and new religious ceremonies.

For George this has been a wondrous experience because until this trip he had never taken the time to consider anything other than his personal needs at any moment in time. This book has given him and will hereafter give him a different perspective on many things.

# 7

# WINTER 1976

We have reached the beginning of September.

First thing this morning George and I scampered up onto the roof and cleared the snow. The wind blew hard enough today to make it uncomfortable on exposed skin.

George managed to shoot a duck along the West River while hiking this morning, and this is what we will eat for dinner tonight.

Once more we live in this moment of nothing, nothing to break up the dull hours of quiet. Nothing occurring to make our blood pump hard. Sitting in the warmth and security of our cabin, we are bored and expectant both at the same time.

\* \* \*

September creeps through its first week, and the start of the long, dreaded winter begins. The weather has turned colder during the past few days. George complains that both his elbow and his leg ache when it's cold. He spends most of his day in the cabin now. I, on the other hand, like to climb the rock formation behind our cabin and spend time scanning the valley.

Our meat supply to date is not a problem, but with the prospect of winter to come, we have contemplated another hunt. We have agreed that the weather is much too unpredictable to go far from the cabin, much less for an overnight jaunt. We have decided to ration the food, with the idea that eating smaller portions now is better than running out of food later.

\* \* \*

Our cabin stays cozy to the point that we wear only long johns and jeans, while outside it is freezing. A storm has entered the valley and is dropping snow as I write.

During the day, we have seen fewer animals, as they have either migrated or are in their dens sleeping. Recently, we eyeballed a snowshoe hare, a single fox, and two or three squirrels burrowing into the snow.

We have spent most of our time playing Stratego or poker. When we tire of that, we eat dinner and then spend the evening talking about whatever races to mind.

The snowstorm has not abated, and since late afternoon yesterday several inches have fallen.

The temperature that accompanied the storm has dropped, now reading 29 degrees, which, taking the wind-chill factor into consideration makes it feel much colder.

George has become engrossed reading the book and is apparently most interested in the ways of the Lakota. He now has good questions about them, questions that I find both amusing and rewarding to answer.

In one regard it is funny. When we came here the joke was that we would be living like mountain men, but in truth, we live more like Indians, doing virtually everything by hand. George has even hinted at trying to make a pair of buckskin leggings.

He has shown a keen interest in the religious theories of the Lakota, and we talk for hours on that subject. He agrees that it is not blasphemous to believe in the spirit of nature, especially when it is so easy to see it flow and know its power in what we see here every day. This spirit is referred to as Skan, something in motion, by the Lakota nation.

Coming from George, who was a weekend Catholic, repenting on Sundays, this is an interesting change in his opinion. Not that George was ever one to preach. He has admitted that he was like most others who call on God at times when they are about to get their ass beat by a gang of crazies. The lessons he now reads about pertain to protecting the integrity of Mother Earth, while knowing where he fits in.

Because we normally sit at the top of the food chain does not mean that we own the Earth or hold any more power than any other creature that we encounter. This is not to say that we are at any real disadvantage, either.

\* \* \*

Raging for a fourth day, this enduring storm has left a substantial amount of snow on the ground. If I let myself dwell on the snow, I get a sick feeling in my stomach, knowing that we could not leave if we needed to. We are entrenched here until spring.

In some places, the snow has been blown into drifts higher than I can see over. On the windward side of the cabin, the drifts have built up to the level of the roof. Needless to say, we will have to remove the snow from the roof at our first chance. Scanning the landscape, the only things that are not white are the pine trees, the horses, and the soon to be frozen river, which is a tan color.

\* \* \*

I am particularly happy today. The storm that stayed with us for four days has now passed, leaving behind sunshine.

George and I went out early and cleared the snow from the roof. We used stiff branches with limbs spread out on the ends, using them much like a rake. It took half of the morning, but we finished the task.

We thought it a good idea to create three escape paths leading from the cabin to the West River in different directions. In the event we needed to get to the river to escape some unforeseen life-threatening situation, this would provide a path. So we spent the afternoon cross-country hiking in our snowshoes, going from the cabin to the West River. We cut three different trails, each taking a marginally different route to the West River. The first trail leads from the cabin heading north, bending tightly around the granite rock formation behind the cabin and down to the West River. The second trail leads from the cabin almost directly southwest to the West River, this having the sharpest incline of the three trails. The third pathway leads from the cabin due south, meeting the West River three quarters of a mile away.

Later in the afternoon we sat on the bank of the West River soaking in the crisp fall air and stunning scenery. Along the bank across the West River, we watched a lone deer scratching for whatever might hide beneath the snow, though she is not bound by the grass. She will also browse as she migrates through the area. In fact, she will get most all of her food browsing throughout the winter. This is another day in the struggle for life for this animal.

In the tree next to the one where we store our meat, new residents have moved in in the personage of a pair of great gray owls. These owls have a wingspan of five feet, I would guess. We heard a faint hooting sound last night, but we dismissed it. This morning, we saw the couple where they are now. We love the idea of having a permanent pair of birds of prey nearby, as we hope they will act as an early warning signal for us. They will also reduce the rodent population during spring and summer.

Besides the owls, jays and finches are the birds we see most often now. We heard the call of the wolf pack, though it was far enough away as to be scarcely audible. As always, whenever I hear a wolf, I feel a touch of anxiety, remembering the chaos of that night not too long ago. Wolves are wild and are truly the masters of this domain. I do not dread being killed by a wolf, but rather having to kill one.

\* \* \*

Today George cut the pattern for his buckskin leggings. With his two tools being a knife and a leather punch, it was not easy. I guess the fact that the seam will be on the inner leg will hide the imperfections in the cut. He will use the punch to make holes down the legs through which to run laces. We brought a lot of these leather end pieces with us to use in crafting.

Speaking of supplies, each time we use an item that we brought with us, we feel clever for having thought to bring it.

We have been eating sufficiently enough that I rarely feel hungry. Both George and I drink huge amounts of water daily to avoid dehydration and some wicked side effects that it brings.

\* \* \*

## SEPTEMBER 17

This morning as I left the cabin to take my bath using one of the escape trails, I was greeted by a herd of doe's, standing inside the tree line. I imagine that they were curious about me and so concentrated their attention on me during my morning routine.

I try to make it a point not to move hurriedly when I encounter wildlife, so I leaned against the cabin and watched them for a while. I wondered if I might see them again, under different circumstances.

They moved deeper into the trees and eventually out of sight. I felt certain that they did not feel threatened by me, and I hope they will return.

I jogged the rest of the way to the West River and was ready to jump in when I saw hundreds of crimson red salmon swimming in the water. For a second I could not believe my eyes. I rushed to the cabin, shouting for George to grab his bow and hurry to the stream.

With our bows in hand we rushed to the West River and shot willy-nilly into the water. Within 10 minutes we had bagged 20, 15-pound salmon. We cleaned the fish right then and there and transported them to the storage box.

We could not stay away from the West River as thousands of healthy, huge fish swam by. Scanning the river in both directions, we did not see any bears along the shore.

Our other guests, the owls, are enjoying their new home. When we need to get meat from the box, we have to scare them away or keep them at bay until we have closed the box.

George has begun to build a smoker, which we will use to dry meat and fish. He has crafted a box five feet tall and three feet wide, and he has put two-inch diameter limbs within to hang the meat from as it dries. The top is assembled using fresh pine limbs spaced three inches apart, thus allowing the smoke and heat to escape the smoker. The front of the smoker is open, thus permitting us to build a fire in the box and toss wet wood chips on the coals. We will attempt to use the smoker tomorrow.

Mother Nature has at her discretion provided life to us and those others who inhabit this valley. Soon the feast shall begin for the bears.

Storm clouds build on the horizon.

\* \* \*

The clouds that we reflected on yesterday brought snow during the night and into this morning, dumping more snow on the ground... and the cabin.

We remained in the cabin for the majority of the day, emerging briefly to watch the salmon run, feed the horses, get meat for dinner, and try out the smoker.

It is clear that the grizzly bears have been fishing, as we stepped over half-eaten salmon scattered all along the West River. The bears are interested in eating the fatty parts of the salmon, the eggs, the brains, and the skin. They are storing fat for the winter.

George spent the afternoon putting the finishing touches on his pants, and they fit well everywhere but the waist, which is too large. He used his belt to resolve the problem for the moment. He said that he will deal with it tomorrow.

We cooked salmon for dinner, which was quite the change from what we have been used to.

* * *

This morning it appeared that the salmon run was far from over, as the West River ran red from the vast number of fish clogging the waterway. Some of these fish were three feet long and weighed 20 to 30 pounds. Others lie dead on the bottom of the West River. More are becoming fertilizer for plants as they rot on the sandy shore. This has been an exhilarating three days to see this unrelenting run of fish.

We ate salmon steaks for dinner this evening. George cooked them to perfection, the meat falling off the bones. What a change of flavor to go from venison to salmon.

We began smoking the salmon this morning, and it will take until tomorrow to finish.

* * *

During the night a bear happened by and located the smoker, destroyed it, and consumed the fish inside.

George and I could do nothing but remain inside the cabin, with the door closed, rifles trained on the door, until morning came and we could appraise the damage. With no sign of the bear around, we emerged from the cabin. We guessed that 20 pounds of meat was lost. It is clear that we will have to guard our smoker from this point on, once we rebuild it.

The snow fell throughout the night and into this morning. We have kept the escape trails to the West River maintained throughout these snow events.

We thrilled at seeing a male grizzly as it waded in the water along the West River and ate its fill of dead salmon from the sandy bottom. This animal had perfected the art of diving to the bottom and retrieving a fish. I had heard about this phenomenon, and had even seen some photos, but to witness it first-hand was beyond compare.

For reasons that I do not know, George has become somewhat irritable.

"I am sick of being stuck inside this cabin, and I need to get out. I feel so restless," George whined.

So this morning he took some meat and his saddlebag and rode off toward the north without a word about where he was going.

I wonder if I have done something to make him angry. You know what? Screw him if that's the case. I have no idea what his problem is.

I decided that I would follow him for a short ways, and so at a comfortable distance I rode in his horse's tracks. After a mile or so, I stopped and listened. Somewhere farther to the north, I heard the call of a wolf. I decided to turn back. After all, George was armed, had food and water, and had warm clothes. Why should I worry? He too was living a dream of his choosing that I need not invade.

After cleaning my weapons, I spent the rest of the daylight hours cleaning the cabin. It was not dirty, simply dusty. I took the opportunity to wash my clothes, and they now hang in front of the fire on the rope I strung across the room.

As winter goes on it seldom gets above 40 degrees in the daytime. I rolled and smoked a cigarette and sat back, reflecting on the events of the short summer with happiness and a touch of smugness.

\* \* \*

George left two days ago, and I have become somewhat concerned. I have gone about my normal routine of feeding Canoni and the packhorse and re-filling the canteens.

Later I took a ride.

Advancing at a steady pace, I rode farther than where I stopped when following George yesterday. I halted at a point where the tracks of George's horse led across a wide-open landscape, a huge treeless area, to the hills, and over them to the north.

I have decided that if George does not return before noon, I will ride out and attempt to find him. This should be easy enough in the snow. I spent the late afternoon eating and being entertained by the quiet of the forest.

\* \* \*

I write now as I sit in the cabin hearing thunder crashing outside after a cold day away from the cabin.

While saddling Canoni this morning I noticed tracks in the snow some 20 feet from the cabin. Two wolves had been close, and I did not hear them. I was surprised to find the tracks. Canoni and the packhorse were oblivious as well, since they did not make any noise, either.

Taking the packhorse along I rode out to find George, proceeding via the same tracks that I had followed previously. I pursued the tracks to the north for three miles, at which time the tracks turned to the west. The tracks led me to a stream that George had crossed. As luck would have it, the stream, which did not appear on the map, was shallow and allowed Canoni, the packhorse, and me to cross. I led Canoni across rather than riding her across. She was reluctant to cross out into the ice-cold water, so I tugged her reins, and she followed across.

Once on the other side, the land became a maze of thick pine and cottonwood trees. George's horse's tracks meandered through the trees, and it was evident that his pace had been reduced. No way could George have cantered straight through this forest.

A mile later the tracks led over a rise and into the valley below. From the top of the ridge I could follow the tracks with my eyes through my binoculars. I rested Canoni and her mate for 20 minutes while I scanned the terrain below. On this side of the pass the snow was not as deep, which made travel much easier.

For the next hour after that, I trudged through the snow, wearing my snowshoes, while the horses followed in line.

George's tracks led me in a semi-circle, going from west to southeast. It appeared that George was returning to the cabin. Then just as abruptly, the tracks turned to the north, then a few minutes later, back to the southeast. I now believed that George was lost!

As the afternoon wore on, inky clouds gathered to the east. I had followed the tracks to a rise in the land, which was the high point in the area. I found an overhanging ledge in an outcropping of rocks where I could take shelter for the night.

I gathered some firewood and used a lighter to start the tinder for a warming fire, which I built a few feet from the overhanging ledge. I tied Canoni and the packhorse to a stake near me and the fire. As I scanned down the valley, I saw a twinkle of light, which I thought could be a fire in George's camp.

\* \* \*

At first light this morning I awoke and rekindled the fire to warm myself. It was cold during the night, and I was stiff. Scanning through binoculars in the direction from which I saw the light last evening, I could see no sign of smoke or fire.

I rode, following the tracks, and after two miles, I rode into George's campsite. The ground around the fire pit was warm. The tracks led to the west, so I rode in that direction at a steady pace. After riding for another hour, I brought Canoni to a rise in the landscape and located George a short distance ahead.

I rode at a canter, and within five minutes I had caught up to him.

"Hey George!" I shouted. "Are you all right? Man, where are you going?"

"To the cabin."

I simply handed him my compass and watched the strange look that came over his face as he realized that he was traveling away from the cabin.

"Why didn't you follow your tracks to get to the cabin?"

"Upon entering this valley, I became disoriented and was not sure in which direction to travel. Since it was cloudy, I planned to wait for sunrise and then ride south.

To my regret, the sun was obscured by clouds."

When I found him he was riding north. He said that he planned to build a smoky fire in the afternoon if he had not seen any familiar landmarks; in the hope I would see the smoke and investigate. He clearly had not seen my fire last night.

We talked for a while longer and then turned in the direction of the cabin. During the ride home we stumbled upon what must have been an ancient Indian burial ground. Standing partially erect was two scaffolds, which at one time supported the bodies of those set to travel the Spirit Trail. The wood had long ago become too weak to support any weight, and so only one pole stood fully erect.

It was so quiet and mysterious. I felt eyes upon me as we inched past. The air seemed to hang still and heavy from the sacred past. Somehow when searching for George, I had missed this burial ground by less than a hundred feet, I noted from the tracks that I had made riding in. Perhaps in the spring I will return here and devote some time to locating relics in the surrounding area.

Upon reaching the cabin in the afternoon, we consumed a meal and smoked a bowl of weed.

George explained to me why he left. "I find myself dwelling on my daughter. I am beginning to feel isolated, and as a result, depressed. Sometimes it seems that we are too far away to ever get back to her and my relatives. With each passing day, I feel less content to be here."

The two days away had helped occupy his mind, though perhaps too much, as he had gotten lost!

"George," I shared my two cents, "from my perspective this experience is ours alone, to treasure and appreciate. It has a limited duration, it has lessons to impart, and we are learning new lessons all the time. Life here is every bit as priceless as life in the city, and since you made the choice to come here, you must live with your decision.

"George, appreciate this time, and keep the memories for when you are with your daughter, so she too may hear about your journey. As a result, you will begin anew the process of storytelling. Keep a positive mind for this time will pass too soon in the grand scheme of things. Of course it is challenging not to think of what is waiting in the city, but I find it easier if I trust the Great Spirit. The Great Spirit will keep safe those we hold dear."

I don't know if this talk helped George at all, but I gave him some things to think about.

\* \* \*

During the two days that we have been back to the cabin, I have seen a dramatic change in George's demeanor and attitude. He is once again gregarious and in good spirits. He is pulling practical jokes. This morning I trudged outside to feed the horses. When I returned and opened the cabin door, I was hit in the head with some kindling that George had balanced above the door. George's dark eyes twinkled as he chuckled. His beard partially concealing his smile.

Outside the snow in the meadow is knee deep, but it is well compacted, enough so that we played catch with a pine cone, as if it was a football.

I have decided to try and make an arrow by hand, so I hunted for a couple of super straight cottonwood branches. This will be a time-consuming project, as it will be challenging to make the arrows straight and perfectly round, so they fly true. I will attach the feathers using tree sap and sinew. Once the shafts are made I will fasten the arrowheads, which I brought with me. They are three inches long, made of metal, and razor sharp.

George made a nice soup of venison and spices. Among the meat chunks and broth, marrow from the bones awaits my attention. Congratulations, George, on your excellent chef-dom.

\* \* \*

Over the past four days the weather has relegated George and I to staying inside, other than to take care of chores.

George has spent time reading while I have started work on my arrows having found several straight tree limbs.

We have smoked and dried 15 pounds of salmon that has been stockpiled for consumption during this ongoing winter.

George made an observation today. "I am surprised at your dedication to your journal. I thought that you would have abandoned it long before now."

Although it does get monotonous sometimes, it is a labor of love. It will have benefits in the future.

* * *

We live to see the start of October today.

I have come down with a cold and am fighting it with high doses of vitamin C and iron.

George boiled a fine bone marrow soup from the leg bone of a deer. It was quite tasty with the chunks of venison that he added. It was a fine repeat of last week's dinner.

I am bundled in a blanket in front of the fire as I write.

George has finished reading his book and asks interesting questions.

He understands the philosophy of the Indian ways and sees the association with our survival quest. "The Indians knew something more about the spiritual side of life's equation than we know. They understood the balance needed between isolation and community. They had learned that sometimes it was best to be alone with ones thoughts in order to calm ones undesirable emotions.

"They realized that it was easier to support a single family during the winter than many families. This is why they tended to winter in family clans. "They knew also that it was necessary to gather as a community in the spring so that they might have their spirit lifted by the collective group."

I would say that George has grasped the concept well.

* * *

I have been recovering from my cold for the last two days and, in fact, feel pretty good today. I migrated outside for some fresh air this morning. Though it was cold, the sun shone, which felt nice on my face. It was good to be outside. By now, all of the bears in our valley have gone into hibernation.

My appetite has returned, and I crave venison. I secured a chunk from the reserves and it is thawing in front of the fire now. Pine needle tea warms my throat as I sip it from my tin cup.

George spent today out among the horses. He has checked on me a couple of times today but has remained away for the most part.

\* \* \*

Two days later, I went for a hike, as I am fully recovered from my cold and felt that I needed the exercise. The weather was icy, and the sky was gray. Outside, the smoke from the chimney hugged the ground, indicating more bad weather on the way.

Our supplies are ample at this time, including our firewood. For our dinner tonight we will eat salmon and a strip of venison. While all of nature slumbers, we find things to do to keep from getting cabin fever.

While I am on that subject, it seems that the phrase cabin fever denotes that one has literally been stuck inside a room for an extended period of time. While this is true, I submit that one can feel similar effects in a rather short amount of time. I begin to feel depressed, and to a degree lethargic, if I am stuck inside even for a few short days.

I will further say that it is possible to feel those effects even if one is able to spend some time outside. Time inside the four walls of this cabin seem to creep by. If I claim to feel cabin fever, it is more likely a case of being cabin bound.

\* \* \*

A cold front inched its way through the valley, bringing a blast of arctic air as the first week of October ends. We know that the day is fast approaching when we will be more or less cabin bound. The ice covering the West River is now thicker, but below the ice the water is moving.

What was at one time a simple chore of bathing in the river has now turned into a time-consuming, physically demanding task. I now use a heavy rock to break the ice, fill three canteens with water, and carry them back to the cabin, where I heat the water in our cooking pot.

I then take the warm water outside and pour it over my head and body. I have enough water to wash my hair and sponge off my body. Since I cannot live with dirty hair, I go through this ritual every third or fourth morning. George bathes on a bi-weekly basis at a minimum. I anticipate springtime when I can jump into the West River to bathe each morning.

George said that he will make a pancake batter and put bits of venison in it and cook it on the griddle. He hopes that it will be like bread when it is finished. I told him that I was anxious to try it.

I am entering this supplemental note to say that the bread did not rise and appeared more like a true pancake with meat protruding from top and bottom. All in all, however, it was not bad fare.

\* \* \*

Early this morning, before the sun came up, we heard wolves howling close enough to wake us up. I am convinced that we are situated on the edge of their home range, and as they move through their territory, they check in on us. Most often they are heard from a great distance away, but it is not uncommon to see wolf tracks near the cabin.

Oh, the elation of seeing the sun! After a solid week of gloom, the rays of the sun warmed the earth today. A slight breeze blew, making it feel chilly if we removed our jackets. I can imagine no better setting to be in unless of course it was summertime.

George and I spent time throwing the pinecone football and later took a hike into the forest.

George pointed out the deer tracks in the snow, and we both recognized this as further security for our survival. Our source of meat is within hunting distance, if needed.

\* \* \*

The weather this morning was mild and clear, with lots of sun. George and I took a morning ride along the edge of the forest, surveying the valley as we rode. We saw signs of many different animals; most using game trails to move around, which requires less energy. Tracks of deer, fox, rabbit, and coyote crisscrossed in the snow. In more than one location we saw tracks of the pack of wolves that claims this territory.

We were less than two miles from the cabin when we saw signs of a recent kill. Only the rib cage of an elk and the stained red snow remained. Perhaps 10 noisy black-billed magpies picked at the remnants of flesh left in the snow.

The many different tracks verify that life moves forward in this frozen wilderness and that we are along for the ride, even though we seem to lay eyes on the animals less often these days.

Farther along on our ride, we stopped and were forced to turn around by the results of an avalanche that obstructed the trail. Trees that once stood tall now lay fragmented in a massive pile of debris and snow.

We returned to the cabin late in the afternoon. George cooked dinner, and I make this entry as we both consume a cigarette.

George has finished reading the book and is now starved for more knowledge about the Indians to whom he now feels connected. We chat about different things, such as how the Indians managed to feed the whole tribe during the winter on the game available in places like this.

I explained that one of the traditions among the nations was to have a great jamboree at the end of summer, when the tribes prepared to split up into close family groups in five or six teepees and camp along different parts of the rivers. They each had their hunting area and were within a day's commute of relatives. They would be able to have gatherings, as before, however they were close family gatherings until the spring returned and the tribe came together in a great circle of teepees.

As George absorbs the information his mind forms new questions, which keep the conversation perpetuating.

\* \* \*

After seeing the wolf tracks yesterday, George and I decided to go back and see if anything had changed. The ride out was quiet, the scenery appealing, and we led our horses at a sedate pace. Once at the site of the kill, we searched for fresh tracks.

As if to give warning, a snowy owl took flight from its perch high in a Lodgepole pine tree. It swooped down for a closer inspection before turning south and soaring out of sight.

We dismounted and climbed the sloping mountain to a point where we could get a better view of the immediate area. As always, we carried our rifles. As we approached the crest of the ridge above us, we heard snarling wolves.

I do admit that I was nervous as I cocked the hammer of my rifle back. We remained silent as we struggled to determine where the sound was coming from. It sounded like they were on the other side of the ridge that we were approaching. Glancing at George, I motioned for him to follow me as I crawled in a semi-circle toward the top. We were downwind of the fighting but were cautious, nonetheless.

With my heart speeding, I raised my head and peeked over the sharp edge of the ridge. My eyes were met by the sight of the pack taking down a bull elk. There,

25 yards from us, were five gray wolves and a single black one pulling down the animal.

The black wolf snarled. As the alpha male, it kept the pack coordinated. The violence was at full throttle. There would be no surviving elk after this attack. As the pack finished the kill and moved in to eat, the alpha male took his place and packed his belly before any of the others touched the kill.

I was shocked and astounded all at the same time. The ever-present thought stayed in the back of our minds that there were no fences between us and these wild creatures.

We surveyed this scene for a time and then scaled down the ridge and to the horses. George called out that he did not see the horses where we had left them. They were, in fact, nowhere in sight.

While I stood guard, George clambered up a tree to survey the area. After a few minutes George hopped down and gestured toward a clearing in the center of a stand of trees a hundred yards from us.

As we retreated I saw that one of the gray wolves had topped the ridge and now meandered down the slope. We kept moving but knew straightaway when it caught our scent, as it jolted its head up and trained its nose into the wind. It then put its nose back to the ground and seemed to focus on the odor.

We retreated further and in so doing caught the attention of the wolf. This animal was not timid at all, glaring at us as it made its way down the ridge to the level ground. We quickened our pace toward the clearing. George trotted, then sprinted as we tried to increase the distance between the wolf and ourselves. Glancing back over my shoulder, I could see that the wolf was closing the gap. We had a hundred-yard lead with 50 yards to go to reach the horses.

It's amazing how the mind functions at a moment like that. I thought of the old movies where the monster is chasing someone, and you just know that that person is going to fall down.

This was my only focus, not falling down in the snow. I noted that the wolf had slowed no longer closing the ground between us. We mounted our horses and after checking the location of the wolf rode back toward the cabin, no longer worried about the wolf.

After we arrived at the cabin, we thought a lot about what we had witnessed, to be specific that we must make sure that we are never surprised by this wolf pack.

They were, I believed, more dangerous than grizzlies, in as much as we encounter them more often.

George said that the whole encounter felt like a rollercoaster ride. All the way up the incline he felt nervous, at the top he felt scared, and on the way down the rails he felt exhilaration and couldn't wait to feel exhilarated once more.

I was uneasy when I saw the pack, nervous during the time that the single wolf was trailing us, and finally after we had escaped, I felt the elated, oddly wishing that I could relive the situation.

In reality, today we were in little danger, since only a lone wolf came to investigate us, and between us we had 20 rounds of ammo for a last stand. The Alpha black wolf really impressed me today, with its absolute dominance over the pack and his ominous cold, yellow eyes.

For the first time in a long time, it was clear tonight, no moon, but a million unnamed stars shone in the heavens.

George and I sat near the fire pit outside looking into the ebony sky. From time to time, a meteor streaked through on its way to parts unknown. This night was cold and silent. The vast Milky Way covered the entire sky, from north to south.

We are back in the cabin now, with me wishing that I had brought a guide to the stars, but we saw a spectacle tonight in any event.

\* \* \*

Three cabin-bound days later, we're trapped by both the temperatures and a blizzard that arrived yesterday afternoon. The wind blows ever stronger today, trying to break the cabin door, it seems. I went out to relieve myself and could see snowdrifts developing against the exposed wall of the cabin. I froze my ass off out there! Maybe in the spring we will build an outhouse, after all.

\* \* \*

October has reached the midway point today. The storm has raged on outside for a third day and displays no signs of letting up. George said he thinks that it has snowed two feet since yesterday. We understood that we had to brush the snow off of the roof, as it was deep and was putting a strain on the structure.

As we had done previously, we fashioned a rake using a straight branch that retained shrubbery at the end. This allowed us to clear the roof without climbing up on it like we did last time. This was a much safer way to remove the snow. The battle today to clear the roof of snow was fought in the wind, Mother Nature mandating that she would not cooperate with us.

Although some snow remains on the roof, we have eased the burden and should be safe until we have improved weather to attempt the feat in.

The horses are fine, all clustered in the corral. Nothing of note occurred today involving wildlife.

George decided that he is going to cook salmon for dinner.

\* \* \*

Thankfully, after four days, the storm broke! The panoramic vista outside our door is a winter wonderland. Snow was heavy on every branch of every tree. The slightest warmth of the sun, softening the snow, caused mini snowfalls in the trees.

The air today was crisp and fresh, so we could see our breath. The smoke from the chimney wafted through the air, serving to remind me of where I am.

George and I now plot to take a short hike wearing our snowshoes.

We arrived back at the cabin from our hike alive.

The world was so quiet today. Staring up at the mountains, it was easy to see the deep, heavy snow forming a ledge on the ridge. I am sure that there will be avalanches at some point, I hope on the other side of the West River.

We smoked a pipe load of weed while hiking and upon returning did our daily chores.

We planned an early dinner of rice and smoked fish, trout I think.

We are getting ready to sleep.

"I'm hoping for more sun so that we may spend more time outside. This cabin is driving me nuts." George grumbled.

\* \* \*

Two days hence, the sun was radiant for a third day in a row. Having made the decision to cook a meal outside for a change, we dug a hole in the snow, 18 inches deep, and then lined it with green tree branches. We put rocks on top of the branches. Next we erected a frame to hold a spindle and built a fire.

We piled the wood on and had an impressive blaze going. After allowing the flames to die down to coals, we cooked a portion of venison.

I love the sound of the fire spitting as drops of fat fall into it. The smell of cooking meat fills the air, and it is something I won't forget.

In our winter paradise, all remains peaceful.

I recollect that when the first snow came, I was apprehensive about how things would work out. But somewhere along the way, I let go of the stress and worry, and today, being isolated and stuck here is not something that we fear in the least. We fit into the norms of nature.

Both George and I have decided that when the time comes, we will observe Christmas with a tree (of which there are plenty), which we will trim with handmade ornaments created from pinecones or wood. I carried beads with me, so we will use those as well.

George and I have agreed to exchange a single gift in the spirit of the day. I will make George an antler-handled knife as a gift. I brought six throwing knives, and I will use one of those.

The venison roasted for two hours and was a wonderful, filling meal. We had some left, which I put in the tree box. We will re-heat it tomorrow.

What I wouldn't give for a couple of eggs!

\* \* \*

Today as we approach the third week of October, we are greeted with light snow falling. It is not windy, so this event serves to make the landscape a lovelier postcard.

We take our daily hikes along the escape trails to the West River, succeeding for the most part in keeping the snow packed.

Animals are using these trails to move from one area to another, as evidenced by the tracks and scat we find when maintaining them.

Because of the snow, no color breaks up the vast whiteness. I have persuaded myself that depression will be a partner at times during this never-ending winter, which has us effectively trapped.

\* \* \*

The weather was frigid yesterday and is today as well. The lingering cold has for the most part kept us in the cabin, but our spirits remain high.

Though we snowshoe on the escape trails for exercise rather than ride the horses, they follow us on their own as we hike the trails, and so they too get their workout.

I imagine that it would be more cheerful if we had brought a lantern, but all we have are candles and the fire, both of which provide soft light.

\* \* \*

Three days later, the snow that covers the ground is hard on the eyes when we venture outside of the cabin. We must wear our sunglasses to prevent our retinas being burned by the glare.

Wearing a jacket is mandatory now as the temperature slips well below freezing on most days. While we remain healthy, as do our horses, we must remain focused on their wellbeing. They are far more susceptible to becoming victims of the cold than we are. Our lives depend upon our ability to keep our horses alive. We do what we are able to do to keep them happy, such as putting a blanket on them at night.

\* \* \*

The weather has been milder over these past three days, the sun aiding in making the days more pleasant.

We spent the day doing tasks such as clearing the lingering snow from the roof. After completing those tasks, I washed my hair and sat for two hours in front of the fire drying it.

Our supply of grass is adequate, as is our food supply.

We have many reasons to be satisfied in our cabin in the wild.

\* \* \*

This morning, a dusting of snow fell. With each passing day we feel somewhat more entombed by the weather. In my mind it is always better to be outside, however, risking exposure to the elements forces us to remain inside.

George found tracks at the base of the tree that holds our meat. The tracks were small, so there is no telling what they may have been. Nothing appeared to have been out of place.

\* \* \*

A cold front pushed through late yesterday, carrying with it the coldest temperatures that we have experienced since we have been here. Outside, the snow has crystalized, and the ground crunches beneath our feet.

Inside the cabin, we have kept the fire going and have relished the warmth, which translates into security for us. The horses seemed none the worse for wear, as they cuddled close together for survival. We saw their breath as they exhaled.

As is my custom, I washed my hair this morning in the West River, and before I made it to the cabin, it froze. It took two and a half hours to dry it in front of the fire.

As October approaches the end we speak of celebrating Thanksgiving by cooking some extraordinary meal in the fire pit outside. We both feel that this would be a welcome relief to roast something outside and celebrate our own kind of Thanksgiving. The obvious choice for dinner would be a turkey, but we have not seen any turkeys. Among our stores we have a mallard duck, which will work as an alternative.

With more than a month before Thanksgiving we have time enough to finalize our plans.

\* \* \*

This, the first day of November, saw our negligence almost cost us.

This morning, we mounted up and took a ride in the foothills nearby, traversing along the bank of the West River where the snow is not as deep as in the forests.

As we left the corral, George did not close the corral gate all the way, leaving the log that locks it on the ground. I was not paying attention, since he was the last to leave it and was accountable for putting the log across the gate to lock it.

We had ridden to the top of the ridge across the West River and had dismounted to view the surroundings. Though at first just a faint din, we heard a horse neighing. Using the binoculars, I peered toward the cabin and could clearly see the packhorse fending off four wolves in the corral. The horse kicked and stomped to defend itself.

I jumped onto my horse and without a word George followed suit.

As we raced down the slope and across the valley, I yelled, "The wolves are at the cabin!"

We drew nearer the cabin with rifles blazing, making a racket to raise the dead.

One wolf lay on the ground, having been kicked by the horse. As we fired, the wolves scattered. We reached the cabin in time to see the one wolf that had been kicked stagger off and join the others. We pursued them, taking shots along the way.

Once we were certain that they were far enough from the cabin, we returned to the corral to assess the damage. The packhorse had puncture wounds on its hind legs, which were open and bleeding. This was the result of one of the wolves attempting to hamstring it.

I could see that George felt bad about what had transpired. He tried to calm the horse. I said nothing, but instead rode in the direction in which the wolves had fled. I rode for 15 or 20 minutes and found no hint of the pack.

Back at the cabin, I found that George had dressed the wounds and waited for me. He apologized for the mistake and assured me that it would never happen in the future. This was not to say that the horse would not have been assaulted had the fence been closed, but it showed us both the consequences of being careless.

We have kept a close eye on the horses and on the horizon, scanning for signs of the wolf pack.

Dinner will consist of trout and boiled rice, one commodity that we are running out of.

This is bound to be a long night of apprehension and guard duty.

\* \* \*

Three uneventful days have passed since the wolves attacked the packhorse. He does appear to be on the mend. I see no indication of infection around the wounds.

We have not seen nor heard the pack since that morning. Happenings such as this one are tough to digest, as the true viciousness involved in the struggle for life overwhelms us. As the astonishment wears off, we realize the true gravity of living among free-roaming animals.

At every turn the potential for death is real.

\* \* \*

I am making this record at the end of a day that brought the wolf pack within earshot. Even as I write, we hear the calls floating back and forth.

George has become protective of the horses from the time when the attack occurred until now and presently leans outside against the wall of the cabin standing guard. Even wearing a number of layers of clothes, I am sure that he must be cold.

It has become evident that we possibly will need to kill these wolves to protect our source of transportation.

They are clever, and they come near to see if we are in the cabin. George noted a lone wolf near the trees sizing up the situation.

We may need to trap a deer and use it to lure the wolves close enough to eliminate them, once and for all.

I do not want to do that, but we cannot think of an alternative plan to keep our horses safe. If it was possible, I would choose to trap them and relocate them, but, of course, that is not probable.

I will cook the meal tonight, a combination of venison and elk meat and some pine needle tea.

\* \* \*

November begins its sixth day today.

George stayed outside safeguarding the horses until late in the night. This morning, I told him of my idea to ambush the pack and asked if he thought that we should proceed with it.

"I don't think we can do much else." George agreed with reluctance.

After debating the subject further, we decided that maybe we could shadow them the next time they approach and chase them much farther away from our lodge. We stupidly assume that they will find a new territory. We both know that the chance of succeeding at this is minimal, since they travel up to 50 miles over their home range as it is. It is more likely that they will keep roving through their entire territory.

We organized our saddlebags with dried meat and fish to follow the pack anytime it returns. Our heavy coats, guns, and extra clothing all wait inside the door.

George thought out loud. "We shouldn't leave the packhorse unattended when we go, so we will take it with us."

He feels guilty for the presence of the pack and indicated that he should hunt it alone. After much conversation, George persuaded me to remain here with the packhorse, and he will go alone to do his penance.

\* \* \*

We did not have to wait long for the pack to reappear.

George and I heard the wolves howling this morning. George saddled his horse and tied some firewood in his blanket, which is on the back of his saddle. Armed with matches and the rest of his goods, George saluted and rode out of camp.

My last bit of advice could have been left unspoken. "Keep a wary eye on the wolves at all times, and keep the fire burning bright. Find a sheltered rock formation under which to sleep, this will limit any attack from the rear."

With that, George vanished into the forest, following the sound of the wolves.

He has been gone for a few hours, and my sole option is to patiently wait for him to return.

It is my intention to keep guard on Canoni and the packhorse.

* * *

George has been away for a full day. A subtle snow falls as I make this entry. Although it is cold, it is not blustery.

I have eaten my daily meal, and in an effort to pass time, am in the process of finishing the arrows by binding the arrowhead to the shaft. For this job I am using pine tar and sinew. I am struggling to keep myself occupied so that I don't worry about George. But I do worry about George, and concentrating on anything else is challenging. I hope the Great Spirit is riding with him.

* * *

Today makes two full days that George has been away.

I feel that it may have been a blunder to let George ride alone against the wolves. Perhaps I misjudged his abilities. Perhaps he has not learned enough to outsmart them.

I am encouraged knowing that the depth of the snow on the ground varies from valley to valley. From previous rides we have found that the valleys to the north hold less snow. Crisscrosses of animal trails lead in every direction and permit easy navigation through the snow. Obviously, if the conditions are too severe, George would abort his mission. At least I hope he would.

There remains nothing for me to do apart from completing the daily chores and wait.

In a few short hours night will settle in, cloaking the valley in a refrigerated grip severe enough to dishearten even the heartiest of men.

* * *

Three days have passed, and I feel a heavy burden pondering if George is okay. The more time that he is away, the more apprehension I feel about his safety.

The weather has stayed cold, though without the snow of the previous few days.

I am of a mind to ride out and find George, but I cannot, for this is his assignment alone.

Today I cleared the remainder of the snow from the roof and cleaned the fireplace. I located a dead pine tree and broke it up to replenish the firewood.

I ran the cleaning rod through my handgun and rifle.

\* \* \*

It is day four, and George has not returned.

Late last night I heard an animal rummaging around outside. Upon investigation I found that it was a fox scavenging for food. I was unable to sleep, so I remained awake, listening and speculating about George.

With the morning came the warming rays of the sun and a new day. I have the feeling that something has happened to George, perhaps an accident.

Many thoughts have whirled through my mind, but it all comes down to his choice to go unaccompanied. I thought of his brother, who predicted that George would die in the wild. Is this prophecy perhaps coming true?

I did not eat at all today, as my concern for George has caused me to lose my appetite. I can only wait, wait, wait.

\* \* \*

We have come to the midpoint of November. I felt less concern for George today for unknown reasons. Perhaps it was the sunshine, which was warmer today than it has been in a few weeks.

At any rate, since the snow has been kept packed throughout the transient storms, I was able to focus on doing chores around the cabin, going as far as adding another railing around the corral. This will make it more difficult for any animal to get between the rails. Any intruder will have to break the rails or jump over them.

To get the trees, I had my pick of those located along the escape trails leading to the West River.

I tidied up the cabin and aired it out. I washed a pair of pants and worked on my arrows.

The owls linger as our neighbors and do not even give us a second glance any longer. They keep us company more or less, hooting on occasion, as if saying hello.

\* \* \*

Today when I woke up, I ambled outside and was greeted by brilliant sunshine and no wind. Today marks six days that George has been absent.

I took a ride using a well-worn trail to the place on the ridge top where we had first seen the wolves attacking our packhorse. As I sat on a rock peering out over the valley, I viewed a hawk flying high above me in a wide circle without effort, as it sought nourishment.

From this vantage point I saw range after range of mountains, with valleys hidden from my view separating them. The background sky was powder blue, and only a few high clouds disturbed the palette. After an hour, I became bored with this and clambered up on Canoni.

I rode in a semi-circle, intent on returning to the cabin. Breaking the quiet was a blast that I knew could only have come from George! I hurried toward the trees from which the sound originated.

Upon reaching the trees, I saw George leading his horse, something unknown tied across the saddle.

I raced up to him, jumped off Canoni, and gave him a hug. "George, I'm glad that you're back alive. How did things go?"

"I'm anxious to tell you, but let's smoke first."

We paced to the cabin, where we smoked a pipe full of weed and then sat back touching the cabin wall.

George finally spoke. "When I left our lodge, I rode straight into the woods, hoping to catch sight of the wolves. The tracks in the snow were fresh and easy to follow. They led north, winding among the trees. Following the tracks to the next basin to the north, I made better time, as the snow there was less than three feet deep. I did not want the wolves to recognize that I was trailing them, so I kept my distance and trailed them until it got dark. I then made camp. I napped fitfully trying to stay on guard, while at the same time trying to sleep."

"I caught sight of the wolves in the morning, half a mile ahead of me, in a clearing flanked by two forested areas. At that point I didn't know if they knew that I was following them, so I trailed them on foot. The fresh tracks in the snow made it easy to focus on the pack."

"Whenever I was able, I hurried my pace to make up ground on them. By afternoon, I was so caught up in the exhilaration of the hunt that I didn't notice how far I had trekked. I thought of you and tore off strips of my bandana and tied them to the trees to ensure that I would return safely.

"It got dark and colder. Shit, my fingers were getting numb. I searched for a place to make camp. I succeeded in finding a downed tree that offered some protection from the snow. I draped a blanket over the tree to serve as a roof. I covered my pony with a blanket and secured the reins to a thick branch. All night I kept the fire going, sitting close, praying to Jesus for morning to come.

"I slept, but only because I was so tired, not because I wanted to. When daylight approached, it was hard to get up. My legs were so Goddamned stiff that they did not want to move. I stood close to the fire and soon felt warmer.

"I saddled my horse and hunted for tracks in the snow. I had no idea how far the pack had roamed, so I followed the tracks, leading my horse. Later, I found the location where the pack had slumbered, five shapes in the snow where they had curled up. Farther along, the tracks split and went in every direction. I assumed that this was where the pack had played tag. The whole area was disturbed.

"It took another 10 minutes to find the tracks, and they led north, farther away from the cabin."

George loaded the pipe, hit it a couple of times, offered it to me, and after I pulled on the pipe once I presented it to George. He then hit it a few more times. "After I found the tracks leading away from the area, I trotted my horse, trying to make up ground.

"One thing I knew for sure. They did not know that they were being followed, or they wouldn't have been playing and relaxing.

"As the day wore on, the weather turned colder. I saw a cave at the base of a rock formation.

"I know what you're thinking, but a bear did not live in the cave. It was unoccupied.

"I determined that this would be the perfect place to spend the night. I started a fire by the entrance of the cave and fell asleep. When I woke up I was feeling refreshed and ready to fight! Let me at them bitches now!

"I made up my mind that I would catch the wolves and deal with them on that day. Picking up the trail was no problem, although the wind during the night had rounded the tracks and made them less evident. I could see no wolves in the distance."

George drank from his canteen. "Farther along, the trail turned west and led me to a frozen beaver pond. On the other side of the pond, the pack had made a kill and feasted on it.

"I dismounted and inched my way ahead, taking advantage of every tree and bush to conceal myself. I crept to within 50 yards of them and lay there in the packed snow, allowing my breathing to steady. I trained my scope on one of the wolves. It moved among the others, and I kept it in view.

"Brother, I decided at that moment that I was not going to kill the wolves since when it came right down to it, I lacked the courage to do it. Everything inside me told me that they should not be killed. That voice within me told me to let them live and pursue another solution, so I aimed short of the target and squeezed the trigger. The silence of the mountains was shattered by my Marlin. I stayed still for a minute to see what the wolves would do."

George took a second drink from his canteen. "Three wolves ran into the forest, each going a different direction. One wolf edged toward me, not realizing I was there and when it was 30 feet away, I jumped to my feet. The wolf stopped in its tracks, staring at me with its tail between its legs.

"I raised my rifle and fired at the feet of the wolf. It snarled wildly and bared its teeth.

"I took aim and fired again. Nothing happened! Shit, I had fired five rounds, and the gun was empty. But the wolf was backing away, turning and running into the trees."

I had to ask George to slow down, as I could not write as fast as he was talking. I wanted to get the entire experience down in my journal, so that at least I would remember it the way he said it happened, even if this did not interest George.

Once again, George lit the bowl and took a hit. "After re-loading my rifle, I thought about following the other two wolves, but it was clear that they were not going to stop until they reached California! I raised my voice to the sky, proud of myself, and let out a loud yell! I had my revenge on those fuckers! Though they now remain alive, it was my judgment to allow them to do that.

"I composed myself and mounted my horse, following the different tracks with my eyes. I rode north through the trees until I found four sets of tracks, where all of the wolves reunited."

George paused for another drink of water. "The way back was difficult going, and I knew that I had to be patient and follow the pieces of cloth that I had tied to the trees. I rode as far as the cave in which I had slept the previous night. There I spent a comfortable night, protected from the elements.

"I thought about my decision not to kill the wolves. I thought that it was as you said, we are the intruders here, and even at the risk of losing our remaining horses, we could not kill these wolves.

"Surely, I reckoned, another pack could take over the range. And would we have to kill all of the bears to be assured that they didn't attack our horses? I was not going to upset the balance that exists in the wilderness that we briefly call home.

"Even though I did not kill anything, I felt like the ultimate hunter! When morning came, I was in no hurry to eat breakfast in a cave, so I mounted up and rode in the direction of the cabin. I left the strips of my bandana in the trees, so I can show you the cave sometime.

"As the afternoon passed, the sun faded. I knew I had to spend at a minimum one more night in the open, so I took my time, striding ahead of my horse, until I found the fallen tree under which I had slept before.

"I stopped while it was still light and ate dried fish." George puffed the bowl back to life with a single ember. "The wind blew harder, the dust making it difficult to see the trail. I thought it best to make camp. Using the blanket, I made a roof and slept beneath it.

"By then I was out of firewood, and everything outside was wet and wouldn't catch fire." George stood and stretched, then reclined against his backrest. "Yesterday, when I awoke and exited my shelter, I found that my horse had gotten loose. It took 10 minutes to find her. She was a hundred feet away, and she stood behind some trees and blended in with them. The sun came out, and I felt better, knowing that I would be able to sleep in the cabin tonight.

"I led my horse by the reins between rides and questioned if I had gotten off the trail and maybe had somehow passed the cabin. Nothing looked familiar at that moment. As it turned out, I had traveled farther than I thought, meaning that I would spend another long, cold night outside.

"Man, I hate the fucking cold at night! Anyway, this morning I rode south and eventually recognized the West River from a distance. I knew that I was home. I fired a shot, and the rest, as they say, is history. So listen, let's eat!"

As George said, we did not eliminate our wolf problem, which was heroic on George's part, but that meant that we would have to defend ourselves and our horses against them forever.

\* \* \*

I was bummed out today because I realized that I have lost my camera somewhere! I spent the morning searching every inch of the cabin and the surrounding area outside. I couldn't remember when I had it last, but I must have lost it on one of my rides. I must have set it down somewhere and forgotten it.

I was so disappointed because pictures of our home and our life in the wild were on that film. Now we have no pictures, only our memories. It is buried somewhere beneath the snow. I can do nothing about that now, and life will go on.

Over the past eight months that we have lived here, we have had no problem securing food and water, which is abundant. We have stayed healthy, and for the most part, warm. The fishing has been consistent, although we have not fished since late October when the West River froze over.

George has learned much and has put that knowledge to use, relying less on me for advice. Together, we have faced danger and overcome it without serious injury. George has twisted his knee on two occasions, which has healed entirely. I have been more fortunate and have not suffered any significant injury.

With the exception of the wolves, we have had few complications with the animals with which we share the land. Outside of being a teeny bit skinny; our horses are fine and happy. Soon enough, spring will come, and the grass will make our horses strong.

\* \* \*

A storm passed during the night, bringing several inches of fresh powder to our valley. The day dawned cold and windy. By mid-morning, the wind had died down, and we scrambled outside for an hour or two, jogging from the cabin down to the West River, thus continuing the practice of maintaining the escape trails after each flurry.

We have gone to some extremes to stave off the dreaded cabin fever, sometimes venturing out while it snows and sitting in front of the cabin for a period of time. We sit there determining if the cold or the cabin is worse.

It does not take long to feel hemmed in when the space we called home is so cramped. I think that this is a cumulative thing. It has built up over the months, and when we were forced to be inside for days on end, we felt uncomfortable. What we wouldn't have given to have a third person around to offer a third opinion, to tell stories we didn't yet know.

Our space would have seemed smaller with a third person, though we knew that we would have built a more significant cabin had a third person made the trek with us. I supposed that this feeling was magnified by the dreary, overcast sky inspired by the storm.

It was hard to rid ourselves of the gloom, so we talked about anything that we haven't already talked about.

For dinner George is roasting venison and a can of peas.

The stock of food that we carried in with us is dwindling.

\* \* \*

Late last night, an avalanche occurred across the West River, upstream of our position a quarter of a mile.

The night was quiet, and then the earth reverberated. We both sat upright and reached for our guns. My first thought was that it was an earthquake, but it was not. The noise grew louder and louder as seconds passed. After what had to be a full 15 seconds, quiet prevailed.

We dressed and went outside to view the damage, but it was too dark to see anything. We went back to sleep.

This morning we climbed to the rock formation behind the cabin and scanned the valley. We were staggered to see that the damage caused by the avalanche was so extensive.

The slide began high up on the mountain. Peering through our binoculars, we followed the path of broken trees and displaced boulders all the way to where the avalanche not only reached the West River but altered the path of it. The snow and other debris forced the water up and out of the riverbed as it flowed around the wreckage, finally dropping back to its original course.

Dead trees littered our side of the West River, and a huge pile of boulders and broken tree limbs rested against the banks. We were fortunate that the slide did not block the riverbed, which could have dammed it up.

This was another event that Mother Nature heaped upon us, in case we were losing our respect for her. We were not!

\* \* \*

It feels like it has been cold and snowing incessantly since we have been here. The nights seem colder now than at any time previously. Our horses are in fair condition, still losing weight as we run out of the grass bundles that we thought would last for the entire winter.

We have, for the past few weeks, been rationing both our food and the horses' food. We have, as is our custom, been eating once daily.

On days when the sun does shine, we allow the horses to wander around, and they manage to scratch up enough food to supplement our supply, but just barely. To be honest, they are a sad looking bunch, skinny and malnourished. They burn as little energy as possible, clustering close together both day and night. Canoni is showing more rib cage than at any time up to this point.

Our own meat supply is down to three sides of venison and perhaps 20 pounds of dried smoked salmon. We can hunt for our food, but the horses cannot.

\* \* \*

## NOVEMBER 26

There's finally some relief from the boredom that we normally endure. Today for the first time in weeks the sun was warm enough to allow us to take off our heavy coats. The bright sun reflected off of the snow, requiring sunglasses and suntan lotion on our faces.

We found a way to have some fun today. We took our rain dusters and rode a short mile to a sloping hill, where we climbed to the top. I arranged my duster on the snow and then sat on it, holding it over my crossed legs. I pushed off and slid down the hill, picking up speed with every foot I traversed. I lost what control I had and tumbled head over heels, skidding to a stop face down in the snow.

I rose, laughing so hard that my sides hurt. By then George had already begun his climb to the top of the hill. His slide was no better than mine, ending with much the same result.

Over and over we raced down the hill. Each run was faster, because the course grew more compact, and we got better at balancing on the duster.

With each run we sounded like kids shouting in unison, "Let's do it again!"

We spent hours playing before returning to camp and taking care of chores. I do believe that we will be drawn to the hill to entertain ourselves in the future.

George and I have decided to cook our Thanksgiving meal in the meadow over an open flame in our fire pit.

We will celebrate Thanksgiving in four days. Our meal will consist of roasted goose and smoked salmon. This is the closest thing to a turkey dinner that we have.

If the weather allows, we will build a fire and stay up late into the night.

George has taken an interest in how the victorious Indians recounted their exploits through dance and mime. He mentioned that he would like to try that sometime. I told him that I would like to do it as well but that we should not tell each other what event we were acting out ahead of time. We will see if the other person can guess what story is being told.

We will try and construct a drum, something to help us feel the beat of our heart. Something to accelerate the trance-like state the drum beat brings to some people.

The elders felt that one goes into a remarkable personal trance when one dances in this manner, and I too am anxious to experience it.

George queried me about the Sun Dance ceremony and what it was all about. I explained that sometimes a man had reason to offer thanks to the Great Spirit for having had some good fortune come to the tribe. He offered up his flesh, his endurance, and any of his earthly possessions. He was sometimes tethered to a pole and danced around it for days in some cases until the leather thongs tore from his chest. Only a great man who loved his people undertook such a feat.

\* \* \*

As I predicted, we already went back to the sledding hill. Though it was a scant 12 degrees outside according to the thermometer, we could not fight the urge to glide down the hill. We found ourselves trying to improve the course by walking in a zigzag pattern, compressing the snow, trying to make banked turns instead of a straight run. We got in a couple of rides before the wind came up and blew the snow around, so we returned to the cabin.

We remained inside for the rest of this afternoon. While we had idle time, we each turned to our respective hobbies. I have a full quiver of arrows now, six in all, each handmade and only needing a final painted decoration, or in our case, berry juice. George is starting a new book today. It is a book about the Korean War.

For dinner we ate smoked salmon.

I make this entry noting that Canoni and the other ponies health is acceptable, huddled close together, their heads facing away from the wind. They are not exhibiting any sign of illness or stress. Enough for now, I will fetch some clean water.

* * *

Thanksgiving in 1976 — a day that we could not have imagined! What I mean is that a melancholy atmosphere permeates this cabin. I would have predicted that George and I would be motivated by sharing the spirit of the day. There is much to be thankful for, and yet it seems similar to any another day.

We did our chores as usual and then placed fresh pine boughs in the fire pit in preparation for cooking the duck. George will roast it using a spindle and rotating the bird as it cooks.

While George worked with the food, I spent a short time snowshoeing on the packed ground beneath the trees near the cabin. As I reminisced about my life up to this point, I recognized that I have accomplished a lot in a short amount of time. I don't ever want to look back and wish that I had done something when I had the opportunity.

Sometimes, it is hard to take time and appreciate things, as there is always one more hill to climb, so to speak.

During my brief stroll, I saw a bald eagle, quite close up for the first time in the wild. It was a striking bird with a huge wingspan. It flew down and passed me at an altitude of 20 feet. Its eyes followed me as it flew by, its dark talons sharp and poised. The majestic bird flew on over the pass and into the next valley. This stately bird is another example of the blessings among which we live and yet another reason to be thankful.

We finished our meal, and despite my expectations, George made the duck taste better than palatable. It was tasty, not at all dry. George and I did have a Thanksgiving to recall.

Over the past five days we have been effectively isolated within the cabin. The cold wind relentlessly blows, and the deep freeze endures. Snowdrifts get deeper by the day in places where it is blown against fallen trees or other obstacles.

The supply of grass that we stored for the horses is now half gone. Our own meat supply is sufficient for the time being. In our view, the worst of it is that the remaining firewood is buried beneath a snowdrift. We will be forced to dig it up as we use it, something that we had not considered when we stored it.

We have no way of knowing how much longer the cold and snow will go on. Something has got to change, or we will be in trouble. There remains more winter than food, and that is not good. We have not yet reached December, and we can feel the burden of the long enduring winter staring us in the face. We do not have many options when it comes to food for our horses. What remains is what they will survive on for at least three months.

* * *

November has expired, and today is December first.

This morning we awoke to find freezing fog dressing the landscape, producing an eerie, unseen, silent presence. We heard not a sound from the surrounding forest.

Visibility was 50 feet, if that. A light mist draped ice over the already heavy branches and boulders below. Icicles hung from many of the tree branches.

The scene reminded me of when I was young and lived near the ocean. My sisters and I played hide and seek on nights when the fog rolled in. Today I wondered what might be hiding in the fog.

By noon the veil of fog had lifted, and a blend of sun and clouds dominated the rest of the day. The top of the mountains remained shrouded all day.

We ate smoked salmon for lunch today and had a cup of pine needle tea. Canoni and the other horses are safe and seem to tolerate the ongoing cold, thankfully!

* * *

Three days later we were greeted by another blanket of fog and an accompanying icy mist. These long dreary days keep us inside for the majority of time, forcing us to find ways to entertain ourselves. While we are both entirely bored we find relief in playing cards or Stratego. Everything else remains the same. We long for the return of the sun.

* * *

This morning the sun broke through a thin layer of clouds and warmed the earth a bit, but not to the point where we could take off our heavy jackets. This is the first time we have seen the sun in a week.

The sunshine obviously perked up our spirits, and for a while we sat outside and absorbed the rays shining down upon us.

The moon rose full and bright this evening, something I love to see whenever possible. The snow seemed so dazzling, boasting a bluish hue that appeared to embrace the trees and bushes. We sat outside for an hour taking it all in.

We ate fresh venison for our meal, along with a cup of tea.

I am full now, so now I will go to sleep with anticipation for tomorrow and what it might bring.

In the far distance we heard the call of the wolves, reminding us that it has been a while since they were last nearby.

\* \* \*

The sun has not made an appearance over the last two days. All signs indicate that the deep freeze of winter remains omnipresent.

As the snow flies from time to time, drifts form, and we hike the escape trails toward the West River to keep the snow compressed.

We spent the morning moving snow out of the corral and the area between the cabin and the fire pit. We hope this will encourage the horses to remain calm and feel less restricted.

My Canoni appears skinny, and I feel sorry for her. She looks at me with her black eyes but does not give away her frame of mind. George and I finished work late in the afternoon and led the horses into a clean corral.

Once in the corral, we gave them the daily ration of grass.

They always appear glad to see us and follow us closely any time we emerge from the cabin. It is obvious that they consider the corral their home and us the leaders of the herd.

\* \* \*

Two uneventful days slid by and another dreary December morning greeted us. The thermometer reads 16 degrees, which is the warmest we have seen over the past several weeks.

Though it pained us physically, we completed our daily chores, replenishing the firewood and refreshing the water, as well as hiking the escape trails to the West River.

With a cup of hot pine needle tea, we found a suitable place near the corral to absorb the condition of this land.

The scenery does not change. It is a shroud of white interspersed with green dots.

The wind blew stiff this afternoon. The chill in the air significantly reduces our level of comfort. I feel bad for Canoni and her companions.

With nothing more to write about, I will wait for nightfall and go to sleep.

\* \* \*

Three days have passed agonizingly slowly since my last entry. Snow has fallen off and on throughout the days, dusting the land multiple times.

The horses are healthy enough, and they demand our constant focus and attention. I am thinking that our horses were born in Canada and have spent three or four years in the weather conditions that we now experience, and that brings some relief to us.

George and I raked the snow off of the roof, a task made easier by the light powdery snow that has fallen. After refreshing the water and re-supplying the firewood in the cabin, we spent time playing Stratego. George beat me this time, three games to two.

George then cooked two pieces of salmon over the fire, searing them on the griddle. We eat well considering the circumstances.

George and I have decided that we will celebrate Christmas by exchanging gifts. This will be an opportunity to take part in a familiar custom that will bond us with our distant friends and relatives.

I have been giving some thought as to how I will construct the knife that I am making George. I brought along five practice throwing knife blades, which are just that, a knife blade balanced to throw. I will use one of them and insert it into an antler that is thick enough to encase the blade. I will use pine sap to glue the blade in place and sinew to bind the antler to the blade.

This knife will appear fine as well as be practical.

\* \* \*

As we glide through the mid-point of December, things have pretty much remained the same with snow showers from time to time dropping a few inches of new powder. We respond by hiking the escape trails from the cabin to the West River. The wind has been a constant companion of late, retelling us of its potential, lest we forget.

Our horses are not stressed, and they seem to be content. With each passing day my concern grows that we may not have stored enough feed for them. With no other option, we will adjust to whatever situation arises at the appropriate time. Between George and me, the overriding sentiment is that it is good to be in the warm cabin.

George is on a winning streak having defeated me three times in a row playing Stratego. I don't mind losing, which is a part of the experience of playing the game, and I enjoy learning to make adjustments to turn the tide.

I just faintly heard a wolf howl. I am immediately pulled back to full alert mode, seeing George confirm that he heard it too. I do not anticipate any misadventures tonight.

\* \* \*

The temperature has held steady below freezing, not rising above 20 degrees during the past two days. Little occurs outside of the cabin that either catches our or requires our attention. The semi-daily chores are accomplished almost blindly, as they have become routine.

Our horses remain in decent health to these amateur eyes. Their winter coat of heavy hair does its job of keeping them from losing body heat.

It is a relief not to have to be alert for bears constantly, although the threat of encountering a mountain lion or a wolf is ever present. As stated previously, predators own the long winter.

In general, our home range sports a veil of snow while at the same time ushering in arctic wind that chills us to the bone. High on the mountaintops, one can see snow blowing off the slopes. And so winter lingers

\* \* \*

Four days have inched passed as December rolls by. Our patience is tested daily by the weather. It is cold outside of the cabin, cold enough to allow hyperthermia to set in should we be exposed for any length of time. We find it grim being confined to the indoors, while our spirits long to be outside.

We tend to want to fend off the danger, insisting that it's not that cold while the reality is that it is that cold...and dangerous. George and I cannot be outside for longer than 30 minutes without our fingers and ears freezing. As always we play Stratego and tell jokes and stories to fight off boredom.

It is one thing to read about cabin fever and another to feel symptoms of it. One of the least enjoyable moments occurs when one of us opens the door in the morning to the blast of cold air that grips our valley. We have second thoughts about going outside.

Since we estimate there to be three days before Christmas, we put up a Christmas tree inside the cabin and decorated it, and it is uplifting. We revel in the fresh smell of pine in the cabin, which makes it feel festive.

Despite the cold, George took a ride this afternoon, which allowed me to work on the knife. I cut a nice, slightly curved six-inch antler, and using a rock, I smoothed the edges. I intend to polish it until it is shiny. I have no way of knowing how it will turn out, but I will give it my best effort.

Our horses are doing well. They are alert and do not seem stressed. Life in the winter carries on, and we endure.

\* \* \*

## CHRISTMAS EVE

For the first time in a while we heard the sound of the wolf pack in the valley some distance away as they called out in the night.

Lying in my sleeping bag listening to them was both concerning and stimulating. The night seems longer when the wolf pack is in the area, and last night was no exception.

At daybreak I peeked out and checked on the horses, finding that all was well. George is going to hike to the West River to compress the snow. While he is out I will work on his knife. I need to gouge a slot in the antler into to which to seed the blade. I will use a chisel blade on edge to accomplish this.

I was not able to dig into the antler as I had desired, and as a result, I was forced to cut the antler in half and scrape hollow the inside. Once the blade fit snugly I used tree sap, wood shims, and sinew to hold the blade in place. It looks impressive and will work fine.

For dinner George cooked a piece of venison and the last can of beans. In one way I am glad that the beans are gone.

\* \* \*

Christmas Day we awoke like a couple of excited kids, not knowing what to do first.

We stepped outside to answer nature's call. A light snow, more like ice crystals, drifted down on the soft breeze. This is, I believe, my first white Christmas.

Inside we were warmed by the fire. Candles diffused a soft light throughout the cabin.

We stopped for a moment of silent prayer and then prayed aloud, giving thanks to the Great Spirit. On this morning, it was good to rejoice in the spirit of the day.

I presented George with the knife, and he paused before speaking. "This is bitchin! I'm going to use it as my primary knife."

He in turn extended to me a quiver, made from rabbit skins sown together with sinew. It was fine looking. I didn't think George capable of such craftsmanship.

Today was special and different from the rest of these winter days. An unspoken feeling of camaraderie exists between my brother and me. I will reminisce in the future about this Christmas, not for what I received, but for the atmosphere, the surroundings, and the sentiment inside of me.

I feel certain that this is the mood that all of those Christmas movies try to convey, and it really is a tangible thing.

\* \* \*

Winter is not letting loose her grip, as is evidenced by the temperature hovering near zero during the last two days.

Our horses are all doing satisfactory. Canoni looks healthy, though remaining skinny. They stay clustered together in the corral, shielded by the cabin from the wind.

Spending warm days in the cabin is soothing, but something is missing. Of course that something is family and friends, and we both feel it. My sister's birthday is today and I silently wish her well.

Our talk turns, in time, to those in California, causing our mood to grow gloomier. I think that if it wasn't impossible, we might ride to civilization and celebrate with anybody we could find!

\* \* \*

Four days later, New Year's Eve dawned, radiating light on the last day of 1976. This has been the best year of my life so far. Aside from making a dream come true, 1976 was also a year in which we both grew stronger, braver, more in tune with our environment.

Over the past few days the snowfall has been light, but the deep arctic cold persists.

We cooked an early dinner this afternoon, eating venison. I have eaten so much venison that I think I feel antlers sprouting from my forehead!

Our horses are holding up well, and nothing has occurred to threaten them recently.

We look forward to the year ahead with the renewed pledge of living one day at a time, minute by minute, and striving to live in harmony with nature.

We took the Christmas tree outside and lit it on fire, enjoying the warmth as it burned.

Now we wait for tomorrow, as yesterday is gone and today's light fades before our eyes.

We have neither seen nor heard anything more from the wolf pack in the past several days.

New snow showers pass through our valley almost daily, and as always, we respond with escape trail maintenance and snow removal from the cabin roof.

Thankfully, we have not seen the fabled whiteout blizzards that history shows have struck this region in years past.

This afternoon George took the horses down to the West River, both exercising and watering them.

We can hear the sound of the wind picking up outside. It is a kind of whistling sound that comes and goes. It is our good fortune that the wind blows from the northwest, allowing the cabin and rock formation behind the cabin to shelter our horses.

* * *

**JANUARY 1, 1977**

Outside it is sunny, but the thermometer displays 15 degrees.

George inquired immediately upon rising this morning, "Who is playing in the Rose Bowl today?"

Of course, I couldn't answer, but that started a long conversation about the many bowl games that we would miss watching today. In years past George and I watched all of the major games along with his brother and friends. Everyone brought food or drinks. By the end of the day the place was pulsating from the noise.

Yes, we are missing the entertainment of the college bowl season, but tomorrow I will open the door and appreciate this lovely land while our friends must go to their job.

I am not the kind of person who makes resolutions at the start of the year. It seems to me that if a man lives his life the way the lord says he should, there would be no need for a resolve to do anything. We are expected to comfort those resolvers as we see them fall off the wagon and revert to familiar ways.

Like many other things that man finds challenging, committing to change is comparable to climbing Mount Everest.

George and I took the horses and hiked around the escape trails and then in the meadow near the cabin.

George sighted a snowshoe hare, which he brought down for dinner. I sit now in elated anticipation of eating something other than venison.

It felt good to be outside the cabin for a while, even in 15-degree weather. Every live thing saw their breath turned to vapor in the cold air.

After finishing our hike, George and I cleaned the fireplace, where he is now preparing the fare.

I am entering this note as a reminder of how grand our meal tasted! I can't describe the flavor, but believe me; the difference between hare and venison is like night and day.

\* \* \*

The weather refuses to be pleasant; rather seeming determined to keep us penned inside the lodge for the last three days.

A deeper cold has engulfed the surrounding countryside, and all forms of life wait for a change, as the environment is brutal.

George has gone outside to build a fire in the corral for the horses. As I glance out the door I see that he has been successful, as he is currently immersed in smoke as he blows the grass into a flame.

Canoni and the other horses stare at him in wonder. The word that best describes our home is frigid.

\* \* \*

I know that it is a cop-out to describe the weather as monotonous, but what we have here is the textbook description of monotonous. Day after day it is cold, and when we think we have felt the worst, it gets colder.

We try to find both a reason and a way to make it from one day to the next. We must fill our minds with busy work to pass the time sanely inside. Outside we must find shelter from the cold. We were blessed to snare a hare near the West River, and so we will relish a tasty meal tonight.

\* \* \*

We are outside the cabin soaking in the crisp morning air. I hear a crow in the distance cawing at some annoyance. Closing my eyes and inhaling deeply, I could feel the fresh mountain air bring life into my body. George sits on his saddle to my right sipping on a cup of pine needle tea, the steam visible above the rim of the cup in the frosty air, and a cigarette in his other hand.

On this morning I send my voice to the Great Spirit and ask him to keep us safe and healthy. I ask that he bring game and birds into our valley. I ask for the wisdom and logic to survive, as we have survived so far. I ask that he keep watch over our horses and keep them safe from predators. I ask that he walk with George and me along each step of this arduous journey.

It is now evening, we have completed our meal and played a game of Stratego, and George took this one.

The wind is picking up in intensity, and we hear it through the door. Falling asleep will not be easy this night.

\* \* \*

Indeed sleep did not come easy last evening. At first I lay awake watching the shadows bounce off the walls, and then I lay awake listening to George snore, the sound of the whipping wind tossed in for good measure. I have no sense of when I fell asleep, but I was drained this morning.

We went about our normal routine; finishing mid-morning we opted to go for a ride.

We rode north along the West River in the direction of the Driftwood River. We did encounter a few animals, a badger and a lone elk standing in a grove of pines.

We circled the meadow near the Driftwood River and then turned south along the same trail upon which we set out. We rode until mid-afternoon.

Upon arriving at the cabin I gave Canoni a rubdown and brushed her flanks and mane. I then placed her blanket on her. I did the same for George's horse and the packhorse.

Since we have been back we are both is a good mood, and our lodge feels peaceful.

\* \* \*

The cold and wind have not slackened at all for the last three days, forcing George and me to stay in the cabin. We have gone out for short periods to refresh the water, replenish the firewood, or answer the call of nature.

Our horses are faring well and do not seem to be anymore stressed than in other recent days. The hours elapse incredibly slowly sitting inside. We try and find the usual things to keep us occupied, such as playing cards or Stratego, but after what seems like days we discover that there is light left in the day.

Dinner today consisted of venison and pine needle tea. I have come to appreciate this mixture of pine needles and water, boiled into a vitamin rich drink that is an option to drinking water. Aside from containing vitamin C, the drink adds subtle pine freshness to plain water.

We try to keep our spirits high but at times find this a difficult chore considering the loneliness that surrounds us. Another night will dawn into another day, and no matter what the daylight brings, we will be appreciative.

\* \* \*

The previous two days of January are now history, without incident, framed in total boredom.

Yesterday late in the afternoon, George and I could make out the sound of the wolf pack in the distance. Over the course of the evening, the calls became louder as they neared. George and I sat up late into the night waiting to see what might occur.

This morning so far we have not heard any more calls from the pack. We did see scat and other signs of the wolves nearby as we hiked the escape trails this morning.

The weather has been a nonstop bitter fan, allowing little relief from the arctic wind. Currently the thermometer reads 19 degrees. At times gusts force smoke down the chimney and into our cabin. We must then open the door and refresh the air, suffering the cold to which we are exposed during that time.

George is preparing our meal, a mallard duck that has been in our store box for several weeks. George has speared the duck with a straight stick, and it is roasting over the fire. After dinner we plan to play cards until it is time for sleep.

Life in this cabin is no easy endurance test, especially for a person such as me, someone who lives to be outside. I don't think that I am going crazy, but the need to get out of this cabin is real and tangible. We feel like hostages in our own cabin.

* * *

During the last three days, the weather did break at least for one afternoon. We were able to spend the day outside yesterday without the fierce wind that has kept us constant company.

We cleaned the cabin and the corral, refreshed the water and firewood supply, and threw the pinecone football around.

We led our horses down to the West River to drink and to stretch their legs. They seem happy. At one point they ran through the snow in the meadow in front of the cabin, seemingly for the fun of it. They all get along well together, which is a blessing for all concerned.

We have seen no animals in the past few days, nor have we heard the wolf pack.

As I write, George is frying venison on the skillet.

With much thankfulness in my heart for the milder weather yesterday, I ask the Great Spirit for another day of the same, however, I have a suspicion that it will not last.

* * *

As we navigate through the ongoing winter, we suffer in the icy grip in which Mother Nature embraces us. No beast, man or animal, should be exposed to the intense, burning cold that cloaks the landscape. The temperature dropped back into the single digits, this morning reading a scant six degrees.

The saving grace during the past week has been the lack of snowfall in our valley. We have done our best to protect the horses by throwing a blanket over them. For the most part they are out of the wind, thanks to the cabin blocking the gusts. They are more stressed, and we realize that they are losing even more fat. We can make out their rib bones when viewing them from the profile view. We ration their food as much as we dare, as we still fear the chances that we will exhaust the supply of grass before winter's end. Our own supply of meat is sufficient for now, although the variety of meat is now limited to venison and a few salmon steaks.

In scanning the surrounding meadows and forest, I see no wildlife.

Our spirits are as high as I could expect given the conditions we face daily. It sometimes seems that the days repeat themselves over and over with little happening to make one day distinct from any other.

So we will go about our chores, have our conversations, play our board game, and wait for this long season to end.

\* \* \*

Three uneventful days have passed and it's now into the third week of January. We have the same concern that we have had for a while now: will the supply of food for our horses hold out until winter ends?

Both George and I feel bad for the horses, as we give them less than they would like to eat. We calculate what we can afford to feed them and still make the food supply last through the winter.

It is not as blustery today as it has been recently, bringing relief to all who reside in this valley. While we can clearly see the wind blowing snow on the tops of the peaks, it is calm in the valley.

George revealed a secret today. "My daughter's birthday is this week, I believe. If I were in California, I would throw the biggest party for her, allowing all of her friends to come to the house and share the cake, games, and memories of the day. I would buy ice cream and balloons to decorate the table. I am sick about missing her birthday. I feel so guilty for not being there."

I chose to let the subject pass in silence.

George is going to cook a salmon steak for our meal today.

Another long cold day persists as we sit in our refrigerated sanctuary hiding from the elements, waiting, always waiting for this winter season to end.

\* \* \*

The pattern of cold and wind is replayed daily. We go about our repetitious daily chores and try our best to make our horses comfortable.

We took a brief ride on the escape trails; both to keep them maintained and to give our horses some much needed exercise.

I have noticed that the crisp air seems to amplify sounds. I heard a limb crack in a nearby tree, and the sound split the silence like a gunshot. It was by far the loudest noise in that second. Immediately after, the silence returned, no sounds carried on the soft breeze. I heard nothing to indicate that life is present, nothing to provide a clear sign that we are not alone in this land.

I know that the most difficult challenge we face on a daily basis is trying to keep our sanity and stay positive while all around us Mother Nature conspires to kill us. She goes about her task ever so deliberately, and we do not notice the cumulative effect of fighting the elements until we feel as if we cannot go on. Depression then set in, unexpectedly changing our outlook on life. I know that we are strong enough to win this battle, but it is difficult to say that I would want to face another winter like this one in the future.

* * *

Three days have passed, and George, our horses, and I forge ahead in our determination to survive this dreadful winter.

A snowstorm passed through last night, leaving two inches of fresh powder across the landscape.

It seems as though every passing day brings fresh doubt as to whether we will indeed survive this harsh season.

Our food supply remains adequate, but we do not feel the same about the food for our horses. The horses lose weight daily; however, they remain alert in the corral.

George brought up an interesting topic of discussion today. "What would happen if we both found that our horses had died? What would be our best course of action?"

"I think that we would have to face the reality of knowing that we would have to trudge those many miles back to civilization. I think we would discover the real limits of our capability by the time we reached our fellow man. But only being able to take what we could carry with us would make for a less than ideal journey."

George chortled. "I don't think that I could walk that far, Tonweya. Somewhere along the trail I would sit down and never get up."

Of course, we both believe that the drive to survive would carry us eventually to our destination. But it is interesting to me to hear George say that he would not make it out because in my mind, if we let even the smallest doubt linger in our mind, it will haunt us at the worst possible time.

In my mind, there is nothing I can't do if it ensures my survival. I am strongest when the thoughts in my mind are positive, constructive ones.

As this day wears on, I pray for the strength to stay upbeat and to keep only those positive thoughts in mind.

* * *

Over the last three days, the weather has been milder than in recent days, allowing us to venture outside for the better part of the day.

On days such as this where the sun is shining and the wind is light, we find our chores to be more entertaining. We donned our sunglasses, hats and jackets and joyfully hiked the escape trails to the West River.

We have heard crows in the trees for the first time in a month at least. Their loud obnoxious calls actually are welcome, assuring us that we are not alone today. Even the horses seem to be engaged this day as they wander around the meadow in front of the cabin, making their way to the remaining grass supply. We allowed them to feed as they wished on this day, let them get their fill for a change. While we may indeed regret this in the future, I believe that to make them contented for one day is not the worst thing we can do.

George and I will eat venison for our meal today, a fare that is increasingly wearisome.

I estimate that I weigh somewhere in the neighborhood of 150 pounds. I have lost weight, at least 10 pounds, as evidenced by the fact that my Levis would now fall to my feet if I didn't tighten my belt. George too has dropped much more weight than I and probably weighs 240 pounds.

We will endeavor to outlast the boredom and hunger that seems to be our lot in life.

* * *

## FEBRUARY 1

No indication of fair weather is in sight. The weather has stayed mild, with the temperature at 35 to 40 degrees during the day and sinking well below freezing at night. Our horses seem to be maintaining their weight for the time being.

We spent two hours outside today, hiking the escape trails. While at the water's edge, George discovered a doe some 100 yards away, across the frozen West River. He took aim and in that moment provided us another week or two of meat.

Around us we see nothing to indicate that this season will end anytime soon. I can honestly say that I have never been so happy to spend time in the elements as I am on days like this when the sun is warm enough to remain outside of the cabin for a few hours.

George and I worked up a sweat as we burned energy tossing the pinecone football around. We have taken care of the required chores and are now inside the cabin, George cooking our meal while I make this entry in the journal.

The overwhelming feeling in this cabin is our yearning for the weather to warm up and for life to return to our valley.

\* \* \*

We've had three mild days and we took advantage the weather today by hiking on the escape trails.

We led our horses to the water and allowed them to drink, though they did not seem to need water. Our horses appear lean, and I use that word generously. Both George and I feel so bad that they have to endure hunger and malnourishment for the foreseeable future.

We then paced through the meadow south of the cabin, compacting the few inches of new snow that has fallen over the past few days.

Our food stock is adequate, and we do not fear starvation.

Having taken inventory of our situation, it is clear that things could be worse, so we forge ahead in a manner that will make us proud of ourselves.

\* \* \*

It is morning as I write this entry, and I have been compelled to note that since early this morning the wolf pack has been in the vicinity. We have taken turns safeguarding the horses from a position on the roof of the cabin.

So far we have scared them away twice with shots fired into the air, but twice they have circled the meadow and closed the distance between the lodge and the forest.

George is now on watch as I warm inside.

I am of the belief that the pack is finding it difficult to locate prey, and our horses make a tempting target in their minds. It is unfortunate that the pack may learn a difficult lesson if it insists on pressing this situation.

The days are short and the nights long, so the pack has every advantage. It will remain our most important job to protect our horses at all times.

It is now evening, the end of a long, tense day. After sparring with the pack for most of the day, playing a game of how close the pack can get to the cabin before the humans respond, it would seem that the wolves have lost interest.

Later in the afternoon they simply jogged into the forest as if they had never seen us.

George and I have made the decision to keep a fire going in the corral and guard our interests. It is my turn to go out and stand guard. I will write tomorrow.

\* \* \*

Last night was a long, wakeful night, alternately spent in the freezing cold or the warm cabin.

Without the fire blazing in the corral there is no way that we could have spent the night outside.

We neither saw nor heard the wolf pack during the night, much to our relief.

I smell like smoke and feel grungy. I need a bath.

Both George and I are hungry this morning, and so while I fetch water for drinking and bathing, George will climb up the storage tree and get some fish to cook.

I predict that this day will not pass without a long nap.

\* \* \*

## FEBRUARY 8

I observe my birthday. And I can't think of another place in which I'd rather be celebrating it.

This day brings cause for reflection on a young life that has already been filled with adventure that most will never experience.

I have faced danger, which in retrospect, could easily have turned out tragically had I made different choices in those moments.

I feel the presence of almighty God as he watches over me and always provides the right options to see me through the danger.

I have grown up to be generous and logical. I have been blessed with having a good family and decent friends. As I advance to the future I find it hard to imagine anything else in my life that will be as inspiring and fulfilling as this journey has been to date.

How terrible would it be if the highlight of my life comes when I am 22 years old? What will the future hold for me if this is the pinnacle of my life?

George has embraced me and wished me a happy birthday, as a brother would do.

So now it is headlong into the next year of life, waiting with bated breath for this dreadful winter to end.

I am one fortunate and content man on this day.

George and I now feel confident that our horses will not perish from hunger, as we are now past the first week of February, and the supply of grass appears that it will last until the snow melts.

It could likewise be that we are gazing through rose-colored glasses and seeing what we want to see.

I believe in the Great Spirit, and I know that he will keep our horses alive until spring.

I have learned my lesson. We could never have enough food stored for Canoni and her friends. Rest assured that we will not be lazy when it comes to pulling grass next summer.

We were fortunate enough to spy a herd of deer as they passed through the meadow across from the cabin, skinny and scrawny-looking though the doe's might have been.

We were encouraged to see them passing so close to the cabin once more. It has been at least a month since we last saw potential provisions nearby.

Both George and I now sit outside, him reading and me writing. All things considered, today is a wonderful day. We will eat venison for our meal later this afternoon.

I try hard to think of another place that I would like to be, and I come up blank. There is no better place in the world than our log cabin in the wilderness.

* * *

Three days have come and gone and we've relished the slightly milder weather, spending some of the daylight hours outside without our heavy jackets.

The sky has stayed clear, although it is below freezing after sunset.

While out hiking today George found an arrowhead stuck in the base of a tree. There was no sign of the shaft itself, only the head. It appears to be made of some kind of rock.

George and I wonder how old this arrowhead could be, though we think it is most likely from the 1800s.

The fact that he found this artifact encourages me to keep my eyes open for other such exciting treasures.

Over the course of the past three days we have kept our horses fed, and they appear healthy.

We have attempted to maintain our own weight by eating larger portions when we have our daily meal, though at best we have stopped losing weight.

It is our hope that the weather will stay mild and that the remaining weeks of winter pass without haste. Nothing would make us happier than not seeing another snowstorm hit our valley.

We strolled to the beaver ponds directly east of the cabin to check the thickness of the ice covering the pond. It is a solid inch thick, meaning that we won't be fishing there for some time to come.

Our supply of food consists now of venison alone, as we have exhausted the supply of smoked and frozen fish that we set aside. It would be groovy to have a pizza and bread sticks for a change!

* * *

Thankfully the weather has remained mild for the last three days, without the cold wind that plagued us earlier in the year.

George scouted the area on a short hunting excursion yesterday for half the day and failed to secure meat.

The snow on the ground has begun to get harder and icy as a result of the softening and re-freezing that occurs almost daily, although the thermometer rarely rises above 40 degrees.

Most areas along the West River are extremely slippery and dangerous. No longer do we ride our horses to the West River, instead we lead them on foot.

We noticed a few new tracks in the snow around the meadow, most likely deer, judging by the size of the tracks. We have not had a visit from the wolf pack recently, which is fine with us.

We have seen the first two weeks of February pass without any real drama.

* * *

A cold front passed through for the duration of the night. The thermometer reads seven degrees at the moment. With the front came several inches of new snow.

Overall, we adapt to the cold by adding layers under our heavy coats. I will write later.

We have returned from executing our chores. Everything is in order, and we are preparing our meal, which, you guessed it, is venison.

Our horses are fed and watered, now clustered close together in the corral.

Gazing up I see that the sky is cloaked in a dreary gray color, indistinguishable cloud formations drift by in the soft breeze.

Maybe we have become spoiled by the recent fair weather. I, for one, can tell you that I have been over the cold for some time now.

Of course, Tonweya, you do not call the shots here, so prepare for the unknown. As sure as the sun will rise, winter will hang on for as long as it hangs on.

\* \* \*

We were forced to stay in the cabin all day yesterday while a front rolled over the valley, bringing with it severe wind.

After the sun had risen, the thermometer read eight degrees. Add that to the wind chill, and I am confident that it was well below zero outside.

This morning dawned without the storm or high wind, bringing us a frosty day.

We went about our chores and then took some target practice. We climbed the ridge behind the cabin and picked out targets across the West River several hundred yards away.

After we had finished, we trekked around the meadow south of the cabin. While hiking George spotted a fox sporting a white coat, making it all the more impressive that George even saw it.

Returning to the cabin we each found things to do to keep us busy. George is cleaning his rifle as I make this entry. We will eat our daily meal in the next couple of hours and then call it a day.

\* \* \*

## THIRD WEEK OF FEBRUARY

We have begun a new day, and our hearts have been lifted by the appearance of milder weather, which has kept vigil through this morning.

Trekking near the cabin earlier, it was plain to see that the snow has softened in a few places exposed to the direct sun and become slushy.

We can only pray that this pattern repeats itself going forward. On this pretty day, we have elected to take our horses out for a ride. I will write upon returning.

We have come full circle, and I now sit near the fireplace making this entry.

Our ride was actually quite fun with the calm weather. We rode south of the cabin around the meadow there and proceeded to loop northwest in a circle around the cabin.

It was easy to tell that Canoni enjoyed the time, as her gait was one of a pony, a lot of stops and starts. She trotted around as if on display. I would like to see her weigh more but she is acceptable.

The snow in the area around the cabin was disturbed by the ride.

We are now contemplating our meal. Will it be venison or deer meat?

This day was one of the more pleasant ones of this long winter.

* * *

The sun has shone brightly over these couple of days. The milder weather pattern did not repeat itself today but rather brought yet one more cold front, plunging the temperature into single digits.

The snow is icy from thawing and re-freezing over the milder day's just past.

Most of the snow in the vicinity of the cabin has, in fact been compressed, and the escape trails, though icy, are ready for use if needed.

We caught sight of a snowshoe hare as it made its way across the meadow and into the forest beyond.

Our daily chores were completed without incident earlier in the day, so we have no pending requirements of our time.

As a result, George has taken to reading one of his books while I sit and make this entry. A cup of warm pine needle tea makes for a nice afternoon treat.

Canoni is wandering alone in the meadow in front of the cabin while the other two horses stand close together in the corral.

The lethargic pace of winter goes on without pause, making each minute seem longer than it is. It seems like 48 hours make up a single day during the winter. God I am bored.

* * *

Our valley has seen a transformation in the weather as of yesterday morning. The wind blew hard enough to force the smoke down the chimney and into the cabin.

As is the case in this situation, we were compelled to open the door and allow the fresh air to circulate in the cabin. Of course, this let all of the heat out of the cabin, but that is a small sacrifice to make to breathe the clean air.

Along with the wind, this morning brought a heavy but brief snow shower, which left an inch of new snow on the ground. The wind blew all of the new snow into drifts, so we will not be required to compress the new snow.

We bundled up and went about our chores without incident. But we have stayed inside since we completed the chores.

The horses are fine, showing no indication of distress. I have come to admire their ability to subsist in such harsh conditions, even more as they soldier on as their species has done for thousands of years.

As I write the wind rattles the door, and we hear the gusts outside quite audibly. It would appear that wildlife is scarce today due to the conditions. For our meal, George will cook venison over the open flame.

\* \* \*

## FEBRUARY 28

This day dawns to reveal that the weather has become worse. A cold front brought with it a storm that dropped several inches of snow since yesterday morning. The gusty wind has accompanied the snow, making for a miserable day any life form outside.

We tolerated the cold long enough to hike the escape trails from the cabin to the West River and complete our daily chores.

Once finished we wasted no time racing into the warm cabin.

I would guess that there is a 30-degree difference between the temperature inside the cabin and the temperature outside.

George says that he cannot remain cooped up in the cabin much longer. He said while smoking a cigarette that he will lose his mind if he doesn't see the sun pretty soon.

I am truly running out of things to keep my mind occupied as well. I know every single inch of this cabin by heart. A woman would surely be a comfort in this dreary winter land.

What a pleasure it would be to have a third person on our journey. The obvious reason is that another viewpoint could enhance the conversation during days such as today.

We will eat our meal later and retire for the night.

\* \* \*

George has come down with a cold and is slumbering as I write. I threw an extra log on the fire to make the cabin cozier and have some pine needles ready to brew a cup of tea when George wakes up. In the meantime, I will take care of the chores by my lonesome today.

I have finished replacing the water and the firewood and feeding the horses. Outside it is cold and still. I did not hear a sound while I outside.

I hear George snoring rhythmically as he rests. I am not too hungry, and I doubt that George will want to eat, so I will forego a meal today.

An image of my mom and dad comes to mind, permitting me to daydream about them. It has been three years since I last saw them, due mostly to life moving on, as it does for everyone. One day rushes into the next, and before you know it a year has slipped by. I tell myself that I will make a point to get home and visit, but sometimes things don't go as planned. I must say that I miss them both dearly and wonder how they are.

When I leave this place I will go and see them, if I do nothing else.

George is stirring. I will stop writing now and heat up a cup of tea for him.

\* \* \*

Three days later, and George is feeling much better today. He appears to have a spark in his eyes. He insisted that I allow him to take care of all the chores today, since I had carried the burden the previous few days. News of note, it is my youngest sister's birthday today.

The weather has eased somewhat, the sky a clear blue and the temperature at 32 degrees. I sit outside the cabin appreciating the day the best I can.

George took Canoni, his horse, and the packhorse horse for some exercise, riding in the meadow south of the cabin.

I find that it is challenging to be satisfied during the winter, as the weather is a constant roller coaster ride, and the cold never seems to leave us. On days like today, our spirits soared, only to be crushed by the next drop in temperature. I keep telling myself every day that we are one day closer to spring, even if it does not feel that way. I never knew that I could be so mentally tough for so long, enduring stressful times and remaining true to myself.

By that I mean that I my personality has stayed the same. Of course, by mere exposure to this environment I have become better at adapting to the ever-changing world that I face in this untamed place.

\* \* \*

As the days of March scoot past, our spirits are higher with each passing day, knowing that the winter days expire one by one.

The sky has stayed sunny during the day. Gradually, as the hours pass and the afternoon draws on, we see a trickle of water dribbling toward the West River, as all runoff tends to do. Right now it is nothing more than an inch wide and scarcely noticeable, but as the days warm, the ground will become soft and muddy.

Canoni and the other horses unite in the meadow, absorbing the relative warmth, moving around the area in a search for food. George and I have permitted them a full ration of grass each day, and as a result, they do not appear to be losing weight, as was the case only a scarce few weeks ago.

We have noticed the return of some of the creatures that we have not seen in a while, such as a fox that we saw along the West River and a bull elk that we spotted making its way through the snow near the forest opposite the cabin. We also see more animal droppings in the snow. While it is the beginning of March, we do believe that there is more of winter left before spring arrives.

\* \* \*

Three days later, the thermometer read 46 degrees, which is quite warm for a March day in British Columbia. I make this entry as the sun approaches setting.

Around us, Mother Nature directs a growing amount of water towards the West River basin.

As we approach the middle of March, we hope, we wish, we pray that the worst of the winter is over, at least as far as the brutal cold is concerned.

The trend in general is that the heaviest snowfall occurs between October and February, according to the material I read.

George has spent a lot of time with the horses as they wander the meadow in search of grass. He gets his exercise and makes sure that no animals attack the horses.

Late in the afternoon while we ate dinner, a quick snow shower passed through, dropping a thin dusting of snow.

Soon, the bears will wake from their long slumber, and we will become reacquainted with them.

From hours of study at the library, I learned that cubs are born in the den at this time of year and weigh about one pound at birth. The cubs normally remain with their mother for at least three years.

Bears will not be the only neighbor returning that we need to worry about. The wolf pack and mountain lions will also be cause for concern.

\* \* \*

A new cold front delivered light rain to our valley overnight. Things outside are slushy and slippery. The thermometer proclaimed 40 degrees by mid-morning.

We took an hour-long ride and found signs of an elk herd passing through the valley.

Canoni was in a spirited mood today. A couple of times during our ride, I barely touched her flank with my heel, and she broke into a gallop, an apparent expression of joy.

I too reveled in the sensation of speed and so did not pull on the reins. Aside from George, Canoni is one aspect that I relish most about this excursion.

Of course, this season belongs to the wolf. From October through spring is when the pack dominates the hunt. They control life and death in the valley.

\* \* \*

Today, as has been the case this week, the sun warmed the earth. After completing our chores, we washed our clothes and placed them on the rocks to dry. They did not freeze to the rocks, as happened to George last time he washed his clothes.

The horses are now discovering short shoots of grass in the thinning snow-covered ground, but it will be another few weeks before they will see their search yield reasonable results.

We have seen deer feeding on willow buds and other soft vegetation that is beginning to sprout.

Algae and moss have taken root on some trees and other vegetation is growing along the West River in places.

George set out hunting this morning and at noon returned with a fine buck over his horse. He butchered the meat and estimated that the buck netted us 60 pounds of meat, which will see us through the next few weeks. If I said I wish that he had killed a cow, I would not be lying!

As the weather grows nicer, we will have to hunt more often and store less meat.

\* \* \*

Two days later, the rain has returned for the first time in a week. The snow that covers the ground is slick, and in some places objects lie below the surface, making the world dangerous for us outside.

Some snowdrifts remain wedged against the foot of the rock formations all up and down the West River.

We have been in the wild for most of a year now, a fact not lost on George and me.

Family and friends have lost bets with us, as most who knew what we were going to do did not think that we could last for an entire year.

I have devotedly kept up with my exercise routine, and it shows. My body is hard, with little fat.

We have continued our vitamin consumption of 500 mg of vitamin C every other day, as well as 500 mg of iron.

I feel that I am strong enough to face the challenges of the seasons ahead.

Canoni and the other horses took a stroll of their own accord, promenading to the West River, where they spent part of the morning along the bank in search of food. They have returned and now stand in the meadow in front of the cabin.

We will eat a venison steak for our meal today, thanks to the hunting skill of George. We smoked a pipe load of weed as the afternoon waned. Sometimes that is a nice way to end a day.

\* \* \*

As we face the day today, we have one situation to work through. George wounded his right forearm yesterday afternoon when he slipped on an icy rock. We do not think it is broken, but it is swollen and bruised. This is an inconvenience for George, as he is right-handed.

It rained this morning, but then the clouds cleared, and the sun showed itself.

The weather pattern seems to be repeating itself, much the same as we experienced last year at this time.

When we arrived in Canada, it rained almost every day for the first two months before giving way to the summer months.

The grass growing at this time is less than an inch tall, but the horses eat it where they find it without prejudice.

As the snow in the high country melts, the West River rises gradually.

Gone now is all of the ice that had covered the West River from bank to bank. We can hear the rapids from the cabin door.

We are limited now to where we travel, at least with the horses.

They will remain on this side of the West River for the near future. We are able to ride in any other direction than west.

In the afternoon, we hiked the forested area along the West River, north of the cabin, heading to the ridge overlooking it.

The first thing I noticed was the enormous amount of water being diverted into the rocks at the location where the avalanche ended. On the backside of the blockage was a major waterfall, 50 feet tall and thunderous.

We came across a dead elk half submerged in a feeder creek that merges into the West River. This will be food for scavengers over the coming weeks.

As the snow melts along the banks of the West River, we have discovered several antlers of elk that evidently died during the avalanche or by some other ill-fated incident.

Above, we notice more ducks flying overhead. George was able to bag one mallard duck with a lucky shot, something we will enjoy for a meal. George is pretty good at hitting flying targets, better than I am, but he took this shot from the hip as the birds came out of nowhere. As we progresses on our get-away, we steered east toward the Driftpile River, and after 20 minutes we passed the pond in which the beavers have made their dam.

We have now returned to the cabin, and while George cooks the mallard duck, I am making this entry.

I am so looking forward to this non-venison meal!

It is good to be alive. Gone is the cabin fever that we both felt a few short weeks ago.

\* \* \*

Today when we woke up, the sun already shone. We decided that it was so nice outside that we would take a morning outing.

A check on the thermometer affirmed that it was 47 degrees, with a hint of a breeze.

As we often do, we rode below the ridge, stopping to climb the rock formation to scan the valley now and then.

From one such vantage point we peered across the landscape and through the binoculars we saw a herd of elk, perhaps 30 strong, climbing toward the pass on the far side, intent on crossing into the next valley. They were steering into the valley that I wish to explore in the spring.

The entire West River is free of ice, although it is presently moving much too fast to fish or cross.

Upon returning to the cabin, we found deer tracks right in front of the door.

\* \* \*

This morning Mother Nature fetched us a measure of rain. With each day the layer of snow remaining on the ground becomes thinner and thinner. More and more, blades of grass appear, and the hillsides have taken on a light green hue.

George chose to ride his pony, while I hiked to the beaver ponds east of the cabin. I make this entry sitting near the pond.

All is calm on the surface of the pond, and mother beaver is assessing the situation in the pond. Two kits poked their heads up from the water to see what was going on. When the mother noticed me, she slapped her tail on the water, and all three of them disappeared into the lodge.

At this same time on the other side of the pond, a red fox watched the action with interest, its ears perked up and its head cocked to one side.

I observed for a while and will now stroll back to the cabin.

I make this entry sitting outside the cabin. As the snowmelt increases, the West River rises and is now 75 feet across and at least 15 feet deep, swift water that is to be respected. There is no mistaking the roar of the building rapids that were once peaceful.

When George returned he told me of another avalanche that occurred south of the cabin where the West River turns east toward the Gataga River.

Today, up close, we saw our first grizzly bear of the spring. It was late in the afternoon as we stood outside the cabin, close the trees, watching the owls attending to their new owlets.

As bold as it pleased, the bear sauntered up from the direction of the West River. It paced up to the cabin, sniffed at the door, and pushed the cabin door open, breaking the hinges with no effort at all.

George and I both fired shots into the air, which frightened the bear, causing it to run away to the north, not looking back until it reached the cover of the forest.

George has since hammered the hinges into place on the door, pounding in more nails, and fashioned a new lock.

I have no expectations that any hinge or lock will stop a curious grizzly.

We are into the third week of March now, and gradually more and more signs of animals are evident. In the distance across the meadow in front of the cabin, we spotted a coyote that paid us no mind, as it was concentrating on searching for food.

We have seen quite a few squirrels and more birds in the trees. Soon, within a few weeks, the rabbit and mice populations will explode, and the coyotes will fatten up. We will then see the game return to our valley, coming within easy hunting range.

* * *

The temperature has rocketed to 48 degrees, and without wind, it feels quite warm outside.

We rode toward the Gataga River, northeast, and much to our surprise found little snow left on the ground upon entering the neighboring basin. Short grass shoots abounded, and the ground was soft from the plentiful moisture.

It appears that the herds know about this place, as we spied several deer and elk herds along the way.

We rode cautiously, observing the many tracks in the forgiving earth. Some measure of knowledge has been gained as we have now filled in the blanks as to where the game disappeared to over the past months.

After a pleasant ride home George prepared a meal while I gave the horses a rubdown.

* * *

The weather fluctuates between mild, sunny days with temperatures near 50 degrees and daily showers. The temperature drops perhaps 10 degrees when the showers roll through the valley but rebounds once they pass.

From inside the cabin we noticed a dribble of water coming from the roof and will patch it once the rain clears up.

Regardless of the rainfall, I took a ride this afternoon, first going to the pond east of the cabin to check on the beavers, which are growing larger and appearing less like playful pups and more like attentive adults. It is no longer easy to sneak up on the family.

After watching the beavers for a while, I turned south along the Gataga River, scouting for a location where I could cross. Along the ride I caught a glimpse of additional babies too.

First, a fawn trying to keep up with her mama, then downstream, on the other side of the Gataga River, a mother grizzly and two cubs patrolled along the bank.

A number of birds are present now, which were not visible even a week ago, and songs can easily be heard if we concentrate.

I was not able to find a safe crossing on the Gataga River and so proceeded on to the cabin.

I viewed a hawk sitting in a tree not too far from the cabin. It had been some time since I had last seen one, last summer as I recollect.

Upon arriving at the cabin, George informed me that he had caught a trout from the West River, this being the first one this year! What a welcome relief this will be for dinner.

\* \* \*

A funny event occurred worth noting. As is our custom, before turning in, we tossed a few logs on the fire, so that the heat would keep the cabin comfy and the coals would last until morning.

Sometime after he fell asleep, an ember popped and landed on George's sleeping bag. It smoldered late into the night. When the ember burned through, George hopped up and yelled at the top of his lungs, jumping around the cabin like a mad man. I thought the wolves had visited again!

Then I saw the smoke coming off of the sleeping bag and howled with laughter. He showed me the singed spot on his thigh. Once the glowing ember was out, we stood guard outside with the door open, airing out the cabin.

This was the second time that George had set his sleeping bag alight. The last time we went camping in Sequoia National Park, he buried some coals several inches below the ground and slept on them, saying that they would keep him warm. They sure did, and I roared with laughter through my tears that time too.

\* \* \*

As it has during the last couple of days, the rain fell today, light but steady.

Living through the final few days of March is easy enough, with the exception of the rain. We dressed as is appropriate in dusters, rainwear popular among cattlemen, and scampered out and did our chores. We devoted some time to patching the leak in the roof which we fixed by stuffing a piece of canvas into the joint that leaked and heaping natural material from the forest over the canvas.

Notwithstanding the light rain, we took a ride into the forest. I don't mind the rain so much. It is the mud that I don't like. Sometimes, Canoni seems to lose her footing, and for a second, I feel like I will fall off.

The mud cakes on our boots and Levi's as well and tracks into the cabin.

I can hear my mom saying, "Well, if you didn't live in the damn forest, you wouldn't get so muddy. If you're getting muddy, it's your own fault."

We set up a couple of snare traps and will check tomorrow to see how our luck is.

New grass has sprouted throughout the meadow, not yet long enough to consume but growing.

I love the shade of green that the grass displays in the mountains, a perfect touch from Mother Earth.

Our beautiful horses have been putting on weight, which is a huge relief to George and me. Gone now is the constant worry that the horses would starve before the grass grows.

We will eat a meal of venison and pine needle tea this evening. Another day will soon end in this wild place.

* * *

## APRIL 1

George and I have played hide and seek with the daily pattern of showers and partial sunshine during these tranquil days. We accept as true that it is April fool's day today.

This morning a light rain fell, really just a mist, but everything is damp. From inside the cabin George spotted a moose crossing the meadow next to the cabin, most likely heading for the beaver ponds or points beyond.

While the snowmelt at lower elevations is well under way, the snow on the high mountaintops remains, in beautiful contrast against the gray cloud cover. In the distance we hear the ever-present roar of the West River, the rapids tumbling southward.

We will take a ride now, and I will write later.

Having returned from our ride to the beaver ponds east of the cabin, we sit now absorbing the brief ray of sun that broke through the clouds. The beavers appear healthy, two kits following mama through the water, learning the skills that they will need to someday take over maintenance on their home.

Grass grows an inch tall on the now fully exposed soil, Canoni and her mates more content as they graze the meadows. It seems so long ago that we were cabin bound and near the limit of our sanity.

* * *

Three days have passed, and we have witnessed mild weather and sunlit days.

We expect a milder month in April as far as temperatures are concerned. Daily rain showers drop amounts of moisture on the land, but the cabin embraces us, making it so much more bearable than when we were riding into the wilderness last year.

George tried his luck fishing on the Driftpile River today, and he brought home a fine trout, which will be a nice flavor change from the venison that we consumed throughout the winter. George has a flair for catching fish in less than perfect conditions, which I both envy and admire.

While George fished, I rode Canoni south of the cabin along the West River searching for a place to cross. Finding no suitable crossing venue, I looped northeast and visited the beaver ponds.

I spent a quiet hour there observing the environment before I rode west to the cabin.

George and I performed our tasks in the afternoon, and we now sit at the cabin door about to consume our meal.

Long live the approaching spring!

* * *

Three days later, George and I took a jaunt along the West River, following it south until it turns east a mile south of the cabin.

The ground is quite soft from the daily showers, the grass now covering the ground in full.

As George and I headed east along the West River, we spied an elk cow and a yearling browsing without concern for our presence. The baby had not yet lost its goofy appearance, legs seemingly too skinny to support the body, the long face appearing too long for the short neck.

Farther along the trail we witnessed a black bear with three cubs as they moseyed toward the beaver ponds. Mama appeared thin, having recently come out from hibernation. A flock of Canada geese flew overhead at one point, bringing a smile to our faces as we made comments about their fine flavor and made a promise to harvest one as soon as we are able.

Every day brings us one day closer to the sun-filled days of summer. Yet, minute by minute, we never know what to expect from the climate.

Our chores are finished, the horses fed and happy, and we need only eat our daily meal to bring another day in heaven to an end.

\* \* \*

The rain that had been with us for the last three days is nowhere to be found today. It was a picture-perfect day.

We took a ride this morning, but for a change we rode separately, going in different directions.

I chose to ride south along the West River. Though some snow is present in shady spots, the trees hold no snow and thrive. The forest floor is carpeted in grass and moss, creating a display of varying shades of green. In places where the sunlight filters to the ground, the moss appears neon-like.

I heard a lot of noise in the forest, and much of the wildlife that vanished over the winter has returned.

A raccoon chattered at me as I passed the tree in which it lived. Songbirds sang in every tree, or so it seemed. I followed the trail to a location one mile from the cabin, yet I could still make out the general shape of it in the distance. It was like an ink spot in a forest, a dark blemish on the green terrain.

Riding south along the West River, I searched for a place to cross. It would be easy enough to cross on a raft (oh, the memories!), but I wanted Canoni with me.

In any event, I plan to ride in the valleys that lie on the other side of the Omineca mountain range, across the West River later in the spring.

During the past few days, George has appeared a bit quiet, perhaps depressed again. My guess would be he is homesick. He sits or rides alone, which is unusual for him. We normally ride together.

Much of his conversation lately has focused on his daughter.

He came clean. "I feel like I'm caught between two worlds, the slow, ever-evolving world we live in here and the fast paced world where my daughter lives."

He has, I think, become fed up with this place. Or perhaps, more accurately, bored with the routines. I have dedicated myself to staying here for another year, and if George elects to leave, I will wish him well and anticipate seeing him out there in the world at some time in the future.

After we had both returned we ate dinner, which consisted of rabbit meat cooked in a flavored broth along with some greens that George managed to scavenge.

We have seen many different mushrooms growing in the area, but we are not willing to take a chance eating any of them.

# 8

# SPRING 1977

We have been blessed with warm, sunny days for these last two days. We much appreciate it. The temperature at night remains near freezing, but it warms up during the day into the mid-fifties. I think it is safe to call it spring.

Canoni and the other horses are putting on weight, as they graze freely during the day, never wandering beyond our view.

George has remained somewhat lethargic and has done little more than fish in the West River. He has had some success and fun I'm sure, but it is obvious that his mind is in Los Angeles.

We spoke about how he feels, and he said that he misses his daughter and his brother. It was that simple.

I recall the words that he spoke before we left. "I have nothing behind me and everything in front of me."

"I miss the variety of life in the city, the many games that people have to play to get to the top of the heap, the bad news on the doorstep every day. You know, I miss people doing what they have to do to get by. I miss being a part of that hustle." George fumbled with the laces on his boots.

"You ought to listen to your inner voice and follow it, man. If you're uncertain about staying here for another year, you should ride out of this wilderness before summer begins, or you will be miserable during the rest of the time that you stay.

"Even riding at a hard, steady pace, it will take you at least 20 days to reach civilization from here."

Without saying a word, he mounted his horse and rode off toward the ridge, no doubt to ponder his situation. I took the opportunity to ride north along the

West River for an hour, searching for a location over which I could cross. Finding no suitable crossing, I returned to the cabin.

George was still quiet, and I will not push the issue.

Knowing George as I do, my feeling is that he will leave before the end of the summer. I support whatever he decides.

\* \* \*

## THIRD WEEK OF APRIL

There is nothing earth shattering to report. However, as I make this entry I sit with George in front of a spectacular scene.

We rode our horses together to a place a mile south of the cabin, a place that we call Deer Creek because we have always seen a healthy population of deer drinking there. We then followed the creek as it wound its way up a canyon. As we rode, the trail got steeper, and in the distance we saw a frozen waterfall. Water dripped into the creek, and then proceeded to the West River.

Never in my life had I seen anything like this.

Then, as if to punctuate the moment, a large owl took flight from a tree somewhere above the falls and swooped down along the gully. As it neared us, it banked its wings, passed overhead, and turned away. We heard the soft rush of air against wings that have touched the heavens. It was a sight that I will long remember.

Riding farther along, we followed the trail as it curled to the top of the falls. We have been sitting here now for half an hour, admiring the scene.

George is deep in thought. I see the agony in his eyes, torn between the raw beauty of this place and his longing to be in the city.

In all the years that I have known George, I have never seen him in such a mood. He looks tired, his normally smiling face absent this day.

I want to say to him, "Why don't you go visit your daughter and brother. You can come back here next spring."

But I know that that would never happen, mostly because the preparation necessary would be impossible for George to accomplish alone.

We sat in silence until George asked, "Are you going to stay here if I leave?"

"I will be here to greet you, my brother, if and when you come back."

I then steered the conversation to the trip coming here because I wanted to gauge whether George could make it out alone. He assured me that he will have no problems. So, is the matter settled in George's mind?

We rode in silence to the cabin, where George cooked our daily meal of rabbit meat.

\* \* \*

Three quiet days have passed, quiet in terms of both dialogue and weather. George and I have not talked about his leaving at all since the other day.

Today, sunshine flooded our valley, and the entire length of it is now painted green with grass.

George and I took a hike today, and while out George told me a story about his military service that still affects him today.

He told me about being discharged from the army for a drug offense. "I was caught trying to send a package of drugs back to the United States from Japan. Upon being caught, I was court-martialed and dishonorably discharged."

Now, he is only able to get jobs as a laborer or in the trucking industry. It was easy to see how this incident would limit his future.

"During my messy divorce, my wife made me out to be a big drug dealer and user, while in reality, she was as heavily involved as I was."

I have no doubt that this was true. Who do you think the judge believed?

Of course, his ex-wife was granted a divorce, and now the two of them share custody of their daughter.

George was sentenced to six months in jail and dishonorably discharged.

"How do you think that things will be different now, since the same people are waiting for you now as when we left?" I felt that I should give George food for thought.

Change affects us all, but only as in getting old. All else remains the same. If we were less than honorable yesterday, would we be any more honorable today? I am not saying that people are not above redemption, but rather, rarely do people change behaviors that they have grown accustomed to.

Without another word, I motioned to George to follow me. He mounted his horse, and I mounted Canoni. Together we rode to a place that I had discovered early on and to which I have sojourned often. This was the first time George had been there.

This was a place where I had often observed a family of grizzlies as they roamed their territory. They happened to be there today.

From this position, it was also possible to see the entire valley, as it wound to the left and then opened into a wide, flat plain.

I opened my arms wide. "Watch the cubs carefully, and you will notice how insecure they are when they get too far from their mama. They become distressed and are then prone to panic, wailing as they seek her out."

This behavior is similar to the way some humans act when they are faced with ambiguity.

The cubs acted differently when they were in close proximity to their mama.

It is the same with humans, feeling insecure outside familiar surroundings and distressed when away from family.

Once the choice was made by the cub to seek out his mother, his world suddenly expanded, making the old location where he had been seconds earlier seem irrelevant.

"Notice also that the cubs never look back to the place where they were before, not unlike humans, never glancing back once they are on their own in the world.

"Why then should you halt now and regret a choice that you have already made? What will be different from before?"

The talking ceased as the bears wandered beyond the West River and into the dense forest. Of course, we must all do what our inner voice commands, even if it goes against all that is sensible. Never go against your nature.

George attempted to puzzle it out. "What it is about this place that makes you so at ease and content, so inclined to stay?"

My answer was the same as always. "This place is pure, without the destructive influence of mankind. The power of nature brings life and beauty to this place that I now call home, and it is the same force that drives me forward.

"Though this is the hardest journey that I have ever undertaken, it does not seem like a chore or something that I resist. I can see the benefits of my struggles become clearer when I enter a situation I feel at ease in today that would have confused me in the past."

I then invited George to recall the many camping trips that we had taken, to recollect the trash along the streams, how the few animals that we found did not fear humans.

I suggested that he remember the loud, drunk voices of people partying late into the night, the lack of nature there. Nature, that which is natural!

Those intrusions by humans took away all that is natural, and this pained my heart. Here there is the sound of nature, George, and me. Another reason that I will stay, though less important, is that I may never be physically fit enough to participate in such a feat again. For these reasons, I plan to persist here.

George revealed that he feels somewhat the same way, however, he feels as lost in this vast expanse of wilderness that is British Columbia as I feel at home.

Part of me thinks that George should stay here and experience this once-in-a-lifetime opportunity. Another part urges me to send him back to what is familiar.

"My brother, you can have it both ways, if you keep the memories of this place alive in your heart. Even when you are a thousand miles away, or 20 years from now man, you can be transported to this place." I closed the subject for today.

We led our horses to the cabin, mostly in silence, each of us lost in considerations about our future.

\* \* \*

The seasonal rain comes and goes, keeping things moist. George has decided to sleep in, so he will not ride today.

The thermometer reads 40 degrees, which is warm enough to take a jaunt on Canoni. I will write upon my return.

I spent a good part of the day searching once again downstream for a spot to cross the West River. I finally found one where the water runs deep and, therefore, has no rapids. It is three miles south of the cabin.

Many trees line the river bank at this point, and I will cut several to use as a bridge, if I can make them fall in the right direction.

I will carry my supplies across first and then lead Canoni across the deep six feet water, which is 20 feet wide.

I will return here later in the month.

The population of offspring has exploded, as is evidenced by the number of species I saw today.

On the way to the cabin, I stopped to check on the beavers, finding that the family had lost one of the babies. I saw no sign of it anywhere around the pond, while I did see the rest of the family. Nature has thinned the colony.

I have seen many areas of standing water, which later in the summer present an issue with mosquitoes should they not dry up. I have insect spray with me, but the problem with this is that animals are quick to detect the unnatural smell of it and may then locate me without trouble.

I need all the advantages I can get, particularly when hunting, so I will use the insect repellent sparingly.

I have spent some time mapping out a route to take an extended field trip, in which I will go northeast some 180 miles, to a point west of the Laird River, near where it intersects the Alaska Highway. I will cross the highway and then traverse a southerly loop as far west as Tuya Lake. From there, I will turn east and then south, crossing the Cassiar Highway, and re-trace my trail the final hundred and 20 miles to the cabin. I will take with me all of my important, necessary equipment.

Despite his dark mood, George cooked a venison steak, which was superb.

\* \* \*

I have decided to leave on my outing in three weeks. I have advised George of my plan. "Are you going to ride with me?"

"No, I am not going to ride with you Ton, and I am not sure if I will spend the summer around the cabin or return to civilization."

I can only imagine the struggle George that is going through at this time. On the one hand he is here, right now, in this place on the adventure of a lifetime, while on the other hand he feels the despairing pull of separation from his daughter.

I don't know what it is about me that I do not feel that same sense of separation, but that does not mean that I do not love my relatives any less.

I feel sure in my heart that George could never find his way back to our cabin, even if he tried.

I comprehend all too well the prospects that await the careless or preoccupied traveler in the mountains, and I assure you that they are not good.

I believe that George will regret his decision at some point down the line, if only because the reasons why he left Los Angeles will be there waiting when he returns.

Eventually the love and excitement of being with family will be replaced by the return to old habits that may keep one from progressing upward in one's life.

I will awake tomorrow and in foreseeable days among my animal brothers.

A strange dynamic has developed between George and me that is somewhat akin to a marriage dissolving. Neither party wants to speak. It feels awkward to be in the same room. Both parties are either silently offended or offending.

George has been quiet, and it is not in my nature to draw him into talking, so this dynamic goes on.

\* \* \*

April moves forward, taking all creatures towards abundance. Mentally I have organized the items that I plan to take along on my ride, as I explore the unknown. I will return to the cabin later in the summer.

Although the sunrise was specular this morning, the rain is with us as often as not.

The West River has receded a bit, and I feel good about the prospects of crossing it safely.

George and I talked some more this afternoon about his intentions.

This time he brought up the subject. "Ton, I am leaning toward riding out of this place soon."

This is acceptable to me, since it is plain to see that this is what he needs to do.

We mentioned something about meeting up in the city later on, but deep in my heart I know that I will never return to south Los Angeles, and I know that that is where George will end up. Even 10 years from now, he will be there.

Secretly I wonder if George brings up the subject more often now for his benefit or mine. I wonder if he is trying to convince himself that he can make it to civilization alone. I wonder if perhaps he is preparing me for his departure.

In any event, I say little about that subject since in my mind the decision has been made.

George will cook a venison roast for our meal.

\* \* \*

## LAST WEEK OF APRIL

Tonight, we will savor fresh meat, as George killed a deer and will cook steaks over the open fire.

All of my gear is inventoried and ready to be tied to Canoni when the time comes.

For the next couple of weeks I will try and assure George, should he need assuring?

George and I fished in the West River today and had marginal success. George caught one trout that is enough to feed us both.

I feel relief on days that we catch fish or harvest meat, because that assures us of another day of survival. At times when we have a stockpile of food, we feel a sense of assurance.

Later in the afternoon George and I cleaned the corral and refreshed the wood and water supply in the cabin.

As the weather gets better, life is easier on all concerned. George and I only focus on feeding ourselves since the grass is suitable for eating for the horses, and we no longer expend huge amounts of energy clearing snow. On the other hand, we now spend energy moving around our environment in search of food and on defense against our predator neighbors.

George decided that he would take a final ride and make up his mind whether to stay or go.

He will ride the trail that we took when we crashed the raft on the Gataga River. He expects to be gone for a week or less. In the meantime, he asked if I would wait at the cabin until he returns. I have agreed to wait for one week.

I do find some comfort in knowing that there is a slight possibility that George will be here when I return in the fall, if he changes his mind and stays here.

I will leave in one week, regardless of whether George has arrived. The sun has blessed us with warm days, and it is a good time to be alive.

\* \* \*

## MAY 1

George has been absent for those same three days.

The weather has remained mild and sunny, without any cold fronts passing through.

I suspect that George has reached the outer limits of his outing by now. I wonder what his decision will be.

As for me, I have cleaned the cabin, to the point of obsession, the corral is clean, and the woodpile is stacked high.

I snared a rabbit this morning, cleaned it, and hung the meat to cool and drain. Later I will take it down and make my dinner.

As I have since day one of this adventure, I spend as much time during the day as I can observing the animals, as the never-ending cycle of the seasons goes on, taking them from newborn to adulthood, sometimes in a single year.

All around, I see the babies learning simple yet important lessons.

I saw a pup coyote cross paths with a porcupine. The coyote rushed in and darted out, nipping at the curious thing in front of it. But once the coyote felt a quill in its paw, the lesson was learned, the session over.

The coyote will take this lesson with it, as it may save his life. If a coyote got quills in its mouth, it could not hunt or eat, and would, of course, die.

I will cook my meal now and wait for the night to descend before turning in.

* * *

## MAY 3

A storm blew in and dropped a lot of rain in a short amount of time. It rained hard for a couple of hours. It cleared up early in the afternoon, but everything was so wet outside that I lingered near the cabin.

For a while I pondered when George will leave for civilization. I have estimated that he will need at least 30 days to reach any populated city, and if he left tomorrow, he might make it by the middle of June at the earliest. Knowing George, he will wait until the last minute to go.

I have everything ready to load on Canoni, things that I will need as I explore the northwest quadrant of this province. I will take just the essentials with me, as I have only Canoni to carry the load.

Aside from my weapons and a compass, and dried meat, I will take several knives, an axe, a rope, a sleeping bag and my tent, clothing, a saw, and a blanket for Canoni. I have also packed a few medical supplies, and as always, my binoculars. I will hunt for the majority of my meals.

I estimate that the course I have charted on the map may take up to 90 days to complete, so I need to set out in the next few days to be back by the end of autumn.

* * *

This morning, the seventh day, George rode into camp. "I'm going to go back to Los Angeles, Tonweya. I hope you don't hate me."

And with that, it is official.

I admit that I am pained by his decision. But I imagine that a heavy load has been lifted from his shoulders and that he will find happiness. He will leave in the next two weeks.

I told him that I will be leaving to go north in the morning, and with that, it was done. Our eyes met and locked for a brief moment before George looked to his pipe load of weed and lit it.

The trip of a lifetime with my best buddy was about to come to an end.

From now on, I face this wilderness alone. I guess deep down inside, this was what I had always wanted, a chance to test my skills against nature.

I will miss George and will keep many great memories of him with me always until we meet again.

Tonight we talk and say good-bye, perhaps for the last time.

* * *

It is early morning, and the sun is not yet above the horizon. Before I forget anything, I want to make an entry about what we talked about last night.

George and I spoke about the things that we have accomplished here in this stunning land, about the many challenges that we have faced and how we overcame them.

We spoke of the night of the wolf incursion, the terror of that moment, George's hunt, and last but not least his pardon of the wolf pack.

We recalled those predictions regarding our longevity here, and we laughed. We felt tears well up in our eyes as we talked about the small victories, like the first rabbit we snared, the first fish we caught, and the day we shot our first duck on the wing.

We tried to avoid using the word good-bye.

"We should meet back at my brother's house when you journey out of the wilderness."

"Sure, let's do it."

But we both know that I will never return to that place, as I've declared before.

I am ready to slip out the door and follow my inner voice, while George lies sleeping. Good luck, Georgie…

* * *

It is afternoon, perhaps five hours since I left. I am five miles from the cabin. I have reached the Driftpile River and am camped above it. I led Canoni the entire distance to the Driftpile River, letting my thoughts drift. As the afternoon sun dissolves, reflections on a swirling eddy appear as a painting, rose in color.

I will eat venison for my meal and perhaps smoke my pipe and contemplate.

I have thought about nothing but George's decision to leave. I have tried to stay focused on my surroundings, but my mind wanders. I am truly concerned for his well-being and not at all confident that he can find his way to civilization. I recognize that it is not my place to interfere in George's choices. Yet I am torn by not interfering.

As the sun sets behind the range of Omineca Mountains to my west, the final rays of sun streak upward from the horizon to the clouds partially obscuring the sky.

The temperature is mild, and the fire reflects heat onto my face. Soon it will be dark, and the owls will own the night sky.

* * *

This morning, I was up and riding as the sun crested the Rocky Mountains to the east. This terrain is not unknown to me, as I have ridden here in the past. It is hemmed in by steep mountains on either side of green valleys, where water runs everywhere, and plants and grass grow high during the peak of spring. Trees cover most of the valley floor. Snow still adorns the higher peaks.

I rode past a herd of elk and several herds of deer.

It is impressive to see 30 elk moving through the open slopes of the mountains.

I saw small creatures scurry across the trail as I led Canoni. Chipmunks darted about in the brush, curious about this huge alien invading their territory.

Ground squirrels darted from tree base to tree base, seemingly out of control, in a panic. They stopped only to sound a high-pitched squeal designed to threaten me. They vanished into holes in the ground as I passed.

A red fox stalked across an open meadow in search of food. It is good to walk, as sometimes I ride too much and miss details.

I made camp five miles from where I was last night, now near the base of Mt. New. I have a trout cooking as I finish this entry.

I hear it calling to me. I will not keep it waiting any longer.

* * *

I have stopped riding for the day and have made camp 10 miles north of last night's campsite.

I am camped north of the Gataga River, which was belly deep for Canoni while crossing, so that helped me stay dry.

Along the trail today I spotted deer, elk, and a moose.

The weather has been comfortable, reaching the warmest temperature by midafternoon. After tying Canoni to a picket line, I set up the tent and got dinner going, boiled rabbit. The fare tasted bland, but it was filling.

As with other things, I must learn to distill my own fears and not let them overwhelm me, because it is these fears that could cause me to hesitate in critical situations.

I see all around me that the creatures that I encounter know their place in the food chain. Some, therefore, fear many, while others fear none.

I am second on the chain, after the grizzly, and so it would seem that all animals would fear me, but that isn't so.

Is it that I have become so in tune with the Earth that I no longer walk with heavy feet? Perhaps I am Wakan, something mysterious in these animals' eyes, a mysterious thing at which to marvel.

Few animals now seem to dash off, unless I startle them. They, more often than not, stop and study me.

Still, everywhere I go I carry my rifle in hand.

\* \* \*

## MAY 9

I will set off now and write when I am camped. I have ridden five miles from last night's campsite and will prepare my meal in a few minutes. Before I do I want to write a few words about what I have seen today.

In this land it is easy to be humble. I sense little fear in the animals that I meet on the trail, mostly, I believe, because they have never seen a human being.

All of this drama plays out on the stage that awaits me around every bend in the trail. A play in which at any moment I could become the object of some, as yet unknown, life threatening situation, a drama put in motion by my last action, always my last action.

This mini adventure has begun very well for Canoni and me. I see no reason that it should not progress in the same fashion.

Now it is becoming quite dark and hard to see, so I will stop writing and rest.

\* \* \*

I am writing from my newest camping site. The morning dawned with a sunny flushed and steely sky. I packed the tent and rode south, five miles to the Gataga River. It is a beautiful river, light blue water flows, running about 10 feet at the deepest.

It runs smoothly in most places from what I have seen. As I make this entry I am relaxing in my tent after eating a trout that I caught in the Gataga River.

Tomorrow, I will ride north toward the Toad River, taking my time, being vigilant not to tire Canoni.

I saw a moose today, from a fair distance away, but I was still able to tell that the animal was a prime specimen.

As I finish this entry, a stiff wind begins to blow from north to south, right through the thin walls of the tent. I will put a blanket on Canoni to make put her at ease.

\* \* \*

Last night was a long, frigid, terrible night. High wind gusts shook the tent, much in the same manner that George and I experienced before. I estimated the gusts at 50 miles per hour. The gusts made Canoni uneasy, and she moved often.

Alone in my tent I felt little warmth or security, more vulnerable than secure. The wind finally calmed down long after midnight.

As morning dawned, I stuck my head out of the tent to find the clouds hanging two feet above me. There was no point in trying to ride through the fog, so I stayed in the tent for several hours.

Once underway, progress was sluggish, and I traveled a few miles before stopping to rest Canoni.

Out of nowhere, I heard a roar and knew instantly that it was a grizzly bear fight. I jumped on Canoni and rode the short distance to where I could clearly see a sow fighting with a male.

I watched as the sow rushed in, avoiding the swiping paw of the male, to deliver her own bites and blows. Quite literally, bear shit was flying everywhere! The male backed away, turned his flank to her, and cowered away. Mama bear then collected her cub and moved on her way.

I loped to the spot where the fight had taken place and found clumps of fur on the ground, a testament to the violence of the meeting.

After riding another three miles, I stopped, and I am now camped just north of the West Toad River.

Dinner tonight consisted of jerky and water. I'd give anything for a beer right about now.

\* \* \*

As the days creep past, May begins to produce the tiny shoots of what will become wildflowers throughout the valley.

Grass grows plentiful. Gone are the wind and the clouds that had hung around the previous two days.

The air seems fresher than usual. The ground is soft from the recent rain, and abundant bird life may be seen in the trees.

The contrast between yesterday and today astonishes me. Yesterday I felt like I was on the defensive. The fog had draped the land in melancholy, making it difficult to get a clear view of the surrounding area. Today, I felt superior, like the ruler of all I survey.

I rode an easy pace, taking in my surroundings.

The snow on the passes is all but gone, though glaciers may be seen in a few places. All other exposed terrain is either grey or green.

On the side of a mountain I saw mountain goats, their white coats standing out in stark contrast to the granite gray and tan landscape.

At any rate, I covered three miles, after having spent part of the afternoon studying the goats.

I am camped atop a rise in the terrain, overlooking a vast, narrow valley, above what the map shows to be the Rabbit River.

After setting up camp, I fished in a small feeder stream nearby and caught a single fish, which is now cooking over the fire.

I thought about George today, wondering if he has left yet, what equipment he will take with him, and how the cabin will fare in our absence.

My brother is welcome to take anything he desires with him, though he is limited to what he can carry on his riding horse and one packhorse. He pressed me to keep the packhorse, since I would need it to carry meat when hunting. I refused the offer, and I insisted that he take it, along with everything he could carry. He also requested that I keep his shotgun, saying that he would be back in civilization soon and wouldn't need it.

All of the times that we shared rides and had good conversation are stored in my memory, and it seems that something always triggers those memories, bringing them to the forefront of my mind.

\* \* \*

Today I made 10 miles, riding most of the day at a casual pace. I strolled less and sang more to the throng of onlookers hiding in the forests through which I passed.

There came a point at which, after not talking at all for so long, I sometimes did not know if I was thinking or speaking out loud. Perhaps this is a landmark on the road to insanity, but it seemed a strange thing. Nevertheless, I sang loudly, the Beatles' song She's A Woman, to let all of nature know that I can carry a tune.

Today I saw an eagle flying above me, and I called, "Wambli, come closer to me, show me how great you are."

Wambli is the Lakota word for eagle. But he flew on, circling the land, until he was out of sight. It occurred to me that maybe I only thought the phrase and did not speak the words aloud. I then tried to direct my thoughts to the eagle, catching myself and chuckling.

I spend too much time talking to myself and talking to Canoni. I see her turn her ears back when I talk to her, but other than an occasional glance at me she appears indifferent.

I caught a trout in a nearby nameless stream, and I will soon prepare it for my meal.

Canoni is eating grass, her head bent toward the lush morsels waiting on the ground as she glides about.

* * *

Today I was able to ride another 10 miles, along the same fork of the Rabbit River as I rode yesterday.

I saw a herd of 15 mountain caribou during the day, the first such herd that I have seen since last fall. I would like to hunt one during the fall.

Studying the maps, I determine that I am 20 miles west of Muncho Lake and 10 miles west of the Alaska Highway.

I have no intention of getting any closer to the highway, so I will travel in a northwest direction from here. The late spring weather of May remains favorable during the day and somewhat chilly after the sun sets.

Canoni is, in my opinion, feeling like a pony as she plays with imaginary friends, similar to the way she plays with me. Her faking a charge only to stop within feet of me, and then running in a circle, is a conspicuous pleasure for her.

This evening millions of stars break up the dark cloudless and moonless sky. It will be colder tonight for sure, so I have covered Canoni with her blanket and will now gather enough wood to keep the fire going all night.

* * *

This morning began with a glorious sunrise, set against a cloudy, inflamed horizon.

The wind blew, making for a brisk early morning ride. In its time, the sun warmed the land.

As I left the campsite, I shot a duck and will eat it for my meal later today. I saw it waddling along and bagged it on the trail near an unmarked stream.

As planned, I traveled more northwesterly today, away from the highway, which now lies to the east.

Having covered 10 miles on this day, I made camp in a suitable location. I am a hundred yards from the shore of a nameless lake surrounded by a stand of spruce.

I will travel almost due west tomorrow, and to avoid the Alaska Highway, which is located, 10 miles northeast of my location.

Where I have set up camp in is incredible, with tall spruce trees abundant and green grass between the trees.

The shoreline of this nameless lake consists of gravelly sand, and the water is clear enough to see 10 feet deep.

Ahead and to the west lays the Rabbit River, which makes a turn to the east, farther north of my location. I will attempt to cross this river tomorrow, if possible.

I find myself thinking about the future and becoming more and more concerned about hunting game in the fall during this month of May.

In my mind, I play out the many possible things that could go wrong. I guess it is natural to think about every possibility.

There is little chance of me not finding meat and less chance of me letting it get away. So I tell myself to shut up and live today.

As I write this entry, I sit by the campfire with my back to the flame.

Like so many before it, this night will be cool, as no clouds drift in the sky, and neither is the moon present.

I ate the duck for dinner, a fare I truly relished.

Canoni is fine. She finds plenty of grass to eat on the trail and grazes when we camp.

Game trails, both old and recent, crisscross the ground in this campsite.

This could be a migration trail that I have stumbled upon.

\* \* \*

## MAY 16

The day is coming to an end, and I find myself camped on the north side of the Rabbit River.

Crossing the river was uneventful. The water rose to Canoni's shoulders, but she swam across like a champion. I held her tail as I swam behind her.

I am situated west of the Coal River by 20 miles, and the Alaska Highway is a mere seven miles to the northeast.

It has clouded up and I anticipate rain, so I am thankful for having crossed the Coal River before any rain falls.

Along the bank I found it sandy, while farther away from the water the landscape is strewn with boulders.

This kind of terrain is dangerous and makes for slow progress, but it is peaceful and pleasant camped here.

The Coal River moves over a set of rapids a short ways upstream, and I hear the faint sound of the water as it rushes over the rocks.

Many other sounds of nature fill the air, including many bird species.

I shot a rabbit during the afternoon, and it is roasting over the coals as I make this entry.

For unknown reasons, today it took longer than normal to start the fire. But once started, the heat feels good, and the meat smells excellent.

Another sight I caught today was the vapor trails of an airplane, high above the Earth. This was the second plane that I have seen in my time here. I was somewhat curious about the destination and somewhat irritated by the intrusion.

\* \* \*

Evening has come as I sit in front of an enjoyable fire after another full day of travel, a day that saw a taste of excitement.

This morning, I traversed south along the Rabbit River, to scout around. As the countryside opened up and the valley between the mountains widened, I found myself striding among knee-high grass over rolling hills.

I let Canoni stroll at her own pace, and we covered 15 miles.

During the late afternoon, I found a location at which to camp, shaded by thick, tall trees.

I noticed a few squirrel dens around, but nothing too obtrusive.

I had started the fire and filled my canteens and had placed them on the ground next my sleeping bag when out of the corner of my eye I saw a flash of black coming my way.

In the instant that I turned my head to see it, I knew that it was a badger, and in reaction I took a step backwards to increase the distance between us.

My second step happened to be into a hole, which sent me down in an awkward manner.

Straightway I jumped up as the badger snarled and pressed me, with its teeth bared and its head close to the ground.

I threw a rock at it and hit it squarely on the head, causing it to stop in its tracks, somewhat dazed. I used that few seconds to free my foot from the hole and hop up.

I backed away some more, and the weight on my foot caused pain. I fell to the ground. I drew my pistol and aimed at the badger in time to see it scamper off, leaving me sitting on the ground in anguish.

I have since crawled to the Rabbit River and dunked my foot in it to reduce the swelling. It is just a sprain, but it could have been much worse. I have wrapped it in an elastic bandage, part of the meager medical supply that we brought with us on the trek, and which thankfully I brought in my saddlebags. I will have to stay off of it for a day or two.

* * *

It was no surprise that I woke up with a swollen ankle this morning. I hopped to the bank on one foot and soaked it in the frigid water of the Rabbit River. I will not ride today, instead I will give Canoni the day off, and I will rest my foot.

I make this entry from the comfort of the soft pine needle floor covering the forest.

This is an example of one of the dangers that the pioneers faced, an injury that would prevent someone from hunting for an extended period of time.

I have venison jerky and vitamins, so I will be fine.

I am appreciative that it is sunny today. The sun feels good on my face.

Just a moment ago, a flock of geese flew overhead, honking noisily as they passed.

I have one problem. My fire. I will need to gather more wood if I want to have a fire during the night. I see lots of driftwood, which may have to do me. I will do my best to collect firewood now.

Once more I sit near the campfire, having finished collecting firewood. I was able to locate and throw a lot of driftwood into a pile.

I used a hand-fashioned crutch to aid in skittering around.

I have enough wood now to last the night. For the remainder of the day I will sit back against this rock and elevate my foot.

\* \* \*

It is early morning, and the sun has crested the horizon enough to light the landscape. I am unable to ride today and so will soak my foot in the Rabbit River a few times, but otherwise relax.

I will once again have to gather firewood, but that will be my only task. I will wait until later in the day to collect the firewood. The weather so far today is nice, no wind to speak of.

In the distance this morning, I saw a black bear near the bank of the Rabbit River eating grass with its head down. I had my rifle close, but there was no trouble as the bear moved away from my campsite.

Sitting still for the whole day, observing, was much like watching a movie. If I looked hard enough, it was easy to find some creature monitoring me, maybe from a tree, a bush, the Rabbit River, or even above me, silently flying.

If I listen closely, I notice that the forest is a symphony of musical notes sung by the natural owners, the little winged creatures. The important thing is to listen. I know that when I don't hear a sound that is the time to worry that danger is near.

My meal today will consist of water and dried venison jerky.

\* \* \*

Today, I awoke and found that my foot was still swollen.

I will spend this one last day soaking my foot in the Rabbit River and keep it elevated for the rest of the time.

During the night I heard a wolf howl, the first in a few weeks.

This campsite is pleasant, and I will use it for one more day.

I will also eat venison jerky for my daily meal, which I am growing tired of.

Tomorrow, I will ride north and anticipate further exploration.

\* \* \*

## MAY 21

This is the 16th day on this outing.

My ankle is better today, well enough that I will ride. I will proceed to the north as planned.

The sun is intense this morning, the wind light. The temperature feels like it is in the mid-forties.

I will ride now and detail it later.

I was anxious to ride today, after being laid up for the last three days. Canoni too seemed anxious to carry on our adventure.

It is now late afternoon, and I have covered 10 miles. I am camped at the base of the Deadwood River, where it runs into the Kechika River.

I have watered Canoni, freeing her to graze, and I have collected firewood. I am now preparing a meal of fresh-caught trout.

To the south, I see a front moving across the valley from west to east, though it appears to be far enough away that it will not inconvenience me.

While fishing earlier this afternoon, I saw a family of coyotes. A mother and three young pups barked and carried on across the Rabbit River.

The Deadwood River runs swift at this site, so I will proceed southwest in search of a place to cross.

I frequently remind myself to be cautious, to not take any chances, especially when it comes to river crossings.

That voice inside always tells me the correct thing to do in any situation. It reminds me of the problems that arise when I do not heed that voice. I will faithfully head that voice and seek another place to cross.

Of all of the natural occurrences that I experience, I think my favorite is the soft cooling breeze evident along most rivers. It is soft enough to lift my hair yet does not blow my hat off. It is the kind of breeze that I could relax and fall asleep in. Today the breeze is agreeable.

Having eaten earlier, I will put my pen down and enjoy the sunset, the making of a memory never forgotten.

\* \* \*

I rode southeast, for approximately five miles, before I found a place shallow enough to safely cross the Deadwood River. I crossed at a location 30 yards wide and four feet deep at the deepest. Canoni handled this crossing with no trouble at all. Once across, I advanced north for two miles, before stopping for the day. Having found a campsite surrounded by Lodgepole pines I set my tent up in an opening in the forest.

Canoni seems content, as she has so much to eat, and she looks fat again. Water is abundant, so she does not have to travel far to drink. While fishing earlier I was able to land a fish, so I will eat fresh trout for supper.

The landscape has remained most consistent over the past few days, flat land along the rivers and lakes and high rising mountains on either side of the valley.

I see wildlife every few minutes, and when I stop to think about the different creatures, I find myself pondering how these animals remain so well concealed during the day appearing only briefly as they migrate through the valley.

Each has found its own hideaway over the eons past, by evolving and adapting to their surroundings.

* * *

Today is the 18th day that I have been out on the trail. A surprise rainstorm last night released a lot of rain, which has made the ground soft and to a certain degree slippery in areas not covered with grass.

I kept steady my pace riding north today, and according to the map, have positioned myself 15 miles south of the Alaska Highway.

This was a quiet, slow riding day, the sounds of the forest and nature itself dulled by the damp ground.

I covered 10 miles while riding for eight hours. The ride was uneventful, though I did see many birds migrating north, mostly ducks, but also an occasional flock of Canada geese.

I glimpsed a grizzly bear with an older cub, ambling several hundred yards east of me. It was easy to tell the age of this cub, as it was larger than the newborns that I have seen, and yet it was obviously still with mama, which would make it two years old.

It is difficult to describe how it feels seeing a grizzly stroll to within a hundred yards of the spot I stand on, with nothing separating us apart from green grass and a few trees.

As is always the case, I felt a combination of exhilaration, the potential for panic, and the explicit desire to remain unnoticed.

At that moment, I sensed my legs become less steady and the urge to flee well up from within. I always fight those instincts and remain motionless, as an observer of this great predator.

I assure you that there is no more of a raw, punch-you-in-the-gut emotion than to realize that a grizzly bear has seen you.

Swarms of mosquitoes and gnats buzzed above my head, wanting to go into my ears, my mouth, and my nose. To combat this I am wearing a mosquito net over my hat, another item I am happy to have brought.

So far the insect repellent is working and I pray that it continues, as otherwise this whole summer adventure could be miserable. I intentionally made the fire smoky by placing green pine branches on the flame. The smoke helps keep the mosquitoes at bay.

After I finished eating and cleaning up the campsite, I sat back and smoked a pipe full of weed, letting my mind wander, as I took in my surroundings. I watched a beautiful white moon rise in an indigo sky free of clouds. I now sit inside the tent as I make this entry.

I am 20 miles south of the French River and will try to cut that distance in half tomorrow. I will sleep early tonight, happy to wake to another day.

\* \* \*

It is early evening, and I am camped four miles east of the Cassiar Highway. I covered 10 miles today, on this 19th day of my ride. Riding today was like every other day, an adventure movie playing out before my eyes.

Along the trail a coyote dashed out of the brush chasing down what I'm guessing was a rabbit. In the brief few seconds that it was in view, it changed directions several times while in hot pursuit. Later I rode past a moose standing belly deep in a marshy pond, enjoying the bounty of aquatic roots that the pond offered.

My camp is situated on the bank of the French River. This river is flat and slow moving at this location. Many small streams feed into it. I heard a loon calling from the forest somewhere, the sound was such a bummer that it brought me down. I must admit that the call of the loon is one of my favorite birdcalls.

Crickets seemed to be abundant everywhere here, so I used them as bait and caught and released a lot of fish. I caught four trout in half an hour.

The weather was good today, mild, not too windy, and, in fact, pleasant. Canoni, my lifeline, remains fat and content to go in whichever direction I point her.

Tomorrow, I will cross the Cassiar Highway and resume my westward swing.

\* \* \*

I started early this morning, and traveling at a modest pace I advanced five miles in two and a half hours.

I have come upon the Cassiar Highway in a somewhat surprising manner. I didn't realize that I was so near to the road, and then the forest opened up, and the Cassiar Highway ran across my path.

I halted Canoni and stalked forward on foot to the road to check it out. In both directions, as far as I could see, the road was void of traffic. I mounted, and after checking once more, rode across the highway and into the dense forest on the other side.

It was a peculiar feeling, one of anxiety and unease.

Once I had progressed deeper into the forest, I dismounted and smoked a pipeful, calm and secure in my element.

I followed a fork in the Blue River to a pretty knoll on a butte overlooking the water.

I will stay here tonight and embark upon the trail tomorrow. As has been the case recently, trout is my dinner tonight, having caught several of them earlier this afternoon, keeping the largest for my meal.

I wonder to myself how many fish I have consumed since George and I arrived in Canada. I have no idea, but I am growing gills!

\* \* \*

## MAY 26

Today I rode Canoni a full 20 miles. This morning I followed the Blue River as it snaked south and west.

Several times this waterway turns back on itself, making for some curious attempts to locate a trail by which to follow it. As it winds its way to places unknown, it abruptly turns, and I find myself looking over the edge of an incline leading to water and am then required to find an alternate path.

I stopped riding and made camp an hour ago and caught two average sized trout in rapid succession. Having finished eating, I am now relaxing. Out of nowhere, George came to mind, and I wonder why.

I have been busy, and I don't think of him too often, so why today? I imagine that he has by this time begun riding south. I can't help but wonder if he will find his way to civilization. I believe that as long as he rides south, he will make it out okay.

My journey, however, progresses, so I will follow the Blue River until it reaches Tuya Lake.

\* \* \*

This day began with rain and a gusty thunderstorm rolling across the valley. The thunder was loud as it rumbled through the land, bouncing off of the mountains, sharp cracks followed by a boom.

The sky cleared and I completed the day under blue sky, having ridden 10 miles.

I am now camped 10 miles north of Tuya Lake.

The forest has become noticeably thicker since I traversed the Cassiar Highway.

I find myself having to ride a zigzag pattern around trees following game trails. Most game trails are between two and five feet wide, but often they are less than two feet wide in thick forest such as I am in today.

I saw another herd of elk during the day, heading in the direction of the Cassiar Highway.

I managed to shoot a rabbit with my bow today, and I roasted it over the open fire, enjoying my daily fare.

I now sit near the fire writing these details of my day. Soon it will be too dark to write, but at this moment, a touch of navy blue light is smudged in the western sky, and to the east I see stars in the heavens.

I heard a wolf calling from somewhere far to the north of me. I have no fear of meeting wolves here, as they seem distant, yet the call gave me things to ponder.

I am reminded how insignificant I am in this universe.

\* \* \*

Today marks the 23rd day of my ride, and today was comparable to no other.

I cleared my campsite early this morning soon after sunrise, riding south at a steady pace.

As always, I reveled in the scenery as much as the act of riding itself. After traveling for most of the day, I caught the faint odor of smoke on the breeze and stopped Canoni. I surveyed the skyline for smoke but saw nothing. The breeze wafted from the south, toward me.

Moving cautiously, I took a route that kept me concealed in the trees, rather than riding in the open valley. In the distance, I clearly saw smoke rising from the pines. I recognized this as smoke from a campfire.

I turned Canoni west, feeling like an Indian scout and crested a ridge, then rode onto the other side of it.

Once I had a clear view of Tuya Lake, I saw that the smoke came from a spot at the north end of the lake. Using my binoculars, I could scarcely make out a person sitting at a campfire.

I decided that this person was no threat to me, so I made my way down the ridge and got to within a hundred feet of where he sat.

I shouted, "Hello?"

The man cocked his head and cupped his hands around his ears, trying to locate where the sound came from.

"Hello." I waved my arms.

An old man acknowledged me by waving back and then gestured for me to approach.

I walked, leading Canoni into his campsite. It felt strange to speak out loud, but I was long ready for it.

The old man smiled. "Hello, I am Milich."

"I am Tonweya."

We shook hands, and he motioned for me to sit by the fire. I scanned the campsite and sighted a black mule staked nearby, and so I tied Canoni to the stake as well.

This encampment sported a large white tent, the kind one sees in the western movies, typically used by the horse soldiers. It was four times as roomy as my tent.

Milich offered me a cup of coffee, which I gratefully accepted. What a treat after drinking only water and tea for so long.

He was cooking scrambled eggs and asked me to join him in his meal, which I did without hesitation. I didn't ask him what species of eggs I was eating, both to be polite and potentially to not get sick if the answer was something that I didn't want to know.

Milich spoke with a heavy accent, which sounded to me like Norwegian or Swedish. "Where are you coming from, Mr. Tonweya? Where are you going?"

I considered my answer. "I am spending the summer riding in the backcountry, on land that my uncle owns, north of here. I've been on the trail for three days, having traveled from the ranch on the upper Laird River.

"How about you, where are you coming from?"

"I have spent the last 10 years in these mountains, roaming between the Yukon River country and British Columbia provinces." Milich's eyes darted about, as if he didn't want to miss a thing.

Milich's white hair and beard and deep steely blue eyes contradicted his solid frame, excellent for a man 62 years old. He was born in Oslo, Norway, in 1915.

He shared the odor of his mule. His clothes were tattered, holes in both knees of his pants. He wore a thick red wool shirt over red long johns. He also wore a heavy tan coat and thick winter gloves with the index finger having a hole in it. Next to him sat a rifle, a 30-30 with a scope. Hanging from the rifle was a hat that he had made from rabbit skin.

"How is it that you ended up in Canada?" I inquired of Milich.

"I fought in World War II, after which time I moved to Canada and eventually married. My wife died in a traffic accident after 23 years of marriage, and then I took off for the mountains. With my horse and mule, I have journeyed for the past 10 years.

"I like camping in this part of the country because it is a popular trail for hikers, and I meet people from time to time. You are the first person that I have laid eyes on since last fall. I spend the winter months in a chalet that I built on the Meister River, in the Yukon Territory, about a hundred miles north of here.

"How about yourself, young man?"

I built upon the fabrication about spending time in the backcountry as I did not know anything about this man and was not inclined to disclose much to him.

As we talked, I pulled out my gun cleaning kit from the saddle I leaned against and let Milich clean his rifle, which showed slight signs of neglect.

He noticed my bow. "How well can you shoot?"

"I hit a rabbit at 30 yards and took a buck with the bow as well." I didn't want to boast but felt compelled to tell the truth.

He revealed that in his earlier years he was quite good with a bow.

Later, he inquired how long I was staying in the backcountry, and I told him that I was meeting my uncle in five days along the Cassiar Highway.

As I observed this old man I could not help but imagine myself in his place. In fact, he seemed too old to be out in this wilderness alone. I knew how hard it was to exist here as a young man, I couldn't begin to conceive how intimidating it must be for him. The simple act of gathering firewood turns into a chore for an old man.

We spent a few hours chatting, me listening to his life story and his love for the land. Milich, I could tell, was a lonely man.

"Why don't you find a companion in the city and live an easier life, which surely would be better than living here alone?" My curiosity got the better of me.

Milich fired back rhetorical questions at me. "Wouldn't it be healthier to be with people my own age who would care for me? Would it not be better to live in an apartment in the city?

"Other people my age don't care at all about me or you for that matter. They are all too busy trying to reach their next birthday, all the while dreading tomorrow.

"I don't care about that at all. If the sun does not shine tomorrow, who will care? Who is going to care about an old man like me, sitting in an old folk's home? Here I am loved and nurtured by all that I encounter.

"Long ago, when I made my choice to live in these mountains, I made the commitment to die here as well."

"Well, I am going to care if the sun does not rise tomorrow," I replied.

After several seconds of thought Milich retorted, "That is the work of the young, to make sure that the sun rises every tomorrow. You are tasked with saving the world each day so that tomorrow the sun will rise."

Admittedly, I was not at all sure of the point that he was attempting to make, so I did not push him.

Having become more comfortable with him, I would have liked to ask him some more questions, but having told a gigantic lie, I chose to remain silent.

Finally, when the sun dropped behind the mountain range west of us, we smoked a cigar, supplied by Milich.

He picked up a knife that he had been sharpening, which he said was, until it broke last month, a fine hunting knife.

I turned and I dug in my saddlebag and pulled out one of the throwing knives inside and presented it to Milich. "A gift comes to you from the relatives, from the invisibles."

Taking it from my hand, I saw his eyes water, but being a proud man, not a single tear escaped.

He looked at me and dipped his head.

Milich disappeared into his tent and a few seconds later returned carrying a tan burlap bag tied at the top. He opened it and pulled out a metal coffee pot and a cotton bag containing ground coffee. He handed them to me and smiled, not saying anything.

I dipped my head as he had done. Sufficient thanks had been given.

I was joyful that I had made his life better in some small manner, I hope making his days more comfortable.

Having been invited to stay the night in his camp, I set up my tent, unrolled my sleeping bag, and placed it inside.

Five minutes later, I glanced across the fire and saw Milich asleep.

What is sad and interesting at the same time is that tomorrow Milich will be one more memory written about in my journal. I will be a world away.

I am for sure a better man for having met Milich.

\* \* \*

I woke up this morning before dawn and stole out of Milich's camp. Untying Canoni, I led her away into the dark as I took one last look at the campsite. After 15 minutes of walking, I mounted Canoni and watched three miles pass us by. I make this entry while permitting Canoni a short break before we move on. I spotted a bull moose ambling into the forest, after browsing since sunrise, I imagine.

I will recollect Milich, and I ask the Great Spirit to watch over him and provide him with what he needs. It would be good to see him later; who is to say that our paths won't cross at some time in the future. He seemed a humble man who had seen a lot. He did not preach to me or try to convince me of anything.

I can say that he was a generous man and quite sure of himself. During the moment when we exchanged gifts, I felt an emotion that I can't remember feeling before. It was like God was watching me give this stranger a new knife. I felt fulfilled by the act. And his gift to me was beyond my expectations. I think it proved that generosity begets generosity. Karma is what goes around comes around, good or bad.

I will ride on now and write later.

Evening has engulfed the land, and I am stopped for the night. Earlier in the afternoon I came across a stream named Canyon Creek, where I made a turn to the east. I have examined the map closely, and from this point I will not travel any farther south but will go instead to the east, in the general direction of the cabin, which is now 160 miles away.

Today is the 25th day of this ride. I will eat dried venison tonight and drink some of the great coffee that Milich gifted me.

\* \* \*

Today I rode four miles before stumbling upon this fabulous meadow. I have pitched the tent and will stay here tonight. As I scan the landscape, I am encircled by high mountains that hold an ocean of rich green grass in their valleys. I see water in every direction. This is a perfect place to let Canoni graze on the grass. In the center of this particular meadow is a shallow lake that offers her a place to drink.

The grass is eight to 10 inches tall near my tent and taller closer to the lake.

The sun shone warmly the whole day, and it felt like a lazy summer day. As I sit and observe, ground squirrels race from place to place, hurrying to do what ground squirrels do.

\* \* \*

## FINAL DAY OF MAY

This morning I cut across the Cassiar Highway, and I am again east of the highway. The trees are dense in the region since I crossed the Cassiar River.

Traveling 10 hours today, Canoni and I covered close to 25 miles. While traversing through the mountainous territory, as a rule I try to keep in the shallow valleys to make it easier on Canoni. It is less rocky and grassier away from the sloping hills. I found a prime location along the Eagle River to camp, on an elevated rise overlooking the water.

I am not hungry today, and I don't feel like doing anything else, so I will climb into my sleeping bag and go to sleep.

The wind has begun to blow, and it feels cool, but my tent and sleeping bag can easily handle anything that comes my way this night.

\* \* \*

## JUNE BEGINS

This morning I took a bath in the Eagle River. The water was extremely cold, and I didn't stay in it for long, just long enough to rinse the soap lather from my hair and body. Then I hustled to the roaring fire to get warm.

After loading Canoni, I rode on, steering east. Before noon, I came to Dark Mountain, which is two thousand feet high. I covered 10 miles today, through pristine land shaped with narrow, rolling hills and lined with stands of tall spruce trees and meadows of varying sizes.

I detected a mountain lion while riding along the trail. This is the first one that I have actually had eyes on, though on several occasions I have seen the tracks. I would say that this is the animal that I am most wary of, because like all cats, the mountain lion is sneaky and is a master predator.

Farther along, I rode through an area where there had recently been a fire.

Although shoots of grass grew in places that had burned, it will take the next few years for this area to recover and support life.

Once I passed through the burn area, I found myself once more riding in tall grass, which swayed in the breeze.

Riding at a leisurely pace, I covered 10 miles in eight hours.

A late thunderstorm gusted through the valley an hour ago, passing in 10 minutes. I set up the tent and coaxed a fire to life, over which I cooked a Canada goose that I harvested earlier.

My dear friend Canoni is recovering from a run-in with a porcupine that intersected our trail.

While we were riding through a stand of trees, a porcupine waddled onto the trail. It did not budge as we came closer, so I stopped Canoni. Not content to merely watch the porcupine, Canoni felt the need to smell this creature. She got too close, and the porcupine slapped her leg it with its tail, leaving a dozen quills stuck there.

As I pulled them out one by one, Canoni was tense and at times reared, kicking her front legs out, making for a perilous situation. There doesn't appear to be any permanent effect on Canoni at this point, however.

I sit in the tent writing this entry, and my campfire is the only light for who knows how many miles.

\* \* \*

Upon awakening this morning, I checked Canoni's leg and found some swelling. It was drizzling at that moment as well, so I decided that we should remain here for the day. I threw on my duster and scouted around the area to relieve the boredom and then spent some time cleaning my weapons. I sharpened my knife as well.

I am making this entry because of a flashback I had today. Out of the blue, for reasons unknown, I found myself remembering the gory scene in the corral on the day that we found the dead packhorse.

Intestines were scattered around the corral, and a large pool of congealed blood sat in the middle of the corral. The entire side of the animal had been eaten.

What really freaked me out were the horse's eyes, which were locked open wide, and in a word, looked terrifying.

The violence that took place was unrelenting and proved fatal for the packhorse. In retrospect it would have been a better idea to take the horse with us that day, but that was not our normal routine. We never took the packhorses when we went riding for pleasure.

That scene will always be somewhere in my memory.

I took a hike around the area and saw signs of where a grizzly bear had dug into an animal den, earth scattered in a wide arc around the hole. After scouting for a while, I returned to camp. In the early afternoon, I caught a fish and ate it along with some venison jerky. What I wouldn't give for a fully dressed hamburger and French fries!

\* \* \*

I am so pleased with the weather, which has remained perfect, an occasional stray thunderstorm the solitary change.

I am camped in a pretty spot, after riding five miles today. I got a later start than usual, as I woke up hungry, and it took a while to catch a fish and cook it.

Once I did set out, I rode slowly, wishing to take in everything across the landscape. I also wanted to make sure that Canoni did not feel hurried.

I kept my head on a swivel as I rode, wanting to catch every sight and sound around me.

In the distance I caught movement out of the corner of my eye and saw a lynx using the same trail upon which I rode.

Further along the trail, a fox that had found some kind of round object and rolled it along with its paws, pouncing on the object from time to time, entertained me.

My camp tonight is located along the bank of the Turnagain River. There seems to be an abundance of pyrite in the water, also known as fool's gold. This river is aptly named, as it snakes back and forth, with many small rapids. It looks like a good river to raft. The weather was warmer today, and the ground, though soft, was easy to traverse.

Today I heard the faint sound of a bush plane in a valley somewhere beyond mine, most likely bringing in fishermen or hunters. As I rode, I crossed a set of mountain lion tracks, quite large and made in recent days. I did not follow the tracks, as I did not want to leave Canoni unattended. Mountain lions are one of several animals that will track and attack a man.

Fishing in the Turnagain River was excellent, with the average fish being in the neighborhood of two pounds.

Having caught six fish in an hour and a half, I ate the largest one early this afternoon, returning the others to the life-sustaining water.

Since the day still had a couple of hours left, I took a walk, away from camp, to an outcropping of rocks nearby.

I spent some time re-evaluating my journey and my journal. I fear that if this journal was ever turned into a book, or a movie perhaps, few would want to read it, due to the lack of action and excitement occurring from one day to the next.

In truth, I have done much exploring, with the occasional moments of danger thrown in for good measure.

I have tried not to overstate or overly dramatize the events. I have tried to describe things as they are, keeping in mind that I must paint a picture that is vivid yet not fantastical.

This journal would possibly appeal to a naturalist.

Those who hold a similar dream that they failed to act upon in their life might like it as well.

On the other hand, perhaps someone who intends a journey such as mine could view this journal as an aid in preparing for their excursion; use it as a guide for what they might expect.

At the very least perhaps, my family and friends will gain a better understanding of who I am and why I do the things I do, why I believe as I do.

In the long run, though, if I never do anything with this journal, I will have it to read, to re-live these most cherished moments of my young life.

In the darkening sky, far to the north, I hear a pack of wolves howling. I am reminded of how lucky I am to live here for a time.

\* \* \*

This morning dawned to an incredible sunrise. The eastern sky held flame-red billows that reflected the light all along the horizon in every direction.

I took a stroll and climbed a ridge for a better view of this part of the landscape. At the top of the ridge as I examined the amazing colors, the breeze picked up my hair and held it out behind me. After the sun had fully risen, I packed Canoni and rode directly south for three miles before turning east.

I traveled 15 miles in total and the trail led to a lake, which, according to the map, is nameless.

I will call it the Way Home Lake. It is not large as lakes here go a couple hundred feet long and slightly fewer across. At the south end of the lake a stream feeds into it, while at the north end the terrain rises sharply, forming a dam. A stream flows out of the lake to the east. All the way around trees line the lake, evergreens mostly, with cottonwood trees mixed in. A heavy growth of algae rings the shoreline to a depth of maybe three feet. Geese and ducks gather here in imposing numbers, there seems to be constant motion on the water.

As I approached the shoreline, a few deer jumped up from their daybeds and bolted away from me. Several of the does ran back and forth in an obvious attempt to gain my attention. Proceeding to the area in which I spotted them, I could see four perfectly shaped daybeds. As I moved I kept an eye on the does, and I almost stepped on a fawn lying still in the taller grass. The fawn bolted away, joining her herd. I apologized to mama for the near miss and advanced on.

I took one of the ducks that ventured too close to me, thanking the Great Spirit for this gift of life.

I just finished giving Canoni a good rubdown, something she truly revels in. She has performed beyond well for me and deserves my show of appreciation. This day has been superb.

Flowers in the meadow nearby are close to full bloom. Unfortunately, the warm weather means insects galore, so I am forced to swat insects and will sleep in the tent rather than outside, as I would prefer to do. There is plenty of grass, and everyone is content for the night.

* * *

I made a sickening discovery this afternoon. Nauseating both in what my eyes saw and in the thought that the actors could still be in the vicinity.

The day started much like any other as I rode south from last night's camp toward the Cassiar River. The sun felt good on the side of my face, and the forest was alive with sounds.

I rode for 10 miles and then began scoping out a place to camp, which is never hard to find. I set the tent up along the raised bank of the Cassiar River and let Canoni graze.

I grabbed my fishing pole, lures, and rifle and set out to fish for trout in a feeder stream. The terrain along the un-named stream was steep and uneven, forcing me to sneak along skinny game trails at sharp angles. At one point, a large boulder blocked the trail, and I had to scoot around it.

I detected another old game trail arching its way toward the top of a ridge above the Cassiar River.

This seemed like a good vantage point from which to see the trails leading to the stream, and I followed it up.

Just below the crest of the ridge, another trail intersected the one I was on and headed directly to the top of the ridge. As I moved I saw strands of silver and black hair hanging on the trunk of a tree. I spied dried blood and diminutive pieces of flesh along the trail.

I brought my rifle into firing position and scanned the area for any movement. Reaching the ridge, I peered over the top and saw the footless remains of a grizzly bear splattered on the rocks several hundred feet below.

Peering through binoculars from my vantage point it appeared as though the top of the bear's head was missing, as were the paws. I was shaken at the sight, having to coax myself into action.

My heart beat fast as I made my way back in the direction from which I had come. Scurrying along the trail down and around to the spot where the bear lay, I examined the damage to the head. It had been hit with a high-powered rifle bullet, which took the top half of its head off above the eyes.

The carcass was wedged between the rocks. Blood no longer dripped from the body. Flies infested the open skull.

A feeling of dread surged into my stomach as I sprinted to camp, thinking that the killer or killers might be at my camp or stealing Canoni! As I neared camp, I scanned the terrain for any sign of movement. I saw none. I have since re-located my camp across the Cassiar River, which provides a better vantage point from which I may look toward the kill site.

I have spent time thinking about the prospects.

What would I do if I did run into a killer?

I would have no problem shooting that piece of garbage and throwing it down into a gulley, as had been done to the bear.

I will not sleep tonight but will instead keep guard from inside the trees until it is light enough to travel.

* * *

# 9

# SUMMER 1977

As soon as it began to get light this morning I readied Canoni for travel. During the long night, I had a feeling that something could be watching me and not knowing where to look for it. I have decided that I cannot leave this place without finding the tracks of the killer so that I may be certain that we are not traveling in the same direction.

Common sense tells me that a person would head back to wherever they came from, most probably the highway. Since I knew that I would worry every night if someone was nearby watching me, waiting to move against me, I crossed the Cassiar River to search for tracks. It took little time to find two sets of horse tracks, leading west.

It now seems likely that these strangers rode in from the highway to the west and after killing the bear left in the same direction. I will not give chase, as karma will catch up with them and dole out what is just.

I am camped on a bluff, a quarter of a mile from the Tucha River. My dinner will consist of fresh-caught trout and pine needle tea.

The more I think about what I saw, the more I feel disgusted by it. The image of the open skull is carved indelibly in my mind. I try to comprehend how someone could kill such a magnificent animal in such a callous way.

Clearly this act was not one of a sporting nature.

I will not sleep tonight but instead will remain on guard for anything that may come in the night.

\* \* \*

As I sit in front of my campfire, along the same Tucha River next to which I camped last night, now 10 miles farther downstream, I make this entry. I enjoyed riding today, once I was sure that I was not being followed. Numerous times I doubled back on my tracks, and another time, I rode to the top of a butte but found no sign that I was being trailed.

Much of the ride today was in the sand along the Tucha River. A fine rolling vapor has moved in from behind the mountains, seemingly as if a fog wave had stopped in place as it splashed over the mountaintop with mystic gray-white foam.

The common sounds have faded to quiet, and the forest is tranquil. It is early evening as I write, and in the foggy distance a wolf lets out a long, lonely howl, sending a familiar chill up my spine.

I imagine that this sound would bring such a feeling to any man alone in the wilderness. The wolf was well off in the forest and was no threat to me, but still I asked the Great Spirit to help me to remain brave.

Once again tonight my meal consists of trout and pine needle tea. This night I am exhausted and will sleep well.

* * *

I have been more than a month on this exploration.

I awoke this morning to dense fog, the visibility virtually zero. Wishing for a new experience, I rode Canoni into the fog. I used my compass to stay in the general southerly direction of the Pitman River. I want to look upon that waterway.

As I rode today, Canoni consumed her fill of the mature grass that is so abundant at the moment. Wildflowers are in full bloom, adding color to the otherwise green landscape.

I happened upon a grizzly sow and her two cubs while riding today. Even from afar, it is easy to tell a grizzly from other bears by the hump on the back and the curved face. This one was blonde in color, though one of her cubs was dark brown and the other light brown.

I am resting Canoni but will soon resume the afternoon ride. I will write more later.

The ride for today is over, and I am camped on a beautiful rise along the western bank of the Pitman River, which runs swift but is not too wide. Upstream, a hundred yards or so, a set of rapids looked like a good place to fish.

After half an hour of tossing out a lure, I caught a trout. I made a pot of coffee from the supply that Milich gave me, and as I write, I am enjoying a cup.

The trout is sizzling in the pan on the coals, ummmmmm.

The fog that covered the valley this morning is not present tonight, which predicts it will be colder.

From a tree behind me, an owl lets me know that he does not like me being here, repeatedly calling hoot-hoot.

I plan to follow the Pitman River east in the general direction of the cabin while searching for signs of the familiar. Thank you Wakan Tanka (Great Spirit) for giving me this day.

\* \* \*

This day of exploration started with a moment of whew! I make this entry as I prepare to ride so I do not forget the details.

During the night, an undesirable visitor slipped under the not-quite-fully-zipped tent flap and found a warm place at the foot of my sleeping bag, where it slept. It was a skunk.

Beautiful in its white and black coat, yet a most unusual threat. I spoke in soft tones to it, trying to wake it up without startling it. I could feel it stir, and I tugged the sleeping bag up over my head, just in case. To my amazement, it left the tent unalarmed. I am a happy camper! I will write in the afternoon.

I rode eight miles today, meandering through thick forest and absorbing the wonders of this land. I rode under a clear sky, the sun shining bright. I would guess that the temperature was in the mid-fifties. I came upon a lake that looked familiar. I dismounted and moved around the shoreline, and finally I recalled this place. I spent one night here while on my return from the fall hunt with George. I recognized this place on the map as being near the Frog River.

While I rode today, meandering through the trees, a fox and three kits paced me for some time, keeping an eye on me from a hundred feet away. The mother was most inquisitive and kept up the charade. Shortly thereafter, they vanished into the forest and did not reappear.

I am camped along the shore of an unnamed lake. All is peaceful at this time, and the three-quarters-full moon will allow me to see a fair distance once it rises completely.

The moon was considered a great mystery to my native brothers and revered at night in place of the sun. It was considered the female equal to the sun.

At night, the entire sky displayed the way to the spirit trail beyond the pines, where the departed reside after life has left their body. The moon, it was further believed, could light the way to this spirit land. The Grandfathers knew that a particular star person in the sky never moved and that all other star people moved around this one. We know this star person as the North Star, or Polaris.

Enough for tonight, tomorrow waits in the wings.

\* \* \*

This morning the sun rose into a clear azure blue sky, warming the land. I found a place to pitch my tent for this evening and will now recount the day.

After cleaning up my campsite and preparing Canoni, I set out north, in the direction of the Jack Stone Creek, riding at a leisurely pace. Twenty minutes into the ride, I spotted a grizzly across the meadow, which was traveling in the same direction as I was, so I stopped and rested Canoni for a while.

I wanted to let the bear travel far ahead of me. I re-commenced riding through marvelous stands of Lodgepole pine trees, listening to the birds sing as they do. Often I tried to memorize their song and mimic it.

Canoni had a case of gas today and farted with each step she took. In that moment I wished that George was here to comment on the situation with the ghetto-isms that he is so fond of.

After traveling until mid-afternoon, I am now camped along a stream not displayed on the map. It is two feet deep and 50 feet wide. I proceeded to set up my tent and build a campfire ring.

Later, I padded downstream away from the small set of rapids located near the campsite and managed to catch a small trout, which I cooked and enjoyed.

I remain hungry, as one trifling fish is not enough to fill up a guy of my size, five-feet, eight-inches tall and 160, at last check before we left Los Angeles. But I'm sick of eating venison, so I will be happy with the fish.

It is getting dark now, too dark to see by candlelight, so I will climb into my tent for the night.

Canoni seems at peace, as does the valley.

\* \* \*

With the morning light came sunshine and a slight breeze. I rode southwest until I come up to another river that is not shown on the map. I could tell that it flowed from north to south, at least along this stretch.

Out of necessity I followed it north, since I knew that I could always turn south and not miss the trail I used last fall.

Finding streams and rivers that do not appear on the map is quite common and causes concern for me because it makes for unexpected obstacles, such as hazardous crossings and detours, which could, if I am not careful, increase the chance of getting lost.

After riding for five miles, I ventured upon a spot where I could ford. The water was waist high, and Canoni and I crossed without incident. I unpacked Canoni and laid my clothes on rocks to dry in the sun. Ahead of me, narrow valleys feeding in from my right separate one range of mountains after another.

A moment ago the unusual struck. As has been the case since I have been here, I never know when something might happen, and as I relaxed on my sleeping bag against a rock, a black bear strolled out of the trees and advanced on the tent.

I fired a single round into the air and observed the bear disappear into the forest.

I recalled that when George and I were first on the trail we used empty food cans to make a primitive alarm system for the perimeter of our campsite. By running a string through the can and tying a small rock to the string, attached in the middle of the can, we effectively had a barrier around camp. If a trespasser hit the string, the rock rattled in the can, and we knew we had an intruder. We also knew where the invader was based on where the rattle came from.

Somewhere over the hundreds of miles and the places we had been, we lost track of the rig. It would be nice to have it now.

\* \* \*

This morning I woke up to four deer calmly eating grass a few feet from my tent flaps. I couldn't conceive what would prompt them to get so close, but it was okay by me. Once before, in California, I had witnessed this behavior.

After packing up, I traveled onward in the general direction of the cabin, now a mere 50 miles away according to the map. At midday, I was crossing an open meadow and ran across a herd of elk.

I focused on a particular cow wallowing in a bog, obviously tying to coat herself with mud to ward off the mosquitoes. She seemed to be having as much fun as it is legal for an cow elk to have.

I rode until the sun was two fingers from sitting on the horizon and then found this nice spot, where I have set up the tent and eaten some venison.

The Indians of the plains used the above method to calculate how much time was left before the sun sets. If you extend your arm straight out toward the horizon and hold your hand so the fingers separate the horizon and the sun, each finger is equal to 15 minutes. So, four fingers would indicate an hour before the sun sets.

* * *

On this day of my ride, Canoni and I navigate the second week of June, longing to be home. I make this entry while sitting near my campfire after sipping a cup of pine needle tea.

I have grown tired of the routine of sleeping on the ground in the tent; however, riding six to eight hours a day remains the best activity in my life. I rode northeast today, covering 10 miles. I arrived at the Kechika River, where I am now camped.

I look forward to possibly hunting in this area sometime and fishing this same stretch of the Kechika River.

As I travel south, I will link up with the Rainbow River, 30 miles downstream. Once I connect with the Rainbow River, I will be 40 miles from home.

Having found this pretty spot at which to camp earlier in the afternoon, I took a hike through the forest. The mountain range facing me is tall; snow and glaciers reside at the higher elevations.

I peered through my binoculars and viewed a heard of caribou near the top of the highest pass, on a slope exposed to the sun. They were relaxed, with no risk of attack from predators.

The slopes of the mountains are filled with thick stands of pines and evergreens. Except for the few avalanche shoots, gulches that have been stripped bare of trees in the path of an avalanche, there is little open space. A person could spend forever in these trees and never be seen.

I came upon a tree with a hole in the trunk, drilled there by the many woodpeckers that populate this range. The hole was today being occupied by a nuthatch. This tiny bird wore blue feathers above his wings, had a brownish-red chest, and proudly wore white and black strips along his head.

Farther along, I was followed by a group of four stellar jays, which squawked loudly, flying from tree to tree, and keeping pace with me. Rabbits and other animals appear to be abundant here as well.

I really like to hike, as I did today, slow, my ears alert. I feel better somehow, as I have all of these creatures to keep me company. In the distance a thin line of gray clouds is visible.

* * *

Morning has come, and rain falls against my tent. It began early and has fallen harder as the morning has progressed. So with the lull in the day's plan, I now sit inside the only dry spot for hundreds of miles and relax, deep in thought. I'm trying to tune into a feeling that I have had during the past several days.

I'm sure that everyone has thought about someone else at some time or another. Hey, I wonder what so and so is doing? Then you feel it again and then more frequently.

I have that feeling today, and I have no doubt about who is thinking about me or what the thought is. George is thinking about me.

After returning from a hike and hanging up my duster, I had some thoughts concerning perspective, which I expressed aloud. "Who am I trying to impress by living out here? Why is it so important to be here and so what if I do not stay forever? Why should I let the people I care about worry about me? One cannot stop a person from worrying. Where would anyone be if they had no worry?

"I recognize that participating in the activities that I have on this journey is imperative to me. After all, this has been my destiny for many years. I am nourishing a need that lives deep inside of me. It is ingrained in me, but I can't explain it. I only know that I could not have gone through life without having passed this way.

"The whole pattern of my life altered and geared itself to this place at this time. Certainly one cannot change the course of events, nor can one re-live past moments, any more than we can be something that we are not. If I was an alcoholic, I would be drinking in a bar, or if an artist, I would now be painting. I am here today because this is where I am destined to be."

The rain against the tent reminds me that I am not yet finished with the journey.

* * *

Another day is nearing an end. Riding today was not as much fun as usual, as all day long I felt tired, and had a headache for a good part of the day. I estimate that I rode eight to 10 miles.

I set up my tent in the middle of a huge meadow surrounded by pine trees. I am not hungry; I am simply tired tonight. I don't feel well for some reason, so I will go to sleep early. The sun is setting over the mountains to the west.

Tomorrow is another day, so I will turn in now.

\* \* \*

This morning, I rode south toward the cabin, which is now 25 miles away. I found a nice spot at which to camp, under a canopy of tall pines. I am intent on reaching the cabin tomorrow, if possible. It has been almost a year ago that I camped near this place on the fall hunt. Time seems to pass quickly in retrospect but slowly when one recounts specific events.

I am cooking a rabbit over the coals, hoping that George might be there when I arrive, though I have no reason to expect that he will be. He made his decision quite clear before I left on this extended sojourn. This saddens me, but this is how it is.

Tonight the wolves sing their songs to the night, perhaps to the moon. Either way I am entertained by the concert. The sounds are coming from far away, so I will not be concerned.

Dinner is finished now, and it is time to retire for the night.

\* \* \*

I have ridden 25 miles and reached a point above the Driftpile River. The cabin is a short five miles beyond. I have come full circle. I will ask Canoni to give me a few more miles today.

I have let Canoni graze, and I set up my tent two miles from the cabin. She did not want to go any farther. I am chewing on a piece of venison jerky trying to fill my stomach, with little success. As I consider what tomorrow holds, my mind races through the many possibilities.

Night will enclose this valley soon enough, and so I will sleep.

\* \* \*

I rode Canoni to a location one mile from the cabin, where I dismounted. Through the binoculars, I could detect no sign of life at the cabin, no horses, no smoke from the chimney, and no movement. Disappointment beset me, though I knew that it shouldn't have.

I will ride to the cabin now.

I sit inside the cabin making an assessment of my situation. When I rode up and opened the cabin door, as expected, I found that George, and all of the belongings that he could carry, were gone.

The cabin was strung with spider webs, and a couple of mice had burrowed in, as evidenced by the droppings on the floor.

The cabin was dark and cold, a dank smell of dust, stale air, and smoke, which was not pleasant at all, hung thick from the walls.

Having the window and the door on the same wall of the cabin does not allow for a cross breeze to freshen the space.

On the floor was a note that George had left:

> *Tonweya, I am sorry to leave you here alone, but I cannot wait any longer to see my daughter. I have to go. I am riding south today. I will see you in the city when you return. Take care of yourself and stay strong.*

I have cleared the cobwebs the best I can and have lit a fire. I am back at the cabin, having caught my meal in the West River. While fishing, many thoughts and memories paraded through my mind. Looking around me, it is plain to see that the season of plenty is coming to an end, and soon enough winter will return. It is late-June now, and my food supply is exhausted.

George took almost all of the dried meat and fish with him.

Having chased all of the critters out of the cabin, it feels more like home; it feels like my place in the woods again. I will take the next few days to rest and then gather the grass necessary to get Canoni through the winter months.

I will have to hunt and pack in my own supply of meat for the immediate future.

I now regret my decision of not keeping the packhorse. It would have made things easier, but that is water under the bridge.

I took inventory of the remaining supplies in the cabin and found four books, three knives, and two boxes of shells, 50 rounds in each, one box for the rifle and one for my side arm. I have an additional hundred rounds buried outside close by, so I am set on ammunition.

Beneath the blanket I had left on the floor were a few other personal items. Both of the backrests that we made sat neatly propped against the wall. Outside, George had the woodpile fully stacked, so that is one less chore that I will need to do.

As I sit cross-legged outside in the grass now, I am trying to grasp the concept that I am truly here alone. I am sure that I do not appreciate the enormity of this reality, but I reassure myself by the fact that I just survived 45 days on a trail alone.

I am not sure if I am more concerned for George or myself. I do wonder how far along the trail he is and how he has fared so far, while at the same time I scan the grounds and see only Canoni's familiar face.

I recognize that this was my choice. Being alone is not so bad, except for the times when the isolation and self-doubt creep into my mind. In some ways being alone causes me to work harder to stay positive.

Wow, I am alone in the wilderness! It is as if all of my visions of the mountain man have come true. Those who sought out the mountains for the bounty and the solitude, those like me, who have to know what lies over the next hill, advance, regardless of the sacrifice. Those who proceed know that every step takes them farther away from what is normal and closer to their destiny.

Sometimes, that feeling manifests itself in the pit of my stomach. This is like no other challenge. Scream as loud as you want, no one will hear you. Injure yourself seriously enough, and your fate is a long, slow, painful death.

I talk to the animals, as they are the only life around me. I lean against the backrest and fill my pipe. Ah, my pipe. It soothes me and brings my mind back to ease.

The wind is blowing a bit harder now. I will go inside the cabin for the night. It is so good to be in the cabin again.

\* \* \*

I sit outside the lodge after another gorgeous day. After I retired last night, the sky turned hostile, and high gusts of wind rumbled from end to end of the valley. As suddenly as it began, the wind calmed again and is totally quiet. In the next minute, I ventured outside, and straightaway the rain soaked me when the shower became a downpour.

It sounded like a waterfall outside the door, as the liquid ran off of the roof.

Lightening slashed across the sky, thunder boomed through the valley, echoing from one mountain range to the other. The downpour lasted for 20 minutes, and it caused a lot of runoff. The rest of the night was uneventful.

Canoni spent her morning grazing, as she loves to do. I took a bath in the West River and took the necessary time to dry.

I set up a snare trap and snared a rabbit, which will be my meal today. Nothing more of note has occurred today, and so it shall fade into obscurity like others before it.

\* \* \*

The sun warmed the earth from a cloudless sky on this day in late-June. The ground was quite soft from the previous rain but did not hamper my routine. I set about my daily chores of feeding Canoni and refreshing the water and wood supply. Later, I spent several hours pulling and bundling grass for Canoni. With each bundle I reminded myself that Canoni can never have too much grass.

As the summer has waned, the wildflowers have bloomed everywhere in shades of blue, purple, white, red, orange, yellow, and different combinations thereof. The animals do not seem to favor any of them as a food source.

Late in the morning, I took a short ride, zig-zagging my way up the side of a mountain near the cabin. Part way up I crossed paths a male grizzly bear making its way along the base of the mountain. I wanted no interaction with it and kept Canoni moving at a comfortable pace. Once at the top of the mountain, I found a vantage point to observe the bear, making sure that he passed my location.

I had traced a trail down on the opposite side of the mountain by which to escape, if necessary.

As it turned out, the bear did pass below me without seeing me and moved on through the valley, passing but not stopping in front of the cabin.

I still get a rush of adrenalin knowing that there is only open space between these enormous creatures and myself. I casually wonder what would happen if he sees me. Sometimes, a bit of fear is mixed in too, and I go from being thrilled to being nervous in a split second.

I spent this afternoon lazily fishing along the Gataga River, while enjoying the warm sun. I took some target practice, spending 25 rounds from the handgun and a dozen rounds from the Marlin.

I finished dinner a while ago and after cleaning my weapons, I smoked the pipe. As twilight approaches I thank the Great Spirit for this good day in this land.

I shared a thought with Canoni. "I think that man was made not to be alone, but rather was meant to converse."

Of course, she did not say anything in response. Instead, she looked at me with her big, dark eyes with indifference.

I heard a coyote barking not too far away, and in the tree behind the cabin the owls hoot to each other. It is rewarding to see that they have stayed in the area. I am sure that they are keeping the mouse population under control, with the help of the coyotes and the wolves.

\* \* \*

I had a nightmare last night that I will document here. In my dream I was moving in the direction of a cliff overlooking an anonymous river. Crawling to the edge and peeking over, the earth all of a sudden crumbled, and I fell, plummeting head over heels to certain death.

Upon impacting the water, I was stunned by the cold, and I sank to the sandy bottom. I tumbled along in the swirling current. At that moment I came face to face with the mutilated bear that I discovered during my recent ride. The skull was infested with maggots and worms, white bone clearly visible through the partially eaten flesh.

The head rotated in the water, and the eyes moved, staring straight at me. I was at the bottom trying to get to the surface. I woke in a sweat and urged the fire to life. Sitting now in front of the fire, I wonder if any significance is inherent in the content of the dream.

\* \* \*

I now sit in front of the glowing fire after a long day. The heavens were flamered when the sun rose through the clouds that lined the horizon. I caught and ate a trout for breakfast.

I then chose to take a short ride east of the cabin, and much to my surprise, I discovered three sets of horse tracks on the earth. Upon investigating the tracks, I realized that the horses were not shod.

Farther along the trail, I caught up with the three horses, which appeared to me to be unattended. They paid little attention to me as they grazed in a canyon that extends east from the main valley. If they linger in the area, perhaps I can formulate a plan to catch one of them to use on the way out of here next year.

As I advanced, they kept their distance but did not run away. Riding to the cabin, I came across a set of mountain lion tracks, leading toward the forest that sits between the Gataga River and the cabin. A slight chill ran through me, and my rifle, as always, was close at hand.

I have little fear of any animal other than a grizzly trying to get into the cabin, as inside I have a distinct advantage. However, fear of attack outside the cabin is a constant concern.

Cooler air settled in this afternoon, reminding me that fall is not far away.

I redoubled my efforts to gather and bundle grass, bundle upon bundle, storing it for the winter to come.

Reviewing the map, I have chosen to hunt north of the cabin, somewhere near Gataga Mountain.

This hunt will commence in September. For now I am content to kill a deer, or other small game, for meals, at least until the snow flies.

\* \* \*

This morning I expended time scouting the set of mountain lion tracks that I discovered yesterday afternoon. The tracks led from the east into the forest, west of the cabin, and circled the cabin at a distance of 30 feet. I heard nothing during the night, nor did Canoni make any unfamiliar noises. I followed the tracks for half a mile before losing them in an outcropping of rocks. The tracks were the width of my hand and set fairly deep in the dirt, indicating substantial weight.

I feel concern because mountain lions are known to stalk a man. They have been known to circle around and sneak up behind a hunter, turning him into the hunted. I will stay alert, as for signs that it is making its home near this area.

I tried my luck bow fishing in the West River today but was not able to hit anything apart from the sandy bottom. Bow fishing is not really an option here, given the speed of the current and the water depth. I became frustrated not having any luck.

I took target practice, aiming at, and hitting, a tree 250 yards across the West River. Like I said, with this rifle, if you can see it, you can hit it. I squeezed off 10 rounds, and now I sit with an aching shoulder from the kick.

\* \* \*

The sun rose in a cloudless, though chilly sky on this morning in the final week of June. I woke up later than usual because I sat up for most of the night making an effort to classify imaginary noises in the dark on the other side of the door.

I investigated and found no fresh tracks of the mountain lion, then rode to the top of the ridge behind the cabin to scan the valley. From that vantage point I clearly viewed the three horses as they grazed along the West River on the plentiful grass. After observing them for a few minutes, I scampered down to the West River to catch my breakfast.

Once fed, I began my chores, including pulling and bundling more grass. The firewood is once again fully stacked, the water refreshed and the corral clean. While cleaning the corral, I entertained thoughts of allowing Canoni into the cabin at night. She is more vulnerable alone. I will ponder this.

I devoted time today throwing a rope at a tree stump, determining that this lassoing skill is much harder than it seems. It did not take me long to realize that I will not be roping any of these new horses, but rather perhaps luring them to the corral and capturing one there.

I took a bundle of grass and rode to a location near where the horses were feeding. They kept a wary eye on me from across the West River as I laid a bundle of grass on the ground and rode away from it. From a spot inside the trees I waited and watched. They crossed the water and consumed the bundle, then moved on to graze along the bank. I wondered if they would ever get close enough to capture.

I ate trout for my dinner and drank what remained of the coffee Milich had given me. Thanks to Milich, I have a tool to use for making tea.

Cooler air has settled in over the valley as I sit in the lodge, reviewing the day's events. Another day spent alone in the wild.

\* \* \*

With the dawn this morning awoke the wind that had been so mysteriously missing for the past two days. As usual, I took care of Canoni, feeding and grooming her. After eating a rabbit I trapped in a snare, I choose to get a view of the valley.

Climbing the ridge behind the cabin, I looked for a vantage point from which to see down the basin. Below me across the West River, the three horses grazed among the trees, now no more than 200 yards from the cabin, though across the river. They seem to be migrating my way. They stood across the river aware of my presence. While attempting to remain hidden, all advantage was gone when Canoni neighed at full volume, and one of them responded in kind.

As I pen this entry, the horses call to each other from not too far away. As the day progressed I caught a trout from the West River and will cook it later.

The wildflowers painted among the meadows bring together color and fragrance to this valley, each different variety offering a different color to attract a pollinator. Each flower reaches for the sun in its struggle to sustain life. Together they make this land more pleasant to live in.

\* \* \*

## JULY

July brings prophecies of warmer days and fair nights. I make this entry to note that a surprise rainstorm last night has left the earth soaked, water puddles everywhere. The temperature is as brisk as it has been all summer. I will take a ride now and write later.

I am back from my ride. I rode Canoni along the West River to a spot where I often cross and allowed her to drink at her leisure. As always, she is good-natured, a fact for which I am grateful. Canoni is without doubt my best friend. The thought of having to offer her up for sale someday in the future brings tears to my eyes. That is a bridge that I do not wish to cross.

In the mud along the banks I discovered a lone set of wolf tracks, which crossed the West River and picked up on the other side, leading up into the hills.

With the sky so cloudy, it appears that I am in for more inclement weather. During the quiet before the rain, I took the opportunity to remove the ashes from the fireplace, replenishing the firewood and putting clean water in the trough at the same time.

Now crouching at the door of the cabin with a fire blazing behind me, I can't help but feel blessed by all I view around me.

This must be an uncommon weather pattern, as we did not see as much rain last summer.

Dinner will be a white fish, which I caught earlier. For now, I will enjoy this variation in the weather.

\* \* \*

This morning dawned with rain falling, as it did during the course of the night. In the distance, with the cabin door open, I hear the water flowing in the swollen West River. As always, I am impressed by the rapid changes the rain brings about. It is not very windy, nor is it cold. I often persuade myself that Canoni is fine outside and that I am fine inside.

It appears that I will be stuck inside today, so to kill time I will work on tying a few feathers to my rifle. I do this for the decoration. I have been thinking about trying to build some kind of protection in the corral for Canoni. Since she is alone now, she will not have the warmth of the other horses throughout the winter months. I will think about the possibilities and come up with a plan. However, I am leaning toward bringing her inside the cabin at night. It will be crowded, but we will both sleep better and be safer inside. Choosing to stay inside today means that I will be eating venison jerky for my meal today.

\* \* \*

## JULY 4

I took a moment to consider George's status. I imagine him on the trail, cooking a meal in the campfire that lights his campsite in the forest. I imagine him studying his map, double-checking his route. I hope that he is delivered to his family. Over the course of the day, the rain has kept me indoors, though during the lulls I have ventured outside.

Canoni is fine, healthy and stout. I read and sit by the door observing nature to pass time. I have devised a backup plan in the event that I choose to keep Canoni outside. I will build a sturdy lean-to in the corral, which will form a shelter that Canoni may go under to be out of the wind. My plan is to cut 15 trees, long enough to lean against the roof of the cabin. Building the lean-to so that there will be enough room for her to turn about will be the challenge. I will not have to wait for the trees to dry out, as we did when we built the cabin. I will start on this project as soon as the weather conditions clear up.

I caught a 16-inch trout in the West River today, which I will eat later. For now all is well.

\* \* \*

This morning, after three days of off-again, on-again clouds and rain, the sun returned to my valley, transporting with it the clear, clean air that supports life. It is peaceful outside, another postcard day.

I will go for a ride now.

I have returned to the cabin after spending much of the day outside. I am fully revived!

As always, the vistas in these mountains are spectacular! The hills are thoroughly soaked, mini waterfalls tumble from the rocks everywhere. In the meadow in front of the cabin, rabbits enjoyed the sun and the green grass provided by Mother Nature.

Since the ground and the grass are wet, I will have to wait to pull and bundle additional grass so that it does not get moldy.

I see clouds forming in the west as I write, so there could be more rain soon.

The wildflowers throughout the valley lift my spirits when I take a moment to closely observe them. Though they are small in contrast to the trees and brush, they are most hardy, each living to attract a pollinator, bees or perhaps a hummingbird or other winged wonder. Each with a precarious hold on the earth is determined to survive the alpine summer.

Canoni was especially spirited today for unknown reasons. She pranced with each stride, stepping high in some cases and generally appearing frisky. I rode until late afternoon, at which time I reverted to the cabin.

For now the light is beginning to fade, and I have not yet cooked my dinner, so I will stop writing and accomplish that task.

\* \* \*

From the heavens above, a sprinkle falls, as the new day begins. As the first week of July plays out, the summer goes on without excitement.

I take notice that all of the animals are doing their best to consume as much food as possible in preparation for the impending winter. Sitting inside the door of the cabin, I see three deer, which all sauntered right up to the corral and now eat the grass that I bundled for Canoni. I scared them away, and they now gawk at me from the edge of the forest. Canoni did nothing to stop them, allowing them to eat as they wished.

As I sit in the cabin, roasting the fish provided by the West River, life beyond the door goes on.

\* \* \*

Three days have passed, and today Mother Nature brought another gorgeous day.

The scent of evergreens wafted on the breeze today. I climbed to the ridge behind the cabin to have a look down the valley. The West River has begun to recede, although it remains possible to see the areas flooded when the banks overflowed. The water remained cloudy, so there was no sense in trying to catch fish today.

I took a ride to the Gataga River, and I caught sight of two of the three roaming horses there. They looked good and well fed. I still have aspirations of capturing one of them. I do wonder if perhaps they belong to a ranch somewhere in these mountains, but I have covered virtually every foot of this entire region and have seen no sign of human activity. I will monitor them as long as they remain in my valley.

I expended a lot of energy this afternoon bundling more grass, as I did last year. I pulled out large chunks of the two-foot tall grass and tied it together with vines from the forest floor. I want to put away much more grass this year than I did last year because without the oats, barley, and alfalfa that the horses had on the ride in last year, Canoni will not get enough nutrients. I ate a Canada goose for my meal earlier, finishing the better part of the bird. Now I will rest.

\* \* \*

I am back in the cabin after working during the course of the day. I bundled and stored a lot of grass today, placing it on the protected west side of the cabin, knowing full well that I am inviting snakes, mice, and other critters to dwell in the piles. It is better than having the grass under six feet of snow during the winter. Speaking of the corral, I built the lean-to, and it will serve its purpose.

I dug a trench 10 feet long and 12 inches deep. I then stuck the thin trees in the trench at a 45 degree angle, leaned them against the cabin roof, and then filled in the dirt around the trench. I compressed the dirt so the trees will not move in the strong wind that occasionally blows.

I then took one thin Lodgepole and nailed it to the roof, after laying it over the trees leaning against the roof. This formed a method to lock down the top of the trees. This modification to the cabin is sound and will safeguard Canoni, and if I decide to bring her into the cabin, it will serve to keep the grass dry during the coming season.

I spent the last hour of the afternoon riding Canoni along the Gataga River, where I spotted the lone wolf the other day. I have named this gal Vagrant, as she seems to have no home. I recognize that she is a female since I have seen her urinate. She is not shy in her environment, being a predator, but when I look her in the eyes, her ears lay back, and she crouches down, inspecting me. If I move on, she paces along.

I do not want to get friendly with her, as she is wild in every sense of the word. She is a social animal and so may be inclined to show her pack this place on some future visit. This could bring a repeat of the distressing encounters that we had in the past. I will neither provide food nor attempt to get close to her.

Sitting here in front of the fire pit in front of the cabin, the world appears so immense and this lodge so insignificant. Beyond the light of the fire lurk all of my fears. Everything unseen in the night lives there just out of view.

If one was standing in the vast darkness observing those sitting at the circle of light, one could clearly count the bodies in the circle. I have never liked that feeling of not being able to see into the darkness while feeling vulnerable by the back lighting. In this backcountry, a fire may be seen from many miles away.

As I sit, I hear in the distance the call of the true dog, the wolf, while closer, I hear a family of coyotes yipping at each other.

I wish that some of those who live in the concrete jungle could be here with me tonight, to witness what they have never known before. Once the mountains have touched you, no other place is as good. At no time in my life will I cherish living among tall buildings or in the decaying inner cities.

It is now, and evermore will be, my desire to live in the center of the mastery that is these mountains.

I agree that in order to get by in the city, it is necessary to play the game and that this is the natural thing to do. I do that well also. However, life is far better for the person who hears the call of the mountains, lays eyes on the flowing rivers, and hears the birds sing in the trees. Even better off is the person who knows the land and never underestimates its potential.

Those who fail to know before they choose where they live are typically victims. Those who fail to see the signs presented by the predator are also destined to be victims. This is true as much in the city as it is here. For people like me the world shrinks more every day. With each new building put up, more of my world, the grizzly's world, and the wolf's world are lost. I fear that in my lifetime, wild places may no longer exist.

* * *

Two days have passed, and this afternoon featured a clear sky and a dazzling sun, which allowed me to gather grass. My hands have become tired from gripping and pulling so much grass. Today, I produced 20 bundles, which I would estimate weigh five pounds each. The pile is getting substantial, and I feel confident about the quantity that I have stored lasting the entire winter. I would like to double the amount I have gathered, and I plenty of time to finish before I go hunting for my winter supply of meat.

During the past couple of days while on my rides I have not seen Vagrant, which is a relief. I am hopeful that she has returned to her pack and that it is roaming away from me. I have no way of knowing, however, so I remain vigilant.

With the warm summer days come afternoon thunderstorms, the impressive tall clouds demanding attention. Other than re-stocking the wood pile, I have little to do in the way of chores.

Having caught a white fish in the West River today, I will soon cook it and enjoy my daily meal.

\* \* \*

Today has been an especially beautiful day. The morning started cloudy, but by noon the sun was out, and it was 70 degrees.

I rode south of the cabin into the canyon where we let our horses graze last year, and I saw a cascading waterfall spilling into a creek, which was by now more like a river. This was the same canyon where the avalanche happened during the winter. The overall damage to the once-pristine canyon is stunning. Huge quantities of debris have been lodged against the walls, trees stuck in the rubble, an indication of the immeasurable force unleashed.

It appears as though it will be quite some time until this waterfall runs dry, as the depth of snow is deep in the chute of the slide. The sun shone on the walls, making the day seem much brighter. The mist drifting away from the falls created a rainbow. I took in the sight for half an hour before riding on.

As I swung east toward the Gataga River, I did not see either the wild horses or the lone wolf. Returning to the cabin, an afternoon wind kicked up, and a thin band of clouds blossomed on the western horizon. The sun radiated through the clouds as it set, the tops of them outlined with a band of gold, making for a spectacular sunset.

Days such as this one were made to be filmed. Mile after mile of spectacular color of the wildflowers is painted on the green canvas of our Mother Earth.

\* \* \*

Today has brought excitement that I did not expect. After waking up and donning my clothes, I opened the cabin door to pee, and directly across from me, 30 yards away, stood a full-grown male grizzly bear, standing on its hind legs sniffing the air. I ducked into the cabin and grabbed my rifle. I reappeared at the door, and seeing the bear move a few steps toward me, I yelled and waved my arms. The bear stopped and again sniffed the air. I shouted and fired a round into the air.

This frightened the bear, and it sprinted the 40 yards into the forest. I guess we were both lucky that it chose flight rather than fight. I don't think the grizzly knew that I was there until I shouted.

The bears, I suspect, have nothing to fear out here, and so perhaps they wander around carelessly in their search of food. I was somewhat embarrassed, recognizing that I initially exited without my rifle, as I have done for some time now, breaking the one rule I promised myself that I would keep.

I avowed today that my hand will not leave my rifle. After the incident with the bear this morning, I bundled more grass. I am now more confident that Canoni will not go hungry this winter. In the afternoon, a brief thunderstorm rolled through, drenching the earth.

I managed to catch a white fish in the Driftpile River and am listening to it sizzling in the pan on the coals of my fire.

I had to laugh at myself, remembering the encounter this morning. My first thought after picking up the rifle was why didn't I build a back door to the cabin through which I could escape? Here I am, a mountain man, and the dreaded invasion of a grizzly bear found me wanting to run! I would not have wanted to shoot that bear unless I had to.

It is getting dark, so I will quit writing now and eat my meal.

* * *

**THIRD WEEK OF JULY**

I resolve to go about planning my fall hunt over the coming weeks.

This morning I took Canoni out. I rode north to the Driftpile River and crossed. I then looped to the west and sat across the West River facing the ridge that obscures the cabin. Abundant signs of animals are present, including deer, elk, rabbit, and ground squirrels. It's both stimulating and frustrating when I see such a maze of tracks, and I can't follow a single set.

Riding on I arrived at the beavers' dam and found the male repairing a leak. I took two trout from the pond and returned to the cabin.

I have gathered pine nuts but have no way of knowing how to cook them. The squirrels will find a windfall before the summer ends. I do wish that I could grow some greens here. I see a lot of natural greens, but I cannot distinguish which are safe to eat and which could kill me.

I now sit cross-legged at the outside fire pit, across from the cabin door enjoying the heat and smoking a pipe load of weed. From somewhere nearby, a loon calls out and is by coincidence answered by the hoot- hoot of the neighbor owls in the tree.

This music is heard almost every night in this valley.

Staying in tune with the evolving seasons and being aware of any change that this land demands is a full-time job. I come to be mentally tired by the end of each day, from the intense concentration and focus needed on a daily basis. I imagine that the instant I relax my guard, something will happen. This was obviously easier when George was here, two sets of eyes being better than one.

The sun is about to sink behind the ridge to the west, bringing a close to this day. Thank you Wakan Tanka for this splendid day.

\* \* \*

I move forward, living the reality that was one time my dream. I spent the better part of this morning gathering grass bundles and storing them. I have decided to use the lean-to on the side of the cabin to store the grass, as well as the opposite side of the cabin. I will be able to store far more grass using both locations, thus assuring Canoni's survival.

During the day, I fished the West River and managed to catch a decent fish, which I will eat later.

As I write this entry, I note how dramatically my eating habits have changed ever since I have been here. In the city I ate three meals plus snacks every day. I had a lot of fat on my body. In this place, it is not easy to prepare three meals, nor do I want to prepare three meals per day, so I eat one large meal on most days.

During winter it is difficult to cut the frozen meat, which is another reason for what has become my custom. I take my vitamin C and vitamin D supplements every other day.

Canoni is enjoying the summer, and we value each other's company.

As it is getting dark now I will cook my meal and then turn in.

\* \* \*

Two days have passed, and of note today is that I found a new set of mountain lion tracks, north of the Driftpile River, a quarter mile up on the other side. I will keep alert to its presence in the area.

I was awakened by the crack of thunder that split the silence of the valley at daybreak. This early morning storm soaked the valley. Lightening flashed in the sky for half an hour before moving into the valleys beyond mine.

Later, the sun showcased its warmth, and the forest filled with sounds. The West River swelled as a result of the runoff and is too swift to think about crossing. Instead of riding today, I alternately took short hikes and collected more grass for Canoni.

Later, as I sat in the cabin, I spent an hour studying the map, deciding where I will hunt in the fall. As the day turns to night, another group of nocturnal creatures takes over the landscape.

I retreat inside my fortress in the vastness of the untamed landscape surrounding me, alert for danger, waiting for sleep.

\* \* \*

Four days have passed, and during this time it has been rather quiet in the neighborhood.

With nothing better to do, I wondered to myself about the likelihood of life after death. If a man is born twice, what would be the purpose for it? What is the prize? Perhaps we would be here to finish some business from a previous life, as some Indian tribes believe.

Impossible you say? Who regulates when in the course of time we are to be born again? If we are not born more than once, are we to live for this short amount of time for reasons mysterious to us? If there is no goal for it, why live at all?

Perhaps the questions cannot be answered. I recognize that sometime in the past I knew this same life, only the landscape has changed. My mission is to understand these questions and to seek answers.

To me, however, the questions are no longer important. I have grown-up. Seeing the world through a child's eyes and seeing the worlds through the green eyes of this man are two different things. Through my man eyes, I see reality, not the imagined. For the time being, I determine the course of the living man, and nature determines who will survive to see the outcome.

\* \* \*

The weather was pleasant today, the temperature reaching 73 degrees. I took a hike after re-stocking the firewood, down to the West River, first to fill the canteens and then to stretch out under the trees that shade the bank.

I found a stick perfect to make a walking stick. I have furs to cover it with, and this project will give me something to help kill the time this winter. It will be a useful item when trekking.

At the West River, the moving water provided a gentle, cool breeze, which was soothing as the temperature rose. All the while the sound of birds singing and chasing each other through the trees filled the air, even over the drone of the rapids upstream. It was a perfect day to be lazy and act like a kid. I took several dips in the river throughout the day and feel clean.

As the afternoon wore on, I cooked what was left of the venison supply. It does not get any better than this.

My hair is too long now. I never thought I would say that, but it now falls in everything. I suppose the bandanas will reign supreme.

After dinner I watched the sun set over the mountains. The earth smells dry tonight, the usual smell on a hot day, which is just as noticeable as the smell of the earth after a summer rain. Gnats fill the air and fly blindly into my face. My only defense is to wear the mosquito net.

As twilight encroaches, the sounds of nature roar to a climax, crickets cricketing, owls hooting, and coyotes yipping. 10 minutes later all becomes silent, as the inky night dissolves over this land.

\* \* \*

## JULY 26

It is so awesome to wake up to perfect days in the mountains; I cannot find words to accurately define the scene! The sun shines. Birds sing in the trees. Canoni, happy to see me, nuzzles her nose against my face from behind.

I sit in outside of the cabin now, making this entry for the day in the journal.

The temperature was warm enough, that I swam in the beaver pond twice today. While down at the West River re-filling the canteens earlier, I caught a 12-inch trout, which I will eat this evening. Canoni is fine, she seems to enjoy the sunny days as much as I do, though she contends with the flies more than I do. She grazes as she wanders the area.

A thought ran through my mind today, a phrase that my grandfather used to say often: be nice to people.

I have been thinking about that phrase, be nice.

I wonder what it is that makes a person inclined to be nice. The obvious answer is reputation. I wouldn't want my friends to say what a jerk I am. To many it is easier to get what you want through intimidation than by legitimate means. I see this first-hand in the city.

Could it be that niceness is a by-product of a good environment rather than a character trait?

What if a child grew up seeing only crime, could he grow up to be nice? I am as nice to people as they are to me.

I think I think too much. Perhaps it is time to let go of this thought.

\* \* \*

As has been the case for weeks now, the weather has remained warm making for memorable days. This morning I rode for a few hours, as always enjoying Canoni's company. I spectated as the world passed by, marveling at the geography.

I found a kill two miles from the cabin. It looked as if the wolves made this kill. The earth was stained with blood, which appeared to be a few days old. Only scattered bones and torn fur were left of the victim.

Riding on I spied a mallard duck on the shore of a small lake. Using my handgun, I was able to hit it on the third attempt. I dressed what was left of it and took it to the cabin. Since the weather has been so pleasant I will cook the prize outside.

It surely takes some effort to pull the feathers off of the duck, making a big mess of the immediate area. I hope that the wind will blow them away.

Enough for now. I have food to cook and have nothing else to say.

\* \* \*

This day began with a sublime sunrise, a brilliant kaleidoscope of red and pink and orange, bordered in gold.

I rode Canoni south down the valley five miles on a trail that I know well. I rode halfway before I got off and sat down among the trees and evaluated the countryside. Gazing south I saw elk in the distance, as they try and pack on weight in preparation for winter. I watched squirrels as they hid the windfall of nuts I had scattered at the base of the trees. I noticed that all too soon the wildflowers have begun to wilt, their mission in life complete for this year. The lazy days of the alpine summer are fast disappearing, and the time to prepare for the cold and the lean times is close at hand.

I now lean against my backrest at the door of the cabin, having returned from my ride. The wind has begun to blow hard enough to hear it through the trees. It is cold enough to make me want to close the door and sit near the fire. So I will spend the rest of the day inside. Dinner will be the remainder of the mallard duck that I cooked last night.

\* \* \*

## JULY COMES TO AN END

This day began with another glorious sunrise. Shortly after sunrise the wind picked up and has been blowing steadily ever since. Cold air from the north equates to a chill factor that may make the day uncomfortable. I glanced at the thermometer and deciphered 44 degrees.

Canoni no longer uses the corral; instead she prefers to wander around the meadow, never straying out of sight of the cabin. I replenished the wood and the water and dug the rain run-off trench deeper. Soon enough the late summer rain will return.

I also made a list of the things I need to accomplish before the snow flies. The list includes things like cleaning the cabin one final time and securing enough food to last the winter.

I feel that I have become knowledgeable about the preparations necessary from being here last winter. The list will grow if I dwell on things. For now, I need to do my daily chores and enjoy the remaining summer days and eventually prepare for the fall hunt.

As I make this entry, it is mid-afternoon, and across the meadow I see a hundred little birds eating in the grass. They seem to travel as one, flying in short bursts from one spot to the next. I also noticed five black and yellow birds flying through the trees.

I have a fish ready to cook, and I am hungry, so this entry ends.

\* \* \*

## AUGUST

I sit in front of the cabin, leaning against my backrest, recovering from being flung off Canoni today.

I rode Canoni this morning and was thrown when she faltered while galloping. I sat there dazed for a second before gathering myself up and mountaineering onto Canoni once more. This makes the second time that I have been thrown. I have no major injury, except to my pride, but I do feel stiff in my lower back and hip. Fortunately for me, the ground is soft from the recent rain.

I know that the mishap was my own doing for not riding correctly, being off balance when Canoni tripped, but still it is embarrassing, and I am glad that George was not around to see it. During the brief moments that it took for the whole incident to unfold, many things went through my mind; foremost among them was whether any danger lurked nearby.

Having had my rifle across my saddle, it sailed to the ground when I did.

I scanned the area and saw no bear or other danger. Canoni stopped a foot from where I landed and stared at me, as though it was I who stumbled. Thank goodness that Canoni suffered no injuries.

Now it is time to cook my meal, a fresh trout caught in the West River.

\* \* \*

After two days, my back and hip feel fine, all tenderness is gone.

In order to stay strong, I took a hike today in full gear, meaning that I wore my sidearm, carried two canteens, my sleeping bag, a knife, a compass, some food, and some stones in my backpack to simulate a full pack. I also took the walking stick that I completed, which I like. It is both warm in the hand, and it looks cool when the feathers boogie in the breeze.

I hiked first across the Driftpile River and then east to the Gataga River. I discovered a newly formed series of beaver dams in a feeder stream, lined up back to back. Each pool was five or six feet deep and 50 to 75 feet wide by my estimation. A number of downed trees along the Driftpile River made for slow hiking and more energy expended.

Once through that maze, travel was easier along the flat shore of the Driftpile River. I saw several deer and signs of more on the sandy shore. On the side of a mountain I spotted three caribou grazing leisurely on the grassy slope. A moose waded in one of the beaver ponds, and I made a point to skirt around the pond unnoticed. Moose can grow to a height of six feet tall and weigh as much as 1,200 pounds, or more. This one as tall as Canoni, may be dangerous at any time of year but are most dangerous in late fall when the rut takes place. They move much faster than they look like they can.

Near where I turned west from the Gataga River for the cabin, I noticed a pair of wolves across the Gataga River on a trail taking them up the valley and into the forest.

There is something to be said about how much more vulnerable I feel when walking. A wolf in the distance is a much more elevated danger while I am on foot, for obvious reasons. I must keep my eyes on the wolves so they don't out-flank me.

I arrived at the cabin in the late afternoon, feeling great after the workout.

# 10

# Autumn 1977

This day afforded some intriguing activity, which proved fatal for an elk. I rode Canoni early this morning along the Gataga River. While on a bluff overlooking a set of rapids, I happened to glance at precisely the right second to see an elk cow flash past me, swirling in the current. If it was not already dead, it soon would be. It slipped over the rapids and underwater, never returning to the surface.

A bit later, I rode upon a set of grizzly tracks, which appeared rounded and not sharp at the edges, indicating that they were made days ago. I followed the tracks visually a short distance up the side of a mountain and into a brush pile the size of a basketball court. No way was I going up there.

I rode on for another three miles before turning Canoni around and heading to the cabin. I walked half of the 10-mile distance to the lodge. It is as if around every bend in the trail the landscape is more spectacular. Wildlife most often seems to be present. I saw a porcupine along the trail, close to the Driftpile River, and gave it a wide berth.

The sun sets now as I relax outside by the fire pit.

I noticed a young hare eating grass near the lean-to. I will not bother it. I mean, how much grass can one rabbit eat?

I cooked a relative of that rabbit for my meal and am now ready to enjoy a pipe full of weed.

I have a desire to experience a sweat lodge, but I have no desire to construct one right now. Maybe in the future.

\* \* \*

Nothing of note has occurred over the past two days other than that the adolescent hare has stayed around the cabin and does not appear fearful of me. I have come within just a few feet of it, and it does not run. If it is to be a companion, I will welcome it.

I decided to bathe since I smelled rather ripe.

Trout is again on the dinner menu. As I brought fresh water into the cabin today, the young rabbit that has been hanging around surfaced in the corral.

\* \* \*

This day dawned with another brilliant sunrise, followed by warmth touching the land.

Upon exiting the cabin, I was greeted by the now-familiar hare, which I will name Buggs in honor of his famous distant relative, Buggs Bunny, a star in his own right.

After speaking in low tones to Buggs for a few minutes, I took Canoni for some exercise, trotting to the Driftpile River and back. While riding, Canoni and I were startled by a commotion along a trail to our left, and I looked in time to see a deer racing down the mountain, a cougar in hot pursuit. The deer succeeded to avoid being caught, and the cougar gave up the chase, slinking back into the brush growing concentrated on the mountainside. On this day the deer was faster, but tomorrow, who knows, the cougar might win the game.

I ate a trout for dinner and now sit outside by the fire watching Buggs devour his fill of Canoni's grass supply. While thinking about food, I recalled that George buried some food at the base of a tree nearby, and if I can remember which one, I will consider it a great windfall. He told me roughly where the tree was and said he buried salt and pepper, flour, sugar, a sack of rice, and a pouch of tobacco. George divulged that he marked the tree by chopping a wedge into the trunk, and he tied a piece of red cloth in a branch 10 feet off the ground.

Tomorrow I will devote some time trying to locate the tree.

In the early afternoon I watched in amazement as a peregrine falcon attacked a crow in flight, successfully hitting the crow but not able to hook it in its talons. The falcon spread its wings to slow itself and then dove again, this time grasping the crow and tumbling in a free-fall until it recovered and flew west and out of sight. Its wingspan was at least four feet from wingtip to wingtip. This bird of prey is one of nature's more obscure birds.

\* \* \*

I am in the cabin, flush with excitement that I was able to locate the supplies that George had hidden. It took the better part of the morning searching around before I finally spotted the red cloth hanging from a branch. He buried a master sack, and inside were four smaller cotton bags containing the supplies.

The master bag had been placed inside plastic wrapping and rolled in a cloth. None of the contents were damaged in any way. I will have some welcome relief in my menu.

My new pal Buggs took an interest in my enthusiasm, and while I was whooping it up in the cabin, he sat near the doorway. Canoni stood in the meadow in front of the cabin grazing on grass.

I finished smoking a pipe of tobacco and wound up lightheaded from the effect. It has been more than a year since I last smoked tobacco. Back in civilization I was a pack a day smoker.

I will go try my luck fishing for my meal. More later.

I was able to catch a small fish for dinner, and with the salt and pepper on the floured fish, it was delicious.

It is getting darker, so I will go inside the cabin and turn in.

\* \* \*

## MID-AUGUST

The grass shows signs of drying. It is losing the lush green color in favor of a more yellow-brown hue. Only the evergreen trees remain fully green. The leaves on the cottonwoods are changing color as well showing signs of yellow-gold.

Being such a logical fella, I have decided that it is in my best interests to begin hunting for meat in three to four weeks. This is a monumental decision, because I have no way of storing meat until the cold weather arrives. If I hunt too early, I could end up with spoiled meat that would entice hungry bears. If I wait too long, I could be caught in a snowstorm, away from the cabin. Last year George and I hunted in the final two weeks of August, about this time. We did, however, end up exploring the country for two weeks before we made meat. I will wait two weeks before I hunt.

Dinner tonight will consist of a mallard duck that I brought down today.

\* \* \*

Overnight a thunderstorm dropped heavy rain in a brief period of time. The rain was absorbed by the earth, which left me with soft, moist ground.

I rode to the south end of the valley this morning, again speaking to Buggs while I saddled Canoni. I'm pretty happy that Buggs seems content to stay around here.

I rode with nothing specific in mind to accomplish, letting Canoni canter at her own pace.

A mile down the trail, I spied a mother grizzly and three yearling cubs. That all three survived the first year struck me as miraculous. Before long enough they will seek a place to hibernate for the winter. They were no threat to me, and I continued my ride.

Farther down, high on a ridge top, a herd of caribou descended toward the valley, numbering at least 30, deliberately making the decent. I presumed that they would be staying in the valleys as the season changes.

While returning to the cabin, I shot a woodland duck. I cleaned it and brought it back with me. As I write, it is cooking over the fire outside.

I am leaning against the wall of the cabin making this entry and monitoring the meat. The fire tends to flare up when I cook duck as the grease dribbles into the flames.

I learned enough from George to know how to make the bird taste great, especially with the recent addition of salt and pepper.

\* \* \*

An interesting and fortunate incident occurred today. This morning at the break of day, a thunderstorm dropped rain for half an hour. The high wind that accompanied the storm knocked down more than a few trees, mostly older, tall cottonwood trees. In addition, mud materialized in some places.

After doing my chores, I rode Canoni to the Driftpile and fished for a considerable time without catching a single fish, which is an infrequent occurrence. I then sat in front of the lodge smoking a cigarette when, without warning, wave after wave of Canada geese flew overhead and then circled before landing in the meadow right in front of me, no more than 20 yards away.

I slayed one of them and spent the next hour cleaning it in the nearby forest. I will cook it for dinner tonight. I would guess that it weighs about six pounds. I will obviously not eat six pounds of meat tonight, but I will eat the breast now and save the legs and thighs for another meal.

The flock of geese generated so much noise honking that it was irritating to listen to. That was quite an experience. There had to be a hundred and 50 geese in total.

A quick note to say that the goose turned out excellent, especially since I have not eaten one in a long while. It is dark now, so I will go inside and turn in.

* * *

As August rolls on, yet another thunderstorm hit the valley before noon, soaking everything and swelling the West River to full capacity in a span of 15 minutes. Comparable past events saw an impressive run-off. It took the better part of the day for the West River to return to normal levels.

Due to the sediment in the water, it was too cloudy to fish. Fortunately, I have part of the goose from yesterday left to eat today.

The later afternoon was warmer. In the distance, I hear a clap of thunder signaling the coming of rain. I recognize the pattern, or cycle, occurring here. During the day the sun warms the earth, causing moisture to evaporate, which then meets cooler air coming over the mountains, and as a result thunderstorms form.

Drops have begun to fall, and I listen to them hitting the roof and the ground. Lightening cracks, and for a split second, the flash is bright, both more dramatic than I can convey in this account.

I will stop writing now and close my eyes, witnessing the energy of Mother Nature.

* * *

I make this entry by firelight at the end of another stunning Canadian day filled with sunshine and warmth. No major event occurred today or yesterday.

What I will remember are the existing conditions, crickets chirping in the grass by the hundreds, and from the West River I hear frogs croaking. From the tree right outside, I hear the family of owls hooting. In the background, I hear the faint sound of the rapids of the West River. Fluttering through the air from time to time both at sunrise and sunset are tiny bats, and since I can't see them clearly, it is hard to know what kind of bats they are. They are no threat to me, so I pay them little attention other than to observe their flight.

The air is cooler now, and the fire feels good on my hands and face. Across the fire pit on the edge of the dimming light sits Buggs, he too apparently enjoys the fire.

From out of nowhere my parents come to mind. I imagine their faces, and I recite a prayer that they are okay. I miss them. It is as the saying goes, you never know what you have till it's gone. I miss my mother immensely.

I am tired now and will go to sleep.

\* \* \*

Again this morning, Buggs sat outside the door eating grass when I opened it to greet the day. I am delighted to see that Buggs has chosen to call this his home too. Canoni seems oblivious to Buggs for whatever reason.

I took a ride this morning, going south toward the mouth of the valley, in quest of new fishing holes. I did indeed find a couple. As the morning wore on, the sun warmed and the atmosphere became drier. I caught five trout, releasing them back into the water unharmed, self-assured that I can catch them pretty much whenever I wish. I then rode farther downstream and fished a different new pool. Near noon, the sun overhead caused the biting to cease.

I spent some time relaxing along the shore, appreciating the day. As the afternoon wore on, I caught two additional fish, gutted them and mounted up for the ride home.

I took my time returning to the cabin.

A mile from the lodge, a thunderstorm rolled through the valley, compelling me to find shelter from pea-sized hail.

I located an overhang where Canoni and I could wait out the storm, which ended in 10 minutes, rolling east toward Alberta.

Upon arriving at the cabin I saw that Buggs was wet and ever so pitiful looking, sitting near the door.

Without coaxing from me, Buggs followed me into the cabin for the first time. He seemed to feel right at home, heading into the corner near the fireplace, where he has remained for the short amount of time that I have been inside.

It would appear that, like it or not, I have a roommate.

\* \* \*

Today was another gorgeous August day. The sun warmed the air, and I went to the West River to fish, catching a mature trout, which I cooked and ate for lunch.

I went for a hike along one of the escape trails near the cabin and had the good fortune to see a remarkably large male grizzly bear from a vantage point where he could not see me. With the wind in my face, I was able to safely observe him as he roamed through the trees, eating whatever edible fare he came upon, a few plants, a tall shoot of grass. He even chased a ground squirrel, digging up the hole into which it escaped. This guy spent as much time rubbing his back against trees as he did foraging.

I observed the grizzly for 20 minutes before better sense told me to leave. I crept away and returned to the cabin. As I looked around the valley, I could see that more than a few cottonwood trees are changing color. Still, for the most part, evergreens dominate the landscape. It is pretty impressive seeing patches of brilliant yellow-gold trees among a sea of evergreens. The fall is starting to make a more robust appearance over the past few days.

While I have plenty of time to prepare for the long winter, I have chosen to begin drying some of the fish I catch. I will start tomorrow.

For my meal, I cooked a rabbit that I snared, but somehow it did not taste as good as usual, perhaps because Buggs sat there watching me. I might have to stop eating rabbit.

Meanwhile, Canoni, my true friend, is in fine spirits. Today she wanted to play and ran around me in circles, faking like she was going to charge me and lightly bumping into me.

She ran around the meadow and seemed to be having a wonderful time. All things considered, this was not a bad day.

\* \* \*

I make this record after having had an encounter with a visiting bear at first light. A young black bear, perhaps two years old, wandered through the area, sniffing and grunting outside the perimeter of the cabin. Knowing that Canoni could be a target, I opened the door and slid outside.

I fired a shot into the air, shouting loudly. The bear spun on its heels and ran off toward the trees.

I darted after it. "No man here is frightened of a young black bear. You come back when you are bigger, big enough to cover the whole floor of my lodge."

I scrutinized it as it sprinted toward the Driftpile River.

I fished for much of the morning in the West River, catching six trout, which I cleaned and arranged in the smoker. I cut them in half from behind the head and down to the tail and hung them above the fire on racks. I will leave them in the smoker until tomorrow. Having had the experience last year of smoking meat, I am confident that I can smoke them to perfection.

* * *

I write while sitting near the fire pit, having finished my meal. I ate a trout coated in flour with salt and pepper.

Once I finished my chores today, I rode to the Gataga River and fished in earnest, landing eight trout, all in the two-pound range. After cleaning them at the river, I returned to the cabin, cut the fish into strips, and replaced the fish that were now smoked and dried in the smoker that George built.

After building the fire up to increase the heat, I used wet wood chips to produce the smoke that flavors the meat. When necessary, I put pieces of green wood on the fire to reduce the heat and create humidity. This made for such an idyllic scene, smoke from the smoker drifting along the ground next to the cabin, in the middle of the backwoods.

Today Canoni is in a particularly good mood, frolicking around in the meadow, racing here and there like a young pony. I spent some time playing her favorite game. I faked like I was going to charge her, and she jumped to one side or the other, then she stood considering me until I did it for a second time. This went on for perhaps 10 minutes before she turned and strolled away, suddenly tired of the game.

As darkness sets in over the land, I view the smoker and hope that I am not visited by predators overnight.

I will sit at the cabin door and keep one eye open. I vividly recall the visit from a determined bear during one night that George and I left the smoker unattended.

Buggs comes and goes as he pleases these days. He pretty much goes out when I go out and comes in at twilight. Buggs is docile and is a good partner to have around. I do have to pay attention to any droppings he leaves behind so I may get them out of the cabin right away, but this has not yet been a problem.

Over the next few days I will try to harvest a deer to refresh my supply of red meat.

\* \* \*

I woke this morning before the sun had fully risen and strolled to the West River to fish.

By mid-morning, I had bagged seven decent trout, which I cleaned right there and carried to the cabin. After preparing the fresh meat, I pulled the fish that has been drying since yesterday from the smoker and put the fresh fish in.

As the day wore on, I decided to ride to the beaver ponds near the Driftpile River with the hope of bagging a goose or a duck. Along a stream connecting the ponds, I came upon a fox drinking. It kept a wary eye on me. I was able to shoot a wood duck, but as luck would have it, I had to swim in the pond to retrieve it.

I cleaned the bird and returned to the cabin. I tossed a couple pieces of wood on the smoky fire, along with more wet chips.

It is now early afternoon, and with not much to do, I sit cross-legged against my backrest outside the cabin in the sunshine. It is times like this when I am more likely to think about things that depress me.

My mind drifts to George. I wonder which memories he shares, what the reaction is from those who hear the account. I wonder if he made it out at all. I wonder if I will make it out!

Like I have said before, it is better for me to remain busy. Hiking is good therapy, as it takes my mind off of everything not connected to my environment as I wander through this enormous land.

I will cook the duck now before night sets in.

\* \* \*

This morning, I was awake and at the West River fishing as the sun rose. I managed to land eight fish before mid-morning, one of which was quite heavy. After cleaning the fish and returning to the lodge, I cut the fish into strips and added them to the racks being smoked. I replaced the dried meat with the fresh and put it in a burlap bag, storing it in the tree box.

The dried fish is safely stored in the tree box, off of the ground and away from most who would want at it. I admired my growing stock of food.

During the afternoon, I rode Canoni north toward the Driftpile River, and after crossing it, rode through dense evergreen forests. I was leading Canoni when I realized that I heard no noises. No birds singing, no squirrels chattering in the trees. Something was not right.

I searched around, slowly scouting the landscape, being cautious not to overlook anything. Seeing nothing unusual, I mounted Canoni and turned in the direction of the cabin.

Within seconds, I spotted a grizzly bear, a large brown colored male that had seen me as well and sniffed the air the way that bears do, swinging its head from side to side. He was off the trail about 50 yards, near a clearing in the forest. I turned Canoni again, this time away from the cabin, and galloped off.

The grizzly made a bluff charge in my direction, half-heartedly trying to catch me. I made a wide circle around the bear and cantered my way back.

Thinking about the incident, I wonder how long the birds were silent before I noticed it. I can't say for sure, but it could not have been too long. There is a difference in the air when it is still.

Buggs seems content and appears fat, which could be a bad omen as the winter drags on.

I write with a shrewd smile. Is it possible that Buggs could become supper someday? Just joking Buggs.

\* \* \*

## SEPTEMBER FIRST

This day began badly. I heard noises coming from outside, bear noises. Lifting up the window shutter, I saw a grizzly eating the fish in the now-open smoker. The bear was unconcerned with Canoni or me.

I opened the door so I could have a clear view of the burglary. I was afraid of what the bear might do after consuming the fish. If it came toward me, I was going to dispatch it. In a moment equally terrifying and exciting, the grizzly finished eating and looked toward the cabin, at me.

I fired a shot into the air, and it took off for the trees. I fired another round as I watched it withdraw. I get so damned fearful around bears because they are so big! With no natural enemy, they don't seem to care at all where they go. That is quite terrifying.

In truth, my knees quivered when our eyes locked, as it is a challenge to a bear when eyes meet. Combat is likely to ensue. That I did not have to destroy the bear is a great relief.

Life rapidly returns to normal after such an affair. It is evening now, but earlier an afternoon shower passed over the valley, saturating the valley.

I am calm once more, but the events of this morning are fresh in my mind. This cabin is a death trap with a bear outside, especially if it is anywhere other than in front of the cabin. The fact that I had to open the door to locate the bear was dangerous, except for my knowing how immersed in eating it was. It would be better to be able to shoot through slits in the wall on different sides of the cabin. I will consider this.

Strangely enough, I flashed back to the episode with the wolves that night when George fired through the window. I did not want to hear a loud report again. My intent was to not have to hurt the bear.

Tomorrow I will repair the damage to the smoker and replace the fish. The bear tore through the small logs bound by rope, and the smoker was no longer in one piece. It might be a good idea to remain awake tonight with the fire pit outside going, to deter the bear should it come back.

* * *

I remained awake last night and kept the outside fire going. Twice I left the closeness of the fire to retrieve more firewood. I heard sounds in my own mind, a twig snapping or something unseen moving beyond the perimeter of the cabin.

In any case, I am alive today. I will go and repair the smoker and then go fishing. I will return and write more later.

It is now early evening as I make this entry. I completed the repairs on the smoker and caught six fish during the afternoon, two of which I ate. The other four are on the rack drying.

I have decided that regardless of the season, I will have to use the storage box again to keep my food away from the natives here, all of whom have keen senses.

Since adult grizzlies cannot climb trees very well, I think the food will be safe. I would prefer that a bear steal my food from the tree rather than from the cabin. Of course, once winter arrives, bears will no longer be a concern.

I spent a few extra minutes this evening thanking the Great Spirit for allowing me to be active in this experience. Each day something occurs that makes me glad that I am here, and events such as those of today permit me to know true humbleness. Appreciating these events for the memories and knowledge that they bring, I look forward to tomorrow. I have lost my stop-in-your-tracks fear of these huge and fierce animals and instead now have a healthy respect for them, knowing that they will not attack unprovoked.

Outside the rain falls as thunder rumbles from far down the valley. I sit and write without worry. This night is not fit for man or grizzly. I honor the Mahato, the Lakota term for grizzly as I smoke my weed.

\* \* \*

I awoke this morning to rain falling, making this a morning to stay inside the cabin. However, I did throw a couple of logs and some wet wood chips on the newly-repaired smoker fire and brought the humidity level down, hoping that the fish would dry today. While the rain did not let up much, the fire stayed hot enough to serve the purpose.

I pulled a bundle of grass out for Canoni to feast on. As a final action, before dusk, I transferred the smoked fish to the storage tree.

I am now prepared to settle down for the night, letting the creatures of the night begin patrol as I sleep, secure in my fort in the woods. It is time for mundane tasks, such as polishing my arrows or cleaning the glass on my binoculars.

The world outside is owned by others. From across the cabin I feel an unblinking set of eyes upon me. There Buggs sits, chewing on grass.

\* \* \*

## SEPTEMBER 5

What a change a day makes! This morning the sun rose over the mountains to the east, which was a welcome reprieve after yesterday, cloudy with showers as it was, never warming beyond 40 degrees. As the earth heated up, a light fog was created, and within a few minutes it evaporated.

The clouds and dampness of yesterday will help extend the grass supply for an additional week or two, enabling me to keep adding to the stores.

I trekked through the forest south of the cabin. In the close distance I heard the low whine of an injured animal. Following the sound cautiously, it led me to a coyote that was in torturous pain. It had apparently been mauled by a bear. Its right eye dangled from the socket, and its jaw hung slack. Rather than permitting it to suffer, I put it down. The remains will be food for another.

After returning to the cabin I rode Canoni to the Driftpile River and caught a white fish, which is now cooking over the open fire.

As I write the sun sets behind the ridge, and as the light fades, a chill replaces the warm air of the day.

In the distance I hear a wolf call. The sound is familiar, a low note escalating to the recognizable howl, then another, then another. Buggs pretends that he doesn't hear the noises, but I see his ears focus on the sound. Such is my world this evening.

\* \* \*

As I finish the first week of September, it is easy to perceive the shifting seasons. More and more the animals seek all of the food they can consume. The leaves on the cottonwoods have all but been stripped by the wind. The Great Spirit has brought another perfect fall high-country day.

Over the past three days, I have dried 30 trout, stowing them in the tree box.

While riding this morning, I happened upon a herd of elk resting in the forest. The rutting season is less than a month away. There is little risk from this herd. I sat under a pine tree and listened to the wind rustle through the trees. The ground was soft from rain, so I chose to take a hike. I spied many species throughout the day.

I caught and dried another 15 fish today, bringing the total to 45 now stored in the tree. I have become proficient at finding the correct temperature in the smoker, which dries the meat in nine hours. This smoker has proven to be a valuable asset, for which I am grateful.

Inside the cabin, Buggs has become more at ease around me, allowing me to pick him up. It's nice to have company, even if it is only a rabbit.

I am not hungry, so without much to do, I will go to sleep.

\* \* \*

Two days later, I am resting Canoni, sitting on a rock, five miles from the lodge as I make this entry. I awoke this morning with a hankering to ride some distance. I packed my tent and sleeping bag, along with some smoked fish, and I headed north across the Driftpile, then slightly west. So far this morning I have seen two bears, one a grizzly, the other a black bear. I have seen several herds of elk, mostly cows. Deer trails crisscross the ground in all directions.

If not for a map and a compass, it would be easy to get lost out here. I imagine that the sensation of being lost would cause panic, as it did when George got turned around. So important is a compass that I carry two of them, one secured to my belt and one tucked into my shirt or coat pocket.

I am finished riding for the day, having found a stunning camping spot 50 feet from the shore of an unnamed lake. The lake is maybe a hundred feet wide and perhaps twice as long. This lake is not shown on the map and will remain unnamed. I made quick work of setting up the tent, thinking that by now I could do this in my sleep.

On the shore of the lake, I have a line in the water, hoping to harvest a fresh meal. If not, I will settle for smoked trout and venison. With three hours of daylight remaining, I do expect to catch something.

A gentle wind filters through the air, shaking the few remaining leaves off the cottonwoods. The smoke from the cooking fire wafts straight up, indicating high pressure.

Finally, a fish took the bait. I pick up my journal again with a two-pound trout sizzling in the frying pan in the fire pit. I will eat and pick up my pen later.

Dinner is finished, I feel full, and I am admiring the sunset. Near the shore of the lake, the multitude of mosquitoes that once flourished is no more. I can now enjoy the vistas without a net over my head.

I spotted a beaver on the lake, swimming with a four-foot long branch in its mouth. On the opposite shore, a buck comes to quench its thirst. The light fades, the dusk presenting itself as replacement for the pink hue that disappears in the western sky. The blaze of the campfire casts light 10 feet around me. In a tree near the lake, I hear an owl hooting, waking up for a night of hunting. It will soon be time to sleep.

\* \* \*

I write this entry having returned from hiking south of the cabin, during which time I came close to strolling into a black bear, which was actually brown in color. I was exploring an unfamiliar trail that I had discovered, which led along a ridge and cut into the mountain, leaving a steep slope on one side and a heavily brush-covered slope above me. The trail was five feet wide and anointed with thick berry patches and native ferns, some six feet tall.

As the trail smoothed out, the brush became even denser. Out of the corner of my eye I saw movement, a brown object descending from a five foot tall boulder. The bear scampered around the boulder and peered at me. Being that it was a black bear, I was not as fearful of an attack. I hollered at the bear, and to my relief, it turned and ran into the heavy brush behind the boulder, never to be seen again.

I did not do anything wrong prior to the incident, but I remain disappointed that I did not see the bear before it got within 30 feet of me.

I rode unhurried to the cabin and spent the afternoon doing chores, preparing my meal, and showing affection to Buggs. Canoni is her usual happy self, as satisfied as I am here in the woods.

I heard a rumble of thunder a second ago, but it is not raining. I hear the wind gusting against the side of the cabin. It is a reminder of how nice it is to be inside at night.

\* \* \*

This morning, I awoke to the cabin being chilly for the first time in a long time. After building up the fire, I ventured outside and was greeted by a bone-chilling cold, although the sun shone brilliantly.

During the last few days, I have been feeling uncertain. It seems that I am sometimes just a second away from losing control of myself. What I mean is that I have found it necessary to reassure myself that I am in control here.

The reality is, however, that I am along for the ride, reacting to the day-to-day events that constitute my life. The burden of being continuously on guard every moment that I am out of the lodge does, after a while, take a toll. Putting on a brave face for myself, I convince myself that I can stand against anything. That's what brought me to this place.

I miss George and wish that he had stayed with me. It is a gift to have someone to talk to, but I have no one now who can answer my words.

Every minute, at every turn, I am focused on survival. In practice, survival is harder that you would expect. There are the daily chores of finding and securing meat, hauling water from the West River to the cabin. Keeping Canoni alive is a top priority. I recognize that at any moment I could be killed out here, and in many different ways. The likeliest of them would be a bear attack.

So, I remain vigilant when it comes to my surroundings when out of the cabin. I am no more or less afraid today than any other day. I make this note so that I may remember these feelings in future years.

I have just finished eating smoked fish for dinner. It is silent tonight, and I will sleep now.

\* \* \*

I woke early and coaxed Canoni out for some exercise. While riding to the Driftpile River, I rode across a new set of grizzly tracks in the sand, half a mile from the cabin. I noted the heavy thicket of bushes in an area of fallen trees, inside the dense forest of evergreens. In the many times that I had passed that trail, I had never noticed that undergrowth before today.

The sun felt good on my back as I rode along. I spotted the same small herd of elk that I discovered the other evening, six in all. They ate grass in a meadow halfway between the cabin and the Driftpile River.

I arrived at the cabin a short time ago and now make this entry. For my meal, I will roast a duck that I took and cleaned while returning from the Driftpile River on my way in.

The customary noises fill the twilight hour, a bugling elk, the hoot of my neighbor, crickets. Canoni is calm, and Buggs sits by the door chewing on grass. Everything in my world indicates that no danger is present. I will eat and then sleep.

\* \* \*

## LATE-SEPTEMBER ROLLS IN

It is becoming cold enough to store meat and have it freeze. The end of autumn in the wilderness brings with it the last chance to travel easily from place to place, the concluding days to prepare for the season ahead.

At this time of year, bears are eating anything that they can find, gaining weight for the long winter hibernation.

I consumed part of the day fetching firewood and schlepping new grass bundles to add to the stockpile for Canoni.

I am dreading the coming months with no one to talk to during those storms that sometimes last for days. Buggs is adorable, but he is not a talker.

To pass idle time I worked on sharpening my knife with the wet stone, to bring the razor edge back. I used the opportunity to sharpen my axe and hatchet as well. The sun has set already, but I stayed inside so I did not see it.

I ate smoked fish and venison for my meal. The fire glows across the cabin, creating a warm and cozy atmosphere. The modest, handmade décor is dimly lit by the fire. Flickering figures dance on the opposite wall. I feel relaxed and secure in my cabin.

Enough for today, I am tired. Tomorrow is another day.

\* \* \*

Four days later, I am watching my meal cook over the fire pit outside as I put pen to paper.

This morning I was awakened by the bugling of a male elk. I went to investigate, and I followed the calls to the edge of a meadow, a mile north of the cabin. Through a fresh two inches of snow, I eased my way closer to the herd, moving a foot or two, then stopping for a few seconds, while using the trees as much as possible for cover. Creeping to within a hundred yards of the herd, I stopped and lay prone for a shot. I took my time and dropped a female with a bullet through her heart. The herd deliberately moved away as I approached.

I fetched Canoni and led her to the kill site. I spent a portion of the morning field dressing the meat and carried 100 pounds to the cabin on Canoni. After further butchering the meat and hanging it in the tree box, I took a quick bath in the West River to wash the blood off of myself.

I looked over the map trying to decide where to hunt. It seems a good idea to stay in the valleys, and this valley is as big as any other nearby. Last year was as much about exploration as it was about hunting.

\* \* \*

This morning brought a cold front, dropping the temperature into the low thirties. Now it is sunny and brisk outside.

I am starting to believe that if I didn't have this journal to write in, I might go insane.

With much idle time in the day, my mind races with thoughts about everything and anything. Observing the constant struggles occurring in this land, and seeing the circle of life played out time after time before my eyes, brings to mind topics of conversation that should not go undiscussed. Yet, sadly, I am alone, save for Canoni and Buggs.

So although some entries in this journal lack excitement, the little things are noticed and appreciated by me. It is important for me personally to keep up my practice of recording the daily happenings so I will be able to look back on them in years to come.

I will have an unusual meal today. I took the ribcage of the bull elk and smashed it in half so three ribs were together. I am boiling the bones in a pot to get to the marrow. I will add chunks of meat to the broth to make a hearty kind of stew. I will let it cook for a few hours and enjoy it later.

Several hours are left before sunset, so I will take care of my chores.

I add this entry to note that the broth turned out filling and tasty. Locating the supplies that George buried was a Godsend, but they will soon be gone. I am full, it is late, and I will now retire.

\* \* \*

This morning, a cold front pushed through, fixing the thermometer at 34 degrees. A stiff breeze blew in from the north, making it even colder.

I bundled up in my long johns, a heavy wool shirt, and my heavy coat and spent a part of the morning tending to Canoni and carrying wood into the cabin. I replenished the water as well.

I schemed for ways to block the cold air from sneaking in under the door, but other than using a rolled up shirt or skin, I have not found a solution to this conundrum.

I took a stroll in the forest south of the cabin and viewed a flock of Canada geese near the West River. They are a suspicious and cautious bunch. Once they noticed me, the guards never diverted their eyes. I got to within a hundred feet, and they waddled away. I had breached their comfort zone. I like the way the honking travel through the valley, sometimes getting a reply from another bird somewhere else. If I didn't have eyes on them, I might not be able to locate them from sound alone.

I ate the remainder of the elk stew for my meal this afternoon. It would be better if it had potatoes and corn in it.

\* \* \*

As the final few days of September play out, autumn becomes more pronounced. I woke up with the sunrise, and after watching Buggs sprint out of the cabin, I rode Canoni toward the Gataga River. My intention was to hunt a buck. In a tree nearby a solitary crow cawed at full volume for reasons unknown. After a short ride, I found myself in a narrow canyon with steep walls on either side of me. A stream ran through the center of the canyon, which is what I used as a trail.

I spotted a buck eating along this unnamed stream some three hundred yards in front of me. I dismounted Canoni and cautiously reduced the distance between us. The breeze was in my face, swinging the odds in my favor.

After a few additional minutes, I was 200 yards away and decided to take the shot from there. I used learned breathing techniques to improve my aim, holding steady on the area just behind the front shoulder. Once the buck stopped, I squeezed off the shot. The sound of the discharge in the quiet startled me, as usual.

The buck turned as I fired, and the shot caught it high on the left shoulder, in the low neck area. The shot spun the deer around and down to the ground. I knew I had not killed the animal, but it remained down. I returned to Canoni, mounted her, and rode methodically to where the buck would be.

From 50 yards away, I could see the buck stand and stagger away, though I recognized that it was bleeding out. I was dismounting Canoni when I heard the sound of what was most certainly a grizzly bear, attacking the wounded deer. I jumped back onto Canoni and whirled her about to see the event. I observed as the bear smashed the deer with both paws and bit into its neck. The attack was over in 30 seconds, as the buck lay dead and the bear stood over the body, sniffing the air and looking around.

This was no longer my kill. There is no more sure death than to try and divert a bear from its meal. This kill I gift to the bear.

Back at the cabin, I pulled some meat from the tree box and cooked my daily meal. I swept out the pellets left by Buggs and gave the whole cabin a cleaning. After replenishing the firewood and water, I smoked a pipe full of weed and am now recounting the events of the day. I must say that I am annoyed about not getting my buck, but at the same time, it was an awesome spectacle of plundering by the bear.

* * *

Not much has materialized to write about in the last two days. Hell, nothing has transpired to write about. The month of September continues to retreat, each day bringing this land closer to the inevitable plunge into winter.

The only item of note is that Buggs's fur has changed from brown to off-white, and the weather is staying cold, but nothing else is different or stirring about today. I caught a trout from the Driftpile River in the afternoon and will eat it for diner.

I found Canoni this morning grazing in the meadow, several hundred yards south of the cabin. She trotted to me when she saw me outside the cabin. I sure do love Canoni. As of this night, Canoni shall sleep in the cabin.

I enter this note while sitting on my sleeping bag observing Canoni's reaction to being inside. She is standing along the north wall facing the entry. The flickering light of the fire waltzes across the wall, catching her attention. Buggs is in his usual spot in the corner quietly studying all that occurs.

\* \* \*

## LAST DAY OF SEPTEMBER

Today the wolf pack returned to the valley. I heard them howling late last night. This morning, I rode south to the entrance of the valley and trotted in a circle in the direction of the cabin. I scouted wolf tracks leading from the trees into an open meadow near the Fox River, which runs into the Driftpile River north and west of the cabin. As long as they keep their distance, there will be no war.

Upon arriving at the cabin, the thought of hunting elk crossed my mind, but it will be better to give the pack a day to leave the area and avoid risking a confrontation. Instead, I did my chores and played with Buggs and Canoni for most of the day.

It has become easy for me to judge any danger in my surroundings by observing Canoni. She is constantly aware of her surroundings, from a mouse in the corral to a bear in the meadow. She is an excellent early warning system. Her coat is shiny, and she maintains her health.

When I started my journal, I promised myself that I would describe the log cabin's interior, which will be my prison for the near future. The log walls are not tall and seem to close in each day. I have to stoop when entering or leaving the building or risk being knocked out should I forget to bend.

The bow and arrows hanging from the wall next to the fireplace and the snowshoes hanging on the opposite wall serve as decent decoration. The fireplace has a coat of ash in the hearth and soot resides on the chimney walls. Next to the fireplace stacked wood serves as fuel for the night ahead. Several deer skins lie on the floor against the door, my effort to keep drafts out. My rifle leans against the wall near the door, and the window is propped open allowing fresh air into the cabin. Below the window, two backrests lean against the wall waiting to be used.

In the southwest corner sits Buggs, while I sleep in the southeast quadrant. Canoni occupies the whole north side along the wall.

In the northwest corner hang two canteens, along with the cooking utensils, which lean against the wall in the same corner. Everything seems to smell like smoke, and it seems impossible to get rid of the odor.

This accurately describes the lodge. I will soon prepare an elk steak for dinner and then turn in for the night.

\* \* \*

## OCTOBER

I am memorializing today's events as precisely as possible. It has been an extraordinary day. After doing my daily chores, I chose to hunt along the Driftpile River. On the trail, half a mile from the cabin, I spotted a doe feeding on shrubs. I shot her and field dressed the meat.

I returned to the cabin, completed butchering the meat, and placed it in the tree box. I would estimate that I garnered 40 pounds of meat.

As it was midday, I ventured to where I had previously hunted, and within 20 minutes, I had scoped another doe a hundred yards off the trail. It browsed on a hillside and did not know that I was there. I crept closer and fired from 50 yards, dropping the doe where it stood. I had cut the belly open and propped the stomach open when I glanced up at the hillside opposite me.

I spotted a wolf inspecting me. Within five minutes, four more wolves appeared at the side of the first. I was paying more attention to them than to what I was doing, and I sliced my thumb open. The wolves stalked off in several directions but kept their piercing eyes on me throughout.

By then, I was thinking that this meat was not worth fighting the pack for, so I took a hind leg, leaving the rest on the ground. The wolves owned the field today because they detected me first and had me under surveillance. I did not expect to see a wolf when I glanced up.

Now I wonder if they are inclined to think that they can intimidate me. But I am not intimidated by them. I can outsmart them, and I can strike from long range.

\* \* \*

October advances as I sit with a cup of warm tea and consider my hunting plans. Of course, it is my desire to hunt under a sunny, dry sky, but not being able to guarantee that, I will bring gear for any eventuality. Today, puffy clouds obstructed the sun in places, casting shadows on the mountains here and there. The day has been cold but sunny.

I rode Canoni along the ridge behind the cabin and regarded the landscape. Across the West River, west of the cabin, in the meadow, a group of four does grazed for grass.

I was able to shoot one from the ridge top, and after retrieving it, I expended time cleaning and butchering the meat. I estimate that I now have a hundred and 50 pounds of meat, dried fish, and jerky in the tree box.

Late in the afternoon I took a chunk of meat from the storage box and will soon cook it over the flame in the fireplace. Buggs, ever the perfect guest, lies in his corner of the lodge. It has been another fantastic day in the mountains, which are my home. After dinner I will bring Canoni inside for the night.

\* \* \*

Today was a working day. I spent time patching some places outside where the adobe has begun to wear thin in the chimney. It seems that the side facing east is the most affected. That I have not had to make many repairs to the cabin is a testament to its solid construction. If I could, I would add a porch roof so I could be outside in the rain, but that would be a pointless job, as I expect I will leave the cabin next year. I collected some firewood to re-stock the supply on the side of the cabin.

Early in the afternoon, I took Canoni for a ride, and this time, for the first time, I took Buggs with us, draping him over the saddle in front of me. I rode for an hour and at one point stopped and dismounted. I set Buggs down to see if he would run away, but he stayed right next to Canoni, eating grass. It looks like Canoni and I have a comrade for life.

In the meadow to the south of the cabin, a fat cow elk grazed as I approached and barely lifted her head to greet me.

I now cook a steak over the fire outside as I write. I smell the smoke from fat dripping into the flame. This is one memory I wish to keep. Buggs is outside with Canoni, both of them eating grass in front of the cabin. I wish I had my camera for this one.

\* \* \*

October has burned through the first week. I write this entry while lying against my backrest by the fire, feeling the warmth on my face. The day has been cold, and the wind has raged all day, keeping me inside, other than to execute my daily chores.

I heard a loud flock of geese fly over the cabin today, but by the time I dashed outside with my rifle, they were out of range. Even though the cabin was clean to start with, I swept it out today. Something with which to keep my mind occupied.

I thought about my parents today, about both of their personalities, and I pondered how these two people became my parents. My father is, without doubt, in charge of the house. He supports a family of four on his salary alone. My mother is a homemaker and has not worked since before they were married. Mother is timid, quick to play it safe rather than taking a risk once in a while. My father is a weekend drinker and dabbles in minor gambling. My mother has always seemed to be along for the ride. In this respect, I am more like my father than my mother. I am more like my mother when it comes to my empathy and concern for the human race. I am unlike either of them in terms of my craving for adventure.

\* \* \*

Three days passed, and today I rode to the Driftpile River this morning to fish and on the bank discovered bear tracks. I scouted the shore, and downstream a quarter of a mile, I spotted a male, judging by the size, searching for food. He went on with his hunt, following his nose around the bend and out of my life.

While fishing, I bagged a goose, which had been eating grass near the bank. Having harvested the bird, I stopped fishing and rode to the cabin. The chore of hunting in some fashion for my meals has become preset into my mind. Without thinking, the first thing I consider in the morning is securing food, whether hunting it or retrieving it from the tree box. I do not let an easy opportunity to secure food go by. Once that task is accomplished, a burden is lifted from my mind, and I can go about the day.

Buggs seems attached to Canoni, as he is quick to follow her around the meadow. He does not stray more than 10 feet from her when they are in the pasture together.

The goose was heavy, and it was easier to chop it into quarters and cook it on a stick. Each quarter usually takes about 30 minutes roasting over the flame. I have stored the other three quarters in the tree box. So far the weather has been cool enough to keep the food stores preserved, though not frozen solid.

\* \* \*

I write this entry early in the day. I opened the door, and I see that several inches of snow fell overnight. This scene prompts me to chop more wood for winter. I will complete this chore and write later.

It is now late afternoon. I spent the day gathering firewood, or more accurately, breaking limbs from the many dead trees that litter the hillside. My supply is exposed, but that's fine. It is not snowing enough to bury the wood yet.

Buggs is near his corner of the cabin, settled in for the night. Canoni is content standing close to the wall. Other than the sound of the wind, all is quiet.

My mind without reason brings images of my sisters, and I wonder how they are doing? I am a terrible brother. I have not spoken to them in a long while. We are all so different, so much so that it's sometimes hard to believe we're related. They are all living hectic lives, scattered throughout California. I guess I sometimes do wish that we were closer, and maybe someday we will be. They are blood, and they matter to me, which is why they came to mind. I can only hope there will be a time when commitments allow us to be together in one place again, to go over what our lives have been like.

\* \* \*

October moves onward and I woke up to a cold cabin. Outside the temperature was 16 degrees. I threw three logs on the fire and wrapped my sleeping bag around myself, listening warily. Through the door, I could make out the wind gusting. Upon opening it I was surprised to see a storm raging. I could not see the meadow, which is only 50 feet from the cabin.

My plan for the day was made. I had to climb the tree to get some fish for my meal, but aside from that I have remained inside. Life in the wild does not stop, only time seems to stop. I am bored to death inside the cabin. I have read all of my books often enough to recite them, so there is no point in reading them again. I can't very well play Stratego by myself. I am glad that Buggs is here. Buggs, Canoni, and my journal keep me sane.

\* \* \*

Two days later, I started the day by having a cup of pine needle tea, leaning against my backrest by the open door of the cabin.

As I contemplated what to do today, out of the trees strolled four wolves. They assembled and watched me. I viewed them with my rifle in hand, waiting for their next move. I do not think the alpha male was among them, as it appeared to me that none of the four desired to lead the others toward me. I moved the few feet to the corral and nuzzled Canoni, calming her down. She knew that the wolves were there.

After a couple of minutes, one of the four took a few steps in the direction of the cabin. I squeezed off a round, and all four vanished into the forest. The wolves are in many ways unpredictable, while in other ways, they are reasonably predictable. They were so bold today, appearing out of the woods and inspecting me. The night that George killed the wolf at the cabin door, the instant, intense violence that the wolf brought to the situation was unpredictable.

Yet in seeing a mom with her pups, the mother's moves are predictable. It is unnerving to think that wolves work together to overcome challenges and survive. I wonder what they make of me. I know that they are wary of me, but by no means are they afraid of me. This condition is both scary and exciting, and I am satisfied with how I handled it this time.

*　*　*

I think that there might have been a rockslide or an earthquake during the night.

I felt the earth vibrate slightly. The terrain rumbled, though not to a significant degree. Overnight, a fast-moving snowstorm dropped several inches on top of the base already on the ground.

It has now become essential for me to clear the escape trails from the cabin to the West River. So I will ride Canoni from place to place, up and down from the cabin to the river.

I am back in the warmth of the cabin, after riding in a pattern from the cabin to the West River. I can now get to the water from three directions. One might ask why this was significant to me, and I can only say that it is because I have had a recurring dream in the past.

I am in a circumstance where I have to escape, but my singular route of escape is where the danger lies. I feel safest with several escape routes.

I pulled a venison steak from the tree box and am defrosting it near my fire. Buggs is his usual self, soundlessly taking up space in the corner of the cabin. I think that I will make it a daily task to hike on the three escape trails that I fashioned today to keep them maintained.

# 11

# Winter 1977

The sun never quite made it out today, instead clouds covered the land.

I noticed that I am not the only one using my trails. I have discovered other tracks, and judging by the size of some of them, elk are using them as well. I confirmed this during the afternoon when an elk with an eight-point rack wandered on one of the escape trails from the forest to the meadow in front of the cabin. I caught a glimpse of it when I opened the cabin door to let Buggs inside. It approached the corral, possibly intending to reach the grass stored against the cabin wall.

I stepped outside, and the elk trotted into the forest. I had not considered this eventuality when I stored the grass. I thought maybe mice, deer, and Buggs, but I didn't even consider that elk might plunder the grass store.

The winters usually last from late August through the end of March, which is a long time.

The sun came out in the afternoon, and I reclined against my backrest on a deer skin near the fire pit with Canoni strolling through the meadow and Buggs perched on my lap.

Once the afternoon sun set, I retreated inside.

It will soon be time to sleep and awake tomorrow to who knows what, so I will stop writing now.

Overall, today was a non-eventful day.

\* \* \*

Today, after doing my chores, I rode to the Gataga River and was surprised to see a small number of salmon swimming through. I may possibly try and add to my food supply tomorrow. For now, I am content to sit in the cabin playing with Buggs and honing my knife blade.

It seems as though there is a period of time between the first of autumn and the first significant snowfall when I am antsy, restless. I have a suspicion that it has to do with the anxiety that I experience in dreading the inevitable, in this case the onset of winter. While I take advantage of the weather that October has bestowed, I know that I am running out of time to be fully prepared for the long winter ahead.

The reality is that I have enough food to get through the worst of winter. If I do need to hunt, history has shown that game resides in this area.

I am contemplating how to collect the salmon. Catching them with a hook will be slow. I could try to give them a concussion by hitting the water with a stick, or I could shoot them. I could spear them as well. I am thinking that I will try to spear them first. I imagine myself trying this in my mind.

\* \* \*

I spent the day at the Gataga River viewing the salmon. This is about the same time that the salmon appeared last year, however there were hundreds upon hundreds then. This year there appear to be far fewer, at least today. I did not see any bears, but with the salmon in the Gataga River, they won't be long in arriving.

I decided I have enough salmon and meat stored now, so I will not harvest anymore.

\* \* \*

This morning I went to the Gataga River to view the salmon and while I was there, two different bear materialized. Fortunately, they were both on the other side of the Gataga River and were happy to pick off the weak or injured fish. They wasted so much meat. I watched them eat the eggs and the brains and then let the fish sink to the sand. Nature has programmed them to consume all of the protein they can get. Within a month or so, they will be hibernating.

My pal Buggs has been at my side since I sat down to write 10 minutes ago. He is rubbing his body against my leg. Canoni is sitting on the ground as the shadows jitterbug on the wall behind her. It seems that the more we ignore each other, the stronger the bond grows.

\* \* \*

This morning, I awoke to a beautiful, royal blue cloudless sky. After taking care of my chores, I hiked to the Gataga River and surveyed the now few remaining salmon as they swam past. Three grizzly bears splashed around in the water downstream as they tried to catch the fish. After viewing them, I would say that they are successful in one out of five tries. The bears, however, have an abundance of energy to try time after time, knowing that they have a short time to complete this feast before seeking out a den.

Along the banks, I saw a few dozen headless salmon, which will become fertilizer for the forest, at least whatever the scavengers leave. I recall last year seeing foxes, coyotes, and river otters eating the fish on the banks. After several days, the flesh rotted and was reclaimed by the earth.

\* \* \*

I woke to the sound of the cabin door rattling from the gusting wind outside. This morning it blew from the east, which is unusual. I could feel the draft coming in under the door, so I pressed a deer skin against the door on the floor to seal the gap. As the day wore on, a fast-moving storm dropped a couple of inches of new snow and then vanished as quickly as it arrived.

Where the water along the banks of the West River is less than six inches deep, a thin layer of ice has formed. I have resigned myself to the fact that these conditions will recur numerous times during the coming months and that for a good portion of that time, I may be cabin-bound. At least I have Buggs and Canoni to keep me company.

I am cooking a venison stew, which has been simmering on the fire for a good part of the day. I chopped meat and added a few remaining spices. Buggs sits next to me, enjoying the warmth of the fire. I look over to Canoni, and she is fine. She wears her blanket and faces the cabin door so that her exposure to the fire is maximum.

It seems that on a day like today, everything is keeping a low profile, staying out of the elements.

\* \* \*

I am making this entry after waking up moments ago. I am sick. I have a stomachache and have made several trips outside to use the toilet, as it were. It is cold, and the wind is blowing. I feel hot and thirsty. I need to sleep some more.

I am awake, it is midday, and I made another trip outside. My stomach is still upset and cramping, and I am sweating. My thirst lingers even as I drink water. My head aches as well. I will sleep again.

I am awake, it is late afternoon now. I continue to sweat, and I stink. The cabin seems too hot, and I am tempted to open the door for a while, but I won't do it because I know that I am sick with fever. I am not hungry. I let Buggs and Canoni out earlier, and they have come in now. I have nothing to do but watch the shadows swing and sway on the walls and be still.

\* \* \*

With thanks I feel less ill today, although my stomach is still queasy. At the least, I am no longer sweating, and the Sqershey herts are gone. I am thirsty and likely dehydrated, so I will soon head to the West River to refill the canteens. I have no choice but to drink lots of water today.

The weather is clear and sunny, but cold. No doubt about it, I am going to bathe and wash my hair today.

It is mid-afternoon, and I have finished drying my hair. I feel much better having had a bath and washing my dirty hair. It took a solid hour by the fire brushing it to dry it.

I will take a ride around the meadow in a bit to exercise Canoni.

I have returned from riding throughout the afternoon. I rode first on the escape trails, three laps, before heading north of the cabin, in the direction of the Driftpile River. The newly fallen snow was spoiled only by the tracks of animals migrating through the area. I heard the hammering sound of the woodpecker as I rode. The sound reverberated in the otherwise near total quiet of the forest.

I crossed the Driftpile River and rode east to the Gataga River, not having been there in some time. The Gataga is still flowing and has not frozen over. I did not think to bring my fishing pole, so I could not fish. I thought that the Gataga River would be iced over.

I passed a frozen, half-eaten elk on the return ride, obviously killed by wolves. Scavenger birds, which I think are ravens, picked at the carcass as I passed.

\* \* \*

Two days later, the weather unexpectedly threw me a surprise. When I came inside yesterday it was sunny and clear. This morning, I opened the door to new snow! It is quite cold, but the need to compact the escape trails dictates that I go into the chill. I will write more this morning when I am finished with my tasks.

I pick up my pen after warming my hands, having completed my required routines. The thermometer read a mere seven degrees as I passed it on my way to the West River.

Being here alone in this quiet, uncrowded place has made me appreciate things that I have come to see and know. This latest weather surprise permits me to recognize the swiftness with which things change.

I am familiar with myself, who I am, what my limitations are. I listen to my inner voice, which is why I have survived this place.

Through the seasons past I witnessed simple occurrences, such as seeing hummingbirds battle for the right to own a desired area. At any time I see the sunlight shine upon the wings of a hummingbird, I will recall this place. Each time I smell the scent of pine and the wet earth after a summer rain, I will reminisce about this land. The memories vary from the dark, rain filled days to riding along a ravine while crossing a mountain range to being swept away in the current of the Gataga River that fateful day last summer.

I embrace memories of the day that George and I finished building the cabin and the time that he lost his long johns in the West River. When I think of those things, I will forever be reminded of this place. I know not what the future holds for me, but whatever it is; I will always recollect this place.

Night has come as I write. I have finished eating some smoked fish and jerky for my meal. Canoni is standing in her usual place while in contrast Buggs has been fidgety this evening, moving around the cabin. He normally rests in the corner opposite the fireplace.

\* \* \*

During the past two days, snow has dropped without end, and the cold lingers. Except to hike the escape trails and answer the call of nature, I have remained indoors, mostly talking and singing, at times listening to the wind. Occasionally I hear a howl coming from deep in the forest, but it is soon drowned out by the wind. From the tree outside the cabin, I hear the intermittent hoot of the owls.

Canoni is well fed and seems content as she strolls around the grounds outside. Buggs is happy and seems to be underfoot today, wanting me perhaps to hold him.

I must bundle up and brave the elements and go out to do chores. I will write later.

I have returned from completing my chores, and it feels good to be warm. In most places off the escape trails, the snow could be as deep as three feet deep, although it is compressed in other places as a result of animals moving through their range. On the escape trails themselves, the earth is packed firm, providing traction and saving me energy.

I spent the past hour removing snow from the roof and packing the snow around the cabin. I then led Canoni to the West River to drink and to get some exercise.

I am cooking smoked fish and so will lay down my pen and eat my meal.

\* \* \*

Today, the sun dominated the sky, and though it shone bright, it remains cold. A hush prevailed when I was out suffering through my chores, as neither man nor beast wandered about.

I held Canoni in the cabin for a few hours this morning. She reacted in the usual way, enjoying the warmth while scanning the landscape from the doorway. Buggs seemed to have no problem with the idea as he sat snugly in his corner observing the goings on.

Even while feeling the cold, I took time to thank the Great Spirit for the purity of my slice of this Earth. I so love the silence and the occasional rush of adrenalin that this place offers.

\* \* \*

During the past three days, the weather has kept me isolated within this shell I call home.

Aside from trying to avoid the hell that is found in boredom I have done nothing but sit attending the fire and having one sided conversations with my room mates.

I have finished dinner, and I had an interesting thought. Here I am living in the wilderness, the greatest challenge by far in my life. If I am successful and go back to civilization, I can't imagine anything grander happening in my life. How long and boring might a life be when one has reached the pinnacle, has achieved the one goal they had in life, all by their 22nd birthday. I fear that perhaps I will never again know beauty and challenge such as I know here. It is a sad thought.

\* \* \*

## NOVEMBER

This morning the sun rose with golden rays in the eastern sky. Three deer stood by the corral eating grass meant for Canoni. They do not have enough courage to go inside the corral. I have seen this behavior before as recent as last week. As I appear in the doorway, they run through the snowy meadow and into the trees, stopping to glance my way before moving on.

In fact, something that I keep in mind when hunting deer is that when they are spooked, they always run a safe distance and then turn back to see what spooked them. The time to shoot is when they turn to have a peek.

It is such a wonderful morning that I believe I will take a ride.

I was presented with a moment of decision while out riding. I saddled Canoni and grabbed Buggs, and the three of us navigated south on the snow trail leading to the meadow. Once through the meadow, I heard antler thrashing against antler. I dismounted, and rifle at the ready, followed the racket to a ravine. From above I saw two bull elk, literally gripped in a battle to the death. Their antlers were interlocked, and there was no way that these two elk would be able to free themselves.

To be merciful, I decided to dispatch one of them so the other might live. In that moment, in that place, I was playing God. I would choose which elk would live or die. Without further thought, I shot the one on the right. It fell to the ground, and the other elk managed to struggle free and bolt away.

I was then faced with having to dress and carry the meat from the kill to the cabin. I cleaned and dressed the meat, cutting it in large pieces, and made three trips to collect it all. I stored it in the tree box and then took a sponge bath in the West River.

I left the rack outside and will mount it above the cabin entryway soon.

I ate a bit of the elk for dinner, and I now sit by the door against the wall making this entry. An interesting thing occurred during the excitement with the elk. When I dismounted I left Buggs wedged between the horn of my saddle and Canoni's neck. During the entire episode, Buggs stayed still and did not make a sound.

I would like to believe that God brought me both Canoni and Buggs to help me through on this astonishing journey. They have become my only friends, my constant companions, and they even teach me how to attend to them more efficiently. In return, I provide them with food, protection from predators, and a secure place to call home.

I can't overstate my relief since I have been bringing Canoni into the cabin at night. I can truly close the cabin door at night and forget about what may be lingering outside.

\* \* \*

I awoke to find the same three does as yesterday eating grass in the corral. They were caught by surprise at the sight of Canoni stepping out of the cabin as if she owned the place. They dashed into the forest in a panic.

I will say that allowing Canoni in the cabin is not bad. She is quiet, and she actually lays down for part of the night. I feel that we are in this together, and it's hard enough to survive without having to face the cold on top of it.

The afternoon is young, and so I will take Buggs and go for a ride. I'm curious to see how the West River is flowing heading north from the cabin. I will write later.

It is evening, and a piece of salmon cooks over the fire. Well, warming is more accurate since it is cured.

Buggs took pleasure in the ride. He gets to see places that he would never see on foot when we ride. When I dismount, he gets to explore the area. When we're atop Canoni, he stays right at the base of her neck and the saddle horn.

I spied a bull moose near the beaver pond, standing belly-high in the water.

I hear the owls hooting outside, one of the many familiar sounds of the twilight in the forest. Hoot-hoot-hoot. Night has taken hold of the land again, and so I will eat and then sleep.

\* \* \*

This a.m. I went about doing my chores and within an hour was finished. I sat on a rock outside the cabin deciding if I was going to ride or hike today. I looked across the meadow, and across from the cabin, I saw a beautiful fox, making its way through the snow along the trees in search of food. It saw me at the same instant that I noticed it, and the fox stopped in its tracks to scrutinize me. After sitting and staring at me for a moment, the fox moved south toward the forest.

I decided to follow it. I slipped into my snowshoes, and I was able to keep the fox in sight for the next quarter mile, until it went into the forest and trotted away.

During the time that I observed it, the fox was able to catch a mouse but missed a snowshoe hare.

From the meadow, I moved on southwest toward the canyon in which we let the horses graze those couple of days, since I hadn't been there in a while. I trudged through the meadow without much effort, as the snow was not too deep there. Near the approach to the canyon, the snow became deeper, causing me to sink a few inches into the snow, making the travel somewhat more grueling.

In the canyon itself I found the frozen carcass of a deer half buried in a drift of snow. It may have starved, as I saw no sign of attack wounds. Perhaps this one had been injured internally somehow and couldn't make it. The rest of my hike was uneventful.

\* \* \*

I scared off a lone wolf from in front of the cabin, across the meadow. Canoni was in the cabin, so the wolf could not get to her, but she was nervous, and she alerted me to it. I opened the window and fired a couple of rounds into the ground. The wolf fled north toward the Driftpile River. No big deal, she was making her rounds.

I let Canoni outside, and Buggs followed her. I kept a sharp watch while I did my chores, knowing how sly wolves can be.

The rest of the day was not adventurous in any way. I am thankful for the mild weather that has stayed with us over the past few days. There is something to be said for dry, stable weather. Today the thermometer shows it to be 32 degrees.

Judging by the absence of tracks in the snow, and the fact that I have not spotted a bear for several weeks, I think it is safe to say that they are now hibernating.

It is evening, and the day is nearly done. I ate smoked fish and vitamins for dinner tonight. Canoni now lies in front of the door, like the largest Great Dane you ever saw, and Buggs is asleep near the fireplace. But for the wind blowing, it is a quiet night.

I look forward to another tomorrow, knowing as I do, tomorrow will be another cold day. But that is part of the experience as well. I guess I could never ask why someone would whine about freezing if I had not lived through it myself.

\* \* \*

November has begun with relatively mild temperatures, which makes the difference between loving and hating this environment. I have returned from a long hike, 13 miles in all. I did not intend it to be that long, but I took the long way, as they say.

The sky this morning was cobalt blue, with little breeze. Wearing my snowshoes I trucked to where the Driftpile River meets the Fox River, six miles one way. The ground was frozen solid and icy in places from repeated melting and freezing of the snow. In most other places, I sank four inches into the snow with each step.

In some places where the elk had marched through, the ground was blemished and uneven. I saw fresh droppings, indicating elk in the area. Closer to the lodge, I viewed a fox through the binoculars and watched it hunt its prey. After a few minutes of viewing these antics, I trudged on, my legs tired, and ready to rest.

I finally arrived at the cabin. It felt so good to take the weight off of my feet. When I returned, Buggs was near the corral with Canoni, both happily eating grasses, which by now is drier and likely less, nutritious, but they both look fat and happy.

On days like today, I miss George's company. We used to have so much fun hiking the trails together. He made a game of which one of us would identify wildlife before the other. This kept us entertained but also more aware of our surrounding.

I will eat salmon for my meal tonight. It has been another day full of spectacle and gratification. I thank the Great Spirit for this day.

\* \* \*

I have just slipped back into the lodge after relieving myself. I spotted lynx tracks, I assume from the shape and size, around the cabin. The tracks are to be too small to be a mountain lion, so I guess a lynx. It looped around the cabin, close to the wall, before heading to the tree box. It was not able to open the box, but the trail led right to the bottom of the tree and then off to the east on the other side of the tree. The lynx apparently climbed up, couldn't get any meat, and then departed. He was quite stealthy, since none of us in the cabin heard anything.

I am as thrilled as I was during my first week in the wild every time I see tracks and consider that I am on the inside in this zoo. Even at times when my mind might wander, it soon returns to focus, looking for danger.

It is late afternoon, and I am outside, leaning against the west facing cold cabin wall with the fading sun on my face. It has been another beautiful day, especially considering the time of year.

Buggs almost got picked off a short time ago. As he ate grass in the meadow, a hawk swooped down, narrowly missing him. Buggs dashed into the open cabin and has not gone outside since. I think Buggs was careless in where he chose to eat.

I am thawing out a piece of meat for my meal. I can hear the pair of owls nesting in their tree across the open meadow. They observe me and occasionally fly over the meadow to snatch a meal. The largest prey I have seen them with was a marmot.

\* \* \*

As is true with every day here, I never know what I will wake up to. Today it was snow, several inches of it fell overnight. It is cold now, a chilly reminder that it is November.

Afternoon has come already, and with it blew blustery weather out of the north. What a difference a single day makes here.

I cleaned the ashes out of the fireplace, which was a dirty job. I took my sponge bath earlier before the wind came up. Now I am drying my hair, sitting near the fire, alternately brushing my hair and putting down my thoughts.

Being the only human here, it sometimes gets depressing that I can't have a conversation with someone else. Throughout the day little things occur, like a hummingbird appearing during the summer, that I want to comment on, but neither of my roommates has yet learned to speak. So I talk to myself or write in my journal.

I seriously wonder sometimes what the limit is of my capacity to be alone. Am I putting my mental state at risk by having no company to talk to? Sometimes I have to concentrate on whether I am thinking or speaking out loud. It appears like it would be easy for me to become estranged from others when I lack the companionship that I am accustomed to.

Yet when I think about being with people, I find myself preferring solitude. I am not by nature anti-social, but I have always liked to be alone in nature, and, in fact, lived alone in my apartments with few exceptions. That was prior to this journey, before I sold my possessions and freed myself from all that bound me to the city. Who is to say how this journey will affect me, but the journey will continue, and the story will be told someday.

I will cook my meal and then let Canoni into the cabin to sleep. All is calm and quiet this evening.

* * *

During the long night, Canoni seemed edgy. Her ears were turned forward, eyes open wide as she listened in the dark. I tried to pick up any sound as well but only heard the soft crunching of snow outside. I crouched near the door listening intently, rifle in hand, ready for action. After a few minutes the noise was gone.

This morning tracks in the snow indicated that our visitor was an elk, which grazed on Canoni's grass. I, myself, am hungry, too, this morning so I will cook some fish for breakfast and get after my chores.

Buggs has ventured out of the lodge and is next to Canoni in the corral. I was going to take a ride, but I have decided that I will instead relax by the fire pit with a cup of pine needle tea. Later I will cook my usual meal and call it a day.

In the meantime, I will be a part of the scenery and observe the goings-on in my safe haven in this wild world.

I saw a squirrel in the tree where the tree box is. Although it could not get in today, this little pest will try forever to break into the box. I may have to shoot it if it comes to be too close to the meat, as I can't have it contaminating my rations.

I have finished dinner and now enjoy time with my roommates, all of us settling in for the night. Canoni does not take long to lie down anymore, and Buggs sleeps in his place by the fireplace.

* * *

Four lonesome days have come and gone, and during this time little of interest has occurred. The weather has been relatively tranquil while both my roommates and me are well. As is the case now, each day inside brings a battle to maintain my sanity. The hours crawl past as I listen for any sound out of the normal. And so winter inches on.

* * *

Like yesterday, the snow does not cease to fall, dropping several inches during the past 24 hours. The wind is gusting outside, and through the door I heard it build from a breeze to a gale force wind in a matter of seconds.

I let Canoni out, and Buggs made his getaway too. I will have to do my chores and take a bath in the cold, but that is nothing novel. It will also be necessary to pack the snowfall on the escape trails. The roof touts a layer of snow that is calling my name.

It is afternoon now. All my chores are done, and I sit by the fire drying my hair. The water and air temperature are so cold that my hair froze in the time that it took to go from the West River to the cabin. It will take most of the afternoon to dry...

My hair is dry now, and I have several dreadfully slow passing hours to kill before nightfall. I will cook salmon for dinner tonight and have a cup of pine needle tea.

\* \* \*

## SECOND WEEK OF NOVEMBER

Winter grinds on agonizingly slow. I hiked with Canoni for two hours during the morning, packing the snow on the escape trails, trying to get some exercise. They look more like roads now than they do trails, as the snow is packed on the trails, while off the trails the drifts are deep. I am glad to see droppings on the trails, as this indicates that wildlife is using these trails to move around as well, making any emergency hunt easier.

Animals are wise. They will always travel on a road before they traverse through thick snow, as they use so much less energy on a road.

Soon I will fetch Canoni into the cabin and call it a day.

\* \* \*

Snow showers linger this morning, three days in a row. Several inches fell overnight.

It has occurred to me that I have not done an adequate job of describing my escape trails, so I will attempt now. First of all, each of the three trails begins at the cabin and goes in a different bearing toward the West River, located a quarter mile away. One trail travels along the giant granite rock structure that stands behind the cabin and overlooks the valley and the West River. This trail skirts the rock formation and follows northwest alongside the base for a quarter mile, then right to the bank of the West River. This trail is four feet wide and is used by numerous animals.

The second trail tracks west of the cabin for a few hundred yards and leads directly to the West River. This trail is also four feet wide.

The third trail starts in front of the cabin and courses almost due south to where it meets a bend in the West River half a mile south of the cabin. This trail is six feet wide and is by far the trail most used by animals.

It takes several hours to hike all three escape trails and pack down the snow wearing snowshoes.

Canoni is wise to the trails and uses them during the day to move from place to place in the area. She often ventures to West River during the day.

These escape trails represent security to me in the event that I ever have to abandon the cabin and find safety. However, once I get to the West River, the snow on the other side is not groomed at all, so it would be an instant challenge to make progress once across the river during the winter months.

\* \* \*

I was hoping that this mid-November morning would bring a sunny day, but this was not the case. It is cold and gloomy, and a thick layer of fog hangs 15 feet above the ground. The fog makes the cold feel more intense. New snow fell on the ground overnight but is merely a dusting. Smoke from the chimney travels low to the ground at this moment.

Canoni is now in the corral eating, and Buggs is consuming the grass dropped by Canoni, having his fill.

I will do my chores and write later.

The wood supply is in good shape, and fresh water awaits my thirst. At the West River I watched as the otter family played in and out of the water. They climbed the bank and then slid on their bellies down into the water. They have no problem catching fish at any time of year.

Canoni stands near the door looking in, and Buggs is already settled by the fireplace. We have fallen into a nice routine, the three of us sharing the cabin.

\* \* \*

This day brought another gray, cold day. There was no new snow overnight, but the trees were frosted by the fog draped over the valley. I think this makes six days without seeing the sun. I can tell that this affects my mood because I feel less energetic and more inclined to be lazy. But since lazy is not an option, I will go and do my chores.

I would guess that I expended an hour and a half on chores today. Near the West River I saw a fox using the trail to migrate through the area. When it noticed me, it turned and headed off the trail, through the deeper snow and out of sight. He sported a white fur coat, making his eyes, his nose, and his lips the only features visible. I have no way of knowing if this was the same fox that used to come to the cabin with her kits, but I'd like to think it was the same one, if only to think that I have permanent neighbors.

I must make a note about my own behavior. This afternoon, I caught myself going outside without my rifle. This is the worst mistake I can make. It seems like it would be impossible to forget it, after this long a time taking it with me everywhere. Anyway, I chided myself and once more vowed that I will keep it on me at all times. I think that I should forget my pants before forgetting my rifle.

I have a piece of elk meat thawing near the fire. Soon I will prepare my meal.

Another day in this refrigerator comes to an end. My roomies are settled in, and I am about to go to sleep. I ask the Great Spirit to deliver a good day tomorrow.

* * *

## MID-NOVEMBER

I see the mid-November sunlight shining under the door. I have let Canoni and Buggs go outside.

On this specific morning I give thanks to the Great Spirit for filling my days with the spectacle that I witness around me. I thank the Great Spirit for bringing fish to my lures and game within sight. For keeping me strong enough to do the things necessary to survive, I say thank you. I am thankful for the milder than expected winter that Mother Nature has afforded this valley.

I am most grateful for Canoni and to a lesser degree, Buggs. As days pass and some things become easier, surely some things will become harder, and I am thankful for the wisdom to confront those things.

The air is fresh and clean, brisk, but not extremely cold. It is quiet outside. Maybe all of the creatures are enjoying the sun. As for me, it is time for chores.

I have completed the chores, and since it is so pretty, I will take Buggs and go for a ride. Not far, just around the neighborhood.

We are back from our ride. We surprised a group of four wolves in the meadow south of the cabin, feeding on a kill. I watched in silence, remaining still as they tore the meat apart while snarling and nipping at one another. After viewing them for half an hour, I moved on. Farther down the trail, I saw a moose in the open meadow, scraping the snow away to get to the meager food supply beneath.

I have been in the cabin since we returned. I will prepare my meal now.

Dinner is done. I let Canoni in, and she is getting comfortable on her side of the cabin. Buggs, as always, sits near the fireplace. As the days slip away, my roommates and I continue to prosper, none of us in distress. We stay strong together. I truly believe that Canoni and Buggs have formed a bond that benefits them both.

Finally, before I turn in, I lift my voice to the Great Spirit and ask for guidance and deliverance. I look forward to another glorious day tomorrow.

* * *

This morning, we were greeted by a cloudless blue sky and bright sunshine. Without sunglasses, I would suffer snow blindness from the glare. The wind, what little there was, blew from the east.

In the open meadow across from the cabin, 10 or 12 Canada geese searched the ground for food. I saw them making their way toward the cabin, or more precisely, toward Canoni's stored grass. My chores are finished, and the geese have flown to another place. All I did was run toward them, and they took off. I was tempted to take one, but the thought of cleaning it didn't appeal to me, so I did not. I am going to take a ride to where I saw the wolf kill yesterday.

I am back at the cabin after riding for part of the afternoon. I rode to the spot south of the cabin where the wolves had made their kill. All that remained today were a fox and three crows, bickering over the meatless carcass. Blood stained the area surrounding the kill site, and from a distance, it looked like a massacre had taken place.

I heard birds singing in the trees today for the first time in weeks. I couldn't count the different voices, but I am sure that there were several dozen distinct calls.

I trucked part of the way back to the cabin, letting Canoni stroll behind me, Buggs sitting across her neck. Once at the cabin, I climbed the tree and retrieved a piece of salmon out of the tree box for dinner. I am beginning to hate the taste of salmon, elk, and venison. A stray cow would have little chance if I spotted it.

* * *

I am writing as twilight cloaks the valley. It was a pristine day, a cloudless sky filled with sun, absent of wind.

I set out on Canoni after sunrise and rode north along the West River to the Driftpile River, then farther north to the Fox River. This ride was six miles one way. Riding through virgin snow north of the Driftpile River made for a slow ride, but once we were on flat land the snow was more packed from the animals that visited there.

There is an unnamed lake to the west of the junction of the Driftpile and the Fox River, which is where I went. The lake was frozen, the ice thick enough to support my weight. I did not see another creature and understood that life will be bleak until spring.

While returning to the cabin, I saw a silhouette along the ridge of a mountain. Through my binoculars, I could plainly see that this marvelous animal was a mountain lion. Nothing but muscle defined this confident beast. It is the number-two predator at this time of year. As I observed it, I could see that it would soon vanish over the ridge, so I rode on toward home.

I arrived late in the afternoon and set about getting my meal cooked.

I am now full, warm, and surrounded by my friends.

I visited the john, and while squatting, I was joined by a full-grown wolverine. This trespasser came from the trees opposite my squatting position. With my rifle ready, I hurried the action. I stood, at which time the wolverine spotted me and stopped in its tracks. He sniffed the air and moved his nose from side to side. He took a step toward me, and I fired a round into the snow in front of him. He stopped and bared his teeth. I eased away, keeping my rifle trained on him.

I was soon far enough away that I could make it safely to the cabin. This wolverine took his time, but he came within 50 feet of the cabin before we had our second confrontation. This one I was going to win. Canoni saw the wolverine and watched it closely. I yelled at the wolverine to run away before it was too late. It moved forward, and it was then that I ended the confrontation with a shot to the head.

I cannot bury the wolverine because the earth is frozen, so I took the remains into the forest south of the cabin. Better to let the pack discover it there.

It saddens me to have to kill animals because this is their home. I am the foreigner, and they are doing what they have done for centuries. However, I must defend myself and my territory, as the animals do.

It is evening now. I make this quick entry to note that I hear the wolf pack howling in the distance.

\* \* \*

Overnight, winter resumed, dropping fresh snow. So today I will be required to hike the escape trails, clear the snow from the roof, as well as do my regular chores. I will take Buggs along today and let him ride on Canoni.

I have completed my chores, including compacting the escape trails and clearing the roof. With the escape trails maintained, I have decided to take a short ride to where I left the wolverine carcass.

As I suspected, a lucky animal found the remains of the wolverine, and it is no longer a problem. As is common, the site of the feast looks like a bloodbath, the snow splattered tufts of red fur scattered all about. I would say that nature is working as intended.

Through the door I hear the wind blow, indicating that more bad weather may lie ahead. Canoni stands along the wall opposite the fireplace looking in my direction. Soon enough she will settle down. As is his modus operandi, Buggs is tucked in the corner of the cabin, close to the fireplace.

For tonight I will eat dried fish and stay warm. There is nothing left to write about, it would seem.

\* \* \*

As I do each morning, I clutched my rifle and headed out to relieve myself. I let Canoni out the door, and then I followed her. She went right into the corral and began eating grass.

I walked to the back side of the cabin to urinate and heard a growl. A coyote investigating the grass stores dashed away from behind the cabin, its tail tucked between its legs. In my mind I had already played through this scenario, and I did not fire, since it ran away as soon as I came out of the cabin, as I would expect a healthy animal to do. No need for further interaction with this animal, which eases my mind.

I went about completing my chores and cleaned the ashes from the fireplace.

I spent some time brushing Canoni, first because she enjoys it, and second because she is in the cabin each night. I will no longer allow her to stay out during the night, where she is susceptible to attack and exposure. I don't yet understand why I took so long to make the decision to bring her in. Anyway, the less dirt she brings in, the better.

Except for dinner, this day is complete. I took a piece of venison from the tree box, which I will cook pretty soon. I lift my voice to the Great Spirit asking for knowledge and protection in the days to come.

\* \* \*

As November drags on, I imagine that people in the city are bustling from place to place, trying to complete their Christmas shopping in the weeks remaining before Christmas day. I'm sure that everyone is in the mood to see family and friends and share the holiday spirit.

I can admit that I used to be the kind of person who took those family get-togethers for granted, assuming that nothing would change. I assumed every year that I would see a turkey at Mom's house for Thanksgiving and a ham at Christmas.

This year, it would be bitchin to see the family. However, that is impossible. Instead, I will share Christmas with my two buddies, Buggs and Canoni. They have grown into the friends that interact with me every day, sharing my burdens of surviving here. They bring the comic relief from time to time that I enjoy so much.

I need to complete chores and so will write later.

The thermometer read 36 degrees earlier as I stepped out. Having refreshed the water and firewood supply, I spent an additional couple of hours hiking on the escape trails, both for exercise and maintenance. I found heavy tracks in the snow made by animals that use these trails to move through the area. I discovered a pile of scat on one of the trails. It was likely from a coyote, as hair was mixed into it. Perhaps it had eaten a rabbit or a mouse.

I spotted a fox crossing the meadow across from the cabin. It is passing through on its way to places unknown. It looks healthy and happy. I know that this fox lives nearby, since I see it often from a distance.

Canoni is outside in the meadow in front of the cabin. I see the steam coming off of her back and from her nostrils when she breathes.

All is well in this little valley, all of us living in harmony today. I checked my meat supply, and I found that I still have plenty left. I should have no problem making it through this never-ending winter.

In the afternoon sky I saw a vapor trail from a jet cruising many thousands of feet above me. It made a line across the sky heading from east to west. For a moment or two I deliberated about where it was going. Was this plane full of holiday travelers? This is the only link to humanity that I have seen for some time. As the plane vanished from view, the memory of it faded as well.

I am once again in my own reality, a realism that is ever-evolving and shifting over time. I too am changing. I know that I am a more well-rounded man. I know my capabilities, and they are far beyond what I thought they could be. I now consider things through before I commit myself to something.

Possibly more significant, I now resist the urge to do something on a whim. I have discovered that often times it is better to let a temptation pass than to act on it. I have found that there is time to do those things that are important to me.

My attitude toward survival has changed too. I now believe that it is tougher to survive in the city than it is here. It is relatively easy to gather Mother Nature's bounty once one learns where to find it. Thing do happen out of the blue here, without warning, and in an instant may change from fun and games to a life or death situation.

But how is that any different than the way things are in the city? I have learned how to live more in tune with nature, to the point where I live with two of God's creatures, one of them born wild. I am sure that I will be a better man when I return to the social order.

As for the remainder of today, I will stay around the cabin and cook a venison steak when evening sets in.

* * *

Yesterday, I woke up feeling feverish, so I stayed inside by the fire for the whole day. As I slept, Mother Nature dumped snow over the valley and, in effect, dictated the chores that I will need to complete once I feel better.

It is early afternoon, and I am back from executing my chore list. I took Canoni and rode the escape trails for several hours. Once I finished, I rode her along the West River, then north to the Driftpile River.

At the Driftpile River I sat on the bank and thought about my escapade with George on the Gataga River, when we climbed aboard a raft and drifted downstream. While it ended badly for George, we had fun until things went awry. The memory of building the raft, taking it down unknown waters with my buddy will never be forgotten.

Canoni hears something outside...

I just frightened away a bull moose, which was trekking around the perimeter of the meadow in front of the cabin. I heard Canoni snort and become alarmed. Upon exiting the cabin I saw the moose across the meadow. Tracks in the snow indicated that it came from the area south of the cabin and proceeded in an arc around the meadow. When it saw me it trotted off into the trees to the east.

Where was I? Oh, yeah, building the raft with George. The thing that I will recollect most in the future is the look that we gave each other as we pushed off from shore: Are we really doing this? In one second, we both resigned our fate to whatever lay ahead. In that moment, we made a silent agreement to take a risk and possibly lose our lives. In that instant, we gave only a passing thought to things that could go wrong and decided to go for it.

I am getting hungry and so will cook some dinner.

* * *

**NOVEMBER ENDS**

With this last day of the month came the dawn of a new day and some drama. I sit outside the door as I make this entry.

I awoke as usual this morning, needing to answer the call of nature. With rifle in hand, I opened the cabin door, let Canoni go out, and stepped out into the sunshine. As I scanned the area, I was shocked to see three sets of tracks cutting through the meadow across from the cabin. I examined the tracks, and though the snow was too deep for detailed prints, I knew by the size that they were mountain lion tracks.

My hands shook, though I was not sure if it was from fear or cold. My guess was that it was a mother and her two offspring. The question is what I should do about this. Are they passing through on their way to their home range? I know that they must have smelled Canoni and me. The tracks did not lead close to the cabin, but I remain freaked out.

I had not planned for this exact situation, multiple cats at once. My two options are to do nothing and see if they return. I could track them and see where they went, or I can lure them somewhere and eliminate them. I would prefer not to see them again. I will give it some thought.

My chores are finished now, and you can bet that I did them with one eye trained on the meadow at all times! I must be vigilant always.

Of all of the animals that I have encountered while in Canada, none of them worry me more than the mountain lion. That includes grizzlies and wolves. I have been close enough to these magnificent cats for us to see each other, and although they have always backed off, they exhibited no fear of me. They have no problem baring their teeth in a threatening manner, unleashing a harsh meaningful snarl.

This is an all-too-familiar sound heard in the mountains. I don't want to hurt these animals, but it would seem shrewd for me to have an idea of where they are, and so I will follow their trail and see where it leads.

It is late afternoon now, and I am back from scouting the cougars. The tracks led from West River out through the meadow across from the lodge. From there, they went northeast toward the Gataga River. Interestingly, it seemed like at no time did they step in each other's tracks; there appeared always three distinct sets of prints. The tracks veered south at the Gataga River and followed that river for a mile or so. From there the tracks swung to the southwest and into the foothills. I was content knowing that the mountain lions had moved on.

I guess there is no defense against these cats other than to be alert and on guard for their presence. I was tripping out when I first saw those three sets of prints.

To be honest, I appreciate events such as the one today because they are the happenings that will leave a lasting memory in my mind. Situations like this offer the perfect opportunity for me to test my courage, my determination to be master of this valley.

Canoni is now settled and is observing Buggs as he scratches an itch behind his ear. I hear the wind as it blows outside. It makes me feel colder so I will put on my cotton denim shirt. I will cook some dinner and sleep. Tomorrow is yet another day.

\* \* \*

Morning has arrived, and outside I detected no new tracks of mountain lions. This morning the sky was turquoise blue with no sign of clouds. It was not too cold, either, the thermometer reading 40 degrees.

I have given more thought to the events of yesterday and have come to the conclusion that I may have overreacted a bit. I think a mother cougar would have better things to do than skirmish with me. It is unlikely that mama would attack, unless she or her kittens were in danger, hurt, or extremely hungry. I guess I spent a lot of energy freaking out over nothing.

I am done with my chores and am deciding what to do to occupy my day. I'm thinking that it is so pretty that I will stay here and enjoy it. I have the best view in the valley right here. I can read some and play with Buggs. I can climb the rocks behind the cabin for an even more commanding view. For the moment I will remain here and relish the warmth of the sun.

It is now afternoon. I have finished taking a quick bath in the West River and spending the required two hours in front of the fire warming myself and drying my hair. Since the day has several hours of sunlight left, I will take Buggs and go for a ride on Canoni.

While I write this entry, now sitting near the glowing fire, Buggs waits in the doorway. Looking past Buggs I see Canoni standing in the sunshine. The best thing about this time of year is that no insects bug me! I have an hour before I roast a venison steak.

It feels cool but by no means cold. Clouds are rolling in from north of the cabin.

Wait, I've spotted a fox coming toward the cabin from across the meadow. It is strolling directly toward the cabin. Canoni is eyeing it, as is Buggs...

When it was 30 yards from the cabin door, I yelled, "Do you plan to join us?"

With that, the fox darted out of view. I am repeatedly amazed by the brash, often bold attitude of most of the animals around here. This is not the first time that I have had to shout or fire a round to get an animal's attention when they approached me.

I am curious as to why sometimes the animals act like they don't even know the cabin is here. I have seen a coyote on a trail heading toward me and never stop up until I made a loud sound, then it acted startled. It reacted the way an alert animal would, bolting into the brush and out of sight. Is it possible that they concentrate on one thing so intently that they have tunnel vision? Is it a show of bravado on their part?

I've seen bears do it; I've seen cattle do it. I wonder what the fox would have done if I had remained still.

With the incident over, I turned to Buggs. "You see, I can be mean!"

Mother Nature has designed every creature for the ever-changing environment. During the winter, the foxes wear a heavy white fur, during the spring and summer; they wear a light coat of red.

Anyway, it is time to cook the duck.

Dinner was most tasty, what a gift the land offered today.

I think that I have said this before somewhere in this journal, but you never know what the next moment will bring in this place but I can't wait to experience it.

\* \* \*

This morning started like any other day. I let Canoni and Buggs out and took care of my chores. Since the morning was sunny and mild, although a couple inches of fresh snow fell overnight, I chose to ride across the West River and through the foothills of the mountains to the west.

As Canoni and I moved along the trail, through the snow-covered landscape, out of the corner of my eye I spotted color, white to be exact, against the green background of an evergreen. I instinctively knew that it was a fox, and not wanting to scare it, I kept Canoni on a straight course. I paid it no attention as we passed. The fox waited for us to move down the trail, and then it fell in behind us.

Any time Canoni stopped, the fox stopped too. If Canoni moved, it moved. I wondered how long the fox would play this game, but it did its thing as if I was not present. I rode about three miles before I looped toward the east. All the time the fox followed us at a distance. I talked to it as I rode for no good reason. We passed other game as well. I saw three elk and a whitetail deer.

When we reached the cabin, I turned Canoni loose and sat down to see what the fox would do. For the next 15 minutes we watched each other from maybe 50 feet apart. But I guess the fox got bored. It disappeared into the forest without glancing back. This was not the same fox that I saw yesterday; this one was smaller, about the size of an average poodle.

I will cook dinner and maybe write later.

\* \* \*

I am making this entry during the early morning hours. A furious blizzard hit the valley, the wind is whistling, and it is cold in the cabin. I have the fire raging now, and sitting here in my sleeping bag propped up against the wall listening to the wind is somewhat unnerving.

Canoni is calm; I can't tell if she is sleeping. Buggs is sleeping, without doubt. I will write later. It is close to midday, and what has turned into a whiteout is raging outside. I can do nothing but stay inside and find things to occupy my time.

It is now evening and the blizzard conditions have not eased at all. I cannot see the trees, which are a couple hundred feet from the cabin. I trudged to the tree box a while ago and took some meat out, tying a rope to the corral so I would not get lost in the conditions. I then supposed that I should tie a rope to the tree and keep the rope outside the cabin door so that no matter how bad it gets, I will always be able to find the food source, although I could go many days without food. For water, I melted snow.

It is easy to see how a person might get lost in a storm like this one. Everything is distorted from the blowing snow.

My roommates are both comfy, so it is time for me to sleep.

\* \* \*

As the first week of December crawls on, the blizzard conditions did not abate overnight, high winds blowing the snow around. This morning, however, the wind was a mere breeze, not worthy of flying a kite.

I let Canoni outside, and Buggs scooted out as well. I went to pee right at the edge of the cabin and then climbed the tree to get some food to eat later. I entered the cabin shaking from the cold. The thermometer reads 12 degrees. Neither Buggs nor Canoni want anything to do with the outdoors. They came in with me.

I will spend some time now completing the daily chores as well as clearing the snow from the roof.

The chores are finished now, and with the weather as it is, I will not venture out. I will instead play with Buggs and perhaps clean my guns to pass the time.

As evening arrives I hear the wind picking up, causing the cabin door to quiver. Both Canoni, who stands in her spot in the cabin, and Buggs, who is in his corner, seem alert. It's not so bad, out here with only Buggs and Canoni with me. They are warm and display emotions, both creatures of habit, predictable in their behavior for the most part. They provide company and confirmation that I am not alone. We three are in this together. I feel a sense of responsibility, as I must provide their food and shelter so they might survive. We three are much happier inside the cabin than outside.

\* \* \*

While I believed the storm had left the valley, it resumed with a vengeance. For a third day, the snowstorm continues, the gale force wind increasing to the point that it sounds like a jet. Right now, I can't leave the cabin for fear of being blown into the forest. Canoni and Buggs will remain inside today as well.

Without being able to go outside, I am limited in what I may do. I have been reading a book, and it talked about how the Indians of the plains believed that people would die and reincarnate in another form, such as a beaver or a wolf. A mighty warrior might return as a grizzly bear. The book cited the similarity in which a bear walks upright or how a raccoon washes its food.

I have heard people say that some animal behavior is so human-like. But to see one's self in the eyes of a grizzly, as I have done in a fleeting instant, is to see a dead expression, no sign of anything except wildness. Some other animals, such as the wolf, seem more expressive. One may gaze into a wolf's eye and know its mood, but the bear has the same blank stare at all times.

I comprehend why the Indian would give such reverence to the animals. In every way the life of the tribe was directly linked to the buffalo and other animals. The hunter tribes, like the Lakota, followed the migration of the herds as they moved throughout the year.

I try to keep my relationship going with the animals. I do not harass them or invade their space without cause. So far, for the most part, we have lived in harmony. I had expected that the animals higher on the food chain would be more aggressive toward me, if only to intimidate me, but that has not been the case. The reality is that the major predators are driven by hunger, fear, or self-defense rather than by anger. Though I'm sure it happens, I have not encountered any animal attacks that were not instinctive, predatory in nature.

I spent the day alternately reading and napping, as the storm continued to rage outside. I had to clean up Canoni's poop. I hate scooping poop, but it is natural. I have to keep her healthy. So I opened the door for a minute to refresh the air. In that single minute, the cabin turned cold. Now 15 minutes later, the fire has warmed the cabin. I will cook some elk meat for my meal and then sleep later.

* * *

It is a new morning, and finally the weather has broken. A sunny, azure blue sky void of wind greeted me. Canoni and Buggs were both anxious to go outside. I am going to put on my snowshoes and take a stroll around to assess things.

The storm that raged with so much fury did little damage, other than knocking down some old, dead trees. While compressing the lighter snow on my escape trails, I was quite surprised at how firm the trails are. The drifts are deep in some places where the snow has piled up. I estimate them to be near five feet high against the granite rock formation behind the cabin. I have never been through a longer storm, and I am relieved that no damage befell the cabin.

The fire pit outside was buried by blowing snow, and I will wait for it to melt before using it again. Any object in the path of the storm is now buried to some degree.

I have cleared the roof of snow. It was a challenging task. The snow around the cabin that fell to the ground as I cleared the roof makes it difficult to navigate without snowshoes. After several hours, I finished grooming the escape trails.

Now, after relaxing by the fire for the past half hour, I feel warmer. I cooked half of a duck for dinner.

Evening is upon me, and those who own the night have awakened. I hear the owls hooting, and somewhere far in the distance, I also hear the call of the pack. The moon is full tonight, in an indigo sky filled with monster movie clouds. They pass in front of the moon every few minutes, and with the pack vocalizing, I think about the old wolf man movies that freaked me out as a kid.

I can only hope that tomorrow will be is as pretty as today.

\* \* \*

Mother Nature blessed me with a gorgeous morning. The sun glare will be high today, so I will wear my sunglasses on my morning ride.

I have let Buggs out, and Canoni is ready to ride.

I am back in the cabin after a long ride. Swinging first south, then east, I rode toward the Gataga River. I arrived to find it frozen solid, as I expected. I used a heavy 15 pound rock to try to break the ice, but I did not succeed. I then scurried across the frozen ice leading Canoni. I rode on the other side for a while before crossing back over the Gataga River and returning to the cabin.

On the way in, I spotted several deer in the forest. I watched as they scrapped the ground trying to find anything that might be growing beneath the snow. I know that this is part of the circle of life, and as much as I would like to feed these animals, I recognize that I am not here to interfere in the balance of nature. These deer may starve, but they will provide food for another animal, though they appear healthy at the moment. Where they find enough to eat to remain fit is beyond my comprehension.

As I retrieved a chunk of meat from the tree I glanced at the thermometer, which read 36 degrees. While my meal cooks, both Canoni and Buggs pass the time being entertained by my movement.

\* \* \*

I awoke to a cloudless, sunny day, free of the wind that has dogged us of late.

It seemed like Canoni was all geared up for a ride. I set about doing my chores. While I was at the West River refreshing the water supply, three wolves appeared on the bluff across the way, 50 yards away. I yelled out to them so they knew that I knew they were there. I felt like an animal at the drinking pool that can't drink because he is so busy keeping track of what might be coming to kill him. After filling the containers, I returned to the cabin.

A short time later while I hiked the escape trails, I noticed wolf tracks leading up the southernmost trail from the West River toward the cabin and then turning away near the corral. They repeated a pattern that I have seen month after month.

I now sit by the door of my secure log cabin making this entry. Soon I will get some meat from the tree box for dinner.

\* \* \*

Today, the sun rose against another cloudless sky. It is colder today than it was yesterday, but I need only a jacket and gloves to be warm. I am going to ride for a while and will write later.

Having returned from a morning ride, I can report that everything is satisfactory in my valley. I saw a herd of six elk cows roaming south of the meadow near the West River. Crows made a lot of racket in the nearby trees as they went about their business. Later, I caught a glimpse of a fox as it made its way over the bluffs, across the West River. Although all foxes look alike to me, I'm guessing that this was the same fox that has remained nearby so often.

I took Buggs along for the ride today, and as always, he seemed to be content, never moving once I put him at the horn of the saddle. I honestly believe that he and Canoni have developed a great friendship and that both covet our daily rides.

All is quiet here as we approach mid-winter. The snow is quite deep off of the trails, and the temperature rarely gets to 50 degrees. The snow does not melt much at all. I know that it could be a lot worse, and every day I thank the lord that it is as it is.

For my meal today I will eat smoked salmon and drink a cup of pine needle tea.

\* \* \*

## MID-DECEMBER

This day brings a new layer of snow, which fell during the night. The sun is out, and the wind is calm. I will do my chores now and let the roomies out. A curious thing occurred while I was out. When I went to the West River for water, I saw a coyote across the water standing on the bluff there. When it noticed me it barked and became agitated. I did not understand why this coyote would sit there and bark like that.

In the few minutes that it took me to get the water, that coyote did not stop yapping. I don't think it was protecting young or anything like that. It did not get aggressive or seem like it was crazy. I will go later and see if it is there.

Canoni is fine, as is Buggs. In general, everything is perfect.

I returned from a walk to the West River. I did not see the coyote anywhere, so I can put the episode behind me. Its late afternoon now, time to get my elk steak prepared.

* * *

Another morning in British Columbia, Canada, has dawned, bringing hues of scarlet, tangerine, and mixed shades of blue to the eastern sky. I believe that I prefer sunrise to sunset because of the promise of a new day that comes with each sunrise. The color is spectacular at either event.

It is brisk outside this morning. I am back from my ride with nothing stimulating to report. The sky morphed from the stunning color earlier to gloomy gray as the morning progressed. I saw a fox scavenging on the remains of a crow that had died. While I was near the Driftpile, I caught the odor of what I believed was a bear, but there is little chance that a bear would be awake at this time of year. Once you have smelled that scent, you never forget it. I did not wait around to find out what it was.

I rode on cautiously, expecting anything. Fortunately, the scenery does not change much, so I repeatedly have pleasurable rides. In my mind, I have memorized all of the terrain within a ten-mile radius of the lodge. Often my dreams at night revolve around this place, and I can walk every trail knowing where it leads. That comes from not having too much else to do other than ride and explore. Outside, I hear a woodpecker hammering on a tree close by.

I think I will take a nap.

Awake again, and I'm refreshed but bored. I will go climb up the ridge behind the cabin.

From my perch, a hundred feet above the West River that flows behind it, I can see the valley to the south of the cabin, as far as the Muskwa Ranges, which cut northwest to southeast. Scanning to the west, my view covers five miles, as far as the Omineca Mountains. In between lays rolling terrain with football sized open meadows among the denser forests, making it easy to locate game. Turning my head, down below me, I see the homestead that is the center of my world. Through the binoculars, I see a few elk far across the West River.

The breeze is picking up now, so I will climb down and retreat inside and make my daily meal.

\* \* \*

I am outside in the warmth of the morning sun, feeling quite alone for some reason. Besides the obvious, I'm not sure why I have lost that spark today. I am in a bland mood. Maybe I will smoke a pipe full of weed, put my snowshoes on, and take a hike.

I'm back from hiking for the better part of the morning, and my mood is much improved. While hiking along the West River north of the cabin, I came upon a family of river otters playing in the water. They live like they have no cares in the world. When they are not fishing, they are frolicking all over the bank and in the water. This family consists of two adults and two young.

I spent a few minutes observing the family play before a lone wolf appeared upstream and noticed the otters. The wolf was able to steal an easy meal when one of the otters left a fish on the bank as it fled into the water. Once the fish was gone and the otters hiding out, the wolf moved on, passing me on the other side of the West River.

As soon as I got back here, I set about replacing the water and the firewood. I also used the time to empty the ashes from the fireplace and sweep out the cabin. The worst chore remains clearing snow from the roof. It is so labor-intensive.

I am now watching Buggs and Canoni eat their daily allotment of grass. Soon, I will cook my food as well. After a slow start, the day turned out to be nice.

\* \* \*

## DECEMBER 20

In approximately five days the world will celebrate Christmas. I will let Christmas pass quietly this year.

I sit inside the cabin with the door open, letting the stale air out. As the snow tumbles in slow motion, Canoni stands in her corral. Buggs, meanwhile, is somewhere out of my sight. The snowy, white scene is broken by the gray granite rocks that line the horizon west of the cabin.

I hear crows in the trees nearby, making a lot of clatter, as is their normal routine. They are always bickering about something.

All of my chores are completed now. While at the West River, after I had filled the canteens, a doe came to drink from the hole that I created in the ice. This was odd if only because she was alone. Deer are more frequently found in herds of six or seven. She took her fill and crept back into the forest.

My firewood supply is now half gone, but I have no fear that it won't last until the thaw comes. The grass stores are still in ample supply. I think that one of the things that I do miss out here is the sound of music playing. In the city I always played music. I wonder what new albums have come out in my absence. Elton John was supposed to be releasing a new album last summer. Of course, I sing all of the time, but having music to sing along with would go a long way toward easing the boredom that I sometimes feel. An audience would not be a bad thing, either.

I will eat duck for dinner tonight. In the meantime, I sit and sing.

* * *

Imitating a moron I hiked without snowshoes to a place on the West River where the water is forced into a deep pool. As I walked along the bank, I slipped and landed on my right wrist. I knew that it was not broken, but it swelled up quickly. I spent the next hour soaking it in the near freezing water. Then, over the next 36 hours, I alternately placed it in snow and then wrapped it in an elastic bandage.

I was unable to fire my rifle during that time. I considered how much trouble a mountain man would be in with a like injury occurring in disputed territory. Funny, I never contemplated having such an injury. It has healed now enough that I can write.

Not much has changed during this two-day hiatus. The snow has fallen off and on, leaving several inches accumulated on the roof of the cabin. The overcast mornings that prevail, combined with the short days, make it seem like perpetual night some of the time. Of course, being this far north, the sun doesn't completely set at certain times of the year.

Not being able to climb the tree to get meat since the accident, I have not eaten in the past two days. I will try right now.

Although it took some doing, I managed to scale the tree and fetch some meat. My wrist is sore again, but it is not too painful. I was not able to cut the meat up in the tree, so I have what is probably four pounds of venison thawing by the fire. Knowing that it will be easier to cut once thawed, I will wait before putting it on the fire. I will bury the piece that I don't use in the snow for tomorrow.

Buggs and Canoni are both fine, neither seemingly caring about, nor even noticing for that matter, my injury. In fact, yesterday Canoni had gas and farted throughout the day and into the evening like an old trail horse. She almost farted her way out of the warm cabin. Fortunately for all, she ran out of gas.

My wrist hurts a bit, so I will stop now and pack it in snow.

\* \* \*

Morning has come, and outside the snow has stopped falling. A light breeze blows from the east. The sun is fully visible for a change, and a few birds are already singing in the trees.

I will take some time this morning and groom the escape trails.

I have returned and can say that the escape trails are groomed and well-packed. While walking along the escape trail north of the cabin and down to the West River, I spied a wolf across the meadow that separates the forest from the bank. As far as I could see, this was a lone animal and so was less of a threat to me.

As I paced another of the escape trails, I observed the heavy, wet snow on the evergreens, which caused the branches to bend under the weight. From time to time I heard the sound of snow hitting the ground in a blob. The December days are short, bringing the promise of more winter to come.

George and I built a fine cabin, a sturdy home in the middle of this refrigerator, though it is scarcely more than a box that holds heat and keeps out the wind and most animals. Once the sun goes down, a human would freeze if exposed to the elements. For sure, the one thing I never underestimated was the dangerous cold we would face.

The coats and underwear we brought have been more than enough to survive this place, the cabin notwithstanding. Of course, good boots have made a difference too. Many times I have avoided a twisted ankle because of my high-top boots.

It is late afternoon now, and I have returned from bringing in the piece of meat that I buried last night. As expected, it froze again, but it will thaw soon and will be ready to eat in an hour. In the meantime, I put a rolled up deer skin against the door to keep out the cold wind now blowing against it.

Every so often, a puff of smoke blows down the chimney, which is then dispersed into the room, forcing me to open the door for a minute. Of course, opening the door allows the cold wind to blow in. How many times have I seen this movie? I cannot think of a solution to this problem. We built the cabin so the door faces the east, not knowing that the wind blows from east to west during the winter. Another item that I did not research at all.

* * *

## THIRD WEEK OF DECEMBER

I was greeted by a striking sunrise. The entire eastern sky was bright crimson. Clouds moved in over my valley as I observed. It does not look like snow, but the picture outside is nonetheless quite dramatic. The thermometer shows an even 20 degrees.

As I experience my second Christmas in the wilderness, this one will be solitary. Nothing will be different on that morning than on the previous day, nothing to indicate that the day will be in any way special. Last year George and I had a tree in the cabin, however with Buggs and Canoni both residing inside, it is neither necessary nor safe to bring a tree inside.

I wonder which uncles and aunts will visit and share dinner with my sisters and parents. I wonder if George is with his family celebrating.

It has remained cold, the wind an ever-present companion. Occasional flurries bring fresh snow, but the frigid weather has been mostly a wind event. Buggs and Canoni are both content with the daily routine. They are both easy to get along with. I have spent the entire time in the cabin during the previous two days.

This morning, as my mind raced from topic to topic, I dwelt on what the future might hold for me. I wonder if things in the city will be different in the coming years. Of course things will be altered, but I wonder what I will be doing in 15 years. Will I be living with someone or alone? What will my family be like then? What if I cannot locate my family? Will the races learn to live with each other? Will the police stop terrorizing inner-city residents? Will the corrupt systems in place now be gone in the future? Will I be a better man for having endured this wilderness adventure?

The passage of time will be the judge. One thing I do know is that I want to remember how this time in my life felt when I am older. What is older? Older than what? I can't imagine myself living to be 50 years old. I am most comfortable being young. I can't imagine being so old that the injuries I suffer here suddenly appear in future years as arthritis and bring me to my knees.

I think that these thoughts show that this man is living for the now, not planning for the future.

\* \* \*

This morning, unlike the past two days, which were snow-filled, a gray sky and a glacial temperature envelop me. Thank God that the wind is not blowing. I have released Buggs and Canoni and washed my face.

I will do my chores now and write later. The roof is heavy with snow so I will do that first. I wish that George was here to help with this chore.

I rode Canoni around on the escape trails, which had accumulated snow in the course of the past three days. All three are now in the condition in which I like them. I had bundled up in my heavy coat and my duster and could still feel the cold through them. The day is coming to an end. I had elk meat for dinner. Outside it is freezing. In a steep crash from earlier today, the thermometer now reads three degrees. The cabin is warm. Canoni and Buggs are both ready for sleep, as am I.

\* \* \*

Three days later, during the night the pack came to visit, first howling to announce their presence and then loitering around the cabin for several hours. I could see Canoni shift her ears in different directions as she heard noises. She was keenly aware that the wolves were here and was prepared for any trouble.

This morning, I opened the door a crack to look out and saw many tracks around the cabin. The pack is nowhere to be found. It is next to impossible to know which direction they took, as the prints go in every direction.

I will take care of my chores now, being ever vigilant to the presence of those shrewd wolves.

It appears as though the pack was re-affirming their territory. Many of the trees are marked with urine in the snow around the base, and I noted several piles of scat about. I certainly hope that this does not become another war for territory. The pack would not have a chance.

I will use this time to work on my walking stick. I have a new skin to put on it.

It is evening now. I have finished my cured salmon dinner. I am drinking a cup of pine needle tea, which feels warm inside. I am content today and am in no way losing my sanity, as I'm sure some would think might happen. Of course, I did not plan for George to leave after a year. I have ample things to keep me sane and a lot to keep me on my toes.

I am half prepared to be up during the night, as I would not be surprised if the pack returned. For Canoni, Buggs, and me, the light from the fire is entertainment enough to lull each to sleep. So I will sleep for now.

It is late night or early morning, I'm not sure which. I am writing by the light of the dim fire.

The pack did indeed find its way back and is outside the lodge. The wolves make growling noises from time to time. Perhaps one is being put in its place. I hear an occasional sniffing at the door, which makes Canoni uncomfortable. It is too dark to open the door, so I am sitting near the fire with my rifle on my lap, ready for action. I will wait for sunrise before I make any moves.

I am not intimidated right now, though not knowing how many wolves are here and what they are planning makes for some tense moments.

Morning arrived. I opened the door cautiously and found tracks right at the door. I saw hundreds of tracks in the vicinity of the cabin. This time, however, one of the wolves had dug at the corner of the cabin, three to four inches, but had not breached the cabin. In the meadow northeast of the cabin, I spotted two wolves sitting there, as if they wanted to make my business their business. As long as they keep their distance the quiet will not be broken.

I will do my chores and in addition will fill in with dirt the hole where the digging took place.

I decided, after filling in the hole, that I will place logs along the base of the cabin where the wolf did its burrowing. Since Canoni does not need a corral, I will use the logs from the rails.

I have finished placing the logs against the base of the cabin, covering them under packed snow. I have made a protective barrier that I hope will keep the wolves, and other animals, from digging under the walls.

As I was finishing up, another storm dumped its load of moisture, and now it is snowing heavily. Fat flakes drift down to settle on the earth. I believe that the heat in the cabin has kept the roof from becoming water logged, and the roof has, in fact, done well against the elements. Buggs is outside the cabin, still chewing grass and seemingly refusing to come in.

Soon I will cook my meal, maybe smoked trout and venison tonight.

\* \* \*

This morning it is me, Canoni, Buggs, and our neighbors. It is another day in a string of cold days that make up this winter.

A single day has passed since the incident with the wolves. The pack did not return last night, nor did the snow stop. So today I will have to groom the escape trails. I have to assume that the pack has moved on to another part of its range.

I found no sign of the pack anywhere around the cabin, seeing instead elk tracks traversing the meadow.

While refreshing the water, I saw a badger near the West River, both of us keeping a courteous distance. Peace prevailed. Badgers seem to have the nastiest disposition, seemingly always angry at something. A lot like some people I know. I am somewhat surprised that I have seen badgers as often as I have. I thought that they were more reclusive. I did not expect to see a badger three times this year so far.

The rest of this afternoon will be spent inside lounging about.

Night has fallen over the valley. I have eaten, and both Buggs and Canoni are settled down now, ready to sleep. I can say that even though the days are somewhat boring, I always find something to focus on.

My beard is getting longer. I do not particularly like that, so I will shave it tomorrow.

\* \* \*

## NEW YEAR'S DAY, 1978!

A beautiful morning, free of snow and wind, has made me thank the Great Spirit for gifting me this place to call home.

Already Canoni and Buggs are outside eating. I will do my chores early.

I have returned from riding Canoni, first on the escape trails and then over the frozen West River and through the meadow beyond. In an area where the trail follows right next to the canyon walls, buttes formed at some time in history, and often there are tracks of mountain goats, which use the vantage point to monitor predators. It would be an easy place to sit and wait for game.

As I pushed on through the snow, it became quite apparent that the snow was much deeper in the places where dips formed in the terrain. In the interests of safety, I turned Canoni around and rode cautiously back to the cabin.

I miss the spring and summer so much at this time, for a few reasons. Number one is that I am limited as to where I can ride during this time of year. Number two, I miss the state of heightened alertness under which one must operate here in the wild. I miss the adrenaline rush of a close encounter. I miss having to be aware of every movement in the forest, which at this time is not really a concern.

I miss these things, which is not to say that I thoroughly enjoy them. Keeping my mind busy is hard when there are not many things to be concerned with. During the other seasons, the variety of life explodes as compared to the winter. More animals influence how I go about my day. In particular, of course, is the grizzly bear. Since bears sleep during the winter, only the big cats and the wolves impact my daily routine. During the growing season, danger exists at every turn, and as I said, this keeps a person sharp. In winter, though, the days are short, and the nights are so long.

It will be getting dark soon, so I better get some meat from the tree.

\* \* \*

This morning all that remains of a storm are clouds scattered on the eastern horizon. This overnight event dropped several inches of new snow. It's not easy to make plans this time of year, since without a weather forecast, I never know what to expect.

I am back from what turned out to be an exciting ride. After riding around on the escape trails, I steered Canoni toward the Driftpile River, riding through the snow at a leisurely pace. Halfway there, I rode in the packed tracks of some kind of herd. A hundred feet in front of me and to my left, I caught movement and focused in. There sitting along the trail were four wolves.

I stopped and cradled my rifle, which was slung over my shoulder. The wolves stared at me, and I glared back. First one, then the others stood and began to advance. I shouted at them, my voice shattering the forest silence. They were not deterred and continued toward me. I spun Canoni around and spurred her on, away from the wolves. Looking behind, they still followed me, bounding through the snow. I urged Canoni on, digging harder into her flank, and she responded with a burst of speed. Again, I glanced over my shoulder to see the wolves following me but rapidly losing ground.

The increased distance between us allowed me to stop and fire a shot, meant to startle them, but they did not even flinch. I turned Canoni toward home, and she broke into a gallop, making my progress much easier than that of the wolves. Arriving at the cabin, I put Canoni inside, and I climbed to the roof and waited for them. After 20 minutes, they had not appeared.

It is late afternoon now, up until now, having seen no sign of the wolves. Canoni has been outside for a couple of hours, and thankfully I have had no problems.

My confusion during this encounter was a result of the fact that the wolves did not act fearful when I fired my rifle, as they had in the past. Once the sight of them approaching set in, I turned Canoni and ran. The fact is that during this encounter, I had the upper hand all the way through. Canoni could travel in the snow much faster than the wolves, and from my elevated seat, I had an excellent angle from which to shoot, if necessary.

It would have freaked me out if they had come to the cabin. After the potential killing was finished, I think I would have tripped out. On the other hand, I must suppose what may have happened had they caught me by surprise and been able to catch Canoni. What if Canoni had stumbled and fallen in the snow? I have decided that I will worry about these things if they come to reality.

\* \* \*

This morning I woke up and slipped outside. Sun, a mild temperature, and no wind to speak of greeted me. It was calm and quiet. The storm has moved away.

After letting Buggs and Canoni out, I warmed a piece of smoked salmon for breakfast, as I had awoken hungry. After breakfast I went about my chores.

I will take Buggs and go for a ride.

I am here in the cabin after riding Canoni to the Gataga River and back. I rode south along the West River, riding on the banks of the West River where the snow is far shallower than in the open meadows and forest.

Along the way, I happened upon fox hunting in the meadow. It was not aware of me, so I surveyed it, following it for a while as it hunted for something to eat. This guy was quite intent on what he was doing, to the point that I could get to within a hundred feet of him.

As he made his way along, he stopped every so often, cocked his head to the side as I've seen foxes do on occasion, and then jumped into the air and planted face first into the snow. He was pretty successful, catching a mouse or a mole roughly 20 percent of the time. After a few minutes, the fox saw me and trotted shyly into the trees. It was an interesting encounter to observe.

Closer to home, I saw several deer in a clearing huddled together. They followed me with their eyes as I passed, never moving or showing any sign of fear. I passed tracks in the snow, tracks that crisscrossed and went in all directions. Not surprisingly, the Great Spirit has provided much for the animals to survive on.

I found some mouse droppings in the cabin, and I spent a bit of time looking for mice. I found none, but surely they are around. What they don't know is that they could be eaten if caught. More than anything, it is the health risk I face if I breathe in the dust from dried droppings.

I remember when George and I were traveling to this place; hundreds of mice flooded the land in the spring. I got over any fear of mice then. After all, they are a part of the food chain here.

\* \* \*

Another day has dawned in the wild, and outside it is cold but sunny. The thermometer indicates that it is seven degrees. A slight breeze makes it feel colder.

I awoke this morning longing for pancakes. I sat for a minute trying to recall the last time I had pancakes, and I was not able to recollect. It has been a long time for sure. In place of pancakes I will heat smoked salmon.

I have completed breakfast and I feel better than before eating. With Buggs and Canoni outside eating, I will go about my chores.

I have completed the routine of stocking the grass, the wood, and the water. The top layer of snow is frozen, and it crunches when I step on it. I haven't seen this too much in the past.

It is close to midday. I will grab my snowshoes and walking stick and go for a hike.

I am cooling down in the cabin after spending several hours hiking. Just cleaning up the escape trails is a major workout, and it left me sweating and somewhat exhausted. I saw the owls sitting in the tree behind the cabin as I approached. Earlier, I saw elk tracks leading from the southernmost escape trail into the forest, and following the tracks with my eyes, I found the herd of six inside the trees eating.

From behind the cabin, it is evident looking at the mountains across the West River that an avalanche occurred sometime in the past few days. I see a wide swath of debris in the chute where the slide passed. At the base of the mountain is a deposit of snow, trees, and huge boulders. I did not hear this slide, but it was a sizeable one.

After returning to the cabin, Buggs now sits outside the cabin door while Canoni grazes nearby in the sunshine. The breeze has died down, but it remains cold. I am sure that it will be cold overnight as well.

* * *

I make this entry as the evening dusk appears on the western horizon.

This day dawned with a beautiful sunrise, the entire eastern sky appearing as if on fire. The vista was so very dramatic. It made me wish that I was a painter.

Across the meadow from the cabin, a lone bull elk made his way to the shielded side of a compact car sized rock formation and dug into the snow right up against the rocks. This elk was in excellent condition.

In the forest, some distance away, I heard a wolf howl. I had my rifle ready and moved outside the door, where I commanded a wide field of vision. Wolves are like some people, they prefer to attack from behind. I heard the same wolf howl, a long, low, drawn-out vocalization.

As the afternoon drew on, Canoni stood where the corral rails used to be. Her ears were pointed forward. She stared intently across the meadow in front of the cabin and into the forest beyond. I took a few minutes to scan the area with the binoculars but failed to detect any danger.

I will climb the tree soon and get a piece of meat for dinner.

It is evening now. The day progressed without incident. Buggs and Canoni are in their usual indoor spots, while I am in my bedroll near the fire. The sunset was as pretty as the sunrise was. How blessed I am to see all of this for free. Soon I will sleep and see what the morning brings.

* * *

It is late afternoon, and I will recap this day's events. The sun shone radiantly when I let Buggs and Canoni outside. A crisp, quiet morning greeted us, except for the crows making their usual racket. They had found a dead animal of some kind, likely a squirrel, and feasted on the remains at the base of a tree.

Once I had finished refreshing the water and the firewood, I took a hike on the escape trails, walking the length of first one, then the other, then the last. At the West River, I slipped on the ice and landed on my ass, which is now sore, as is my right wrist again. High overhead I saw a hawk circling, no doubt watching those crows eat their morning fare.

I took Canoni out for a ride around the meadow and then out to the Driftpile River. The ride was relaxing and without drama. I stopped and covered my wrist in the snow a couple of times to reduce any swelling that might result from the fall. On the way home I rode past the lake that I have yet to name, finding frozen ice and no signs of animals.

Once I returned to the cabin, I stoked the fire and thawed out my dinner. This day was so beautiful, so calm. I do not take these days for granted.

\* \* \*

## JANUARY 10

The past three days have each dawned with a wintry mix of snow and wind. On days such as this it is best to remain inside the lodge, which I have done.

Canoni does not seem to mind being outside, but Buggs much prefers the shoebox-sized nest in the corner of the room.

I brought in some kindling the other day and found Buggs resting behind it. I remember reading about how cottontail rabbits do not dig their own nests but rather use woodpiles or shrubs as nesting places. So I brought some grass in and tossed it on the kindling, and Buggs has grown possessive of it. I guess that Buggs feels a natural instinct to be shielded from air-borne attack. The nest does not take up much room, so I will permit Buggs to keep it there.

I have watched Buggs taking short naps. At the beginning, he opens his eyes every few seconds. Then he waits for a minute or two. Finally, when he is ready to sleep soundly, he lies on his side and does not open his eyes for perhaps 10 minutes at a time. He must feel secure in his nest.

Canoni is most happy when the wind is not blowing. She stands right against the cabin wall, observing the meadow when she is out. On some occasions, she wanders, but I have no fear of losing her.

My back is sore this morning for some reason. I will take it easy today, stay around and read, let the chores go until tomorrow.

It is midday, and outside the snow flutters. Within the cabin it is comfortable, while on the other side of the cabin door is a different story. Two things are on the other side of that door. The dark and the cold. It strikes me that there is almost no difference between a cabin and a burrow under a tree in the wild. Both will protect one from the elements and offer safety from predators. But having slept in both, I can say that the cabin is the better option.

\* \* \*

I have allowed four days to slip by. During this time it has remained cold and snowy.

At the moment, Canoni stands in the open meadow in front of the lodge, observing something that I can't see. I will go investigate.

I am back in the cabin after searching the landscape, trying to find what Canoni was looking at so intently. Finally, I noticed movement, and an arctic fox trotted into the forest from the trees. Its white coat made it impossible to see from my vantage point. How Canoni spotted it is beyond me. Only because its eyes and nose were dark and because Canoni was gazing in that direction was I able to see it at all. This is not the first time a fox has tricked me this way.

It is late afternoon now, and outside the light, misty snowfall goes on. A several-inch thick layer of snow weighs down the trees and makes them look droopy.

Closer to the fireplace, it is much warmer. Canoni is content wearing her blanket, and Buggs is snug in his nest, already settled.

I will cook my meal soon and then read until I can sleep.

The days are shorter than before, and there are so many hours in the night. I know that a direct correlation exists between the weather and my moods. So far, being cabin-bound has been as bad as I had imagined it would be. I do get out, if only to hike the escape trails and keep them maintained, which in its own right is mundane, but at least it is outside.

\* \* \*

Yesterday was quite boring with nothing of note to report. Today, however, is a different story. During the night an avalanche occurred across the West River north of the cabin. The earth vibrated.

I will ride over and investigate.

I am sitting on a downed tree at the foot of the avalanche as I pen this description.

All is quiet now. A soft, light snow is falling. The destruction caused by this avalanche is hard to believe. Trees, some 40 feet tall, now lie in shattered splinters at the base of the mountain. Surveying upslope toward the top of the mountain, I see trees sticking up out of the snow, which appear similar to toothpicks. The path of the slide is littered with tree branches and dark brown dirt. I estimate the area of the slide to be 200 yards wide and a quarter of a mile long.

I do not come here often, so this slide has little effect on me other than to remind me of the possibilities. Scanning around I see no animals or even tracks. I do note that a boulder the size of a Volkswagen Beetle rolled into a tree and shattered it. The rock will most likely never move again.

It is getting cold. I will retreat to the cabin.

I have arrived home. I have brushed Canoni and brought some meat into the cabin for my meal later. All is well in my part of the world.

I finished my meal, and as I sit by the fire I started thinking about my favorite uncle. Every family has a crazy uncle, you know, the one everyone like the most!

For me that person is my Uncle John, my mom's youngest brother. I'm sure that he was accidentally dropped on his head as a baby, played football without a helmet, and was probably fond of chasing parked trucks too. He is an amateur full-time comedian. When Uncle John is on a roll, everyone listens and laughs. He and my father have gotten into more trouble together than anyone knows. I think uncle John is everyone's favorite.

He has a flat top haircut. He is skinny, wears glasses, and is a friend to all. All of the kids, regardless of age, think he is hip, so he is always surrounded by children.

It is my desire to be that cool uncle to my sister's children in the future. I imagine that once they learn of this journey the label of crazy uncle will be passed on to me.

* * *

Overnight a fast-moving front dropped new snow. January has reached the halfway point without danger to the residents of this lodge. This morning it is mostly sunny, the air is calm but cold. I see the condensation when either Buggs or Canoni breathe.

I will go about my daily tasks and write later.

Taking my time, I completed my chores in a couple of hours. I took a hike on the escape trails and then proceeded north to the Driftpile River. While I tromped through the snow it occurred to me that the view is entirely different wearing snowshoes than it is when riding. Hiking limits my field of vision to a much smaller area. Since I cannot see as far, my vision is more focused.

Of course, I would have less time to react to an emergency, but in theory since I am more focused, I should not be caught off guard. I paid more attention to the tracks in the snow as I made my way to the cabin. I could tell the recent prints from the ones made a couple of days ago by the sharpness of the edge of the print.

At one point three crow flew above me, calling to each other from the safety of the trees. In the quiet of the morning their sound carries deep into the valley. They are curious as they watch me, occasionally dropping to the ground and investigating my tracks.

I arrived at the cabin in mid-afternoon and brushed Canoni and Buggs. Canoni loved it while Buggs made every attempt to get away from the brush.

I will cook the last of the rice from the buried stash for dinner, along with a venison steak. The stale tobacco that George buried tastes terrible and will soon run out as well. The only thing I can say about it is it produces smokes.

I read that the plains Indians used tree bark and dried herbs for tobacco. Maybe I will try that if I get desperate.

I have not had any signs of withdrawal that I would have expected to have since coming here. I was a pack-a-day smoker in the city. It must be that my mind is always occupied that I am not noticing any physical signs of withdrawal.

It is dark as I have returned from a short jaunt through the meadow in front of the cabin. I wanted to see how the cabin appears at night. It is like a tiny beacon of light in the dark ocean of night. I can see light coming from under the door and from the shuttered window.

I heard the owls hoot from their perch in the tree.

Psychologically, being in the cabin makes all the difference. It is warm, light, safe, and defendable. From the meadow the cabin appears as a painting, the environment dwarfing the tiny cabin in this vast wilderness.

All is well, time for sleep.

\* \* \*

This morning Mother Nature gave me a front row seat to the circle of life. As I trotted to the West River to replenish the water, I noticed a snowshoe hare eating the bark from a shrub. Suddenly the hare broke into a sprint, and behind it, crashing through the shrub, ran a lynx. The hare scurried in a zig-zag manner, trying to lose the lynx. After 30 yards the lynx caught up to the hare, and at the proper distance, stretched out its paw and tripped the hare, which tumbled into the snow. The lynx had caught its dinner. The last I saw, the lynx carried the hare away in its mouth, into the privacy of the forest.

In the blink of an eye, one life was taken so another life could endure. The circle of life played out before my eyes, as it does every day in this land.

It is late in the afternoon as I write this entry. Canoni stands in the meadow, and Buggs is getting into the grass stores.

I have brought in some meat for dinner. I will cook it a bit later.

I noticed that the thermometer outside read 22 degrees earlier. For now, I sit at the door watching the stillness as light transitions to dark. On the horizon I see that the moon will be full, though a cold night will accompany it. In the distance, appropriately, I hear the faint howl of the pack. The wolves must be making their rounds through their territory.

As a kid, the one monster movie that freaked me out was The Wolf Man, starring Lon Chaney. For me it is quite easy to remember that movie on this night of the full moon, with the wolves howling in the distance.

* * *

This morning began with the usual brilliant display of color as the sun made its way into the sky through clouds on the horizon. Outside, I saw no signs of wolves or any other animals that may have passed during the night.

Canoni and Buggs are outside, and I am preparing to get some exercise on the escape trails. I will put on my snowshoes and depart. The forest is alive with bird songs, crows and blue jays among them.

I have returned from a stimulating hike. I headed off toward the Driftpile River. Two large but distinct meadows lie between the cabin and the river, each bordered by thick stands of evergreen trees. As I plowed through the first snowy meadow, from a distance of a hundred yards, a moose sauntered out from behind the trees and glared at me. Since the rutting season is long behind us, he did not present a threat to me.

Not knowing if it was going to be aggressive, I had to assess the whole picture and make my choice. The moose did not fear me, and it sure didn't alter its course. I moved out of the way, giving him the right of way. It is exhilarating to see such a large animal in the wild, close up. These animals show no fear of humans. For a brief second, as our eyes locked while it passed. I then felt a broader connection with this massive animal.

I hiked to the cabin a short time later.

It is late afternoon; the sun is about halfway to setting. I guesstimate that we have two more hours of daylight. It is this time of day that Buggs is most active, hopping from the grass stores to the open meadow and then dashing back to the cover of the grass. He will come inside the cabin before dark.

Canoni is ever the attentive companion, always within an ear's reach of my call, always observing me. Our relationship is complex. She knows that I am the source of her food and protection, while I know that she is my sole source of transportation. Her even temperament has been a fine asset to have, as she is always in good spirits. She is also a good watch horse. I can look at her and know if any danger lurks nearby. She is never hesitant about coming with me when I travel. If I go any distance at all from the cabin, she follows.

Outside now, the world is in near total darkness. Inside, the light and warmth of the fire offer a special glow and cast soft shadows on the wall. Buggs and Canoni are in their respective places, and I am propped up against the wall writing. Buggs has, over time, been adding sticks and grass to his nest, and now it is hard to see him in the milk crate sized abode. No such problem with Canoni, she is a tight fit in this cabin and even lying down she takes up a lot of room. I hear the owls hooting in the trees. Soon they will hunt their meal. This time is theirs to be the top predator of the night.

* * *

As is often the case I am amazed at what a difference a day can make. Morning has come, and with it a violent storm which is blowing snow sideways. Fortunately, the wind is blowing from the north, so the front door of the cabin is shielded from the direct wind and so does not rattle as much as otherwise. I let Canoni out of the cabin, and she now stands close to the wall of the cabin. If I had to guess, I would say the wind is blowing at 30 miles per hour or more. I will bring Canoni in a while. I guess it must be psychological, but I feel more vulnerable when the weather is like this. I feel the isolation of this location. But as soon as the sun returns, my attitude corrects itself, and I am happy once again. I will not go out today for fear of getting lost or worse. Instead, I will stay inside and read and maybe nap. These days get to be so long!

* * *

## THIRD WEEK OF JANUARY

The previous two days were spent cabin bound hiding from the raging storm. This morning dawned with an overcast sky. The storm, which is now moving on, takes the damaging wind with it.

So this morning I must tend to my chores, making sure to clear the snow from the roof. I will then spend as much time as is necessary to hike on the escape trails to keep them passable. This task is becoming a dreaded routine, since it generally takes two to four hours to groom the trails.

I am sporting an injury to the muscles in my right leg. While riding Canoni as we groomed the trails I felt the beginning of a cramp in my inner thigh and so jumped off of Canoni to walk it off. I sat down for a moment, but as I hoisted myself off of the ground, the cramp became severe, affecting my whole inner thigh, and I could hardly move to do anything. If I tried to bend my leg, the cramp became severe just above my knee. If I tried to stand on my tip-toes to stretch it, the cramp became worse in my upper thigh.

I managed to hobble to a tree and lean against it to keep from dropping down. The cramp subsided several minutes after it began. I was unable to ride Canoni, so I ambled slowly to the lodge. Now my entire leg is sore. I am moving with a limp and am not at all comfortable. I have never experienced a cramp as severe before and truly am afraid that if it reoccurs and I fall down, I will not be able to get up. The muscles in my leg are causing me terrible pain.

I will sit on the rock outside the cabin and work the muscles in my leg until I feel that they are normal. The possibility of having a debilitating cramp has never occurred to me, and being out here alone, it could cause issues under the right circumstances.

The day has passed now. I can't say that my thigh feels any better, but it has not cramped again. I am not hungry, and I am not particularly interested in climbing the ladder to the food in the tree. The weather now is calm and cold, but I am cozy in the cabin with my mates. So I shall call it a day.

* * *

Morning has come, and my leg muscles remain sore. I will not attempt to do any work today, but rather I will try and loosen up my leg.

The animals are outside, feeding in the sunshine. Although my whole leg hurts, the worst of the pain is in my upper thigh. Big muscle equals big pain. I will take a stroll in front of the cabin.

I am inside after gingerly walking outside the cabin. I felt pain with every step. I think it will take a few days to mend.

With the prospect of more storms coming through the valley, I must be mindful of the escape trails and keep them maintained, even if it takes all day. At the very least, one trail must remain open at all times between the cabin and the West River.

I am hungry, so I will be forced to climb the tree for meat. I guess I might as well do that now.

I am back with meat, and it was indeed painful to retrieve. I am sure that I have not done my leg any favors by climbing a ladder and moving around in the tree. Anyway, the chore is finished.

I will spend a bit of time massaging my thigh, trying to cure what ails me.

The day has been partly overcast, at times the sun shone through, but for the most part it has been gloomy. As I look outside, I see a few light snowflakes falling.

Canoni and Buggs are both outside, eating their grass. I can see that Canoni has lost weight, but she is still quite healthy at this point. Soon I will bring her and Buggs in for the night.

We three, concealed in our cabin, are safe from those who rule the night.

\* \* \*

Over the last two days, my leg has healed, no longer reminding me of the cramp with each step I take.

This morning dawned cold and gray, like yesterday. Currently, the thermometer reads five degrees.

I will do my chores and get back inside as quickly as possible. Buggs and Canoni will be able to handle it outside until I finish the chores.

I have finished my chores, and after a short time outside, I was literally shaking in my boots. With Buggs and Canoni inside now, the cabin will warm up, and we can settle into a peaceful environment.

Though it is midday, it feels like it should be evening. Minutes drag on like hours, hours like days while we cower in the warmth of the cabin. I have such a feeling of being antsy, not able to relax totally. I have the desire to be outside, though to go outdoors is life threatening. It burns a lot of energy being fidgety, and I am just that.

There is nothing more to write about today, and so I will drop my pen. Today, our valley is at peace, deep in winter.

\* \* \*

Sometimes it is hard to keep track of time accurately, as every day seems like the day before it during the long winter. White dominates the landscapes, thus change is challenging to detect. This morning finds the sun shining, but the temperature is low, hovering around 12 degrees.

While doing my chores I saw my neighbor, the fox, trotting (not foxtrotting, ha! ha!) in the meadow across from the cabin.

As I make this entry, I sit on a rock near the West River, listening to the birds singing in the nearby trees. As I look across the narrow valley, on the trail leading up the foothill mountain, I see several elk, making the trip up and out of sight as the trail winds around the other side of the mountain. As I breathe, I see steam in the cold air.

Life is hard for all creatures at this time of year because of the shortage of food, harsh weather conditions, and the predation that occurs during the short days and long nights.

I hear something. It was Canoni strolling back from the river. She scared the hell out of me! Now that she is here, I will take her for a ride.

I have ridden Canoni to the Driftpile River, where I now relax against a rock, taking in the now-familiar scenery. I feel as if I have lived here long enough to know this valley by heart. I see a lot of tracks in this area that appear to be wolf, but I see no evidence of a kill, nor have I heard any howling, so I feel safe. I notice the breeze picking up a bit, rustling the trees, yet not uncomfortably.

I will tuck away my journal and ride to the cabin.

I am relaxed now, having returned from my ride and rekindled the fire. I have a venison steak for my meal. I will relax for the rest of the day and wait for the night.

I do wish that there was some way to fast forward to the end of winter. I am so anxious to be entrenched in the life that abounds after winter fades.

I consider myself lucky so far that I have not been cabin-bound for extended periods of time, as I had expected, based on things I read before the journey. For me, two or three days inside is like being in a prison cell. The conditions have to be pretty bad to keep me inside. Though the snow is deep in some areas, most of the game trails are well-packed and easy to navigate. The same is true for the escape trails, all of which are packed and maintained.

I will cook my meal now and prepare for the evening.

\* \* \*

I make this entry after what has been another of those unanticipated moments of sheer danger. I took Canoni for a ride, and while we advanced slowly through the trees, she stopped abruptly. Realizing that something had caught her attention, I gave her the reins. She backed up a few feet and rotated her head to the right. Suddenly, from behind and to the right, a wild boar charged across the trail, causing Canoni to rise up on her hind legs, which in turn caused me to drop my rifle. I immediately pulled my handgun from my holster and jumped off of Canoni.

The boar wheeled around in the snow and grunted before ambushing me. By then, I had picked up my rifle. I holstered my handgun and fired three rounds from my rifle into the boar's body, bringing this incident to a speedy close.

As is usually the case with this kind of thing, the adrenaline flowed through my veins, and the metallic taste in my mouth was strong. I had to spit. In this instance, the realization of what had taken place hit me. When I fired my rifle, Canoni got spooked and ran a short distance away from me. She waited for me to catch up to her. I left the boar in the snow, as it was too heavy, perhaps 200 pounds, to carry with me.

I will go out tomorrow and see if I can butcher it. I have no idea how to butcher a pig. George would have no problem with it, I'm sure.

For now, I will take care of my chores and later cook my meal.

In re-living this latest incident with the boar, I don't think it could have gone better, unless I hadn't dropped my rifle. The fact that Canoni knew that something was wrong, and that she looked back when she did, made all of the difference. It would have been a whole different scenario if I had been thrown to the ground rather than jumping off of Canoni. If I had had to fight from the ground, it may have been a different outcome.

To take it a step further, if the boar had not charged me in the first place, two lives would not have been impacted. That is Mother Nature for you. It that seems wild animals are either at ease or in full attack mode, no in between.

It has been a good day.

\* \* \*

## JANUARY ENDS

The preceding three days passed uneventful, but during last night, the wolf pack made an appearance at the cabin, sniffing around the door, scratching in the snow. Sporadically, a brief fight between members broke out but ended in a matter of seconds. I have seen this behavior several times now, and it is always a unnerving episode.

As is the case every morning, I never know what is on the other side of the door. Today, I found the tracks and diggings of the pack. I see many urine spots around the cabin, and why not, I am the intruder in their land.

I let Canoni go out, but Buggs has remained inside. Canoni seems pretty relaxed, so it seems that all is quiet.

In a while I will ride and see if I can butcher the boar. It would be awesome to have pork chops!

I have returned without as much as a slice of bacon! It is obvious that a nighttime predator came upon the dead hog and dragged it off. After looking around for five minutes, I discovered the scattered remains of the boar near a cave, which I had not previously noticed. The carcass was stripped of flesh on one side, and was lying in the snow. It was quiet, and I had the uneasy feeling that I was being watched, so I left the area. It was likely a mountain lion that was waiting to return at some point to devour the remainder of the kill.

The day goes on, somewhat cloudy day with occasional sunshine.

* * *

## FEBRUARY 3

Today brings with it the same cold, crisp conditions we have known over the previous days.

The thermometer read minus six degrees. It is sunny, but the sun does nothing to warm the earth. The sky is bright blue, not a cloud to be seen in any direction. I see the steam as Canoni breathes, and this looks bitchin' because she is in profile.

I will go out and do the chores and then burn some energy maintaining the escape trails. My leg has completely healed from the cramp and the aftermath, so hiking is once again an alluring idea.

It is late afternoon now. I took my time and hiked for several hours. I caught sight of five caribou through the trees lining the meadow across from the cabin. They were at least half a mile from me and totally unaware that I was there. I have not seen many caribou since I have been here. They are easy to identify with their unusual shaped antlers.

So the long winter that seemingly lasts forever wears on. I have done everything there is to do inside the cabin. I have read my books enough to know them by heart. I have examined Buggs' digs to the point of knowing if he has added a new stick. I have cleaned and emptied things to the point of being compulsive. I have become a master of casting shadow animals on the wall of the cabin: a bird, a bear, a rabbit.

I make this entry after dinner to note that it has begun to snow. There is enough light to see the fluffy flakes slowly float down from above the treetops, settling on the earth. My roommates are settled in, so it is time to sleep.

\* \* \*

## FEBRUARY 8TH

I celebrate my 22 birthday today. Alone here in the wilderness of British Columbia, I have thrived and grown wiser.

Today I opened the cabin door to a world of calm. A dazzling sun rose in the east. It is one of those days where the sky is deep blue, with a slight hint of a breeze. It seems that the world is calling my name.

I have returned from my ride, and it is late afternoon now. Today, as so often happens, I witnessed the brutality of life. Taking Canoni and Buggs, I headed out toward the Driftpile River, as usual, traveling along the bank of the West River. Half a mile from the cabin, I found signs of a kill, blood and guts and fur scattered in the snow. It appeared that the wolf pack had made a kill sometime during the previous night.

As I rode forward, I could see a coyote near the carcass, gnawing on a leg bone and trying to break it off of the body. On a butte overlooking the drama, three other coyotes watched the scene.

Suddenly, one coyote barked a warning to the others. I then saw three wolves, including the alpha female and the alpha male, trotting out of the forest. The male made a direct line for one of the coyotes, which did not heed the alarm given by the other coyote, and in an instant, the alpha male wolf had attacked the coyote and killed it by breaking its neck with its powerful bite.

With no trouble at all, the wolf picked up the dead coyote and carried it through the snow, displaying the kill to the rest of the pack. Two young wolves appeared out of the trees and tried to take the kill away but were reminded of their place in the pack by the alpha male. The male picked the dead coyote up once more and carried it farther along, then dropped it in the snow and strode into the forest, leaving the carcass for a couple of foxes that showed up on the scene. They wasted little time in consuming the coyote. The rest of the coyotes left the area as well.

This entire event spanned roughly 10 minutes from start to finish. Within a day or two, as is the pattern, new snow will cover the site of this massacre, obscuring the bones. For now, the foxes, ravens, magpies, and others will consume the carcass. Witnessing this was a case of being in the right place at the right time.

For dinner I will eat smoked trout, which I haven't had for a while.

The day remains clear and comfortable. With a cloudless sky, it may be cold overnight. I thank the Great Spirit for another day in this land.

\* \* \*

As has been the case for the past two days, I awoke to a clear and sunny sky this morning. The thermometer read a favorable 30 degrees.

After letting my mates out, I set about doing my chores. Since it was so nice I decided to hike the escape trails, though they remain in good condition, letting Canoni walk behind me. She willingly follows anywhere I go. I did not use my snowshoes on this hike since the snow was fairly well compressed. The one thing I was glad I brought was my sunglasses. The glare coming off of the snow could easily have caused snow blindness. I imagine that I look like a raccoon when I take them off.

It is midday now, and things are calm. Winter is in so many ways boring, while at the same time, I have a fascinating world out there to see and explore. On days like today, though it is boring, it is also beautiful beyond compare. Life in winter is totally different than it is in the other seasons.

I see how some animals have a distinct advantage, while others do not. An example of this is the elk and the wolf. During the other three seasons, the elk is dominant since it can run faster, fight better, and is in better general health during the seasons of plenty. In the winter, however, the wolf has the advantage.

Wolves have plenty of territory in which to roam. They can run on top of the snow while the elk must run in much deeper snow. By hunting as a pack, the wolves are able to wear down the elk. It is just a matter of how long it takes. Wolves chase and challenge the elk, continuously seeking out the sick, the young, or the old. Once segregated from the herd, the victim faces a slow torturous end.

During spring, summer, and autumn, the world has much more to offer, entertain, or even kill you with.

\* \* \*

The previous two days were spent cabin bound due to the dangerous cold, which has reigned over this valley.

A winter postcard, a perfect day, is how I would describe the scene today. The snow seems lighter than usual for some reason, and as the ice particles in the air fall, they reflect the sunlight and appear as sparkles swirling in the air, all of which adds to the postcard-like image.

Snow covers the land as far as I can see; deepening the layer on the surface.

It is afternoon now. I arrived home from hiking a short time ago. While traversing near the West River a quarter mile south of the cabin I found a deer lying partially submerged in the water. My guess is that it died of hunger, since I did not see any signs of injury or blood in the snow. I am sure that the carcass will not remain there for long. Some predator making its rounds will find and consume the free meat.

The lodge feels warm after being outside. I have the door open, and I see Canoni outside gazing. Meanwhile, Buggs is hidden in his growing lair inside of the cabin.

My food supply is adequate, as is the grass supply for my friends. Plenty of fresh water, pine needle tea, and firewood equal contentment in the wilderness. I will relax for the remainder of the day.

\* \* \*

## MID-FEBRUARY

Today promises more of the restrictive cold that we have endured over the last couple of months. No longer does there seem to be mild days, the temperature seldom gets over 30.

Regardless of the weather, Buggs, Canoni, and I take our daily jaunts on the escape trails and sometimes across the West River and into the meadow on the other side.

I realized that I have been referring to what I have named the West River, the flowing water behind the cabin on the other side of the huge rock formation, as a stream, a creek, and at other times, a river. I guess it is a river because it does have tributaries feeding it, both upstream and downstream. It is deep in some places, and yet it is shallower near where it meets the escape trails, running four feet deep. It is now frozen solid at least three inches thick. These days, I have to use the axe to chop through the ice to get to the water below.

Buggs is somewhat anti-social these days, not coming out of his tangle of sticks except to go outside. He doesn't want to be close to me for some reason. He acts intimidated.

The weather has stayed cold, though no snow has fallen for the past few days. The sun shines from time to time, but for the most part it remains cloudy.

I do my best to stay upbeat and content, though with each passing day, my patience with winter wears thinner. I anticipate at least six to eight weeks more of winter, at a minimum.

I have distracted myself recently with thoughts of how to prepare for the journey out of the mountains, as I have decided that I cannot stay for another ceaseless winter. Perhaps I will leave in late June or early July. To that end I have been thinking about what to do with the cabin. I have always imagined myself standing at a distance and watching it burn to the ground. If I leave it, nature will reclaim it in coming years. It would be nice to think that someone could stumble upon it in the future and use it to survive. We will see what happens at the right time.

I have decided to leave the bow and quiver of arrows hanging on the door, if I do not burn the cabin down. This will be my gift to the next inhabitant.

\* \* \*

Outside the air is ice cold. The thermometer reads minus 12 degrees. Ice particles drift through the air. The sunlight reflects off of these little crystals, and for an instant a flash of light is created.

I see steam rising from Canoni's and Buggs's bodies as they both wander around outside.

I will go about my routine, although I will not take a bath for fear of freezing to death. I average a dunk about every other day. After three days my hair is oily and not at all comfortable. Tomorrow, rain or shine, I will take my bath.

I have taken care of my chores. The water has been refreshed, as have the grass and the firewood. I did not see any animals while I was out, no doubt due to the extreme cold. I climbed the tree and took out some meat for my meal today. The meat is frozen as hard as a rock, so I will set it near the fireplace and hope that it will thaw by late this afternoon.

\* \* \*

This morning finds extremely cold air draped over the valley. The thermometer reads minus eleven degrees, which is a single degree warmer than yesterday. As Canoni struts around, I hear the crisp snow crunch with each step.

I will take a bath in the West River this morning, and so I am heating up some water over the fire. I will take it to the river and use it for rinsing. Before I go out to bathe, I will stoke the fire.

I guess I'm ready, so I will write later.

My body is clean, and my hair is dry, after a couple of hours of brushing it in front of the fire. The amount of energy needed to take a bath in this cold is surprising. First, I had to use my ax to break the ice on the water. Next, I stripped my clothes off and plunged into the water. In a matter of three minutes or so, I was out of the water and running up to the cabin.

Once inside, I danced around in front of the fire, trying to keep the circulation going. When I was warm enough to sit, I did so in front of the flames and dried off. For the time that I was in the water, my body was doing all it could to shut down blood flow to my extremities. Stumbling on numb feet, my one goal being to reach the cabin, made the feat of getting inside all the more satisfying.

Now that I am dry and comfortable, I feel like a million bucks. Of course, I will not go outside for the remainder of the day. I don't want to invite illness. Actually, I think it was my mom who told me that you don't catch a cold from the cold.

With Canoni outside and Buggs here in the cabin with me, I will spend the rest of this day inside. I will make an exception to go to the tree box later to take some meat out for my daily meal. Of course, Canoni will come in then.

Living here in the wild, everything is as it would have been a hundred and 50 years ago. I know that there is land enough for all. It was gold that changed the balance of harmony. Gold and greed in the name of progress changed history.

I have long believed, and believe at this moment, that I was born in the wrong time period. I should have been born during the 1840s. At that time this lifestyle was common. Many men made their life in the mountains. I would have either been a mountain man or a train robber.

\* \* \*

I am considering the journey retrospectively this morning and I am proud of myself, for I have thrived in this land, facing hardships and challenges and winning each battle. I have learned about my limitations and strengths, learned that I have the mental capability to be alone for extended periods of time. I have come to understand over time that if I focus my mind on something, there is nothing that I cannot accomplish.

I recognize that I am the center of my world; everything else is peripheral noise. Trivial events that occur nearby are not the driving force steering me through life. My focus and my desires compel me forward. I intend to remain proactive in my approach to life, if only because I prefer to have a certain amount of order in my life.

My hair has grown to a length three inches above my waist, the longest it has ever grown, and I am proud of it.

Although today I am in good spirits, I wish for one change: spring! February moves forward, bringing with it new things to observe, enjoy, and experience.

On this morning, cold air remains over the valley. Much like opening the freezer and sticking my head inside, the cold air can take my breath away. It does not take long for this weather to get tedious. It makes me long for the days of summer.

My chores won't do themselves, so I will write when I am finished with them.

I am back from executing my chores. I spotted a fox having a drink at the West River. It saw me and wasted no time running into the forest.

In the snow along the escape trail leading from the cabin to the West River, I noticed hoofed tracks, which I believe belonged to a moose. The tracks led from the forest to the river and then into the forest again. Other than the fox and the moose, I have not seen or heard anything for the past several days to speak of.

Both Canoni and Buggs are in good health and enjoy the time they spend inside the cabin. Why wouldn't they? They are free from most dangers. During the past couple of months, I have become accustomed to having them inside during at night. I don't have to worry about something attacking them. Instead, Canoni acts as a good guard horse, letting me know when danger nears the cabin. She has only crapped on the floor a couple of times.

For dinner tonight I will eat a piece of fish.

I must say that I am becoming restless, being cabin-bound for the most part for successive days. I dream of warm, sunny days that allow me to be out for the entire day. I say a prayer that tomorrow will be warmer.

\* \* \*

It would appear that prayers are not always answered. I awoke to a dismal gray day, the clouds hanging low like a thick blanket over my home. Looking at the thermometer on the cabin wall, it shows minus nine degrees.

I am in the cabin, my chores finished for the day. I decided that I need to have some fun today, and so I will take a deer skin to an area south of the Driftpile River, a place with long, sloping hillsides, and go sledding!

I will write more upon my arrival home.

It is late afternoon, and I have returned from a fun day of sledding on skins. On the ride to the hills, I passed a kill site, apparently from a few days ago. No doubt wolves, judging from the amount of blood in the snow. Only scraps of an elk hide remain, and ravens picked away at them.

Farther on, I crossed paths with a herd of seven deer trying to scratch out an existence. They were all so skinny that I could see their ribs. It seems that they would be easy prey for other animals, but so far they have made it through this long winter season.

I got to the sliding hill as the sun was directly overhead. I took the deer skin and made my way up the sloping hillside until I was 50 feet up, and then I sat on the skin and skidded down. I was impressed with my speed and the smooth ride.

So naturally, me being me, I chose to ascend to a hundred feet and try it. Needless to say, I generated more speed, and at times, I wiped out after losing my balance and falling to one side or the other. Of course, awkward plunges through the snow occurred during those instances, and it would have been fantastic if I had had a movie camera. I rolled nearly six times during one crash.

After several rides at a hundred feet, I decided that it was time to go to the top, a good three hundred feet up the slope. At the top, I will admit, I had second thoughts. Then I jumped onto the skin and...zoom! I was a kid again!

There I was, hollering at the top of my lungs as I picked up speed, fighting to keep my balance, until finally I lost control and tumbled head over heels down the slope. I came to rest, laughing wildly, lying on my back, looking up at the gray sky. I took a couple more rides from 100 feet and called it a day.

Lord, how I wish George was here to play today.

I have changed out of my wet clothes. I will definitely go to the slopes again before this winter ends. It was a great time. If I was going to stay here for another full year, I would build a small sled from wood to use next year.

Perhaps one of my worst flaws is my love of speed. Anything that can make me feel the pull of gravity is something I want to experience. I love the sensation of being pushed into the seat that I feel on a roller coaster or in a sports car.

This could one day prove to be the cause of my demise. Be that as it may, it is my sincere hope that I keep my longing for that feeling in the future.

Both Buggs and Canoni are fine, living each day as I do, looking forward to springtime when the meadows will change from white to green.

I will eat a piece of venison for my meal.

\* \* \*

As the season continues February sees its moment, much to my surprise, the sun has returned to our valley. It is early morning, and I have let both Canoni and Buggs out. I now sit on the rock outside the cabin. It is quiet, except for the hammering of a woodpecker somewhere in a tree nearby. The sound echoes deep into the forest and out into the meadow.

I think I will spend the day thoroughly cleaning the cabin. The fireplace holds many pounds of ashes, as it has seen a month of fires since it was last cleaned. It might be a good idea to go through the meat supply and take inventory.

I am back and have taken stock of the remaining meat in the tree box. I easily have 50 pounds of meat, equal parts elk and venison. The math is easy enough, a pound of meat per day for 50 days, which means that I have enough meat to get me through until early spring. Then fishing and hunting will provide the local fare.

I will sit back and play with Buggs. It turns out that letting Buggs into my world has really made a difference. He is a distraction from boredom and is affectionate. That is to say that he likes to be petted. He is entertaining to watch as he bolts from place to place, with no particular reason for doing so. At times when he is outside, without warning, he bursts full speed from one location to the next. It is as though an invisible force is prompting this behavior. I can say that it seems freaky.

This evening I feel lazy. I will sit by the door until I get tired.

\* \* \*

This past year has been the most educational, exciting, challenging, and rewarding year of my life. Obviously, the second half of the year was the most challenging, as I have been alone, with only Canoni and Buggs for companionship.

I don't feel that I am going, or have gone, crazy. Well, I do have conversations with my neighbors, but since they don't answer, I guess you can't say that we're talking.

Learning the ways of nature has been fairly easy, the proof being that I still have all of the appendages that I started out. Each day I awake looking forward to the next lesson taught by Mother Nature. Even though I have yet to use my escape trails, I believe that making them was one of my better ideas. This has taken stress and worry off of my shoulders.

I am young, and I know that the lessons I learn here will follow me for the rest of my life. I don't believe that there will come a day that I would not like to take a hike in the forest and recall my solitude here.

I am still learning lessons in my young life. I know that I do not do everything right in every instance. Many have been the times when a difference of a second has decided my fate. In the days that I used to hitchhike, when I was picked up by strangers, I believe that the Great Spirit guided me. In all of the times that I have faced danger, an escape has always been presented. I believe that they were presented by the Great Spirit.

There was a brief time when I was a bible-thumping hippie, a part of a group of people who were more or less Jesus freaks. For me, trying to convince people to stop the evil was a bit too much. I realized that I did not know my own path and so found it hard to tell others about a different path. God is all around me, the essence of Wakan Tanka in the air. In every drop of water, every blade of grass, every grain of sand, everything on this Earth and everything that flies above it, I find the essence of Wakan Tanka, the Great Spirit.

I wish to remember my thoughts in future years and so write them in my journal now.

Canoni spent the day outside, staying close to the cabin, allowing it to shield her from the mild breeze that kicked up. Buggs is in the tangled pile of sticks and grass that has become is his home. He has added so much to it that I have to look closely to see him. I imagine that he feels secure in his snug nest.

The owls still reside in the tree in front of the cabin, and they remind me of their presence with a soft hoot-hoot every day.

As I make this entry, I am warming water for some tea. It is a bit of a comfort to me that pine needles grow so abundantly.

I guess that that is about all for today. Soon sleep will come, and I will wake to another day in the wilderness.

* * *

## MARCH ARRIVES

March is supposedly the coldest month in this region. Over the preceding days nothing has changed to make me believe we are any closer to the end of this unbearable winter. As another day begins, winter sluggishly plods on for those of us in the wild who call this place home. This day dawned with an overcast sky and a chill in the air. The fluctuation in temperature is quite sobering, with a swing of 30 degrees not uncommon from day to day.

I see no sign of the wolf pack around the cabin this morning, a pleasant relief from two nights ago when they made a brief visit.

Canoni seems quite relaxed as she moves about in front of the cabin. Buggs is somewhere outside as well.

My daily chores await me, so I will address them now.

I chose to wash my hair today, so I took care of that chore as well. After two hours, my hair is once again clean and dry. I like nothing more than riding with the wind in my clean hair, especially on a summer day. Unfortunately, warm days seem a lifetime away.

I shiver to imagine being stuck outside on a day like today. During this season of short days, the earth never gets the chance to warm before the night comes, plunging the temperature most nights to below zero.

I am ever grateful for this log cabin. The care and attention to detail that George and I poured into building it pay dividends daily. It retains heat, and other than the crack under the door, is relatively air-tight.

In a while I will cook some dinner, and after I eat perhaps I will sing to my roomies.

I have decided to write less often since this is the least exciting time of the year. I have read some of the passages, and they become redundant. So now maybe I will go two or three days between entries. I have one pen remaining, having lost several in a river during one crossing, which put a strain on my supply.

* * *

As March drags on, the weather has turned fickle. I have seen alternating periods of snow and sun. Snowfall has been minimal during this time, but the cold has been dangerously pervasive

Buggs and Canoni are fine and are currently outside.

As I indicated in my last entry, not much goes on at this time of year. I did see two geese fly overhead yesterday, the first that I have seen in several months. I have been thinking about how cool it would be to have a dog out here, maybe a Labrador or a German Shepard. Yes, I am thinking of the old Rin Tin Tin and Hondo TV series.

Having a dog could offer protection and companionship on one hand, but it would also be a target of the pack. Ultimately, a dog could fend for itself and be a part of the circle of life. I think the problem with having a pet out here is that sooner or later, it would most likely be killed.

I am not inclined to become too close to an animal out here. Yes, I have Buggs, but he adopted me.

All is quiet in the valley of dullness.

\* \* \*

Nature has brought the reality of the wild to me, rather than me having to go seeking excitement. Late in the night last night, the usual silence was interrupted by a noise from the advancing wolf pack. Having no light with which to step outside, I hunkered down behind the cabin door, rifle in hand, listening to the approaching chaos.

In the near distance, I could hear growling and an obvious attack taking place, but what the facts were, I couldn't guess. For the next hour, my roommates and I listened to the members of the pack committing murder, hearing several fights break out during the mayhem.

This morning, when it was light enough to see, I opened the window shutter and upon peeking out saw blood-stained snow covering a sizable area in the meadow in front of the cabin. Entrails and the hide from what was left of a buck littered the area. Scraps of flesh are all that remain, and certainly the pack will come back to finish their kill today or tonight.

To be accurate, the area appears to resemble a massacre site. Once the wolves finish the meat and move on, I will cover the blood with clean snow. Mother Nature never waits when she is ready to teach.

I think it safe to assume the buck was drawn to the cabin by the stored grass and was an easy target for the pack.

I spent the remainder of this day inside the cabin with Buggs and Canoni. At no time did I see the pack reappear.

\* \* \*

Not surprisingly, the weather has persisted cold for the last three days, though with more sun than not. This morning the thermometer read a scant four degrees. At the moment the wind is calm, so it is tolerable.

I have spent several hours a day hiking on the escape trails, both maintaining them and attaining my required exercise. Canoni has accompanied me on these short jaunts willingly. As always, she brightens my days.

Two nights ago, the pack reappeared to finish off the buck that it killed previously. The wolves reappeared during the morning, so I was able to view them from outside the cabin, safely seated on the roof. Once they had finished and moved on, heading to the north, I threw clean snow over the blood-stained ground. After an hour, the ground was again white as far as the eye could see. It will require a snowfall to make the area pristine.

Yesterday I decided to go sledding, and I had a gas! With a better sense of balance acquired by experience, my rides were longer and faster. I suffered hard crashes as well but experienced no permanent damage. I spent the better part of the day on the mountain yesterday.

Each morning begins with us greeting the sun, or at least that is the hope each morning. Regardless of the weather, the chores demand attention and so are executed faithfully. I do not like drinking day-old water. From an animal-interaction point of view, it has been quiet during these few days.

\* \* \*

March has moved forward and so far it has been a snowy, cold day, a repeat of a pattern that started three days ago. During this time snow has fallen. At night, it has been bitterly cold. This is dangerous cold! Exposed skin would be vulnerable to frostbite in as little as 10 minutes.

I have been out of the cabin to refresh the water and grass supply, to get meat, clear the snow from the roof, and to relieve myself. The same is true of Buggs and Canoni. They go out for short periods before returning to the cabin.

Ravens have found this valley and are loudly protesting something, flying close to the cabin and calling out in a loud, obnoxious way. They fly off for 15 minutes and then repeat the whole thing again.

The further gloom of cold and gray dampens what are already boring, quiet days. Both Buggs and Canoni are fine, and like me, they make the best of the long days inside.

I have allowed Buggs to come along when I hike the escape trails with Canoni. Sure enough, Buggs follows at his own pace. Canoni enjoys the exercise associated with maintaining the trails. She gets to the chance to explore her surroundings. I imagine that she does most things out of reflex rather than making a plan and following it through.

There have been occasions when I have seen her sizing up a situation and making a simple plan of where to escape. This is especially evident when she spots something on the trail. She stares with intention at it until either she feels that it is no longer a danger or until it leaves the area. As I've said before, she is an excellent guard.

Life at this time of year is so damn boring. I am amazed that the boredom hasn't driven me insane, cabin-bound for all intent and purpose by the cold weather for days at a time. I go out for food or to relieve myself. I talk to myself...and answer myself. But with no one around to see it, who but me would ever know?

I find myself thinking back to those sunny days of last summer, when the sun felt so fine on my back. I have seen this land in full regalia, with so many flowers and trees and enough green grass to feed 10,000 horses. The rivers are cold, blue, clear, and full of life. The air is alive with sounds of the creatures living in the valley, each trying to be heard. The full moon even appears different in the summer months, a softer, more inviting appearance, than in the cold glow of winter.

All too soon, the fire dying, I am snapped back to reality. No sunny days or flowers are on the horizon, there is simply white and cold.

* * *

March has reached the midway point. The weather has remained exceptionally cold, for what today would be the fifth day in a row. I have not seen the sun shine for an extended period in a week. Everything seems to have stopped, mired in thick soup. The minutes all seem the same, the nights long and cold.

I have seen a couple of deer during this time, but the lack of game is noticeable. Could this be the middle of winter? I hope that it is far past the middle. Surely I will go crazy with another three to four months of winter!

I keep current with my chores, not allowing a day to pass without completing them. My roomies are both doing well.

I have said it repeatedly, every day is the same old routine, and I can't wait for spring, to have a change in scenery.

Our food supply is beginning to decline, but I am confident that I have enough to last until the end of winter. The firewood is in fine shape. I have more than enough to last until spring.

The one questionable commodity is my sanity. These days, it seems that the cabin is getting smaller, like I have less air to breathe. It seems that the daylight lasts for a brief few moments before darkness comes again. I find myself being tired most of the time. I feel less motivated to do those same chores I that enjoyed doing just a month ago, things like hiking on the escape trails. Nonetheless, the chores shall get done.

I have found myself losing interest in the little projects that I have begun. I have been losing my concentration and not sleeping as well as before. I don't know how much more winter I can take. I don't seriously think that I am losing touch with reality, but on the other hand, who do I have to compare myself to?

\* \* \*

I make this entry while leaning against my backrest, having finished dinner. The cold weather persists. I read that March can be the coldest month in this region, and so far I would agree.

It snowed for a while last night, though this morning the sky is clear and blue. A gander at the thermometer reveals 12 degrees.

I took Canoni out for some exercise, after finishing my daily chores, leading her around the escape trails with Buggs slung over her neck near the saddle. It is nice to work out for hours and not even be the slightest bit sore. To share the experience with both of my friends makes it more special.

The location on which we chose to build the cabin has turned out to be perfect, as the huge rock formation behind the cabin has served well as a windbreak, and as a result relatively little has snow built up on the slope behind the cabin. This makes getting to the slope fairly easy. Gazing out over the snow-covered beauty that is this stark white landscape, the West River with a trace of dark blue color breaks the stark whiteness.

Here, in this setting, as in all wild environments, every creature of the Great Spirit struggles to survive the grip of winter. As the snow has deepened over the season, those grazers have either left the valley or must dig deeper to reach food. The tradeoff falls between calories burned to dig versus calories ingested. This is currently not an even trade. During the long, cold season, many will perish and become food for others. The scavengers wait out of sight to begin the process of returning elements to the earth.

This season is hard on a young man too. The cabin keeps me warm and dry, safe from predator attack. However, I must be outside for some functions, and when the elements get harsh, I am sometimes forced to remain inside for extended periods of time. Keeping dry is important. Frostbite may set in quickly under certain conditions. On days when the sun does come out, it shines so brightly that snow blindness would be a problem without sunglasses.

For all who live in this valley, time creeps ahead, spring seemingly a lifetime away. Aside from the permanent residents, I have seen no animals in the valley. I hear the few crows and owls on a daily basis, but God willing, the spring will come soon, and my freedom will be restored. Such is one price of freedom.

* * *

Outside the thermometer reads a brutal minus four degrees. One cold front after the other has invaded our valley. I have been in the cabin almost exclusively for the past week, going out only to refresh myself, the water, the firewood, and the food supply. Other than that I have tried to keep busy reading, sleeping, and sewing my worn clothes.

I am having little success reading due to a lack of interest. The books no longer have a suspenseful plot. I know them all by heart.

While sitting here in the shoebox that is the cabin, I think about people I have known and perhaps loved. I ask myself some questions. What is it like to really know how to love? Is love not a physical feeling? Is it not to some truly an addiction? What then is love? Is it to know and predict one's partner's mood, thoughts, or feelings? Does love see its culmination in the middle of the worst or the best moment?

If I don't understand love, or can at minimum define the true meaning of the word, why then would I pretend to think that I know what it feels like? How do we profess to acknowledge receiving love when love means so many different things to different people?

Love would never let one down, but the world is filled with unhappy, lonely people. Love would never cause one to shed a tear, but we all know how to cry. Love is said to be a part of our religions, our upbringing, our creed, and yet our brothers kill. Who among us can tell when love is present, considering that we all know how to lie.

Yet, others try to convince us that they know better than most what love is and how it feels. Perhaps they are the chosen ones who politely go about their way in love. Many of these are the same people who fight behind closed doors.

I have become confused, as I have never known what love is, as a result hurting those whom I love, pushing away those who would wish to hold me, ending up, predictably, alone. I am confused until the day comes when the clouds have cleared, the feathers are once again smoothed, and the word love is understood by me. Maybe, if I open my eyes wide, or is it my heart, I will see it? Either way, the liabilities of love seem greater than the rewards in my mind, due in part to the dysfunctional education we received in school.

Everyone is broken. Some hide it better than others.

\* \* \*

It has been three uneventful days, but today I have something to write about. The wolf pack made another appearance before dark last night, and the wolves have been in the area for longer than they normally stay. I don't know the reason for this, but the behavior does not concern me at this point. In fact, I welcome their return.

At sunrise this morning, I crept outside the cabin, leaned against the doorframe, and observed them, as they alternately played and rested in the forest across the meadow.

Canoni has been nervous and has not strayed from the cabin door. She has not eaten as of yet. She watches intently any movements that the pack makes and shifts her weight when necessary to get a better view. Buggs has not made an appearance at all yet today, hiding deep within his lair of sticks in the cabin.

This wolf pack has been a constant companion on this journey, ever since we arrived at this location. I have come to appreciate the line of command that they have established in the pack as well as the cunning that these wolves display. I have a deep respect for their predacious abilities and feel elation when viewing them roaming free. Today, there is nothing between them and me, save for the meadow.

Today is by far the warmest day that we have had in quite a while. The sunshine brings a false hope that this winter could be nearing an end.

My chores are up-to-date, fresh water and firewood sit in the cabin. The escape trails are clear and packed from the almost daily hiking that Canoni and I do to maintain them.

Overall, the last few days have been pleasant, and I look forward with great anticipation to seeing warmer days soon. My mood has rebounded today as a result of this sunny day, including the appearance of the pack. I wish for a sunny tomorrow and thank the Great Spirit for this one today.

I will soon cook my daily meal, which will be trout, dried last fall.

\* \* \*

I am encouraged, since the passage of each day brings us closer to spring. This is a mental boost for me, increasing my chances of survival, since attitude is the greater part of survival. It is truly difficult to keep track of the days because they all seem the same, drab and dreary. Only occasionally am I bestowed a sunny day. Snowy white landscape lies in every direction, as far as the eye can see.

Canoni is healthy and content in her daily routine, going out at dawn and spending the day wandering through the meadow and using one of the escape trails to go for water. Canoni is attentive to her surroundings. I need simply look at her to know if danger is close.

As for Buggs, he comes and goes as he pleases. He sprints from place to place at full speed, even if it is a ten-foot sprint! He is a good alarm, though, quick to pick up on any movement when he is outside and racing into the cabin at the first sign of trouble.

In taking stock of inventory, I find our food supply to be adequate, as is the firewood. After going about the daily chores, I spent some additional time clearing the snow from the roof. This chore is perhaps the most imperative, but it is also my least favorite. It requires a lot of energy and brute force to shake the layer of snow from the roof. Sometimes, when it does break loose, it has a tendency to slide off right in front of the door, giving me another chore to complete. Today, there was not a heavy load, so clearing it was relatively easy.

\* \* \*

This morning, I opened the door to let the animals out, and there across the meadow, sitting at the base of an evergreen tree, was a cougar, not intimidated at all by my presence. Both Buggs and Canoni spotted it right away, and they both gawked in that direction. Of course, my rifle was securely in my hands as I contemplated what to do.

Buggs decided to wait in the cabin and sprinted inside. As the cougar and I gazed at each other, me through the scope on my rifle, I wondered what had attracted the big cat and what its intent was. Hunger no doubt led it here. Perhaps it discovered my meat supply. I crept into the meadow to gage the cougar's reaction and was not surprised to see it sit taller and snarl in my direction.

As I returned to the rock outside the cabin, the cat resumed a crouched position and watched me. I decided to approach the cat, making a loud noise and firing my rifle, hoping that it would retreat. Obviously, since I am writing now, my plan worked.

I grabbed a deer skin and walked in the cat's direction. I shouted at the cougar. I swung the hide around over my head in an attempt to appear bigger. When I was within 30 yards, I fired my rifle into the air. The cougar jumped to its feet and darted away from me, into the thick trees to the east of the meadow.

There are not a lot of places on that side of the meadow for it to live, so I feel certain that it will loop back to the west and cross the West River. The landscape contains many more mountainous cliffs and formations across the river.

I rode Canoni south toward the West River and then a little east. Because the top few inches of this river are frozen, I found no tracks. Perhaps this cougar's expansive territory includes land to the east of my cabin.

I arrived at the cabin a few minutes ago and have documented the event, immortalizing a memory that will live on in my mind until my last day on this earth. I will, of course, keep one eye out for the cougar for the next couple of days.

In the meantime, life in the cold mountains goes on. I will eat the final piece of waterfowl left in the tree box. It is a mallard duck that has my mouth watering.

\* \* \*

Five days have passed, and during that time it has been quiet, with nothing occurring to prompt excitement. March reaches its end, showing no sign of the icy weather easing.

Over the past few days I have noticed that the owls occupying the tree near the cabin have begun to hoot more often and for longer periods early in the morning and at dusk. I don't remember reading about owls in the library while preparing for this journey. I wonder if this could be related to reproducing in some way.

* * *

No earth-shattering episodes have taken place in the area during the last three days. Snowfall has come and gone several times during the last few days, but at no time was there anything more than a average winter storm.

The days seem to be getting slightly longer now, although that is most likely wishful thinking. After all, who would notice an extra minute of sun from day to day?

Canoni goes about life with her usual good nature. If she didn't crap in the cabin, she would be perfect. Buggs, on the other hand, seems to be anxious to get outside more often, when it is not snowing, of course. I think that Buggs is essentially a lazy rabbit.

Somehow I nicked the palm of my hand in the last couple of days, and it is tender and puffy, as if it is infected. I will scrub it and see what happens.

I went to the West River mid-morning. After breaking the ice and filling the canteens, a whitetail deer approached. He waited for his turn, and as I left he moved to the hole in the ice and drank his fill.

The deer are bulky here, compared to the ones I've seen in California, which tend to be about the size of a Great Dane dog. Without doubt, there are by far more deer here than in California. I'm sure that the number of hunters in California dwarfs the number in this region.

Everything is excellent here today. It has been another day of waiting for the fair weather and thaw.

* * *

Two mind-numbingly cold days have gone by, and during the night tonight the wolf pack visited. I could hear the wolves close to the cabin. Several times I heard them sniffing at the door. This was not much to be afraid of, and other than propping a strong supporting stick against the door; I listened to them in the dark. Canoni was nervous, but she stayed quiet, and by this morning, they had gone.

Outside I noted five or six yellow spots in the snow and just as many at the base of the cabin. They had again marked their territory.

The sun is shining now, and though it is still only 27 degrees outside, it feels warmer due to the absence of a breeze. Make no mistake, 27 degrees is crisp and captures my attention, but it has been much worse.

Both Buggs and Canoni have gone outside, and they show no signs of tension. Usually the pack hangs around for half a day or so, but there is no sign of it now.

I will go about doing my chores and write later.

Having run through all of the chores, I am preparing to brush Canoni. This is the one thing Canoni loves most, getting her coat brushed. She would let me brush her for days on end if I didn't stop. She does have a thick winter coat that helps insulate her during this season.

My food and firewood supply are both ample to see me through until spring, which I hope is only eight or so weeks away.

For my meal today, I will eat venison and have a cup of pine needle tea.

\* \* \*

## APRIL

This entry is necessitated by an incident that happened this morning. I was at the West River, refilling the canteens, when I noticed movement in the nearby brush. With my rifle in hand, I looped around the area of interest and found a different vantage point from which to peer into the brush. Again I saw motion, and to my surprise, staring back at me was a moose in the thick brush.

What I saw next freaked me out! As the moose stepped away from me, I saw that it had a long leafless tree branch stuck in its side. The branch dragged on the ground, and inspecting it as close as I dared, I could see that it had pierced the side of the moose. I kept seeking a better vantage point to view from. It was the damnedest thing!

I observed the moose drag the branch as it struggled into the clearing of a meadow. It was plain to see that the moose would not survive with the branch in its side. But I had no way of removing the branch because I was afraid that the moose would charge if I got too close.

The moose left a trail of blood dripping on the snowy ground, blood that any predator could follow. As I had done in the past, I made the choice to interfere in the circle of life. I knew that it was right to kill the moose rather than to let it die from its injuries. With that, I fired the fatal shot into the moose's head, killing it instantly.

I soon found that the tree branch, two inches in diameter, was stuck a full foot into the moose's side. It took hours to dress the meat, and I am tired from the energy that I expended cutting and transporting the meat to the tree box. But I now have a hundred pounds of moose. Thank you, Wakan Tanka.

I have tried to imagine how the moose was impaled, and all I can think is that somehow it ran or stumbled into the branch. I will say that my first thought was that a person had thrown a spear at the moose, and for a brief moment I was uncomfortable, but the feeling soon passed.

The weather has remained calm but not exceedingly cold. My roomies and I are thankful that no big storms have passed through our valley for some time.

Both Buggs and Canoni are fine. They are both currently eating grass in the corral. Aside from the owls in the tree, it is strangely quiet. I hear no other sounds at this moment.

I have taken a piece of smoked fish out for dinner tonight.

All things considered, I am content with how life has played out for us this winter.

\* \* \*

I have taken daily rides for the last three days on the escape trails, seeking out any unfamiliar tracks or sign of any other persons in the valley. I remain bewildered about the tree branch sticking out of the moose. The end of the branch did not appear to be artificially sharpened. It entered at a strange angle, but I cannot picture the event in my mind. From the angle of the wound, the moose would have had to jump or been struck from below. Whatever the method of entry, I have not found any foreign tracks in the valley.

Today, I put my mind at ease and decided that it was a freak accident that maimed the moose. I am indeed grateful for the meat windfall and the fact that no people have invaded my valley.

Today the sun warmed the land, and I notice some, but not much, melting of snow. We have a long way to go before spring.

I will cook a moose steak for my daily meal later this afternoon.

I have a developed a stomach issue today. I have diarrhea, and so I am making frequent runs, no pun intended, to the outdoors. I am trying to drink a lot of water to replace the liquid I am losing. It is currently not a pleasant situation.

\* \* \*

Two days later, I woke up feeling renewed. I feel like myself again. I wanted to do something special, so I decided that I will go to the sledding hill. After spending the last two days in the cabin recovering, I need some time outside.

I have returned from sledding, which was a lot of fun, with no injuries or other adverse occurrences. While on the trail to the hill, I came across the meager remnants of a wolf kill. Blood-stained snow and tufts of hair are all that endured.

I arrived at the cabin in late afternoon. I cut a piece of moose meat, which now cooks over the fire.

I think Canoni enjoyed the outing today. She seemed to be taking in everything around her, while walking with pep in her stride. Buggs, in contrast, seems to be sleeping all of the time these days, spending short durations out of the cabin.

Everything is fine today.

* * *

For the last three days, all remains quiet here in the valley. It was quite windy yesterday, but overall, it has been what I consider mild.

I spent some time this morning rearranging the meat in the tree box, and I found half a salmon hidden at the bottom. This was the second time that I had discovered fish when I thought it was gone. I am now convinced that there is no more fish in the tree box.

I will eat half of this for dinner later.

Canoni spent most of the day in the meadow in front of the cabin. She ran sprints one moment and then paced in a big circle the next. She does seem happy. Her ribs are showing a bit more, but I am not concerned, as the green grass will reappear in a couple of months.

Buggs has not been outside the cabin for several days, and I am wondering if he is sick. He seems rather lethargic, anyway, so it is hard to know if something is physically wrong with him. I would be sad if something bad happened to him. I have become attached to him.

I have made the decision to ride to civilization sometime in middle to late June, which means that I have two months left to experience life here. During the next few months I know that I will battle with myself emotionally about leaving or staying for another year.

I don't think I wish to spend another long winter here. It is so hard to do every chore that needs doing on a daily basis. If I had company, it might be different, but to stay for another year alone might be mentally more than I can take. I consider myself mentally strong, capable of being isolated for extended periods of time, but I'm not so sure that I desire to extend the experience.

For now, I will sit and smoke my pipe and allow my mind to wander where it will.

\* \* \*

While things have been quiet, the temperature has not risen above 30 degrees during that time. Occasionally the wind comes up and makes things feel colder, but for the most part, Mother Nature has taken pity on her wayward children.

During the night I awoke to urinate, and outside the sky was pitch black, crystal clear, and filled with stars. While I urinated, a bright, large, slow-moving meteor lit up the sky, lasting perhaps three seconds before fading. Fantastic! I saw shadows from the trees on the ground as the meteor passed overhead. It was perfect timing.

For a brief few minutes I stared into space, beyond the Milky Way, deep into the galaxies that fill the heavens. To think that we are alone in this vastness does not seem logical to me, but in that moment, I felt totally alone in the universe, so insignificant that I scarcely make a difference in any way. This left me probing for an answer to the age-old question: what is my purpose in the grand scheme of things?

I stayed outside for another 15 minutes without seeing any more meteors, before catching a chill and retreating to my warm sleeping bag.

\* \* \*

## LATE APRIL

If I could change one thing it would be to shorten the winter by half! Each morning I go outside and glance at the thermometer, only to see the same low temperature as the day before and the day before that. New-fallen snow, once such a joy to see, now is depressing. How I long for the days I when can leave my heavy coat in the cabin when I go outside. It sometimes feels like winter is marching in place.

Last night sometime after I went to bed, a new storm passed through the valley and left several inches of new snow. This morning, however, the sun is shining and reflecting off of the new snow. Fortunately, I do have the sunglasses that I brought with me. These have served me well.

Buggs is outside playing in the snow. Well, it appears like play, anyway, and he seems to be trying to tunnel through the snow toward whatever lies beneath. I see snow flying as he digs. Canoni, on the other hand, is farther out in the meadow across from the cabin, strolling around like she hasn't a care in the world. She eats from the shrinking supply of grass whenever she feels the need.

The air is fresh and even a tad cold when I stand in the shade. It is a good day to do my chores, including cleaning off the roof and maybe taking a ride later.

It is afternoon. I spent time hiking in my snowshoes on the escape trails from the cabin to the West River. While hiking I came across some elk droppings, a clear indication that they too are using these trails. Once the chores were complete, I placed Buggs on Canoni and led Canoni south along the bank of the West River. Buggs, wide-eyed as always, took in his surroundings from a now-familiar vantage point. I would say that Buggs is the king of the rabbits in this valley, as I have seen no other rabbits on horseback.

In all we hiked six miles today, a nice workout for all of us.

I now rest against the cabin wall writing these notes of another day that I cherish, in spite of my complaining, creating an account of the sights and sounds that I will wish to recall in future days.

\* \* \*

The weather has been a bit more decent the last three days, remaining cold at night, while the daytime temperature rose into the low forties today.

It is early evening as I write, using the glow from the fire for light. I have eaten my meal, venison, and both Canoni and Buggs are settled in their respective beds.

I rode Canoni toward the Driftpile River, since I had not been in that direction for some time and wanted to check it out. I scooped up Buggs and took him along. I can report that it was striking riding through the virgin snowfields, free of tracks of any kind.

Gazing at the mountain ranges that surround me, it was apparent that heavy snow packs the peaks, and it won't be too long before avalanches could become a real possibility, even a threat. I recall last year's damage done to the West River by an avalanche. Although the snow was firm as I crossed the meadow north of the cabin, it was above Canoni's knees in some areas, making for sluggish travel.

After riding for two miles, I realized that it would be fruitless to continue, so I turned and rode to the cabin. Seeing my single set of tracks in the snow was quite sobering, reminding me that man exists to have company, other than a horse and a rabbit.

\* \* \*

Prompting this entry was another visit from the wolves last night. My roomies and I were all relaxing in our part of the lodge when we heard the call of a pack member not too far away. Instantly Canoni's ears perked up, and she rose to her feet.

I soothed her. "It's all right, Canoni. Nothing is going to hurt you."

I dragged my sleeping bag over to the door, and after climbing into it; I sat back against the door facing Canoni. Throughout the night the wolves lingered outside for reasons known only to them. At no time did they attempt entry. The night progressed with us inside eavesdropping and them outside exploring.

As the sun rose above the horizon, I peeked out from the relative safety of the window and saw no sign of the elusive group, only tracks leading in all directions. I snuck around the cabin, and once I was sure they were gone, I let Canoni and Buggs out.

There is no sign that Mother Nature will release the cold death grip that she holds on our valley any time soon.

\* \* \*

## MAY FLOWERS

May has taken charge and during the first three days the sun drenches the earth on a more regular basis, the snow pack softens ever so slowly. Each day when I check the West River, it is less iced over. Though it is progress, it could just as easily be hope crushed if an unannounced blizzard rolls through.

Canoni has found fresh grass shoots in areas exposed to the sunlight, mainly in the meadows, and she spends her time outside seeking out these rare tidbits of grass. Buggs is always right next to her, partaking in his share of any discovery.

I have perceived the deer becoming more abundant and some bird species returning to the valley that we call home. More and more the signs indicate that the worst of the winter is behind us and that the promise of spring lies ahead.

I tell myself not to get too thrilled about the slight temperature increase because the average is said to be in the high forties for April in this part of Canada.

Today I will eat a venison steak and have a cup of tea.

\* \* \*

Today I rode Canoni all the way to Driftwood Lake, the sun on my back as I rode. Ice still covers the lake, but it is thin enough to throw a heavy rock through. Soon, I will be able to fish again.

In the early afternoon I came upon three minks playing at the edge of the stream running out of the south end of the Driftwood Lake. I watched for a few minutes, feeling good, knowing that life is returning more each day to my heaven on Earth.

I rode south the six miles to the cabin all the while feeling the sun on my face. The temperature was warm enough to allow me to unbutton my jacket.

I caught sight of a skunk crossing the meadow in front of the cabin and happily observed it pass without incident.

My dinner will consist of, can you believe it, venison.

\* \* \*

The days have remained warm, and the snowmelt is beginning. The thermometer reads 44 degrees under a clear, sunny sky. The meadow is still snowbound, but my hope is that the snow in the meadow will melt quickly in the direct sun. Although the ground is hard now, it will soon enough turn soft.

After completing my chores I hiked south along the West River for a mile then did a U-turn and returned. I saw nothing to report on this outing.

I will eat a hunk of moose meat for dinner. In my opinion, the moose taste gamier than other meat. I find it to be tougher as well, which is why is has lasted so long in the tree.

Dinner is complete. I am full and content. Both Buggs and Canoni have settled into their spots and are both staring at me curiously.

\* \* \*

Mother Nature has offered perhaps the biggest shock since I have been in British Columbia. Buggs is a mother! Buggs, whom I've been calling him for all of this time, is a mama!

I woke up and tossed a log on the fire and then tucked into my sleeping bag. By chance, I looked at Buggs, and he...errr...she seemed busy in her nest. I went to sleep again, awakening a while later. I found my way to my feet and opened the cabin door to let Canoni out, and I turned back to see if Buggs wanted to go too. I then saw eight tiny bunnies suckling Buggs.

I still can't believe that he is a her. I mean, she is a mother. I don't suppose that I have a choice in the matter, so I assume that I have eight more roommates. Buggs is for sure a cottontail rabbit. She stayed in the cabin with her young today, but she did take two trips outside the cabin door to eat. Welcome to the world, little ones. I wish you all a long and peaceful life.

Since this curve ball was thrown at me, I feel like I owe it to Buggs to stay and protect her until her litter grows. I will postpone my departure until the bunnies have left the cabin.

The West River behind the cabin is now 20 feet across and five feet deep. It won't present danger when I cross it, especially the longer I wait.

\* \* \*

Three days have passed since Buggs gave birth, and two of them have perished. I have removed them from the lodge. She now has six mouths to feed. The babies' eyes have opened, and they all appear so small, their beady black eyes staring at me. Buggs has sustained her routine of leaving the cabin about three times a day to eat grass, while the babies explore their immediate surroundings.

As May has reached the end of the second week, life in this cabin has remained a nursery.

Canoni has shown no interest in the new roommates. She grazes during the day and sleeps at night.

I fished in a deep pool on the West River south of the cabin, and to my surprise, I caught a trout, the first one of the season. I say surprised because there is a lot of sediment in the water, making it cloudy. I did not think a fish would see the lure.

This fresh trout will be a welcome change for dinner today.

\* \* \*

This morning, mid-morning, a beautifully colored, full-grown lynx strutted right in front of the cabin, perhaps 25 feet from the door, showing no fright at all. It strolled from right to left, examining the cabin and me standing in the door. It never stopped trucking and persisted through the meadow until it was back in the trees.

A handsome coat of tannish-gray fur, hollow yellow-green eyes, and black tufts of hair on the tips of its ears left no doubt about the identity of this feline. I would estimate that the cat weighed around 30 pounds. This was the first lynx that I have seen in the open in all of the time that I have been here, and it was impressive.

Buggs and her six remaining young are doing well. The little ones are growing rapidly. They now come and go from the cabin at will for short periods of time. They are perfect replicas of Buggs. Canoni is, as always, happy and content.

I have been wrestling for a few days over how my mother would react if she saw this place. Being here is the culmination of a lifelong goal that I had, and I realize that my time here is soon enough coming to an end, but I wonder if the splendor of this land would help her understand my captivation with it.

Would seeing a wolf or a grizzly bear touch her soul as it touches mine? Would the range of mountains circling the valley give her the same feeling of security as it does me? Would she understand that my entire life before the journey was spent preparing for my life here? Would she think that two years was a short return on the investment spent?

It is not that I seek approval for my spirit and sense of adventure, but rather I would like my mother to know this happiness, both in this land and in my heart.

It is due to population growth in the United States that George and I had to come here to experience this life. I do know that my mother has the same, though unspoken, respect for nature as I do, however, she seems not to have a need to acquire knowledge about it first hand. It is my hope that she will someday read my journal and that this might heal the wounds that I inflicted on her and my father by being out of touch for so long. I can imagine the questions she would ask me.

By any measure of time, days in the wilderness, especially during the winter, seem to pass agonizingly slowly. Each minute of each day seems longer. In the long run, it doesn't matter how anyone else would judge my choices. After all, this is my life, and I am here by my choice. If I died here, this too would be due to the choices I made. Some people might accuse me of being selfish or not caring about other people's feelings, but the truth is, we get to go around only once in life. You live your life to your liking, and I will live mine to my liking.

On our deathbeds, we will all think about two things: how to stay alive and what kind of life we led.

I would say to any young person, follow your dreams now, and stay away from the crowd. You can stand alone and be strong. Take the time necessary and learn how to be independent. You might be the one others follow. Don't be fooled by passing trends or fashions. Stay true to yourself. Know your limitations and strengths, and know that being prepared in every situation will deliver you.

\* \* \*

As the young rabbits grow, they now spend more time outside of the cabin than they spend inside. They are weaning themselves off of the provided shelter and striking out on their own it would seem.

May marches on, and the snow melt has continued nicely. The grass is more yellow than green, but after a few more sunny days that will change.

I saw a lone male grizzly yesterday while I paced back from the Driftpile River, this one not being close enough to see or smell me. Earlier today, I found a set of grizzly tracks on the shore along the West River. Clearly, the grizzlies have emerged from hibernation and are hungry.

A noisy flock of geese flew overhead a while ago. Much more activity is taking place in the valley than even a few days ago. The sky holds no clouds. I will go fishing later and hope to catch my dinner.

I did not, in fact, catch my dinner, I caught nothing and so now have a piece of venison thawing by the fire.

\* \* \*

I have made the decision to leave by the middle of June. The rabbits are all but gone, as is Buggs, and the snow has melted to a point where shoots of green grass are appearing. I will travel lightly, taking with me only the barest necessities. I have decided to leave the cabin standing rather than burning it down. I will leave the bow and quiver of arrows hanging on the outside of the door. Who knows, perhaps a different young man will come exploring and find it in his time of need.

As the month of May advances, I pay more attention to selecting which items to take and preparing myself mentally for the long ride ahead. I can't believe that I am thinking about leaving this land, but the Great Spirit knows that it has beaten me. I cannot bring myself to face another frigid winter in the wilds.

Today while riding Canoni on the escape trails, I spotted a mother grizzly with three young cubs. She searched for food, and the cubs lagged behind her, learning about the new world around them. They tackled one another from behind, having fun with their mates. Mother was more serious about finding food, and would from time to time; discipline a cub by softly swatting it with her huge paw. As she moseyed along, she ate grass and other vegetation. Mother was a light shade of red, with almost an orange tint to her coat. There was no mistaking that she was a grizzly, judging by the curve of her face and the muscular hump on her back.

They continued their way diagonally across the West River and into the open spaces on the other side. As always, I was happy at the sight of the family, a new beginning for this mother and a new generation to carry on the species.

\* \* \*

Three days later, the sun is not yet fully in the sky, but the air is crisp. Canoni waits outside, fed and ready to go on our daily ride. As I glance around the cabin, I see memories in every item.

Strolling around the outside of the cabin, looking at the chimney, thinking back on the work that it took to build it, I am so proud of the cabin.

I will ride now and write later.

Riding away from the cabin, I did not glance back until I was on the lower side of the valley on a rise, the cabin perhaps a mile away. From that distance the cabin appears as a dot on the horizon.

I rode onward south to Deer Creek and followed it as it made its way to the interior valley. Finding nothing of interest, I headed north toward the cabin. In total, I rode 10 miles. It was a good day of riding in this land.

Dinner will consist of a rabbit that I snared along the West River. I wonder how the rabbit will taste this year. I am hungry, meat is meat, and it will taste fine.

\* \* \*

The days have remained warm, making the chores once again pleasurable. The thermometer reads 50 degrees. This is by far the warmest day this year.

Thankfully, no longer is clearing snow from the roof a daily event. No longer do I hike the escape trails to keep them groomed. I sometimes wonder how many miles I have traveled on those escape trails in the time that I have kept them open. I would be willing to say at least a hundred miles.

I fished in the Driftpile River today and took away three trout. Taken together, the three will make a proper meal.

Canoni is in the meadow in front of the cabin, eating the new sprouting grass, which is becoming more abundant. It is my intention to move the small amount of stored grass away from the cabin and out of the corral. It might otherwise become a dwelling for mice and other critters, and Canoni is not going to prefer it to fresh grass. I estimate that there are fewer than 10 bundles of grass left.

Throughout the forest the sounds of birds, squirrels, and other residents make their presence known, each in their own way. I hear a woodpecker hammering on a tree. I recognize the noise of a flock of crows as they bicker over one thing or another.

Every hour in the day now brings about more activity. This is my favorite time of year.

\* \* \*

For the last two days, the weather has stayed warm, the sun heating the thin mountain air. I note a bit of sunburn on my arms from exposure.

This day will see me spend time here around the cabin. I have finished the chores and sit outside the cabin in the warmth leaning against my backrest. Soon I will go empty the ashes in the fireplace and open the window in an effort to expel the smell of smoke that permeates everything in the cabin. I would go as far as saying that the wood itself is infused with the smell.

My clothes hang from various branches and trees in an attempt to accomplish the same deed.

During the spring thus far, I have had no problem securing food, with plenty of game around and the fish biting well.

In the distance a new fawn is following its mama along the tree line on the far edge of the meadow in front of our cabin. Mama nips at some foliage as the fawn looks on. Mama would do well to move her baby into the forest.

\* \* \*

Luminous days have been the rule recently, as the snow is almost melted.

This morning, as I rode Canoni in the meadow south of the cabin, an elk moved among the trees. He was heading east, toward the range of mountains that lie across the Gataga River.

I set up a couple of snare traps in the forest, hoping that I can catch a rabbit for dinner. I will go back and check them out this afternoon.

It is afternoon, and all three of the snare traps were empty, so I will not eat rabbit tonight. I will eat fish. A cup of hot pine needle tea will round out my meal.

\* \* \*

Aside from one foggy morning, the last three days have been bright. A lot more of the snow is melting and is beginning to run off of the hillsides and into the streams and rivers. The trails are even softer than a few days ago.

I managed to snare a rabbit, which I will eat tonight for my meal. In my head, I have an image of George sitting somewhere enjoying some beef spare ribs, fresh off of the barbecue. In my mind I can taste the meat.

I recall that when George cooked ribs, the meat fell off the bone. That would be, I would guess, a better-tasting meal than my rabbit cooked over a fire. Those weekend barbeques included greens and potato salad. Someone always brought chips and dip, and everyone brought some kind of alcohol. The feast turned into a party. Music played, and people danced. The kids played basketball, and everyone had a great time.

Those events seem so special to me now, while at the time they seemed normal and average. Those memories of neighborhood barbecues are good memories.

As I bring myself to the present, May has warmed the earth, and the snow melt goes on. I can now hear the water in the West River as it descends into the canyon behind the cabin. Rapids now exist in places that were shallow just weeks ago.

Nothing exciting has occurred during the past few days. I take time each day to consider the things that I will take out with me. It is unfortunate, but I will be leaving a lot of things here that cost a lot of money. I do not, and will not, have any regret, regardless of what I decide to take with me. Whatever stays will be a gift to the discoverer.

For dinner I will eat trout, caught in the West River. It took two hours to catch a fish, due mostly to the increased water flow.

The moon will be bright tonight, so perhaps I will sit outside and enjoy the evening.

Canoni is fine, fat and healthy. She spends all of her time outside, now that it has warmed up. She is able to find plenty of new grass in the meadows.

I washed my Levi's today, that pair is now drying. I have two other pair, so this is not a problem. Hanging them in the air for two hours helped freshen them up, but they all need to be washed.

\* \* \*

## JUNE 1

I have decided to ride east of the cabin today, along the Gataga River. I will follow it south for 10 miles. This will take me along the same trails that I traveled when our rafting trip went bad. Of course, I will bring my fishing pole and tent, and I will travel unhurriedly. This ride is to quench my desire to re-trace the trail followed on the disastrous raft ride.

To be honest, I do not remember too much about the lay of the land on the day of the raft trip.

I will eat fish tonight. In the morning, I will take my exploration ride.

\* \* \*

Morning has dawned. I have ridden five miles from the cabin, and I now sit on the bank of the Gataga River, preparing to turn south. I want to make a note about a curious thing I saw a couple of minutes ago. On the other side of the Gataga River, sitting on the bank, was a lone coyote that stared into the water intently. As I followed his gaze, I saw a carcass at the bottom of the river. Upon closer examination, I determined that it was the body of a cow elk. The carcass was pinned under a fallen tree, so only its head was moving, waving back and forth in the current. This action captivated the coyote.

I have made camp five miles farther down the Gataga River from the point where I turned south from the West River at the point the two rivers merge. As I traveled along the bank, I counted many tracks in the sand, although the sand made it impossible for me to determine which animal left which tracks.

I managed to catch a fish and will soon cook it over my campfire.

I will write more after dinner.

The weather today has been spectacular in every sense. It was perhaps 60 degrees outside with no wind or clouds. I sit shirtless near my tent recording the scene. At the moment, the sun reflects off the water and right into my eyes. I feel the heat on my exposed face.

I have cooked and eaten the fish, and the sun is no longer at the same angle as it was before. Now it is two fingers from setting beyond the mountains to the west.

I smell something unfamiliar in the air. It smells like mold, a slightly offensive dirt smell that you might smell if you lifted a carpet that had been in moisture for a while. It is not strong; it just faintly hangs in the air.

I see many shades of pastel colors as I look at the western horizon.

Canoni seems comfortable here. She has spent a lot of time standing close to the water, but she has never gone in.

I will watch the sunset and then turn in for the night.

* * *

I am now camped another five miles farther along the Gataga River, and the scenery is pretty. Across the river, the valley is fairly flat, grass grows tall everywhere. Farther east, the Rocky Mountains rise high into the sky, dominating the horizon from north to south. Snow still caps these mountains, though only on the highest peaks. I estimate that the range is 10 miles or more away.

Riding along the sandy bank of the Gataga River I followed tracks from a small animal as they snaked along the water's edge. I am camped on a rise, 15 feet above the water.

I caught a trout for dinner, which I will cook shortly.

This may be my favorite time of day, the short twilight hour before the sun sets. I see so many animals coming out of the forest to drink. Those who do notice me stare at me for a minute and then resume drinking. I have even seen a few mallard ducks paddling past in the Gataga River. They are so incredibly beautiful when the sun reflects off of their feathers.

Soon, the sun will dip behind the mountains, and dusk will set in ending another spectacular day.

* * *

It was another sunny day, and I found nothing to complain about. I rode five miles today, at times parading through the forest as opposed to along the bank of the Gataga River. Riding through the forest requires that a lot more attention be paid to my surroundings. It is easy to miss something due to the tall trees towering above me, as well as the many trees littering the forest floor.

The animals blend in with the darker environment more so than when they are exposed along the rivers. There is, of course, no way to ride straight through, instead it is necessary to zig-zag my way through the forest maze.

My tent is set up on the crest of a rise overlooking the Gataga River. I will try to hunt a rabbit for dinner. That would be a welcome change from all of the fish that I have been eating lately.

I am back at the campsite, having had the good fortune to find meat. I took a large rabbit from 15 yards using my handgun. I thank the Great Spirit for this fare, as I watch it cook over the fire. I will truly enjoy this meal.

After dinner, I will clean up the campsite, throwing any bones into the Gataga River so as not to attract unwanted guests.

* * *

This morning, the fourth day of my ride, saw a bright sun rise into a cloudless sky. I rode along the bank of the Gataga River until I came to an elevated section of land. From there I could see the Tuchodi River in the distance merging from the east into the Gataga River. This is as far as I will travel along this path. Tomorrow, I will begin the ride to the cabin.

In all, I have traveled 20 miles from the cabin. Fishing is excellent in this river, and today I again caught a nice trout, which after cleaning, weighed at least a pound.

I finished my meal, cleaned up the camp, and now sit on the sand, writing this entry and smoking a single pipe full of weed. Life is good today.

* * *

This morning, I followed Canoni's several day old tracks along the Gataga River and on to the cabin. I hiked a lot today, covering 10 miles in all. During the whole day of hiking I never had to check to see where Canoni was. As always, she followed a few feet behind me.

Pacing along the Gataga River brought back memories of when as a kid I hiked along the Keweah River, exploring as I went. I could imagine myself as a pioneer, crossing the land for the first time. But my family was a short distance away enjoying the pool in a hotel.

Here, I am far away from anyone. Now that I am older, I realize, of course, that the real adventure is always better than a child's memories.

I took a colorful mallard duck during the day, and I am roasting it as I write. I believe that cooking over an open fire does something to enrich the flavor of meat.

I will lay down my pen now and have my meal.

I have finished supper, and being the savage that I am, I ate the entire duck.

A band of clouds is passing overhead, and the sunlight is reflecting off of the bottom of them, turning them a bright marigold. I never tire of watching Mother

Nature dazzle me with her displays in the sky. While the sun sets, I sit here with a grin on my face.

\* \* \*

During the night, it rained for a couple of hours. This morning it is damp, but the sun rising should change that in a few hours. The grass lies flatter than usual due to the moisture.

Canoni, who typically bends her head slightly and pulls grass as we move, has found it somewhat harder today. I think she gets angry, so now and then she yanks her head down, pulling the reins through my hands. She then takes a bite of grass. I can only chuckle at her.

I have traveled six miles today, and I am camped less than five miles from the lodge, just below where the West River joins the Gataga River. It is an easy two-hour ride from here.

I caught yet another fish, which I will grudgingly force myself to eat. I've eaten so much fish here that I may have grown gills and don't know it yet.

The moon is rising over the eastern horizon, while the sun is four fingers from setting in the western sky. So I find my mind wandering, and it has parked itself on another subject about which I have been thinking. Are we alone in the universe?

I don't think that little green men live on Mars or that terrifying creatures will appear from the dark side of the moon. I think that if all of the reports of UFOs are true, there must be something out there. I feel the same way about aliens, if they exist. I want to see one, but I don't want them to see me see them. The same holds true for Bigfoot.

I could spend countless hours reading all of the conspiracy theories regarding the government and alien bodies and space crafts. I prefer to spend my time not worrying about it. If I am destined to meet anything from outer space…or inner space, I will be better for the experience.

It is getting dark. I will stop writing now.

\* \* \*

I am at the cabin, having arrived a short time ago. Six days spent exploring has come to an end. Canoni has gone to the West River to drink, and I have refreshed the water in the cabin.

In a while, I plan on hunting for a doe. I usually get around 30 pounds of meat from one. I am sick, sick, and sick of fish! My body is demanding red meat.

It is early evening now. I did, in fact, take a young deer. I think I got 30 pounds of meat, as I had expected. It is obvious that I can't eat that much meat before it spoils, so I cooked 10 pounds of it and placed the rest in the meadow near the West River. No doubt, some predator will find it and eat it.

I am stuffed! I ate as much as my stomach will hold and took the remaining cooked meat and hung it in the tree. I will eat more tomorrow.

I don't feel that I wasted the meat because at some point, the deer was going to be someone's dinner. I only shortened the process.

The fire in the fireplace sends a soft glow through the cabin. Canoni stands in the door. I guess she is coming in. I will write again soon.

\* \* \*

## JUNE 10

Right after I got to my feet I raced toward and jumped into the West River to wash up, I returned to the cabin, dried my hair, and ate some more venison.

It is mid-afternoon, and the sun is shining as I make this entry. A few high clouds drift by, casting large shadows over the land from time to time. Canoni is grazing in the meadow in front of the cabin.

I will go and bring firewood and fresh water into my home.

While I was at the West River securing clean water, I noticed a fox drinking along the bank opposite me and downstream a ways. I never tire of seeing this awesome animal, just the size of an average dog, yet able to survive with ease in this place.

In the trees I hear so many species of birds singing that it sounds more like noise than it does music.

Today has been a lazy day around here. Perhaps I will fish later, but it seems like a good day to be lazy.

\* \* \*

I awoke this morning to the sounds of the wolf pack, as it has reappeared after an extended absence. The wolves make a lot of noise when playing. Presently beneath the trees across from the meadow, all five of them are lying down in the shade.

I let Canoni outside, being sure to keep my eyes on the wolves. She was immediately alerted to their presence and was quick to locate them.

I must say that I miss Buggs. The activity in the cabin is much less since she moved on. I recollect her trailing Canoni's every step.

As the morning has passed, all parties have been well behaved, the pack staying amongst the trees and Canoni staying close to the cabin. I will not stray from the cabin today for obvious reasons.

It is mid-afternoon as I write. The pack has moved on, I no longer see them under the trees. Canoni has moved farther into the meadow, indicating that she is relaxed. Whatever the reason for the visit, the wolves did not approach the cabin this time, as they have many times in the past. I believe, as I have stated before, that my home sits on the edge of their range, and they pass through on their trips through the territory. They certainly do appear and disappear quickly. Now since they are gone, I will try to catch my meal.

I am back from fishing, having been successful in catching a single trout. Just to be safe, I took Canoni with me to the West River while I fished.

As June drifts on, I find myself becoming somewhat uneasy about leaving this place. I am not anxious to leave; rather I feel anxiety when realizing that I will not wake up to this heaven on Earth each day. I have pretty much selected the items that I will carry out with me, and I have made the definitive decision to leave the cabin standing when I go.

Though I am the intruder in this land, I have come to feel that I have made a truce with all of my neighbors. None of the animals that I have encountered give the impression of being stressed by our chance meetings. I feel that I have blended in quite well and have been an observer of nature, as I had hoped, rather than an influencer. I have tried to live as one with the land, taking what is offered and only what I need.

This land is pristine, and everything living on it plays a part in making it unspoiled. I have tried to do my part in keeping it that way. I have not allowed my presence to interfere with the flow of life unless it was to end suffering. I consider myself fortunate that the Great Spirit chose to teach me lessons in such a way that I was not often in real danger.

Yes, this is a hard place to live, mainly because I have had to have a strong mind and a strong back to match in order to endure. I can think of nothing that compares to being stuck in a cabin for a solid week, with no one to speak to and nothing to do. It takes a strong will to make it through. Believe me when I say that a solitary week in a cabin can send a rational person to the brink of madness.

I make this entry after eating a roasted rabbit. Outside as the sun sets in the western sky I hear the sounds of the night coming to life. I hear the owls hooting softly, I hear geese making noise along the West River. I am again secure in my cabin as the light fades.

\* \* \*

Three days have passed, and this morning has brought a clear sky void of clouds or wind. The thermometer reads 52 degrees.

Since I have been awake today, I have been thinking about something. I wonder if mankind can stop, or even slow, the pace of discoveries. It seems that invention outpaces the knowledge to use the item invented. I think about the rash of inventions that we hear about daily, the microwave ovens now equipping our kitchens to standard transmissions in our cars. One idea begets another, and the ideas become grander.

For example, the space shuttle program being developed by NASA right now will take Americans back into space, but now for extended periods of time. There will be scientific projects, satellite deployments, with the main goal being the re-use of a vehicle for low orbit space projects. This means that someday man will travel to space and return and be able to use that vehicle again.

I wonder what other discoveries will be made and how they will affect me in the future. Mankind does not know how to control many of the powerful things he has created. There are conflicts all over the world. Each side is trying to develop a more lethal weapon, a way to kill more people at a lower cost. Since countries around the world have access to modern-day weapons, there seems no way to reduce the expansion of arms.

Drugs are the same way. There are too many easy ways to get most drugs. In cities like Hollywood, one can find any drug they desire. I don't see how anything will change the pace of life, it can only get worse.

My point is that in 20 years, this grass under my feet may be cement. The world is changing that fast. I can't imagine how this world will be for the coming generations. I may be the lucky one for having experienced this adventure in this land at this particular time.

I make this entry after finishing my meal. The day was warm, and the breeze blew just enough to cool me off. I stayed around the cabin, other than refreshing the water. I ate a white fish that I caught an hour ago. Right now, the owls are stirring, getting ready to hunt. Several Deer and elk have made their way through the meadow from the West River, retreating back into the forest east of the meadow. The sun casts a long shadow of the cabin onto the ground, a mere two fingers from setting.

Canoni has just strolled up from drinking at the West River. She is ready to come inside. I imagine that the cabin must smell like a horse, but like everything else I have grown accustomed to it, I guess.

I thank the Great Spirit for this day, and I will sleep now.

* * *

Two days gone, both were sunny — the kind of which memories are made. Late yesterday afternoon, a thunderstorm popped up and dumped its shower upon the land. It poured for 15 minutes, then it passed, and the sun reemerged.

It is now twilight, and as always, the occupants of the nightshift begin to stir. I hear a coyote yapping. I hear my tree-dwelling neighbors preparing to hunt once again. The now familiar group of deer and elk pass by after drinking.

This pattern has been repeated for centuries. What I am stating is that things have been slow around the neighborhood. No developments worth tribute have occurred in the past two days.

My dinner consisted of a rabbit roasted over the fire outside and a cup of pine needle tea. One might wonder if I feel funny eating a rabbit, considering my extended relationship with Buggs. The answer is yes, I feel guilty, up to the point that my stomach growls and then meat is meat.

I will watch the sunset from the ridge and then sleep.

* * *

A new day has dawned, and I have by this time refreshed the water and restocked the firewood in the cabin. I woke up hungry, and I was able to catch a fish quickly, so I ate breakfast.

I have decided that there is no reason to delay my departure any longer. If I hesitate too long, I could be endangering myself by getting caught in the coming winter season. If I allow myself to doubt my decision, then soon enough I will be thoroughly confused. I could consequently make bad choices to the point that I am caught unprepared by the winter.

I will not doubt or question my decision, but rather I will set about organizing my gear. Having convinced me that now is the time to exit this wilderness; I can scarcely imagine life away from this neighborhood. Today is the last day that I will call this log cabin home.

Of all of the things that I have accomplished here, I am most proud of this lodge that George and I built. It has faced the conditions that this land imposes, and it has stood firm through them all. I tell myself that someday I will come back here to visit, but unless I do it soon, passing time will dull the possibility, life will happen, and I will never find the way back. It is more likely that I will never return to this place. This is such a sad thing to ponder.

But tomorrow will be the start of another adventure, the ride to civilization. My rifle, handgun, shotgun, two hunting knives, binoculars, ammunition, axe, cooking pot, frying pan, canteens, clothes, tent, sleeping bag, and rope, among other things, are the things that I will take with me.

I estimate that the total weight, including me, will be near 200 pounds. Canoni is strong, and she can handle that, but just the same, I will travel unhurriedly, and I will spend time leading Canoni as well.

It is midday; the sun is shining, so I will take a hike.

I am in the cabin after hiking for 10 miles. I went down to the West River, followed it downstream for a half mile, then turned east and made a loop to the Gataga River before heading home. I enjoyed the scenery, listening to the forest sounds, feeling the sun on my back. I thought I heard a turkey call from a distance today, but I don't remember reading about them living this far north. I only heard it once, so I must have been mistaken.

Farther along on the hike, I happened upon two cow elk grazing in the grass near the beaver ponds east of the cabin. It looks like good habitat for moose, though I did not see any today. I spotted a hog on the trail but had no problems with it.

I devoted four hours hiking 10 miles. But for the rest of today I will laze around, think of all of the memories that this land has showered upon me, and in the morning, I will ride south to civilization.

I will eat a 15-inch long trout for my meal later. I have a sunset to look forward to now.

\* \* \*

# 12

# Ride To Civilization

Morning has come, the light outside is becoming brighter with each passing minute. I did not sleep at all, being both lost in contemplation and flush with anticipation. I felt a certain dread creep in as random memories of the cabin and the neighborhood floated through my mind. I recounted different memories shared with George in the lodge during that first year.

My will wavered perhaps, but in what has proven a most difficult choice, I have Canoni saddled up, gear packed on her back comfortably. I now intend to travel due west until I have crossed the Swannell Mountain Range, which is about a two-day ride from here. So now, I go. Farewell little cabin in the vastness.

It is mid-afternoon. I have traveled 20 miles and have found a location to camp for the night. I set up my tent right away. I have a fire going. I am at the place where tomorrow I will cross Thudaka Creek, heading south toward Fishing Lake.

I sense how alone I am and how fragile life is, Canoni being the only familiar thing around me. At least George made for great company when we rode into this wilderness.

I did not set any snare traps, so tomorrow I will have no breakfast. Few things in this world make me crabby, but waking up hungry is one of them.

I hear the wolves howling in the distance. I am reminded, as if I needed to be, that I am not at the top of the food chain.

\* \* \*

## JUNE 19

Riding from just after sun-up, I traveled 25 miles today. Early on I crossed a stream, itself of little consequence, however, grizzly tracks led along the muddy bank. I estimate the front paw print at near 12 inches across. Otherwise the ride was uneventful, save for the ever-expanding vistas along the way.

The scenery is magnificent. I managed to shoot a rabbit and will cook the hindquarters over the fire later. It is fairly cool this afternoon, and there is a slight breeze, which doesn't help.

I made the final five-mile ride to Fishing Lake slowly, while enjoying the wildlife. I am now camped on the bank of Fishing Lake.

Nightfall is a few hours off. I will use the time to try my luck fishing.

It is evening, and I just finished fishing, without any success. I did have a good hit but failed to catch that fish. I will now cook the rabbit and eat.

With dinner finished, I sit facing the west in anticipation of the pending sunset. It appears as though it will be another spectacular twilight. Clouds are scattered along the western horizon, and as the sun sinks, it is turning the clouds from gray to pink, yellow, and gold. I take it in while puffing on a pipe load of weed.

\* \* \*

After riding a short 10 miles today, I have set up camp along the Toodoggone Creek. I am 40 miles from the cabin. I have been forced to backtrack from time to time, due to the numerous what I will term box canyons. Sometimes when riding the land becomes steeper, I am forced to choose which valley to drop into, and sometimes, I ride a mile or two and run into a wall no less than 200 feet tall. So I must backtrack and choose another trail.

I see snow on the distant Omineca Mountains, and I will have to cross them, perhaps in two days. I do not intend to rush back to humanity, partly because I am still convincing my heart that I should leave.

In truth, it is hard on a body living here. I couldn't imagine doing this at 40 years old.

It began to rain a couple of hours ago and mist lingers as I write. From inside my dry tent, Canoni looks pitiful standing in the moisture, and I can't help but laugh. Better you than me, buddy.

I am east of a national wild lands park. Tomorrow I will travel due south, around Thutade Lake, which is 20 miles away. I then intend to head a bit west to explore the Skeena Mountains.

In the distance, I hear the howl of the pack, the sound bouncing through the canyon and coming back around. I wonder if this is the same pack that kept tabs on me at the cabin. Wolves do tend to have a large range.

It seems that my considerations have moved from survival to the future. I find myself thinking about what I have accomplished here other than just enduring. I have learned a lot of things, of course. I have been taught hard lessons and have made fond memories during the past two years. I know that I am not the same person who went into this wilderness. I am much wiser.

I have been thinking about going to South Dakota to see if I can spend some time with the Lakota people. I have nothing to lose, and my intentions are good. I believe that I have a bond with them that is not yet fully developed. If the principals, the tribal elders, listen to my story, I know that they will understand. This too is in my future and awaits a decision.

Again, the pack howls in the distance, the sound first rolling through, passing, and bouncing around for a second time. And then, all is quiet.

\* \* \*

This morning it is not raining, but low clouds drape the landscape. It is chilly to the bone. I will carry on with my ride and enter a note later.

It is late afternoon. I have stopped for the day and set up camp. I am camped at the southern tip of Thutade Lake, roughly 60 miles from the cabin. The fire is going, and a fish hangs over the flames suspended from a stick, caught fresh from a creek nearby. While it cooks I will recount the events of the day.

The trail, what there was of it, was not too bad. The ground stayed firm, which allowed me to safely travel 15 miles. I saw a male grizzly heading up a mountain meadow, eating grass. He did not even notice that I was near. He appeared underweight from the long winter. I watched him for a while and then led Canoni along quietly.

This section of land is in the middle of a wide valley, divided by a series of mounds, with trees dotting the landscape. The distance across the valley is at least two or three miles. My tent sits on top of grass four inches tall. This makes for good padding. The land around my campsite is open, so I feel somewhat safer, not being encircled by trees in this place.

I will keep the fire burning bright during this long night.

\* \* \*

Morning has arrived, and I make this entry. The night rain returned, and for what seemed like hours, it poured. My roaring fire was doused in a matter of a few seconds, and although the tent stayed dry, the noise of the water hitting it was such that I couldn't sleep. I could only feel sorry for Canoni as she endured the downpour in silence.

I encouraged myself and stirred, put on my clothes, and after trudging around in the mud and getting things packed on Canoni, I am ready to start out. I will write later.

Throughout the day I rode south. The landscape again altered to mountains and valleys, as opposed to the openness of the land yesterday. I managed seven miles in all and now sit at the base of Bird Hill, which is actually a decent-sized mountain. Riding in the rain slows everything down. Of course, I traveled at a nonchalant speed, but I mean the whole world seemed to have reduced its pace. I noticed many more things, and for today at least, each trail I followed worked out to my advantage.

Maybe the planets are aligned today. It took two hours, but I managed to get a fire going, which feels so good at the moment. Writing by the light of the fire is tough, so for now I will stop.

I hear the grunting of a bear. Yes, it's definitely a bear. I fired off two rounds from my 40.440, and I can't imagine anything staying around this area after that.

For some reason, a memory of George just came to mind. Among the best of days were the ones that dawned warm enough that we did not need a jacket. How splendid it was to ride to a mesa and view the sunrise.

One particular August morning started out as that kind of day. George and I woke up early and saddled our horses. We rode in the light of dawn to view the sunrise. Feeling extra adventurous that day, George informed me that he would lead the way. Fair enough. All was well, I having been masterfully led to the summit in time to view the sunrise in all of its divine colors.

Sure enough, our interest in the morning changed as quickly as the color in the sky. It was not long before we thought about eating. Being the geniuses that we were, neither of us brought any food. Being mid-August, the berries were not ready, and there didn't appear to be significant wildlife present for hunting.

George led us down the winding trail toward the valley below. Soon, George caught sight of a bee hive in a standing tree, and he decided that it would be worth getting a sting or two to get the honey. He started a fire and sent smoke into the hive. When he was convinced that there was enough smoke, he stuck his arm into the hive. Of course, he got the expected few stings on the arm, but suddenly the hive came alive in a swarm of pissed off bees.

"Oh, now you've done it," I yelled at George, as I dashed for Canoni.

Once up, I waited for George to reach his horse, and we galloped away from the horde. After a quarter mile sprint, we slowed the horses and enjoyed the honey. Unfortunately, George had been stung several times on his face near his eyes, which were now swelling shut. He appeared like a fighter who had stopped a lot of punches with his face. By days end, his whole head had swollen up. I am sure that something bad could have come from so many stings, but by the grace of God, the stings weren't fatal. That was a fair exchange for honey in his mind.

It seems like George could not go long without being the news of the day.

\* \* \*

I have decided to let Canoni have the day off. I will camp here for another night. For now I will enjoy a cup of pine needle tea and relax.

I make this entry as I watch the sun set to the west. The day was sunny and cloudless for the most part. Canoni spent her time eating the grass, which is more abundant each day. Once she had eaten her fill, she strolled back to the tent. I've not seen her stray more than 50 yards away at any time, but I never have to worry, she will always come back to the tent.

Later in the afternoon, I tried my luck fishing in the Mosque River. It would have been great to catch a trout, but it didn't pan out. I have not eaten a lot in the last couple of days. I think Canoni has eaten better than I have.

It is getting dark now. I have set out a few snare traps along several rabbit trails that I located. I feel hungry, but not enough to eat any insects or grass. Tonight I will hear my stomach growl.

\* \* \*

This morning while making my rounds to check the traps, I found a badger, wrestling to free itself from one of them. I was not going to eat the badger, so I had to come up with a way to free it. I considered shooting the wire trap but thought that I would more likely upset the badger.

I didn't want to get too close by cutting the wire by hand. Finally, I decide to cut a sapling, fix my knife to it, and cut the wire from a comfortable distance. To do this would require tension on the wire, which would allow it to be cut easier. The badger had the wire wrapped around a sapling, leaving only about four inches of wire exposed for me to cut. I cut the wire without difficulty.

The badger snarled and made loud noises as it trotted away, obviously angry. I am happy that it did not attempt to attack me.

I found the remaining three traps empty, so I sprang them, collected the wire, and returned to camp. Not having trapped anything, I did not have breakfast today.

In the distance to the west, puffy storm clouds are building, and it looks like I am going to feel the rain today. I will write this afternoon.

Travel was dreadfully slow today because of the rain. Covered by my duster, I rode for five hours before stopping to make camp. I covered a meager seven miles. I am camped at Birdflat Creek. I was able to catch a white fish, so dinner is pending.

I saw signs of deer and elk today. I saw so many tracks that it is impossible to say how many animals may be around. As afternoon turns to twilight, those elk and deer should be heading for water soon. A red fox has decided to investigate my campsite, sniffing at the tent, the campfire, and eyeing the fish cooking over the flames.

No, I am not going to feed the fox. It is wild, although it acts much like a frisky pet. Like every animal, the fox has a comfort zone, his being about one to two feet. If I try to get closer, it will run or bite me. It seems attracted to Canoni as well, seemingly playing, nipping at her and running wide circles around her.

I see five elk, females, slowly exiting the trees and heading to Birdflat Creek. I wish I had my camera right now. The sun is setting over the horizon, reflecting on the ruby water. It is almost gold, outlined by a white border on the foamy rapids. I am viewing the classic western painted sunset.

As if on cue, in the distance a pack of coyotes yip in the fast-fading light. As the sun dips further, the pallet of color changes to burgundy and raspberry, lighting up the clouds that dumped rain for much of the day. The breeze picks up unexpectedly, and smokes from the fire blows into my face.

I have finished dinner, bones from the fish sizzling in the flames now. Minus my fire in this vast, empty darkness, there is only night. I see no moon to show the way. The occasional shooting star dashes across the night sky, but otherwise it is cold and clear.

I will go to sleep now and hope to wake to a sunny day.

\* \* \*

It is early, maybe three o'clock in the morning, and I am still shaking from what just occurred. I was sleeping when I was awakened by a grunt, or more of a huff, right outside my tent. Of course, it was a goddamned grizzly bear!

In an instant, my rifle was in my hands, my mind fighting the urge to panic. I unzipped the tent flap a couple of inches. My deepest fear had come to pass. I could make out the dark outline of the bear from the dim glow of the dying fire. The bear glared at my tent. I cocked my rifle and took aim. The bear sniffed the air, becoming agitated and rocking its head from side to side. We stood not more than 15 feet apart.

Again, he looked directly into my eyes. I diverted my glance quickly. I fired a round into the night sky, startling the bear. The muzzle fire and the report caused it to immediately spin on its hind legs and run into the darkness.

I unzipped the flaps and crawled out of the smoke-filled tent on unsteady knees. I only now realize how large the grizzly was. I tasted the metallic adrenaline in my mouth from the horror of seeing the bear from my kneeling position. The bear was easily five feet tall at the shoulder. Enough with the fucking bears already! I've had my fill of damn grizzly bears.

I have stoked the fire back into a hot blaze and will sit out here for a while. We will see if I am eaten or get tired enough to sleep. As if on cue, a lone coyote howled a melancholy chorus. Maybe he is screaming at me to shut up!

\* \* \*

Last night's excitement left me wondering why Canoni did not alert me to the bear before it was so close to the tent. I can only surmise that she did not see or hear the bear until it grunted, a tribute to the stealth of this great bear. During the incident I do not know where Canoni was, but needless to say, she took the appropriate action as not to be a victim. The bear left many tracks as he made his way toward an open range, low grass luring the hungry bear.

I am seven days into the ride out now, and nothing looks familiar, although I know I am not riding the same trail we came in on. I will trust my compass and not second-guess myself. I estimate that I have traveled 90 miles in seven days. I have many more miles left to go.

I have always had a lack of interest when it comes to memorizing which plants are edible. As a result, I have stayed away from eating anything other than some roots and a few well-known plants. George and I tried eating watercress, which is eaten like greens, either raw or boiled. We tried wild leeks as well, which we also found in forested areas, which tasted okay after the root was cut off and they were boiled.

We ate dandelions in the spring and early summer. George used the leaves as salad, before the flowers bloomed. Neither George nor I ever became sick eating these select greens.

Truth be told, none of them tasted especially good to me, so I ate less of them than did George.

It is getting dark now, and I am becoming tired. I will sleep.

* * *

I spent another day in the saddle, picking a point far in the distance and riding to it and then picking another point and so on. I have covered 20 miles. I traveled south and east, crossing the Sustut River, which was wide but just thigh deep on Canoni. Although the land is more rolling than flat, it does not offer any advantage in seeing farther down the trail.

Beautiful forest surrounded me all day, engulfed me, gently reminding me that I fit into the grand scheme of things.

It is almost sunset, I now sit near my campfire, looking over the valley to the west, and like in a movie, the violet sky fades to dark, leaving my speck of flame the sole light not of natural origin. Not too far in the distance, I hear the wolves howling lustfully, each one trying to be louder than the next.

I find myself smiling as I lean against a car-sized boulder, snuggled as close as one may be to a rock. During the past two years, I have become accustomed to the sounds of the pack, always aware of the distance between us. For now, they are far enough away.

Tomorrow I will spend another day riding and alternately walking through country that I would describe as fresh. Nothing spoils Canada's mountains; nothing pollutes the clear streams that supply life to so many creatures.

I find a kind of freedom in singing as loudly as I wish, knowing that no other human being will hear me. I know that only a couple of animals here have the ability to kill me, while millions of people in the civilized world would not give it a second thought. Out here I can face the threat knowing what it is, while I cannot read all people. Some people are so slick, and lie so well, that one might believe them like they would believe their own grandmother.

Funny that I would think about impermanence as I leave this place that has for so long been home to me.

\* \* \*

I now sit at my campfire, a bit shaken by today's events. The sun came up, revealing a cloudless sky. After eating some smoked fish and washing it down with tea, I started riding. After a while I had the feeling that nothing appeared familiar. Up until then I had passed a few things that I recollected from the ride in.

This morning nothing was the same, and as I rode on feeling sick in my stomach, my mind ran wild with wasted thoughts. What if I am somehow traveling in the wrong direction? What if I am not where I think I am on the map, which is not even close to scale?

I stopped Canoni and got off to walk for a while. I kept checking my compass, steering west by southwest, toward the coast, still days away from here. It took until late in the afternoon to convince myself that everything was all right.

Finally, I got some reassurance, the river Asitka, which I recalled crossing and evidenced by the fire pit that George and I built two years ago. It is strange how my mind can, without warning, lead me on a journey of doubt, not believing even those things that I know to be true. It is weird how, over a period of time, I can go from being calm and assured to being filled with doubt and confusion.

I do confess that getting lost in the wilderness is truly my principal fear, not so much because I don't think that I could find food and shelter but because I wouldn't know where I was. Anyway, the forest has provided another lesson today, a lesson I learned years ago. I need to trust my compass, not myself!

I am tired and so will sleep now.

\* \* \*

## NEXT TO LAST DAY OF JUNE

This month has brought the fair days I've longed for. I traveled 15 miles today and am now camped south of the Omineca River. I will have to cross this river once more as I further my journey south.

While riding today, I made a surprising discovery. As I passed through a small valley, I noticed more trails than I had previously. Many of these trails were packhorse trails. I found an old, rusty coffee can on the ground, and for a few minutes I freaked out! Have I reached the outer borders of civilization?

Sometime in the past, someone visited here. I have mixed emotions about this. It is not comforting to me to know that the world lies in wait, an unknown number of miles ahead. I ask myself how I will respond to people after so long being alone.

Talk about a gift. While I was sitting here writing, a two foot tall hare strolled across my campsite, not more than 20 feet in front of me. Needless to say, I will eat hare for dinner!

Anyway, returning to my thoughts about seeing the trails today. I wondered to myself if this was what a soldier would feel like, after deployment to a jungle or mountains. I feel somewhat anti-social. I am guessing that I have maybe three more weeks of travel before I reach civilization, so I will relax and enjoy it. I'm not even out yet, and I am stressed. Maybe I should turn around and go back to the cabin.

\* \* \*

After traveling six miles over rough terrain today, I sit along a wide, slow-moving stretch of the Omineca River, contemplating the beauty of this scene. The sandy beach feels good on the bottom of my bare feet. The fishing has been steady as well. I caught two keepers, and I threw plenty more into the water.

I intruded on the home of four otters that swam by to investigate my presence in their home territory. They made a lot of chatter letting me know of their displeasure. A breeze feels cool on my skin, my hair blowing along with it. The low-pitched sound of bubbling water is almost enough to lull me to sleep.

With my fish cooking above the coals, I can let my mind wander and smoke the pipe. I am taken to a place near Sequoia National Park, along another river, my eyes closed, and hearing sounds exactly like the ones I hear now. What a fantastic, incredible world I live in, the same as it was a thousand years ago.

I do wish I had my camera, for this is the photo to remember!

For the record, the fish was excellent. I now sit near the fire. Soon enough, I will climb into the tent and sleep beneath the darkest, star-filled sky that you can imagine.

\* \* \*

## JULY

Thoughts floated through my mind about what I would wish to hear someone say at my life's end. I would wish that people would remember how much I was loved by children. There is a reason for this, and it is simply that no matter my age, I am the child's age when I talk and interact with them. I have never scolded a child for being a child. Never raised my voice because a toy was broken.

I would hope that I am remembered as a generous person, one who gave often to those who have less. I want to be remembered as a man who was even-handed to all people, all races, and a man who did not let color bind him to bigotry. I would wish that people might contemplate what it meant to me to live this way.

I would wish that they might know of the countless miles that led me to the place where the final act plays out. Voices may sound like mine but are owned by others, yet the message is clear. I didn't go before my time; I chose this time to go.

I traveled seven miles today, stopping after crossing the junction of the Omineca River and Ominicetla Creek. I got wet on this crossing, so now my Levi's are drying in front of the fire.

Canoni seems to be favoring her left leg, so I will stay here for the next few days and let her heal. This area is rich with wildlife, as is evidenced by the seven does to my left and the many ground squirrels running about. Birds sing in the trees around me, and the Omineca River teems with trout waiting to be caught.

\* \* \*

The morning is inviting me to take a hike, so I do.

I am now in camp. I took an all-day hike through the surrounding countryside. I left Canoni at the tent, free to graze as she will. The grass felt good beneath my bare feet. It has been a long time since I last trucked bare-foot through the grass. As I hiked, I spotted three deer browsing in a meadow, paying more attention to the food than they did to me. I saw a moose in a shallow pool of water, eating whatever was growing below the water. A pair of hawks soared high overhead, riding on the rising thermal currents, so high as to nearly disappear from my view. Only the squeal from far above gave their presence away.

While trudging along I was reminded of an Indian saying: Man rides too often, he sits high above the earth. It is good for a man to walk so he sees the earth from a new perspective. It is true that once one get used to riding, one see things differently.

Canoni met me a hundred feet from where I left her. I ate trout for dinner and will soon watch the daily sunset dazzle the heavens and awe all who see it.

* * *

Morning has come, and once again Mother Nature made a house call. For whatever reason, I don't tend to get freaked out by things, but last night, I was close. I spent the early part of the evening gazing at the stars, feeling small. It was chilly, so I lay under my coat and my sleeping bag. Canoni began to get fidgety, snorting, and moving in an alert stance. Sitting up, I heard footsteps in the darkness, coming from the trees down the slope.

I listened closely, holding my breath, aiming the barrel of my gun at the night, not seeing or being seen by whatever was there. Then I heard a grunt and knew immediately that it was a bear. In the next 10 seconds, my mind raced, my sight and hearing focused, thoughts of past terrors in the back of my mind. I decided in those brief few seconds to fire my rifle in the direction of the sound. The black bear, as it turned out to be, charged my camp, running between Canoni and me. It was definitely limping, hardly using its right front leg.

My heart beat so fast that I took involuntary deep breaths, trying hard aim my rifle! Canoni was going crazy and trotted off a short distance. I could hear the bear, rushing up the sloping mountain to my right. When I could no longer hear it, I collected Canoni and stoked the fire up real high. I sat behind the fire, scanning the slope.

I am sure that the situation made things seem more dangerous than they really were, but this was the second time that I had been close enough to a bear to effortlessly touch it. In both cases, the events transpired so quickly that I could not defend myself had it been attacking.

As soon as it began to get light, I dosed off and woke to the blue jays making a racket well after sunrise. Once again, a bear takes normal to anything but normal in the blink of an eye. I am feeling a bit jumpy about having these more frequent run-ins with bears. I will confess that my nerves are all but shot. The bears are the ultimate players in this land, and I will be happy not to have to worry about them in a few weeks.

This was one of those terrifying moments that are thrown into the hundreds of boring moments that is life out here in this gigantic universe.

* * *

**JULY 4**

I am taking time to recount the day's events. After heading out, I followed a trail south, one that snaked between two steep mountains. I intended to travel to the Fall River. The grass along this trail was trampled and quite recently. Within a few minutes, I saw a herd of 20 or so elk eating in a patch of green grass.

The ride to the Fall River was only eight miles, leaving me a good portion of the day left. The river here flows evenly, at a depth of four feet. I caught a beautiful trout, which I will eat later. I have smoked a bowl, quite aware that my supply is practically gone. I now sit against a tree, scanning the landscape.

Tomorrow, I will try and ride as far south as Tsayata Lake, some 40 miles, though I expect to make it halfway at best. For tonight, it is trout for dinner, a cup of pine needle tea, and then I will sleep.

* * *

This day began with wind escorting clouds and showers throughout this region. It is late afternoon, and I am camped north of Kwanika Creek. I covered half of the 40 miles that I wanted to travel today.

Starting out this morning, the rain fell lightly and constant for the first few hours. Then a mixture of sun and clouds began to dry the land. The ground was soft during the hours that I led Canoni to ease her burden.

Many streams run down from the hills, and it seems like the majority of the time I must ride or hike in water. The location in which I've chosen to camp on today is on flat land. The grass is five inches tall and grows all around, except for along the bank of the creek, which is sand. My tent door faces east. The creek, located behind me, is perhaps 15 feet away. Observing the mountains, I estimate that the sun will set in two hours. I will try my luck in Kwanika Creek and write later.

Kwanika Creek gifted me a fine trout, which is cooking over my fire. I filled my pipe and offered thanks in the four directions, then smoked. The smell of the fish cooking gives hope to my stomach.

I heard a coyote bark in the distance to the west.

Canoni seems content, filling herself with the grass growing so abundantly. She shows no signs of injury, and so we will resume our ride. It will be hard to sell

Canoni upon reaching civilization. She has become as a sister to me, my reliance on her rewarded by her loyalty and camaraderie. For tonight, she remains my one and only friend in this darkening lonely world.

Dinner is ready now, so I will eat.

* * *

Today, I reached the eastern shoreline of Tsayata Lake, utterly amazed by the beauty of this trail. Green grass lines the brown dirt trail as far down the trail as I can see. Pine and spruce trees surround this campsite. The mountains around this lake are tall and sheer.

I carefully chose the spot upon which I set the tent, making sure that it is high above the stream feeding the lake. To the south, I see thunderclouds building. I will gather some firewood and cover it with my duster. If it rains, I want dry wood to have a fire in the morning.

I finished the chore of collecting and covering firewood, which I hope that I can use later. At the moment I sit in the tent. The rain did come, and it is falling hard. Thunder crashed through the air, the lightening streaked across the late afternoon sky, bright enough to cast shadows across the floor of my tent as I sit inside. The stream is flowing faster now, but I am high enough above it to not be flooded. I will wait to see if the storm passes tonight.

* * *

It is morning now. The storm did not pass until late in the night. The one dry thing in sight is the pile of firewood that was under my duster. I intend to ride due south and reach Indata Lake by late afternoon. That would be a distance of 20 miles. Everything is packed and ready, so I will ride now.

Due to the high-flowing feeder stream, I was forced to ride farther east than anticipated, and now I find myself five miles east of Indata Lake. I am approaching Nation Lakes, which is a popular destination, where I will likely make contact with another human being. By tomorrow evening, I should be there.

Trying to gage my thoughts about that, I find myself completely satisfied with how things have progressed on the way out. The log cabin seems a long way from here, and a long time ago. It seems a distant memory, literally.

I know now, more than ever before, that I will be successful in any anything that I decide to do with my life. The few limitations I have are those I put on myself. So tomorrow, if I should meet anyone, I will be happy to see them. For now, though, I will try and catch a fish for dinner.

I am making this entry to note that I see the light of several campfires along the shores of Indata Lake, at the far end of the lake from me, perhaps a mile away. I hear no voices, only the occasional laughter of a camper and the breeze in the pines.

It is time to cook the nine-inch trout I caught earlier.

\* \* \*

## LATE JULY

I made the decision to ride to the west around Tchentio Lake, and now I am camped to the north of Leo Creek. The ride today was slow. I did not see any substantial animals, but I did cross a lot of riding trails. So far, I have not made contact with anyone. I am camped in a flat area, with grass 18 inches tall waving in the breeze. Canoni stands among it having her fill.

I snared a hare, cleaned it, and will cook it in a while. I have a dreadful emotion of anxiety as I comprehend that this whole adventure will soon come to an end. Suddenly, there will be no more danger; the wild will lie behind me. Now those once-abundant animals have become scarce as I near the population of humans that dominate the land that I am approaching.

With foreboding of never again seeing the new babies learn daily lessons, I force myself south. I recognize that each step that I ride my beloved Canoni is one step closer to having to part with her forever. If that is to be the case, I will focus on what lies ahead of me, while at the same time miss what is behind me.

\* \* \*

Today I rode 10 miles, through some of the nicest country I have seen so far. I saw a few small lakes, and several larger ones, as I wound my way south. I am camped on the Shore of Kazchek Lake, one of the bigger lakes in the area.

The fishing in this lake is excellent. In 20 minutes, I caught four rainbows.

As evening begins to set in, I can clearly see smoke from a campfire across the lake. I also see what appears to be a lantern. I am pleased to say that I do not have the apprehension I thought I would have, and for that I am grateful.

I feel so sad knowing that this expedition is all but over. In the next couple of days I will reach the outskirts of Ft. Saint James and from there will make it to Vancouver.

As I look at Canoni standing there, silhouetted against the campfire, I have a heavy heart realizing that she will no longer make my days fun. From this day forward, our rides across the valley become memories. A tear rolls down my cheek and onto the page of my journal.

I will ride the remainder of the trail out of here. I will sell my true friend Canoni and my gear. Perhaps I will travel to Pine Ridge, South Dakota. I will make every effort to find George, and together we will catch up on all that has happened. This will be the last daily entry in my journal.

# Epilogue

I compose this epilogue some 40 years after my adventure concluded. I find it essential to fill in some specifics that you do not yet know but that will help bring closure to the story.

First, it took an additional two weeks to reach Fort St. James, the end of the trail, so to speak.

I imagine that one might wonder about what came to be of Canoni. I am pleased to tell you that I met a rancher in Fort St. James, Canada, who bought Canoni from me. I told him of the things that we had been through together, and he assured me that he would treat her well. He told me that Canoni was going to be a gift for his young granddaughter. I assured him that Canoni would travel well and take care of his grandchild.

I shed tears on that afternoon and carried a sick, empty feeling for quite some time after. Canoni was one of those infrequent gifts that come into our lives, bringing unbridled joy, giving so much while asking little in return. These rare jewels pass too soon. Many have had a dog, I had Canoni.

I made enough money selling my possessions, other than my rifle, to get back to Vancouver and then to go on to the United States.

Perhaps you are envisioning the reunion party that George and I surely had. Upon my homecoming to the United States I reached out to relatives of George by telephone, and I was stunned and saddened to learn that no one had seen him since we left that April morning. The emotions raging in that family ranged from loss and resignation to disdain for me.

Over the years from time to time I called one family member or another to see if George ever came home, only to be told that he had not. Eventually I was asked to call no more.

I am to this day heartbroken that George did not survive the Canadian wilderness. I am saddened further that his daughter lost her daddy and that so many others lost a portion of them as well.

Ultimately, I ended up in Colorado, where I reside today. I am blessed to have one sweet girl who calls me grandpa, a name more significant to me than any other I have ever possessed. I have spent more time with my sisters over the passing years, enjoying their lives and families as well. I am called uncle, dad, brother, and many people care about me and love me, so my life turned out well.

As the years have rolled by, I have told bits and pieces of my adventure to some who have asked about my days in Canada, some fascinated by the act of going to the wilderness itself and others amused by the effort. Questions are asked by the dozen. Overwhelmingly, the most common question I hear is how I got past the fear of going into the wild. Interestingly, in hindsight, I can't say that I ever felt fear where the wilderness was concerned.

Some of the animals that I encountered in the wilderness, on the other hand, scared the shit out of me on occasion. We were prepared by the many hours that I spent in the public library studying in detail what we would need to know. We brought enough equipment to make constructing the log cabin easier than it otherwise would have been. Our firepower was overwhelming in the eyes of anything we expected to encounter.

We were, of course, exposed to danger during the months that we slept in our tents, George in his and me in mine, but I suspect now that we may have been more young and stupid than brave.

I have seen both of my parents pass in recent years. I did allow my mother to read my journal in its original rendering, and aided by more than a few stories that I shared with her, she told me that she did understand my need to prove myself a man to myself. She also said that she would have preferred knowing where I was during that time.

Being the essence of what a mother should be, she forgave my absence and lifted a heavy burden from my shoulders, a burden that I had long carried.

Today this world is not the same place as it was at the time of our travels. Today there is no respect for opposing opinion, poverty in the richest country in the world is worse now than ever, and it seems that nobody is to be trusted.

Music has remained a huge part of my life, and whenever possible I try to share my music with others. It is my expectation and wish that you found enjoyment, amusement, and perhaps astonishment in the places that you trekked with George and me.

To you, the reader, I thank you for sharing my adventure.

www.ingramcontent.com/pod-product-compliance
Lightning Source LLC
Chambersburg PA
CBHW021138080526
44588CB00008B/116